Deep Learning for

MW01129676

A beginner's guide to getting up and running with deep
learning from scratch using Python

Dr. Pablo Rivas

BIRMINGHAM - MUMBAI

Deep Learning for Beginners

Copyright © 2020 Packt Publishing

All rights reserved. No part of this book may be reproduced, stored in a retrieval system, or transmitted in any form or by any means, without the prior written permission of the publisher, except in the case of brief quotations embedded in critical articles or reviews.

Every effort has been made in the preparation of this book to ensure the accuracy of the information presented. However, the information contained in this book is sold without warranty, either express or implied. Neither the author nor Packt Publishing or its dealers and distributors will be held liable for any damages caused or alleged to have been caused directly or indirectly by this book.

Packt Publishing has endeavored to provide trademark information about all of the companies and products mentioned in this book by the appropriate use of capitals. However, Packt Publishing cannot guarantee the accuracy of this information.

Commissioning Editor: Amey Varangaonkar
Acquisition Editor: Joshua Nadar
Content Development Editor: Sean Lobo
Senior Editor: David Sugarman
Technical Editor: Manikandan Kurup
Copy Editor: Safis Editing
Project Coordinator: Aishwarya Mohan
Proofreader: Safis Editing
Indexer: Tejal Daruwale Soni
Production Designer: Shankar Kalbhor

First published: September 2020

Production reference: 1180920

Published by Packt Publishing Ltd.
Livery Place
35 Livery Street
Birmingham
B3 2PB, UK.

ISBN 978-1-83864-085-9

www.packt.com

Packt.com

Subscribe to our online digital library for full access to over 7,000 books and videos, as well as industry leading tools to help you plan your personal development and advance your career. For more information, please visit our website.

Why subscribe?

- Spend less time learning and more time coding with practical eBooks and Videos from over 4,000 industry professionals

- Improve your learning with Skill Plans built especially for you

- Get a free eBook or video every month

- Fully searchable for easy access to vital information

- Copy and paste, print, and bookmark content

Did you know that Packt offers eBook versions of every book published, with PDF and ePub files available? You can upgrade to the eBook version at www.packt.com and as a print book customer, you are entitled to a discount on the eBook copy. Get in touch with us at customercare@packtpub.com for more details.

At www.packt.com, you can also read a collection of free technical articles, sign up for a range of free newsletters, and receive exclusive discounts and offers on Packt books and eBooks.

Foreword

I have known and worked with Dr. Pablo Rivas for more than 5 years. He is one of the leading experts in deep learning and artificial intelligence ethics. In this book, he takes you on a learning journey that aims to bring you up to speed with the latest ideas through a hands-on practical approach to deep learning. In the last few years, deep learning has experienced breakthroughs that have transformed several communities around the world both positively and negatively. It is imperative that deep learning education includes discussions of the societal implication of certain algorithms so that learners and practitioners can have awareness of the tremendous positive potential of deep learning-based technology as well as its possible negative consequences. Dr. Rivas has continued to evolve as a machine learning scientist and educator to meet these needs by educating students and sharing his research through papers that are being read around the world. I have had the privilege of working with him in a study that warns about the impact and repercussions of artificial intelligence being developed, funded, and adopted in only a few places in the world. However, this book stands as an invitation to anyone anywhere in the world to jump in and start learning about deep learning so that more people can have access to this type of specialized knowledge.

Dr. Rivas has done a great job of explaining concepts with practical examples, interesting applications, and ethics discussions. He has made use of Google Colabs, which makes deep learning tools and libraries accessible to anyone who does not have a high-performance computer, enabling them to run the code on the cloud. Further, he has used his skills as a certified online instructor and teacher to convey ideas in a way that is memorable and making thought-provoking questions that will leave you thinking beyond what seems to be obvious. By reading this book, you will be part of an education movement that increases access to resources in artificial intelligence engineering and improves awareness of the long and short term effects of artificial intelligence.

This book will serve you well in your learning journey by providing you with several examples, best practices, and fully working code snippets that will give you the understanding you need to apply deep learning in several disciplines that include computer vision, natural language processing, learning representations and more. The way the book is organized will give you a smooth transition between supervised and unsupervised models that can accelerate your grasp of knowledge and easier navigation between topics if you need to move at a faster pace.

In Deep Learning for Beginners, Dr. Rivas encapsulates the knowledge gained through years as a world-class machine learning scientist, an educator, a community leader, and a passionate advocate for underrepresented groups in artificial intelligence. With his words, step-by-step instructions, source code snippets, examples, professional tips, and additional information, you will learn how to continuously enhance your skills and grow professionally.

Become a deep learning practitioner, professional, or scientist by reading this book and applying these state of the art techniques today; your journey starts here.

Laura Montoya

Published Author, Speaker
Founder & Executive Director
Accel.AI Institute

Contributors

About the author

Dr. Pablo Rivas is an assistant professor of computer science at Baylor University in Texas. He worked in industry for a decade as a software engineer before becoming an academic. He is a senior member of the IEEE, ACM, and SIAM. He was formerly at NASA Goddard Space Flight Center performing research. He is an ally of women in technology, a deep learning evangelist, machine learning ethicist, and a proponent of the democratization of machine learning and artificial intelligence in general. He teaches machine learning and deep learning. Dr. Rivas is a published author and all his papers are related to machine learning, computer vision, and machine learning ethics. Dr. Rivas prefers Vim to Emacs and spaces to tabs.

About the reviewers

Francesco Azzola is an electronic engineer with over 15 years of experience in computer programming and JEE architecture. He is an IoT and machine learning enthusiast. He loves creating IoT projects using Arduino, Raspberry Pi, Android, ESP, and other platforms. He is the author of *Android Things Projects*, published by Packt Publishing. He has reviewed several Packt books covering IoT and machine learning. He is interested in the convergence of IoT and mobile applications and the convergence of IoT and machine learning. He is SCEA, SCWCD, and SCJP certified. Previously, he worked in the mobile development field for several years. He has a blog called Surviving with Android, where he writes about coding in IoT and machine learning projects.

Jamshaid Sohail is passionate about data science, machine learning, computer vision, and natural language processing and has more than 2 years of experience in industry. He has worked in a Silicon Valley-based start-up named FunnelBeam, as a data scientist. He has worked with founders of FunnelBeam from Stanford University. Currently, he is working as a data scientist at Systems Limited. He has completed over 66 online courses from different platforms. He authored the book *Data Wrangling with Python 3.X* for Packt Publishing and has reviewed multiple books and courses. He is also developing a comprehensive course on data science at Educative and is in the process of writing books for multiple publishers.

Packt is searching for authors like you

If you're interested in becoming an author for Packt, please visit authors.packtpub.com and apply today. We have worked with thousands of developers and tech professionals, just like you, to help them share their insight with the global tech community. You can make a general application, apply for a specific hot topic that we are recruiting an author for, or submit your own idea.

Table of Contents

Preface

For years, those who have been faithfully working on machine learning have seen the field grow and flourish, yielding amazing technology and even promising radical societal changes. However, for those who want to join us in studying this area, it might seem a little bit intimidating. Certainly, there is so much stuff out there on the web and it has become very difficult to navigate through all the papers, and the code, to find reliable introductory content for those who want to join us in the field of deep learning. While there are many introductory books on machine learning, most are inadequate in addressing the needs of those who specifically want to work on deep learning and have the minimum necessary mathematical, algorithmic, and programming skills.

This book aims to reach out to those beginners in deep learning who are looking for a strong foundation in the basic concepts required to build deep learning models using well-known methodologies. If that sounds like you, then this book might be what you need. The book assumes no prior extensive exposure to neural networks and deep learning and starts by reviewing the machine learning fundamentals needed for deep learning. Then, it explains how to prepare data by cleaning and preprocessing it for deep learning and gradually goes on to introduce neural networks and the popular supervised neural network architectures, such as **convolutional neural networks (CNNs)**, **recurrent neural networks (RNNs)**, and **generative adversarial networks (GANs)**, and unsupervised architectures, such as **autoencoders (AEs)**, **variational autoencoders (VAEs)**, and **restricted Boltzmann machines (RBMs)**. At the end of each chapter, you will have a chance to test your understanding of the concepts and reflect on your own growth.

By the end of the book, you will have an understanding of deep learning concepts and recipes and will be able to distinguish which algorithms are appropriate for different tasks.

Who this book is for

This book is for aspiring data scientists and deep learning engineers who want to get started with the absolute fundamentals of deep learning and neural networks. Now, about requirements:

- No prior exposure to deep learning or machine learning is necessary, but it would be a plus.
- Some familiarity with linear algebra and Python programming is all you need to get started.

This book is for people who value their time and want to get to the point and learn the deep learning recipes needed to *do things*.

Deep learning can be intimidating if you don't know the basics. Many people are discouraged because they cannot follow the terminology or sample programs they see on the web. This causes people to make poor decisions about the selection of deep learning algorithms and renders them unable to foresee the consequences of such choices. Therefore, this book is for people who do the following:

- Value access to good definitions of deep learning concepts
- Want a structured method to learn deep learning from scratch
- Desire to know the fundamental concepts and really understand them
- Want to know how to preprocess data for usage in deep learning algorithms
- Are curious about some advanced deep learning algorithms

For details about the contents of each chapter, read the next section.

What this book covers

Chapter 1, *Introduction to Machine Learning*, gives an overview of machine learning. It introduces the motivation behind machine learning and the terminology that is commonly used in the field. It also introduces deep learning and how it fits in the realm of artificial intelligence.

Chapter 2, *Setup and Introduction to Deep Learning Frameworks*, helps you in the process of setting up TensorFlow and Keras and introduces their usefulness and purpose in deep learning. This chapter also briefly introduces other deep learning libraries to get you acquainted with them in some small way.

Chapter 3, *Preparing Data*, introduces you to the main concepts behind data processing to make it useful in deep learning. It will cover essential concepts of formatting outputs and inputs that are categorical or real-valued, as well as exploring techniques for augmenting data or reducing the dimensions of data.

Chapter 4, *Learning from Data*, introduces the most elementary concepts around the theory of deep learning, including measuring performance on regression and classification as well as the identification of overfitting. It also offers some warnings about optimizing hyperparameters.

Chapter 5, *Training a Single Neuron,* introduces the concept of a neuron and connects it to the perceptron model, which learns from data in a simple manner. The perceptron model is key to understanding basic neural models that learn from data. It also exposes the problem of non-linearly separable data.

Chapter 6, *Training Multiple Layers of Neurons,* brings you face to face with the first challenges of deep learning using the multi-layer perceptron algorithm, such as gradient descent techniques for error minimization, and hyperparameter optimization to achieve generalization.

Chapter 7, *Autoencoders,* describes the AE model by explaining the necessity of both encoding and decoding layers. It explores the loss functions associated with the autoencoder problem and it applies it to the dimensionality reduction problem and data visualization.

Chapter 8, *Deep Autoencoders,* introduces the idea of deep belief networks and the significance of this type of deep unsupervised learning. It explains such concepts by introducing deep AEs and contrasting them with shallow AEs.

Chapter 9, *Variational Autoencoders,* introduces the philosophy behind generative models in the unsupervised deep learning field and their importance in the production of models that are robust against noise. It presents the VAE as a better alternative to a deep AE when working with perturbed data.

Chapter 10, *Restricted Boltzmann Machines,* complements the book's coverage of deep belief models by presenting RBMs. The backward-forward nature of RBMs is introduced and contrasted with the forward-only nature of AEs. The chapter compares RBMs and AEs on the problem of data dimensionality reduction using visual representations of the reduced data.

Chapter 11, *Deep and Wide Neural Networks,* explains the difference in performance and complexities of deep versus wide neural networks. It introduces the concept of dense networks and sparse networks in terms of the connections between neurons.

Chapter 12, *Convolutional Neural Networks,* introduces CNNs, starting with the convolution operation and moving forward to ensemble layers of convolutional operations aiming to learn filters that operate over data. The chapter concludes by showing how to visualize the learned filters.

Chapter 13, *Recurrent Neural Networks,* presents the most fundamental concepts of recurrent networks, exposing their shortcomings to justify the existence and success of long short-term memory models. Sequential models are explored with applications for image processing and natural language processing.

`Chapter 14`, *Generative Adversarial Networks*, introduces the semi-supervised learning approach of GANs, which belong to the family of adversarial learning. The chapter explains the concepts of generator and discriminator and talks about why having good approximations to the distribution of the training data can lead to the success of a model in, for example, the production of data from random noise.

`Chapter 15`, *Final Remarks on the Future of Deep Learning*, briefly exposes you to the new exciting topics and opportunities in deep learning. Should you want to continue your learning, you will find here other resources from Packt Publishing that you can use to move forward in this field.

To get the most out of this book

You will need to make sure that you have an internet browser and access to Google Colabs at the following site: `http://colab.research.google.com/`.

Although this book assumes no prior exposure to deep learning or machine learning, you have to have some familiarity with linear algebra and Python programming in order to get the most out of this book.

In order to ensure compatibility with future releases of Python libraries for machine and deep learning, we have included a list of current versions produced with the `!pip freeze` command in the code bundle and on the GitHub repository of this book; however, these are only for reference and future compatibility – remember that Google Colabs already has all the necessary setup.

We also have other code bundles from our rich catalog of books and videos available at `https://github.com/PacktPublishing/`. Check them out! Again, the list of libraries is for reference, but Google Colabs has the latest setup.

If you are using the digital version of this book, we advise you to type the code yourself or access the code via the GitHub repository (link available in the next section). Doing so will help you avoid any potential errors related to the copying and pasting of code.

Once you reach the end of your learning journey using this book, celebrate, and pay close attention to the last chapter of the book, which will point you in new directions. Remember to always keep learning: it is one of the keys to success in life.

Download the example code files

You can download the example code files for this book from your account at
`www.packt.com`. If you purchased this book elsewhere, you can visit
`www.packtpub.com/support` and register to have the files emailed directly to you.

You can download the code files by following these steps:

1. Log in or register at `www.packt.com`.
2. Select the **Support** tab.
3. Click on **Code Downloads**.
4. Enter the name of the book in the **Search** box and follow the onscreen instructions.

Once the file is downloaded, please make sure that you unzip or extract the folder using the latest version of:

- WinRAR/7-Zip for Windows
- Zipeg/iZip/UnRarX for Mac
- 7-Zip/PeaZip for Linux

The code bundle for the book is also hosted on GitHub at `https://github.com/PacktPublishing/Deep-Learning-for-Beginners`. In case there's an update to the code, it will be updated on the existing GitHub repository.

Download the color images

We also provide a PDF file that has color images of the screenshots/diagrams used in this book. You can download it here: `https://static.packt-cdn.com/downloads/9781838640859_ColorImages.pdf`.

Conventions used

There are a number of text conventions used throughout this book.

`CodeInText`: Indicates code words in text, database table names, folder names, filenames, file extensions, pathnames, dummy URLs, user input, and Twitter handles. Here is an example: "The `predict()` methods in the latent encoder model, `latent_ncdr`, and the `autoencoder` model produce the output at the specified layers."

A block of code is set as follows:

```
x = np.array([[1., 1., 0., 1., 1., 0., 0., 0.]]) #216

encdd = latent_ncdr.predict(x)
x_hat = autoencoder.predict(x)

print(encdd)
print(x_hat)
print(np.mean(np.square(x-x_hat)))
```

When we wish to draw your attention to a particular part of a code block, the relevant lines or items are set in bold:

```
import matplotlib.pyplot as plt

plt.plot(hist.history['loss'])
plt.title('Model reconstruction loss')
plt.ylabel('MSE')
plt.xlabel('Epoch')
plt.show()
```

Any command-line input or output is written as follows:

```
$ pip install tensorflow-gpu
```

Bold: Indicates a new term, an important word, or words that you see onscreen. For example, words in menus or dialog boxes appear in the text like this. Here is an example: "The first important thing is a new activation function called the **hyperbolic tangent**."

 Warnings or important notes appear like this.

 Tips and tricks appear like this.

Get in touch

Feedback from our readers is always welcome.

General feedback: If you have questions about any aspect of this book, mention the book title in the subject of your message and email us at customercare@packtpub.com.

Errata: Although we have taken every care to ensure the accuracy of our content, mistakes do happen. If you have found a mistake in this book, we would be grateful if you would report this to us. Please visit www.packtpub.com/support/errata, selecting your book, clicking on the Errata Submission Form link, and entering the details.

Piracy: If you come across any illegal copies of our works in any form on the Internet, we would be grateful if you would provide us with the location address or website name. Please contact us at copyright@packt.com with a link to the material.

If you are interested in becoming an author: If there is a topic that you have expertise in and you are interested in either writing or contributing to a book, please visit authors.packtpub.com.

Reviews

Please leave a review. Once you have read and used this book, why not leave a review on the site that you purchased it from? Potential readers can then see and use your unbiased opinion to make purchase decisions, we at Packt can understand what you think about our products, and our authors can see your feedback on their book. Thank you!

For more information about Packt, please visit packt.com.

Section 1: Getting Up to Speed

This section brings you up to speed on the basic concepts of learning from data, deep learning frameworks, and preparing data to be usable in deep learning.

This section consists of the following chapters:

- Chapter 1, *Introduction to Machine Learning*
- Chapter 2, *Setup and Introduction to Deep Learning Frameworks*
- Chapter 3, *Preparing Data*
- Chapter 4, *Learning from Data*
- Chapter 5, *Training a Single Neuron*
- Chapter 6, *Training Multiple Layers of Neurons*

1
Introduction to Machine Learning

You have probably heard the term **Machine Learning (ML)** or **Artificial Intelligence (AI)** frequently in recent years, especially **Deep Learning (DL)**. It may be the reason you decided to invest in this book and get to know more. Given some new, exciting developments in the area of neural networks, DL has come to be a hot area in ML. Today, it is difficult to imagine a world without quick text translation between languages, or without fast song identification. These, and many other things, are just the tip of the iceberg when it comes to the potential of DL to change your world. When you finish this book, we hope you will join the bus and ride along with amazing new applications and projects based on DL.

This chapter briefly introduces the field of ML and how it is used to solve common problems. Throughout this chapter, you will be driven to understand the basic concepts of ML, the research questions addressed, and their significance.

The following topics will be covered in this chapter:

- Diving into the ML ecosystem
- Training ML algorithms from data
- Introducing deep learning
- Why is deep learning important today?

Diving into the ML ecosystem

From the typical ML application process depicted in *Figure 1.1*, you can see that ML has a broad range of applications. However, ML algorithms are only a small part of a bigger ecosystem with a lot of moving parts, and yet ML is transforming lives around the world today:

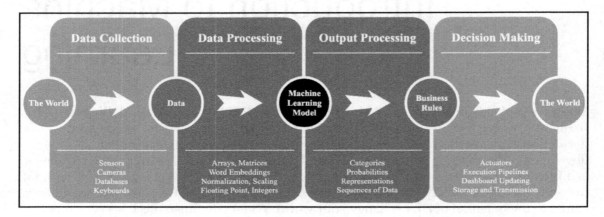

Figure 1.1 - ML ecosystem. ML interacts with the world through several stages of data manipulation and interpretation to achieve an overall system integration

Deployed ML applications usually start with a process of data collection that uses sensors of different types, such as cameras, lasers, spectroscopes, or other types of direct access to data, including local and remote databases, big or small. In the simplest of cases, input can be gathered through a computer keyboard or smartphone screen taps. At this stage, the data collected or sensed is considered to be raw data.

Raw data is usually preprocessed before presenting it to an ML model. Raw data is rarely the actual input to ML algorithms, unless the ML model is meant to find a rich representation of the raw data, and later be used as input to another ML algorithm. In other words, there are some ML algorithms that are specifically used as preprocessing agents and they are not at all related to a main ML model that will classify or regress on the preprocessed data. In a general sense, this data preprocessing stage aims to convert raw data into arrays or matrices with specific data types. Some popular preprocessing strategies include the following:

- Word-to-vector conversions, for example, using GloVe or Word2Vec
- Sequence-to-vector or sequence-to-matrix strategies
- Value range normalization, for example, (0, 255) to (0.0, 1.0)
- Statistical value normalization, for example, to have zero mean and unit variance

Once these preprocessing measures take place, most ML algorithms can use the data. However, it must be noted that the preprocessing stage is not trivial, it requires advanced knowledge and skills with respect to operating systems and sometimes even electronics. In a general sense, a real ML application has a long pipeline touching different aspects of computer science and engineering.

The processed data is what you will usually see in books like the one you are reading right now. The reason is that we need to focus on deep learning instead of data processing. If you wish to be more knowledgeable in this area, you could read data science materials such as Ojeda, T. *et.al.* 2014 or Kane, F. 2017.

Mathematically speaking, the processed data as a whole is referred to using the uppercase, bold font, letter X, which has N rows (or data points). If we want to refer to the specific i-th element (or row) of the dataset, we would do that by writing: X_i. The dataset will have d columns and they are usually called features. One way to think about the features is as dimensions. For example, if the dataset has two features, height and weight, then you could represent the entire dataset using a two-dimensional plot. The first dimension, x_1, (height) can be the horizontal axis, while the second dimension, x_2, (weight) can be the vertical axis, as depicted in *Figure 1.2*:

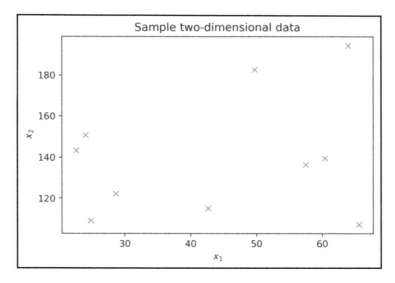

Figure 1.2 - Sample two-dimensional data

During production, when the data is presented to an ML algorithm, a series of tensor products and additions will be executed. Such vectorial operations are usually transformed or normalized using non-linear functions. This is then followed by more products and additions, more non-linear transformations, temporary storage of intermediate values, and finally producing the desired output that corresponds to the input. For now, you can think of this process as an ML black box that will be revealed as you continue reading.

The output that the ML produces in correspondence to the input usually requires some type of interpretation, for example, if the output is a vector of probabilities of objects being classified to belong to a group or to another, then that may need to be interpreted. You may need to know how low the probabilities are in order to account for uncertainty, or you may need to know how different are the probabilities to account for even more uncertainty. The output processing serves as the connecting factor between ML and the decision-making world through the use of business rules. These rules can be, for example, *if-then* rules such as, "If the predicted probability of the maximum is twice as large as the second maximum, then issue a prediction; otherwise, do not proceed to make a decision." Or they can be formula-based rules or more complex systems of equations.

Finally, in the decision-making stage, the ML algorithm is ready to interact with the world by turning on a light bulb through an actuator, or to buy stock if the prediction is not uncertain, by alerting a manager that the company will run out of inventory in three days and they need to buy more items, or by sending an audio message to a smartphone speaker saying, "Here is the route to the movie theater" and opening a maps application through an **application programming interface (API)** call or **operating system (OS)** commands.

This is a broad overview of the world of ML systems when they are in production. However, this assumes that the ML algorithm is properly trained and tested, which is the easy part, trust me. At the end of the book, you will be skilled in training highly complex, deep learning algorithms but, for now, let us introduce the generic training process.

Training ML algorithms from data

A typical preprocessed dataset is formally defined as follows:

$$\mathcal{D} = \{\mathbf{x}_i, y_i\}_{i=0}^N$$

Where y is the desired output corresponding to the input vector $\mathbf{x}$. So, the motivation of ML is to use the data to find linear and non-linear transformations over $\mathbf{x}$ using highly complex tensor (vector) multiplications and additions, or to simply find ways to measure similarities or distances among data points, with the ultimate purpose of predicting y given $\mathbf{x}$.

A common way of thinking about this is that we want to approximate some unknown function over **x**:

$$f(x) = \mathbf{w}^T \mathbf{x} + b = y$$

Where w is an unknown vector that facilitates the transformation of **x** along with b. This formulation is very basic, linear, and is simply an illustration of what a simple learning model would look like. In this simple case, the ML algorithms revolve around finding the best w and b that yields the closest (if not perfect) approximation to y, the desired output. Very simple algorithms such as the perceptron (Rosenblatt, F. 1958) try different values for w and b using past mistakes in the choices of **w** and b to make the next selection in proportion to the mistakes made.

A combination of perceptron-like models that look at the same input, intuitively, turned out to be better than single ones. Later, people realized that having them stacked may be the next logical step leading to multilayer perceptrons, but the problem was that the learning process was rather complicated for people in the 1970s. These kinds of multilayered systems were analog to brain neurons, which is the reason we call them neural networks today. With some interesting discoveries in ML, new specific kinds of neural networks and algorithms were created known as deep learning.

Introducing deep learning

While a more detailed discussion of learning algorithms will be addressed in Chapter 4, *Learning from Data*, in this section, we will deal with the fundamental concept of a neural network and the developments that led to deep learning.

The model of a neuron

The human brain has input connections from other neurons (synapses) that receive stimuli in the form of electric charges, and then has a nucleus that depends on how the input stimulates the neuron that can trigger the neuron's activation. At the end of the neuron, the output signal is propagated to other neurons through dendrites, thus forming a network of neurons.

The analogy of the human neuron is depicted in *Figure 1.3*, where the input is represented with the vector *x*, the activation of the neuron is given by some function **z(.)**, and the output is *y*. The parameters of the neuron are **w** and *b*:

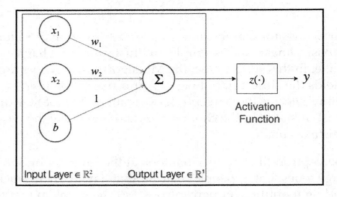

Figure 1.3 - The basic model of a neuron

The trainable parameters of a neuron are *w* and *b*, and they are unknown. Thus, we can use training data $\mathcal{D}$ to determine these parameters using some learning strategy. From the picture, x_1 multiplies w_1, then x_2 multiplies w_2, and *b* is multiplied by 1; all these products are added, which can be simplified as follows:

$$x_1 w_1 + x_2 w_2 + b = \mathbf{w}^T \mathbf{x} + b$$

The activation function operates as a way to ensure the output is within the desired output range. Let's say that we want a simple linear activation, then the function **z(.)** is non-existing or can be bypassed, as follows:

$$z(\mathbf{w}^T \mathbf{x} + b) = \mathbf{w}^T \mathbf{x} + b$$

This is usually the case when we want to solve a regression problem and the output data can have a range from -∞ to +∞. However, we may want to train the neuron to determine whether a vector *x* belongs to one of two classes, say -1 and +1. Then we would be better suited using a function called a sign activation:

$$z(\mathbf{w}^T \mathbf{x} + b) = sign(\mathbf{w}^T \mathbf{x} + b)$$

Where the *sign*(.) function is denoted as follows:

$$sign(\mathbf{w}^T \mathbf{x} + b) = \begin{cases} +1 & if\ \mathbf{w}^T \mathbf{x} + b \geq 0 \\ -1 & otherwise \end{cases}$$

There are many other activation functions, but we will introduce those later on. For now, we will briefly show one of the simplest learning algorithms, the **perceptron learning algorithm** (PLA).

The perceptron learning algorithm

The PLA begins from the assumption that you want to classify data, **X**, into two different groups, the positive group (+) and the negative group (-). It will find *some* **w** and b by training to predict the corresponding correct labels y. The PLA uses the $sign(.)$ function as the activation. Here are the steps that the PLA follows:

1. Initialize **w** to zeros, and iteration counter $t = 0$
2. While there are any incorrectly classified examples:

    - Pick an incorrectly classified example, call it x^*, whose true label is y^*
    - Update **w** as follows: $\mathbf{w}_{t+1} = \mathbf{w}_t + y^* x^*$
    - Increase iteration counter t++ and repeat

Notice that, for the PLA to work as we want, we have to make an adjustment. What we want is for $\mathbf{w}^T \mathbf{x}_i + b$ to be implied in the expression $\mathbf{w}^T \mathbf{x}_i$. The only way this could work is if we set $\mathbf{w} = [b, w_1, w_2, \ldots, w_d]^T$ and $\mathbf{x} = [1, x_1, x_2, \ldots, x_d]^T$. The previous rule seeks **w**, which implies the search for b.

To illustrate the PLA, consider the case of the following linearly separable dataset:

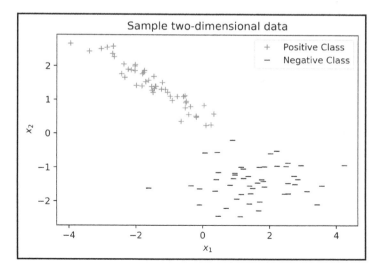

A linearly separable dataset is one whose data points are sufficiently apart such that at least one hypothetical line exists that can be used to separate the data groups into two. Having a linearly separable dataset is the dream of all ML scientists, but it is seldom the case that we will find such datasets naturally. In further chapters, we will see that neural networks transform the data into a new feature space where such a line may exist.

This two-dimensional dataset was produced at random using Python tools that we will discuss later on. For now, it should be self-evident that you can draw a line between the two groups and divide them.

Following the steps outlined previously, the PLA can find *a* solution, that is, a separating line that satisfies the training data target outputs completely in only four iterations in this particular case. The plots after each update are depicted in the following plots with the corresponding line found at every update:

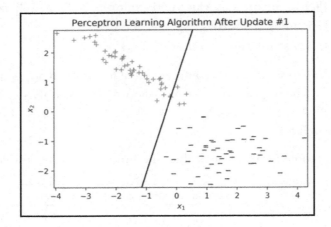

At iteration zero, all 100 points are misclassified, but after randomly choosing one misclassified point to make the first update, the new line only misses four points:

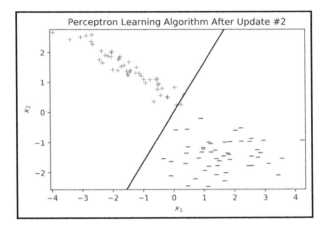

After the second update, the line only misses one data point:

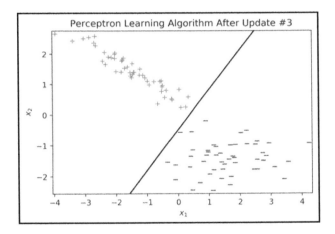

Finally, after update number three, all data points are correctly classified. This is just to show that a simple learning algorithm can successfully learn from data. Also, the perceptron model led to much more complicated models such as a neural network. We will now introduce the concept of a shallow network and its basic complexities.

Shallow networks

A neural network consists of multiple networks connected in different layers. In contrast, a perceptron has only one neuron and its architecture consists of an input layer and an output layer. In neural networks, there are additional layers between the input and output layer, as shown in *Figure 1.4*, and they are known as hidden layers:

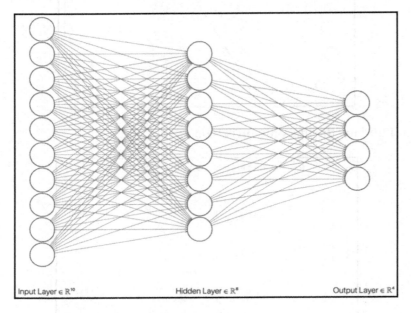

Figure 1.4 - Example of a shallow neural network

The example in the figure shows a neural network that has a hidden layer with eight neurons in it. The input size is 10-dimensional, and the output layer has four dimensions (four neurons). This intermediate layer can have as many neurons as your system can handle during training, but it is usually a good idea to keep things to a reasonable number of neurons.

If this is your first time using neural networks, it is recommended that your hidden layer size, that is, the number of neurons, is greater than or equal to the input layer, and less than or equal to the output size. However, although this is good advice for absolute beginners, this is not an absolute scientific fact since finding the optimal number of neurons in neural networks is an art, rather than a science, and it is usually determined through a great deal of experimentation.

Neural networks can solve more difficult problems than without a network, for example, with a single neural unit such as the perceptron. This must feel intuitive and must be easy to conceive. A neural network can solve problems including and beyond those that are linearly separable. For linearly separable problems, we can use both the perceptron model and a neural network. However, for more complex and non-linearly separable problems, the perceptron cannot offer a high-quality solution, while a neural network does.

For example, if we consider the sample two-class dataset and we bring the data groups closer together, the perceptron will fail to terminate with a solution and some other strategy can be used to stop it from going forever. Or, we can switch to a neural network and train it to find the best solution it can possibly find. *Figure 1.5* shows an example of training a neural network with 100 neurons in the hidden layer over a two-class dataset that is not linearly separable:

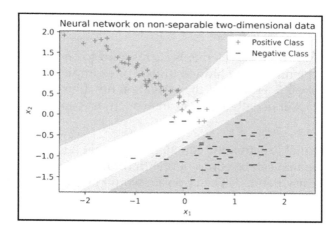

Figure 1.5 - Non-separable data and a non-linear solution using a neural network with 100 neurons in the hidden layer

This neural network has 100 neurons in the hidden layer. This was a choice done by experimentation and you will learn strategies on how to find such instances in further chapters. However, before we go any further, there are two new terms introduced that require further explanation: non-separable data and non-linear models, which are defined as follows:

- Non-separable data is such that there is no line that can separate groups of data (or classes) into two groups.
- Non-linear models, or solutions, are those that naturally and commonly occur when the best solution to a classification problem is not a line. For example, it can be some curve described by some polynomial of any degree greater than one. For an example, see *Figure 1.5*.

A non-linear model is usually what we will be working with throughout this book, and the reason is that this is most likely what you will encounter out there in the real world. Also, it is non-linear, in a way, because the problem is non-separable. To achieve this non-linear solution, the neural network model goes through the following mathematical operations.

The input-to-hidden layer

In a neural network, the input vector x is connected to a number of neurons through weights w for each neuron, which can be now thought of as a number of weight vectors forming a matrix W. The matrix W has as many columns as neurons as the layer has, and as many rows as the number of features (or dimensions) x has. Thus, the output of the hidden layer can be thought of as the following vector:

$$\mathbf{h} = z(\mathbf{w}^T \mathbf{x} + b)$$

Where **b** is a vector of biases, whose elements correspond to one neural unit, and the size of **h** is proportional to the number of hidden units. For example, eight neurons in *Figure 1.4*, and 100 neurons in *Figure 1.5*. However, the activation function z(.) does not have to be the *sign*(.) function, in fact, it usually never is. Instead, most people use functions that are easily differentiable.

 A differentiable activation function is one that has a mathematical derivative that can be computed with traditional numerical methods or that is clearly defined. The opposite would be a function that does not have a defined derivative, it does not exist, or is nearly impossible to calculate.

The hidden-to-hidden layer

In a neural network, we could have more than one single hidden layer, and we will work with this kind a lot in this book. In such case, the matrix W can be expressed as a three-dimensional matrix that will have as many elements in the third dimension and as many hidden layers as the network has. In the case of the *i*-th layer, we will refer to that matrix as $\mathbf{W}_i$ for convenience.

Therefore, we can refer to the output of the *i*-th hidden layer as follows:

$$\mathbf{h}_i = z(\mathbf{W}_i^T \mathbf{h}_{i-1} + \mathbf{b}_i)$$

For $i = 2, 3, ..., k\text{-}1$, where k is the total number of layers, and the case of h_1 is computed with the equation given for the first layer (see previous section), which uses x directly, and does not go all the way to the last layer, h_k, because that is computed as discussed next.

The hidden-to-output layer

The overall output of the network is the output at the last layer:

$$\mathbf{h}_k = z(\mathbf{W}_k^T \mathbf{h}_{k-1} + \mathbf{b}_k)$$

Here, the last activation function is usually different from the hidden layer activations. The activation function in the last layer (output) traditionally depends on the type of problem we are trying to solve. For example, if we want to solve a regression problem, we would use a linear function, or sigmoid activations for classification problems. We will discuss those later on. For now, it should be evident that the perceptron algorithm will no longer work in the training phase.

While the learning still has to be in terms of the mistakes the neural network makes, the adjustments cannot be in direct proportion to the data point that is incorrectly classified or predicted. The reason is that the neurons in the last layer are responsible for making the predictions, but they depend on a previous layer, and those may depend on more previous layers, and when making adjustments to W and b, the adjustment has to be made differently for each neuron.

One approach to do this is to apply gradient descent techniques on the neural network. There are many of these techniques and we will discuss the most popular of these in further chapters. In general, a gradient descent algorithm is one that uses the notion that, if you take the derivative of a function and that reaches a value of zero, then you have found the maximum (or minimum) value you can get for the set of parameters on which you are taking the derivatives. For the case of scalars, we call them derivatives, but for vectors or matrices ($\mathbf{W}$, $\mathbf{b}$), we call them gradients.

The function we can use is called a loss function.

 A loss function is usually one that is differentiable so that we can calculate its gradient using some gradient descent algorithm.

We can define a loss function, for example, as follows:

$$L = \frac{1}{N} \sum_{i=1}^{N} (\mathbf{y}_i - \mathbf{h}_{i,k})^2$$

This loss is known as the **mean squared error** (**MSE**); it is meant to measure how different the target output y is from the predicted output in the output layer h_k in terms of the square of its elements, and averaged. This is a good loss because it is differentiable and it is easy to compute.

A neural network such as this introduced a great number of possibilities, but relied heavily on a gradient descent technique for learning them called backpropagation (Hecht-Nielsen, R. 1992). Rather than explaining backpropagation here (we will reserve that for later), we rather have to remark that it changed the world of ML, but did not make much progress for a number of years because it had some practical limitations and the solutions to these paved the way for deep learning.

Deep networks

On March 27, 2019, an announcement was published by the ACM saying that three computer scientists were awarded the Nobel Prize in computing, that is, the ACM Turing Award, for their achievements in deep learning. Their names are Yoshua Bengio, Yann LeCun, and Geoffrey Hinton; all are very accomplished scientists. One of their major contributions was in the learning algorithm known as backpropagation.

In the official communication, the ACM wrote the following about Dr. Hinton and one of his seminal papers (Rumelhart, D. E. 1985):

> *In a 1986 paper, "Learning Internal Representations by Error Propagation," co-authored with David Rumelhart and Ronald Williams, Hinton demonstrated that the backpropagation algorithm allowed neural nets to discover their own internal representations of data, making it possible to use neural nets to solve problems that had previously been thought to be beyond their reach. The backpropagation algorithm is standard in most neural networks today.*

Similarly, they wrote the following about Dr. LeCun's paper (LeCun, Y., *et.al.*, 1998):

> *LeCun proposed an early version of the backpropagation algorithm (backprop), and gave a clean derivation of it based on variational principles. His work to speed up backpropagation algorithms included describing two simple methods to accelerate learning time.*

Dr. Hinton was able to show that there was a way to minimize a loss function in neural networks using biologically inspired algorithms such as the backward and forward adjustment of connections by modifying its importance for particular neurons. Usually, backpropagation is related to feed-forward neural networks, while backward-forward propagation is related to Restricted Boltzmann Machines (covered in `Chapter 10`, *Restricted Boltzmann Machines*).

A feed-forward neural network is one whose input is pipelined directly toward the output layer through intermediate layers that have no backward connections, as shown in *Figure 1.4*, and we will talk about these all the time in this book.

> It is usually safe to assume that, unless you are told otherwise, all neural networks have a feed-forward architecture. Most of this book will talk about deep neural networks and the great majority are feed-forward-like, with the exception of Restricted Boltzmann Machines or recurrent neural networks, for example.

Backpropagation enabled people to train neural networks in a way that was never seen before; however, people had problems training neural networks on large datasets, and on larger (deeper) architectures. If you go ahead and look at neural network papers in the late '80s and early '90s, you will notice that architectures were small in size; networks usually had no more than two or three layers, and the number of neurons usually did not exceed the order of hundreds. These are (today) known as shallow neural networks.

The major problems were with convergence time for larger datasets, and convergence time for deeper architectures. Dr. LeCun's contributions were precisely in this area as he envisioned different ways to speed up the training process. Other advances such as vector (tensor) computations over **graphics processing units (GPUs)** increased training speeds dramatically.

Thus, over the last few years, we have seen the rise of deep learning, that is, the ability to train deeper neural networks, with more than three or four layers, in fact with tens and hundreds of layers. Further, we have a wide variety of architectures that can accomplish things that we were not able in the last decade.

The deep network shown in *Figure 1.6* would have been impossible to train 30 years ago, and it is not that deep anyway:

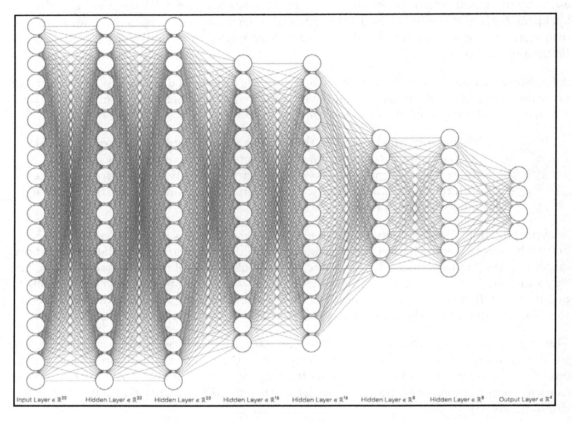

Figure 1.6 - A deep and fully connected feed-forward neural network with eight layers

 In this book, we will consider a deep neural network any network that has more than three or four layers overall. However, there is no standard definition as to exactly how deep is considered deep out there. Also, you need to consider that what we consider deep today, at the time of writing this book in 2020, will probably not be considered deep in 20 or 30 years from now.

Regardless of the future of DL, let us now discuss what makes DL so important today.

Why is deep learning important today?

Today, we enjoy the benefits of algorithms and strategies that we did not have 20 or 30 years ago, which enable us to have amazing applications that are changing lives. Allow me to summarize some of the great and important things about deep learning today:

- **Training in mini-batches**: This strategy allows us today to have very large datasets and train a deep learning model little by little. In the past, we would have to load the entire dataset into memory, making it computationally impossible for some large datasets. Today, yes, it may take a little longer, but we at least can actually perform training on finite time.
- **Novel activation functions: Rectified linear units (ReLUs)**, for example, are a relatively new kind of activation that solved many of the problems with large-scale training with backpropagation strategies. These new activations enable training algorithms to converge on deep architectures when, in the past, we would get stuck on non-converging training sessions that would end up having exploding or vanishing gradients.
- **Novel neural network architectures**: Convolutional or recurrent networks, for example, have been transforming the world by opening the possibilities of things we can do with neural networks. Convolutional networks are widely applied in computer vision applications or other areas in which the convolution operation is a natural thing to do, for example, multi-dimensional signal or audio analysis. Recurrent neural networks with memory are widely used to analyze sequences of text, thus enabling us to have networks that understand words, sentences, and paragraphs, and we can use them to translate between languages, and many more things.
- **Interesting loss functions**: These losses play an interesting role in deep learning because, in the past, we only used the same standard losses over and over again; losses such as the MSE. Today, we can minimize the MSE and, at the same time, minimize the norm of the weights or the output of some neurons, which leads to sparser weights and solutions that, in turn, make the produced model much more efficient when it is deployed into production.

- **Novel strategies resembling biology**: Things such as missing or dropping connections between neurons, rather than having them fully connected all the time, is more realistic, or comparable to biological neural network design. Also, dropping or removing neurons altogether is a new strategy that can push some neurons to excel when others are removed, learning richer representations, while at the same time reducing the computations during training and when deployed. The sharing of parameters between different and specialized neural networks also has proven to be interesting and effective today.
- **Adversarial training**: Making a neural network compete against another network whose sole purpose is to generate fraudulent, noisy, and confusing data points trying to make the network fail has proven to be an excellent strategy for networks to learn better from the data and be robust against noisy environments when deployed into production.

There are many other interesting facts and points that make deep learning an exciting area and justify the writing of this book. I hope you are as excited as we all are and begin reading this book knowing that we are going to code some of the most exciting and incredible neural networks of our time. Our ultimate purpose will be to make deep neural networks that can generalize.

 Generalization is the ability of a neural network to correctly make predictions on data that has never been seen before. This is the ultimate purpose of all machine and deep learning practitioners, and requires a great deal of skill and knowledge of the data.

Summary

This introductory chapter presented an overview of ML. It introduced the motivation behind ML and the terminology that is commonly used in the field. It also introduced deep learning and how it fits in the realm of artificial intelligence. At this point, you should feel confident that you know enough about what a neural network is to be curious about how big it can be. You should also feel very intrigued about the area of deep learning and all the new things that are coming out every week.

At this point, you must be a bit anxious to begin your deep learning coding journey; for that reason, the next logical step is to go to `Chapter 2`, *Setup and Introduction to Deep Learning Frameworks*. In this chapter, you will get ready for the action by setting up your system and making sure you have access to the resources you will need to be a successful deep learning practitioner. But before you go there, please try to quiz yourself with the following questions.

Questions and answers

1. **Can a perceptron and/or a neural network solve the problem of classifying data that is linearly separable?**

   Yes, both can.

2. **Can a perceptron and/or a neural network solve the problem of classifying data that is non-separable?**

   Yes, both can. However, the perceptron will go on forever unless we specify a stopping condition such as a maximum number of iterations (updates), or stopping if the number of misclassified points does not decrease after a number of iterations.

3. **What are the changes in the ML filed that have enabled us to have deep learning today?**

   (A) backpropagation algorithms, batch training, ReLUs, and so on;

   (B) computing power, GPUs, cloud, and so on.

4. **Why is generalization a good thing?**

   Because deep neural networks are most useful when they can function as expected when they are given data that they have not seen before, that is, data on which they have not been trained.

References

- Hecht-Nielsen, R. (1992). *Theory of the backpropagation neural network*. In *Neural networks for perception* (pp. 65-93). *Academic Press*.
- Kane, F. (2017). *Hands-On Data Science and Python ML*. *Packt Publishing Ltd*.
- LeCun, Y., Bottou, L., Orr, G., and Muller, K. (1998). *Efficient backprop in neural networks: Tricks of the trade* (Orr, G. and Müller, K., eds.). *Lecture Notes in Computer Science*, 1524(98), 111.
- Ojeda, T., Murphy, S. P., Bengfort, B., and Dasgupta, A. (2014). *Practical Data Science Cookbook*. *Packt Publishing Ltd*.

- Rosenblatt, F. (1958). *The perceptron: a probabilistic model for information storage and organization in the brain. Psychological Review,* 65(6), 386.
- Rumelhart, D. E., Hinton, G. E., and Williams, R. J. (1985). *Learning internal representations by error propagation* (No. ICS-8506). *California Univ San Diego La Jolla Inst for Cognitive Science.*

Setup and Introduction to Deep Learning Frameworks

2

At this point, you are now familiar with **machine learning (ML)** and **deep learning (DL)** - this is great! You should feel ready to begin making the preparations for writing and running your own programs. This chapter helps you in the process of setting up TensorFlow and Keras, and introduces their usefulness and purpose in deep learning. Dopamine is presented as the new reinforcement learning framework that we will use later on. This chapter also briefly introduces other deep learning libraries that are important to know.

The topics that will be covered in this chapter are as follows:

- Introduction to Colaboratory
- Introduction and setup of TensorFlow
- Introduction and setup of Keras
- Introduction to PyTorch
- Introduction to Dopamine
- Other deep learning libraries

Introduction to Colaboratory

What is Colaboratory? Colaboratory is a web-based research tool for doing machine learning and deep learning. It is essentially like Jupyter Notebook. Colaboratory is becoming very popular these days as it requires no setup.

Throughout this book, we will be using Python 3 running on Colaboratory which will have installed all the libraries we may need.

Colaboratory is free to use and is compatible with most major browsers. The company in charge of the development of the Colaboratory tool is Google™. As opposed to Jupyter notebooks, in Colaboratory you are running everything on the cloud and not on your own computer. Here is the catch: you need a Google account since all the Colaboratory notebooks are saved into your personal Google Drive space. However, if you do not have a Google account, you can still continue reading to see how you can install every piece of Python library you will need to run things on your own. Still, I highly recommend you create a Google account, if only just to learn deep learning using the Colaboratory notebooks of this book.

When you run your code on Colaboratory, it runs on a dedicated virtual machine, and here is the fun part: you can have a GPU allocated to use! Or you can also use a CPU if you want. Whenever you are not running something, Colaboratory will deallocate resources (you know, because we all want to work), but you can reconnect them at any time.

If you are ready, go ahead and navigate to this link: `https://colab.research.google.com/`

If you are interested in more information and a further introduction to Colaboratory, search for *Welcome to Colaboratory!*. Now that you have accessed the previous link, let us get started with TensorFlow.

 From now on, we will refer to **Colaboratory** as **Colab** for short. This is actually how people refer to it.

Introduction and setup of TensorFlow

TensorFlow (**TF**) has in its name the word *Tensor*, which is a synonym of vector. TF, thus, is a Python framework that is designed to excel at vectorial operations pertaining to the modeling of neural networks. It is the most popular library for machine learning.

As data scientists, we have a preference towards TF because it is free, opensource with a strong user base, and it uses state-of-the-art research on the graph-based execution of tensor operations.

Setup

Let us now begin with instructions to set up or verify that you have the proper setup:

1. To begin the installation of TF, run the following command in your Colaboratory:

```
%tensorflow_version 2.x
!pip install tensorflow
```

This will install about 20 libraries that are required to run TF, including numpy, for example.

 Notice the exclamation mark (!) at the beginning of the command? This is how you will run shell commands on Colaboratory. For example, say that you want to remove a file named model.h5, then you would issue the command !rm model.h5.

2. If the execution of the installation ran properly, you will be able to run the following command, which will print the version of TF that is installed on your Colaboratory:

```
import tensorflow as tf
print(tf.__version__)
```

This will produce the following output:

```
2.1.0
```

3. This version of TF is the current version of TF at the time of writing this book. However, we all know that TF versions change frequently and it is likely that there will be a new version of TF when you are reading this book. If that is the case, you can install a specific version of TF as follows:

```
!pip install tensorflow==2.1.0
```

 We are assuming that you are familiar with Python, thus, we will trust you with the responsibility of matching the proper libraries to the versions that we are using in this book. This is not difficult and can easily be done as shown previously, for example, using the == sign to specify the version. We will be showing the versions used as we continue.

TensorFlow with GPU support

Colaboratory, by default, has GPU support automatically enabled for TensorFlow. However, if you have access to your own system with a GPU and want to set up TensorFlow with GPU support, the installation is very simple. Just type the following command on your personal system:

```
$ pip install tensorflow-gpu
```

Notice, however, that this assumes that you have set up all the necessary drivers for your system to give access to the GPU. However, fear not, there is plenty of documentation about this process that can be searched on the internet, for example, https://www.tensorflow.org/install/gpu. If you run into any problems and you need to move forward, I highly recommend that you come back and do the work on Colaboratory, as it is the easiest way to learn.

Let us now address how TensorFlow works and how its graph paradigm makes it very robust.

Principles behind TensorFlow

This book is for absolute beginners in deep learning. As such, here is what we want you to know about how TF works. TF creates a graph that contains the execution from its input tensors, up to the highest level of abstraction of operations.

For example, let's say that we have tensors x and w that are known input vectors, and that we have a known constant b, and say that you want to perform this operation:

$$\mathbf{w}^T \mathbf{x} + b$$

If we create this operation by declaring and assigning tensors, the graph will look like the one in *Figure 2.1*:

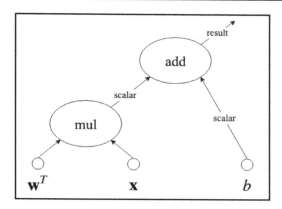

Figure 2.1 - Example of a tensor multiplication and addition operation

In this figure, there is a tensor multiplication operation, *mul*, whose result is a scalar and needs to be added, *add*, with another scalar, *b*. Note that this might be an intermediate result and, in real computing graphs, the outcome of this goes up higher in the execution tree. For more detailed information on how TF uses graphs, please refer to this paper (Abadi, M., et.al., 2016).

In a nutshell, TF finds the best way to execute tensor operations delegating specific parts to GPUs if available, or otherwise parallelizing operations on the CPU cores if available. It is open source with a growing community of users around the world. Most deep learning professionals know about TF.

Now let us discuss how to set up Keras and how it abstracts TensorFlow functionalities.

Introduction and setup of Keras

If you search on the internet for sample TensorFlow code, you will find that it may not be super easy to understand or follow. You can find tutorials for beginners but, in reality, things can get complicated very easily and editing someone else's code can be very difficult. Keras comes as an API solution to develop deep learning Tensorflow model prototypes with relative ease. In fact, Keras supports running not only on top of TensorFlow, but also over CNTK and Theano.

We can think of Keras as an abstraction to actual TensorFlow models and methods. This symbiotic relationship has become so popular that TensorFlow now unofficially encourages its use for those who are beginning to use TensorFlow. Keras is very user friendly, it is easy to follow in Python, and it is easy to learn in a general sense.

Setup

To set up Keras on your Colab, do the following:

1. Run the following command:

```
!pip install keras
```

2. The system will proceed to install the necessary libraries and dependencies. Once finished, type and run the following code snippet:

```
import keras
print(keras.__version__)
```

This outputs a confirmation message of it using TensorFlow as the backend as well as the latest version of Keras, which at the time of writing this book is 2.2.4. Thus, the output looks like this:

```
Using TensorFlow backend.
2.2.4
```

Principles behind Keras

There are two major ways in which Keras provides functionality to its users: a sequential model and the Functional API.

These can be summarized as follows:

- **Sequential model**: This refers to a way of using Keras that allows you to linearly (or sequentially) stack layer instances. A layer instance, in this case, has the same meaning as in our previous discussions in Chapter 1, *Introduction to Machine Learning*. That is, a layer has some type of input, some type of behavior or main model operation, and some type of output.
- **Functional API**: This is the best way to go deeper in defining more complex models, such as merge models, models with multiple outputs, models with multiple shared layers, and many other possibilities. Don't worry, these are advanced topics that will become clear in further chapters. The Functional API paradigm gives the coder more freedom to do different innovative things.

We can think of the sequential model as an easy way of starting with Keras, and the Functional API as the way to go for more complex problems.

Remember the shallow neural network from `Chapter 1`, *Introduction to Machine Learning*? Well, this is how you would do that model using the sequential model paradigm in Keras:

```
from keras.models import Sequential
from keras.layers import Dense, Activation

model = Sequential([
    Dense(10, input_shape=(10,)),
    Activation('relu'),
    Dense(8),
    Activation('relu'),
    Dense(4),
    Activation('softmax'),
])
```

The first two lines of code import the `Sequential` model and the `Dense` and `Activation` layers, respectively. A `Dense` layer is a fully connected neural network, whereas an `Activation` layer is a very specific way of invoking a rich set of activation functions, such as ReLU and SoftMax, as in the previous example (these will be explained in detail later).

Alternatively, you could do the same model, but using the `add()` method:

```
from keras.models import Sequential
from keras.layers import Dense, Activation

model = Sequential()
model.add(Dense(10, input_dim=10))
model.add(Activation('relu'))
model.add(Dense(8))
model.add(Activation('relu'))
model.add(Dense(4))
model.add(Activation('softmax'))
```

This second way of writing the code for the neural model looks more linear, while the first one looks more like a Pythonic way to do so with a list of items. It is really the same thing and you will probably develop a preference for one way or the other. However, remember, both of the previous examples use the Keras sequential model.

Now, just for comparison purposes, this is how you would code the exact same neural network architecture, but using the Keras Functional API paradigm:

```
from keras.layers import Input, Dense
from keras.models import Model

inputs = Input(shape=(10,))

x = Dense(10, activation='relu')(inputs)
x = Dense(8, activation='relu')(x)
y = Dense(4, activation='softmax')(x)

model = Model(inputs=inputs, outputs=y)
```

If you are an experienced programmer, you will notice that the Functional API style allows more flexibility. It allows you to define input tensors to use them as input to different pieces of the model, if needed. However, using the Functional API does assume that you are familiar with the sequential model. Therefore, in this book, we will start with the sequential model and move forward with the Functional API paradigm as we make progress toward more complex neural models.

Just like Keras, there are other Python libraries and frameworks that allow us to do machine learning with relatively low difficulty. At the time of writing this book, the most popular is Keras and the second most popular is PyTorch.

Introduction to PyTorch

At the time of writing this book, PyTorch is the third most popular overall deep learning framework. Its popularity has been increasing in spite of being relatively new in the world compared to TensorFlow. One of the interesting things about PyTorch is that it allows some customizations that TensorFlow does not. Furthermore, PyTorch has the support of Facebook™.

Although this book covers TensorFlow and Keras, I think it is important for all of us to remember that PyTorch is a good alternative and it looks very similar to Keras. As a mere reference, here is how the exact same shallow neural network we showed earlier would look if coded in PyTorch:

```
import torch

device = torch.device('cpu')

model = torch.nn.Sequential(
```

```
    torch.nn.Linear(10, 10),
    torch.nn.ReLU(),
    torch.nn.Linear(10, 8),
    torch.nn.ReLU(),
    torch.nn.Linear(8, 2),
    torch.nn.Softmax(2)
).to(device)
```

The similarities are many. Also, the transition from Keras to PyTorch should not be too difficult for the motivated reader, and it could be a nice skill to have in the future. However, for now, most of the interest of the community is on TensorFlow and all its derivatives, especially Keras. If you want to know more about the beginnings and basic principles of PyTorch, you might find this reading useful (Paszke, A., et.al., <u>2017</u>).

Introduction to Dopamine

An interesting recent development in the world of deep reinforcement learning is Dopamine. Dopamine is a framework for the fast prototyping of deep reinforcement learning algorithms. This book will deal very briefly with reinforcement learning, but you need to know how to install it.

Dopamine is known for being easy to use for new users in the world of reinforcement learning. Also, although it is not an official product of Google, most of its developers are Googlers. In its current state, at the time of writing this book, the framework is very compact and provides ready-to-use algorithms.

To install Dopamine, you can run the following command:

```
!pip install dopamine-rl
```

You can test the correct installation of Dopamine by simply executing the following command:

```
import dopamine
```

This provides no output, unless there are errors. Usually, Dopamine will make use of a lot of libraries outside of it to allow doing many more interesting things. Right now, some of the most interesting things one can do with reinforcement learning is to train agents with reward policies, which has direct applications in gaming.

As an example, see *Figure 2.2*, which displays a time snapshot of a video game as it learns, using policies that reinforce desired behavior depending on the actions taken by an agent:

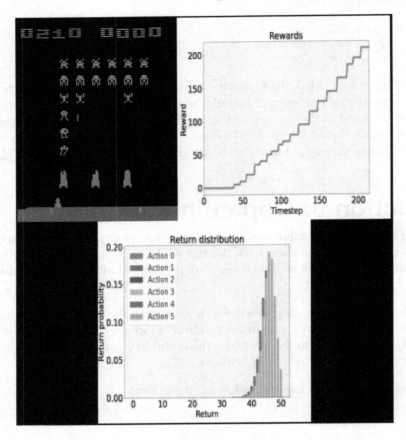

Figure 2.2 - Sample visualization of Dopamine's agent in a reinforcement learning problem in gaming

 An agent in reinforcement learning is the piece that decides what action to take next. The agent accomplishes this by observing the world and the rules of the world. The more defined the rules are, the more constrained the result will be. If the rules are too loose, the agent may not make good decisions on what actions to take.

Although this book does not dive a great deal into reinforcement learning, we will cover an interesting gaming application in the last chapter of the book. For now, you can read the following white paper for more information about Dopamine (Castro, P. S., et.al., 2018).

Other deep learning libraries

Besides the big two, TensorFlow and Keras, there are other competitors that are making their way in the world of deep learning. We already discussed PyTorch, but there are more. Here we talk about them briefly.

Caffe

Caffe is also a popular framework developed at UC Berkeley (Jia, Y., et.al. 2014). It became very popular in 2015-2016. A few employers still demand this skillset and scholarly articles still mention its usage. However, its usage is in decay in part due to the major success of TF and the accessibility of Keras.

> For more information about Caffe, visit: `https://caffe.berkeleyvision.org`.

Note also the existence of Caffe2, which is developed by Facebook and is open source. It was built based on Caffe, but now Facebook has its new champion, PyTorch.

Theano

Theano was developed by Yoshua Bengio's group at the University of Montreal in 2007 (Al-Rfou, R., *et.al.* 2016). Theano has a relatively old user base that probably saw the rise of TF. The latest major release was made in late 2017 and, although there are no clear plans of new major releases, updates are still being made by the community.

> For more information about Theano, please visit:
> `http://deeplearning.net/software/theano/`

Honorable mentions

There are other alternatives out there that may not be as popular, for a variety of reasons, but are worth mentioning here in case their future changes. These are as follows:

Name	Developed by	More information
MXNET	Apache	https://mxnet.apache.org/
CNTK	Microsoft	https://cntk.ai
Deeplearning4J	Skymind	https://deeplearning4j.org/
Chainer	Preferred Networks	https://chainer.org/
FastAI	Jeremy Howard	https://www.fast.ai/

Summary

This introductory chapter showed how to set up the necessary libraries to run TensorFlow, Keras, and Dopamine. Hopefully, you will use Colabs to make things easier for you to learn. You also learned the basic mindset and design concept behind these frameworks. Although such frameworks are the most popular at the time of writing this book, there are other competitors out there, which we also introduced briefly.

At this point, you are all set to begin the journey to mastering deep learning. Our first milestone is to know how to prepare data for deep learning applications. This item is crucial for the success of the model. No matter how good the models are and how deep they are, if the data is not properly formatted or treated, it can lead to catastrophic performance results. For that reason, we will now go to Chapter 3, *Preparing Data*. In that chapter, you will learn how to take a dataset and prepare it for the specific task you are trying to solve with a specific type of deep learning model. However, before you go there, please try to quiz yourself with the following questions.

Questions and answers

1. **Does Colab run on my personal computer?**

   No, it runs in the cloud, but with some skill and setup, you could connect it to your own personal cloud.

2. **Does Keras use GPUs?**

   Yes. Since Keras runs on TensorFlow (in the setup of this book) and TensorFlow uses GPUs, then Keras also does.

3. **What are the two main coding paradigms in Keras?**

   (A) Sequential model; (B) Functional API.

4. **Why do we care about Dopamine?**

   Because there are only a few reinforcement learning frameworks you can trust out there, and Dopamine is one of them.

References

- Abadi, M., Barham, P., Chen, J., Chen, Z., Davis, A., Dean, J., Devin, M., Ghemawat, S., Irving, G., Isard, M., and Kudlur, M. (2016). *Tensorflow: A system for large-scale machine learning*. In *12th {USENIX} Symposium on Operating Systems Design and Implementation ({OSDI} 16)* (pp. 265-283).
- Paszke, A., Gross, S., Chintala, S., Chanan, G., Yang, E., DeVito, Z., Lin, Z., Desmaison, A., Antiga, L. and Lerer, A. (2017). *Automatic differentiation in pytorch.*
- Castro, P. S., Moitra, S., Gelada, C., Kumar, S., and Bellemare, M. G. (2018). *Dopamine: A research framework for deep reinforcement learning*. arXiv preprint arXiv:1812.06110.
- Jia, Y., Shelhamer, E., Donahue, J., Karayev, S., Long, J., Girshick, R., Guadarrama, S., and Darrell, T. (2014, November). *Caffe: Convolutional architecture for fast feature embedding*. In *Proceedings of the 22nd ACM international conference on Multimedia* (pp. 675-678). *ACM.*
- Al-Rfou, R., Alain, G., Almahairi, A., Angermueller, C., Bahdanau, D., Ballas, N., Bastien, F., Bayer, J., Belikov, A., Belopolsky, A. and Bengio, Y. (2016). *Theano: A Python framework for fast computation of mathematical expressions*. arXiv preprint arXiv:1605.02688.

3
Preparing Data

Now that you have successfully prepared your system to learn about deep learning, see Chapter 2, *Setup and Introduction to Deep Learning Frameworks*, we will proceed to give you important guidelines about data that you may encounter frequently when practicing deep learning. When it comes to learning about deep learning, having well-prepared datasets will help you to focus more on designing your models rather than preparing your data. However, everyone knows that this is not a realistic expectation and if you ask any data scientist or machine learning professional about this, they will tell you that an important aspect of modeling is knowing how to prepare your data. Knowing how to deal with your data and how to prepare it will save you many hours of work that you can spend fine-tuning your models. Any time spent preparing your data is time well invested indeed.

This chapter will introduce you to the main concepts behind data processing to make it useful in deep learning. It will cover essential concepts of formatting outputs and inputs that are categorical or real-valued, and techniques for augmenting data or reducing the dimensions of data. At the end of the chapter, you should be able to handle the most common data manipulation techniques that can lead to successful choices of deep learning methodologies down the road.

Specifically, this chapter discusses the following:

- Binary data and binary classification
- Categorical data and multiple classes
- Real-valued data and univariate regression
- Altering the distribution of data
- Data augmentation
- Data dimensionality reduction
- Ethical implications of manipulating data

Binary data and binary classification

In this section, we will focus all our efforts on **preparing** data with binary inputs or targets. By binary, of course, we mean values that can be represented as either 0 or 1. Notice the emphasis on the words *represented as*. The reason is that a column may contain data that is not necessarily a 0 or a 1, but could be interpreted as or represented by a 0 or a 1.

Consider the following fragment of a dataset:

x_1	x_2	...	y
0	5	...	a
1	7	...	a
1	5	...	b
0	7	...	b

In this short dataset example with only four rows, the column x_1 has values that are clearly binary and are either 0 or a 1. However, x_2, at first glance, may not be perceived as binary, but if you pay close attention, the only values in that column are either 5 or 7. This means that the data can be correctly and uniquely mapped to a set of two values. Therefore, we could map 5 to 0, and 7 to 1, or vice versa; it does not really matter.

A similar phenomenon is observed in the target output value, y, which also contains unique values that can be mapped to a set of size two. And we can do such mapping by assigning, say, *b* to *0*, and *a* to *1*.

If you are going to map from strings to binary, always make sure to check what type of data your specific models can handle. For example, in some Support Vector Machine implementations, the preferred values for targets are -1 and 1. This is still binary but in a different set. Always double-check before deciding what mapping you will use.

In the next sub-section, we will deal specifically with binary targets using a dataset as a case study.

Binary targets on the Cleveland Heart Disease dataset

The *Cleveland Heart Disease* (Cleveland 1988) dataset contains patient data for 303 subjects. Some of the columns in the dataset have missing values; we will deal with this, too. The dataset contains 13 columns that include cholesterol and age.

The target is to detect whether a subject has heart disease or not, thus, is binary. The problem we will deal with is that the data is encoded with values from 0 to 4, where 0 indicates the absence of heart disease and the range 1 to 4 indicates some type of heart disease.

We will use the portion of the dataset identified as `Cleveland`, which can be downloaded from this link: `https://archive.ics.uci.edu/ml/machine-learning-databases/heart-disease/processed.cleveland.data`

The attributes of the dataset are as follows:

Column	Description
x_1	Age
x_2	Sex
x_3	Chest pain type: 1: typical angina 2: atypical angina 3: non-anginal pain 4: asymptomatic
x_4	Resting blood pressure (in mm Hg on admission to the hospital)
x_5	Serum cholesterol in mg/dl
x_6	Fasting blood sugar > 120 mg/dl: 1 = true 0 = false
x_7	Resting electrocardiographic results: 0: normal 1: having ST-T wave abnormality 2: showing probable or definite left ventricular hypertrophy
x_8	Maximum heart rate achieved
x_9	Exercise-induced angina: 1 = yes 0 = no
x_{10}	ST depression induced by exercise relative to rest
x_{11}	The slope of the peak exercise ST segment: 1: upsloping 2: flat 3: downsloping
x_{12}	Number of major vessels (0-3) colored by fluoroscopy

x_{13}	Thal: 3 = normal 6 = fixed defect 7 = reversible defect
y	Diagnosis of heart disease (angiographic disease status): 0: < 50% diameter narrowing 1: > 50% diameter narrowing

Let's follow the next steps in order to read the dataset into a pandas DataFrame and clean it:

1. In our Google Colab, we will first download the data using the wget command as follows:

```
!wget
https://archive.ics.uci.edu/ml/machine-learning-databases/heart-dis
ease/processed.cleveland.data
```

This, in turn, downloads the file processed.cleveland.data to the default directory for Colab. This can be verified by inspecting the **Files** tab on the left side of Colab. Please note that the preceding instruction is all one single line that, unfortunately, is very long.

2. Next, we load the dataset using pandas to verify that the dataset is readable and accessible.

 Pandas is a Python library that is very popular among data scientists and machine learning scientists. It makes it easy to load and save datasets, to replace missing values, to retrieve basic statistical properties on data, and even perform transformations. Pandas is a lifesaver and now most other libraries for machine learning accept pandas as a valid input format.

Run the following commands in Colab to load and display some data:

```
import pandas as pd
df = pd.read_csv('processed.cleveland.data', header=None)
print(df.head())
```

The read_csv() function loads a file that is formatted as **comma-separated values (CSV)**. We use the argument header=None to tell pandas that the data does not have any actual headers; if omitted, pandas will use the first row of the data as the names for each column, but we do not want that in this case.

The loaded data is stored in a variable called `df`, which can be any name, but I think it is easy to remember because pandas stores the data in a DataFrame object. Thus, `df` seems like an appropriate, short, memorable name for the data. However, if we work with multiple DataFrames, then it would be more convenient to name all of them differently with a name that describes the data they contain.

The `head()` method that operates over a DataFrame is analog to a `unix` command that retrieves the first few lines of a file. On a DataFrame, the `head()` method returns the first five rows of data. If you wish to retrieve more, or fewer, rows of data, you can specify an integer as an argument to the method. Say, for example, that you want to retrieve the first three rows, then you would do `df.head(3)`.

The results of running the preceding code are as follows:

	0	1	2	3	4	5	6	7	8	9	10	11	12	13
0	63.	1.	1.	145.	233.	1.	2.	150.	0.	2.3	3.	0.	6.	0
1	67.	1.	4.	160.	286.	0.	2.	108.	1.	1.5	2.	3.	3.	2
2	67.	1.	4.	120.	229.	0.	2.	129.	1.	2.6	2.	2.	7.	1
3	37.	1.	3.	130.	250.	0.	0.	187.	0.	3.5	3.	0.	3.	0
4	41.	0.	2.	130.	204.	0.	2.	172.	0.	1.4	1.	0.	3.	0

Here are a few things to observe and remember for future reference:

- On the left side, there is an unnamed column that has rows with consecutive numbers, 0, 1, ..., 4. These are the indices that pandas assigns to each row in the dataset. These are unique numbers. Some datasets have unique identifiers, such as a filename for an image.
- On the top, there is a row that goes from 0, 1, ..., 13. These are the column identifiers. These are also unique and can be set if they are given to us.
- At the intersection of every row and column, we have values that are either floating-point decimals or integers. The entire dataset contains decimal numbers except for column 13, which is our target and contains integers.

3. Because we will use this dataset as a binary classification problem, we now need to change the last column to contain only binary values: 0 and 1. We will preserve the original meaning of 0, that is, no heart disease, and anything greater than or equal to 1 will be mapped to 1, indicating the diagnosis of some type of heart disease. We will run the following instructions:

```
print(set(df[13]))
```

The instruction `df[13]` looks at the DataFrame and retrieves all the rows of the column whose index is `13`. Then, the `set()` method over all the rows of column 13 will create a set of all the unique elements in the column. In this way, we can know how many different values there are so that we can replace them. The output is as follows:

```
{0, 1, 2, 3, 4}
```

From this, we know that 0 is no heart disease and 1 implies heart disease. However, 2, 3, and 4 need to be mapped to 1, because they, too, imply positive heart disease. We can make this change by executing the following commands:

```
df[13].replace(to_replace=[2,3,4], value=1, inplace=True)
print(df.head())
print(set(df[13]))
```

Here, the `replace()` function works on the DataFrame to replace specific values. In our case, it took three arguments:

- `to_replace=[2,3,4]` denotes the list of items to search for, in order to replace them.
- `value=1` denotes the value that will replace every matched entry .
- `inplace=True` indicates to pandas that we want to make the changes on the column.

In some cases, pandas DataFrames behave like an immutable object, which, in this case, makes it necessary to use the `inplace=True` argument. If we did not use this argument, we would have to do something like this.
`df[13] = df[13].replace(to_replace=[2,3,4], value=1)`, which is not a problem for experienced pandas users. This means that you should be comfortable doing this either way.
The main problem for people beginning to use pandas is that it does not *always* behave like an immutable object. Thus, you should keep all the pandas documentation close to you: `https://pandas.pydata.org/pandas-docs/stable/index.html`

The output for the preceding commands is the following:

	0	1	2	3	4	5	6	7	8	9	10	11	12	13
0	63.	1.	1.	145.	233.	1.	2.	150.	0.	2.3	3.	0.	6.	0
1	67.	1.	4.	160.	286.	0.	2.	108.	1.	1.5	2.	3.	3.	1
2	67.	1.	4.	120.	229.	0.	2.	129.	1.	2.6	2.	2.	7.	1
3	37.	1.	3.	130.	250.	0.	0.	187.	0.	3.5	3.	0.	3.	0

```
4  41.  0.  2.  130.  204.  0.  2.  172.  0.  1.4  1.  0.  3.   0

{0, 1}
```

First, notice that when we print the first five rows, the thirteenth column now exclusively has the values 0 or 1. You can compare this to the original data to verify that the number in bold font actually changed. We also verified, with `set(df[13])`, that the set of all unique values of that column is now only `{0, 1}`, which is the desired target.

With these changes, we could use the dataset to train a deep learning model and perhaps improve the existing documented performance [Detrano, R., *et al.* (1989)].

The same methodology can be applied to make any other column have binary values in the set we need. As an exercise, let's do another example with the famous `MNIST` dataset.

Binarizing the MNIST dataset

The MNIST dataset is well known in the deep learning community (Deng, L. (2012)). It is composed of thousands of images of handwritten digits. Figure 3.1 shows eight samples of the MNIST dataset:

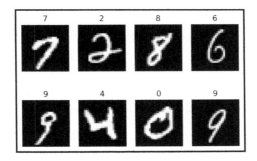

Figure 3.1 – Eight samples of the MNIST dataset. The number on top of each image corresponds to the target class

As you can see, the samples in this dataset are messy and are very real. Every image has a size of 28 x 28 pixels. And there are only 10 target classes, one for each digit, 0, 1, 2, ..., 9. The complication here is usually that some digits may look similar to others; for example, 1 and 7, or 0 and 6. However, most deep learning algorithms have successfully solved the classification problem with high accuracy.

From *Figure 3.1*, a close inspection will reveal that the values are not exactly zeros and ones, that is, binary. In fact, the images are 8-bit grayscale, in the range [0-255]. As mentioned earlier, this is no longer a problem for most advanced deep learning algorithms. However, for some algorithms, such as **Restricted Boltzmann Machines (RMBs)**, the input data needs to be in binary format [0,1] because that is how the algorithm works, traditionally.

Thus, we will do two things:

- Binarize the images, so as to have binary inputs
- Binarize the targets, to make it a binary classification problem

For this example, we will arbitrarily select two numerals only, 7 and 8, as our target classes.

Binarizing the images

The binarization process is a common step in image processing. It is formally known as image thresholding because we need a threshold to decide which values become zeros and ones. For a full survey about this topic, please consult (Sezgin, M., and Sankur, B. (2004)). This is all to say that there is a science behind picking the perfect threshold that will minimize the range conversion error from [0, 255] down to [0, 1].

However, since this is not a book about image processing, we will arbitrarily set a threshold of 128. Thus, any value below 128 will become a zero, and any value greater than or equal to 128 will become a one.

This step can be easily done by using indexing in Python. To proceed, we will display a small portion of the dataset to make sure the data is transformed correctly. We will do this by executing the following commands in the next steps:

1. To load the dataset and verify its dimensionality (shape), run the following command:

   ```
   from sklearn.datasets import fetch_openml
   mnist = fetch_openml('mnist_784')
   print(mnist.data.shape)
   print(mnist.target.shape)
   ```

   The following is the output:

   ```
   (70000, 784)
   (70000,)
   ```

The first thing to notice is that we are using a machine learning library known as `scikit learn` or `sklearn` in Python. It is one of the most used libraries for general-purpose machine learning. The `MNIST` dataset is loaded using the `fetch_openml()` method, which requires an argument with the identifier of the dataset to be loaded, which in this case is `'mnist_784'`. The number `784` comes from the size of `MNIST` images, which is 28 x 28 pixels and can be interpreted as a vector of 784 elements rather than a matrix of 28 columns and 28 rows. By verifying the `shape` property, we can see that the dataset has 70,000 images represented as vectors of size 784, and the targets are in the same proportion.

Please note here that, as opposed to the previous section where we used a dataset loaded into pandas, in this example, we use the data directly as lists or arrays of lists. You should feel comfortable manipulating both pandas and raw datasets.

2. To actually do the binarization by verifying the data before and after, run the following:

```
print(mnist.data[0].reshape(28, 28)[10:18,10:18])
mnist.data[mnist.data < 128] = 0
mnist.data[mnist.data >=128] = 1
print(mnist.data[0].reshape(28, 28)[10:18,10:18])
```

This will output the following:

```
[[  1. 154. 253.  90.   0.   0.   0.   0.]
 [  0. 139. 253. 190.   2.   0.   0.   0.]
 [  0.  11. 190. 253.  70.   0.   0.   0.]
 [  0.   0.  35. 241. 225. 160. 108.   1.]
 [  0.   0.   0.  81. 240. 253. 253. 119.]
 [  0.   0.   0.   0.  45. 186. 253. 253.]
 [  0.   0.   0.   0.   0.  16.  93. 252.]
 [  0.   0.   0.   0.   0.   0.   0. 249.]]

[[  0.  1.  1.  0.  0.  0.  0.  0.]
 [  0.  1.  1.  1.  0.  0.  0.  0.]
 [  0.  0.  1.  1.  0.  0.  0.  0.]
 [  0.  0.  0.  1.  1.  1.  0.  0.]
 [  0.  0.  0.  0.  1.  1.  1.  0.]
 [  0.  0.  0.  0.  0.  1.  1.  1.]
 [  0.  0.  0.  0.  0.  0.  0.  1.]
 [  0.  0.  0.  0.  0.  0.  0.  1.]]
```

The instruction `data[0].reshape(28, 28)[10:18,10:18]` is doing three things:

1. `data[0]` returns the first image as an array of size (1, 784).
2. `reshape(28, 28)` resizes the (1, 784) array as a (28, 28) matrix, which is the actual image; this can be useful to display the actual data, for example, to produce *Figure 3.1.*
3. `[10:18,10:18]` takes only a subset of the (28, 28) matrix at positions 10 to 18 for both columns and rows; this more or less corresponds to the center area of the image and it is a good place to look at what is changing.

The preceding is for looking at the data only, but the actual changes are done in the next lines. The line `mnist.data[mnist.data < 128] = 0` uses Python indexing. The instruction `mnist.data < 128` returns a multidimensional array of Boolean values that `mnist.data[ ]` uses as indices on which to set the value to zero. The key is to do so for all values strictly less than 128. And the next line does the same, but for values greater than or equal to 128.

By inspecting the output, we can confirm that the data has successfully changed and has been thresholded, or binarized.

Binarizing the targets

We will binarize the targets by following the next two steps:

1. First, we will discard image data for other numerals and we will only keep 7 and 8. Then, we will map 7 to 0 and 8 to 1. These commands will create new variables, X and y, that will hold only the numerals 7 and 8:

```
X = mnist.data[(mnist.target == '7') | (mnist.target == '8')]
y = mnist.target[(mnist.target == '7') | (mnist.target == '8')]
print(X.shape)
print(y.shape)
```

This will output the following:

```
(14118, 784)
(14118)
```

Notice the use of the OR operator, |, to logically take two sets of Boolean indices and produce one with the OR operator. These indices are used to produce a new dataset. The shape of the new dataset contains a little over 14,000 images.

2. To map 7 to 0 and 8 to 1, we can run the following command:

```
print(y[:10])
y = [0 if v=='7' else 1 for v in y]
print(y[:10])
```

This outputs the following:

```
['7' '8' '7' '8' '7' '8' '7' '8' '7' '8']
[0, 1, 0, 1, 0, 1, 0, 1, 0, 1]
```

The instruction `[0 if v=='7' else 1 for v in y]` checks every element in `y`, and if an element is `'7'`, then it returns a 0, otherwise (for example, when it is `'8'`), it returns a 1. As the output suggests, choosing the first 10 elements, the data is binarized to the set {0, 1}.

Remember, the target data in `y` was already binary in the sense that it only had two sets of unique possible numbers {7, 8}. But we made it binary to the set {0, 1} because often this is better when we use different deep learning algorithms that calculate very specific types of loss functions.

With this, the dataset is ready to use with binary and general classifiers. But what if we actually want to have multiple classes, for example, to detect all 10 digits of the `MNIST` dataset and not just 2? Or what if we have features, columns, or inputs that are not numeric but are categorical? The next section will help you prepare the data in these cases.

Categorical data and multiple classes

Now that you know how to binarize data for different purposes, we can look into other types of data, such as categorical or multi-labeled data, and how to make them numeric. Most advanced deep learning algorithms, in fact, only accept numerical data. This is merely a design issue that can easily be solved later on, and it is not a big deal because you will learn there are easy ways to take categorical data and convert it to a meaningful numerical representation.

Categorical data has information embedded as distinct categories. These categories can be represented as numbers or as strings. For example, a dataset that has a column named `country` with items such as "India", "Mexico", "France", and "U.S". Or, a dataset with zip codes such as 12601, 85621, and 73315. The former is **non-numeric** categorical data, and the latter is **numeric** categorical data. Country names would need to be converted to a number to be usable at all, but zip codes are already numbers that are meaningless as mere numbers. Zip codes would be more meaningful, from a machine learning perspective, if we converted them to latitude and longitude coordinates; this would better capture places that are closer to each other than using plain numbers.

To begin, we will address the issue of converting string categories to plain numbers and then we will convert those to numbers in a format called **one-hot encoding**.

Converting string labels to numbers

We will take the `MNIST` dataset again and use its string labels, *0, 1, ..., 9*, and convert them to numbers. We can achieve this in many different ways:

- We could simply map all strings to integers with one simple command, `y = list(map(int, mnist.target))`, and be done. The variable `y` now contains only a list of integers such as `[8, 7, 1, 2, ... ]`. But this will only solve the problem for this particular case; you need to learn something that will work for all cases. So, let's not do this.
- We could do some hard work by iterating over the data 10 times —`mnist.target = [0 if v=='0' else v for v in mnist.target]` — doing this for every numeral. But again, this (and other similar things) will work only for this case. Let's not do this.
- We could use scikit-learn's `LabelEncoder()` method, which will take any list of labels and map them to a number. This will work for all cases.

Let's use the `scikit` method by following these steps:

1. Run the following code:

```
from sklearn import preprocessing
le = preprocessing.LabelEncoder()
print(sorted(list(set(mnist.target))))

le.fit(sorted(list(set(mnist.target))))
```

This produces the following output:

```
['0', '1', '2', '3', '4', '5', '6', '7', '8', '9']

LabelEncoder()
```

The `sorted(list(set(mnist.target)))` command does three things:

- `set(mnist.target)` retrieves the set of unique values in the data, for example, `{'8', '2', ..., '9'}`.
- `list(set(mnist.target))` simply converts the set into a list because we need a list or an array for the `LabelEncoder()` method.
- `sorted(list(set(mnist.target)))` is important here so that *0* maps to 0 and not to have *8* map to 0, and so on. It sorts the list, and the result looks like this - `['0', '1', ..., '9']`.

The `le.fit()` method takes a list (or an array) and produces a map (a dictionary) to be used forward (and backward if needed) to encode labels, or strings, into numbers. It stores this in a `LabelEncoder` object.

2. Next, we could test the encoding as follows:

```
print(le.transform(["9", "3", "7"]) )

list(le.inverse_transform([2, 2, 1]))
```

This will output the following:

```
[9 3 7]

['2', '2', '1']
```

The `transform()` method transforms a string-based label into a number, whereas the `inverse_transform()` method takes a number and returns the corresponding string label or category.

 Any attempt to map to and from an unseen category or number will cause a `LabelEncoder` object to produce an error. Please be diligent in providing the list of all possible categories to the best of your knowledge.

3. Once the `LabelEncoder` object is fitted and tested, we can simply run the following instruction to encode the data:

```
print("Before ", mnist.target[:3])
y = le.transform(mnist.target)
print("After ", y[:3])
```

This will output the following:

```
Before ['5' '0' '4']
After [5 0 4]
```

The new encoded labels are now in `y` and ready to be used.

 This method of encoding a label to an integer is also known as **Ordinal Encoding.**

This methodology should work for all labels encoded as strings, for which you can simply map to numbers without losing context. In the case of the `MNIST` dataset, we can map *0* to *0* and *7* to *7* without losing context. Other examples of when you can do this include the following:

- **Age groups**: ['18-21', '22-35', '36+'] to [0, 1, 2]
- **Gender**: ['male', 'female'] to [0, 1]
- **Colors**: ['red', 'black', 'blue', ...] to [0, 1, 2, ...]
- **Studies**: ['primary', 'secondary', 'high school', 'university'] to [0, 1, 2, 3]

However, we are making one big assumption here: the labels encode no special meaning in themselves. As we mentioned earlier, zip codes could be simply encoded to smaller numbers; however, they have a geographical meaning, and doing so might negatively impact the performance of our deep learning algorithms. Similarly, in the preceding list, if studies require a special meaning that indicates that a *university* degree is much higher or more important than a *primary* degree, then perhaps we should consider different number mappings. Or perhaps we want our learning algorithms to *learn* such intricacies by themselves! In such cases, we should then use the well-known strategy of one-hot encoding.

Converting categories to one-hot encoding

Converting categories to one-hot encoding is better in most cases in which the categories or labels may have special meanings with respect to each other. In such cases, it has been reported to outperform ordinal encoding [Potdar, K., *et al.* (2017)].

The idea is to represent each label as a Boolean state having independent columns. Take, for example, a column with the following data:

Gender
'female'
'male'
'male'
'female'
'female'

This can be uniquely transformed, using one-hot encoding, into the following new piece of data:

Gender_Female	Gender_Male
1	0
0	1
0	1
1	0
1	0

As you can see, the binary bit is *hot* (is one) only if the label corresponds to that specific row and it is zero otherwise. Notice also that we renamed the columns to keep track of which label corresponds to which column; however, this is merely a recommended format and is not a formal rule.

There are a number of ways we can do this in Python. If your data is in a pandas DataFrame, then you can simply do `pd.get_dummies(df, prefix=['Gender'])`, assuming your column is in `df` and you want to use `Gender` as a prefix.

To reproduce the exact results as discussed in the preceding table, follow these steps:

1. Run the following command:

```
import pandas as pd
df=pd.DataFrame({'Gender': ['female','male','male',
```

```
                                      'female','female']})
        print(df)
```

This will output the following:

```
  Gender
0 female
1 male
2 male
3 female
4 female
```

2. Now simply do the encoding by running the following command:

```
pd.get_dummies(df, prefix=['Gender'])
```

And this is produced:

```
  Gender_female  Gender_male
0             1            0
1             0            1
2             0            1
3             1            0
4             1            0
```

 A fun, and perhaps obvious, property of this encoding is that the OR and XOR operations along the rows of all the encoded columns will always be one, and the AND operation will yield zeros.

For cases in which the data is not a pandas DataFrame, for example, MNIST targets, we can use scikit-learn's OneHotEncoder.transform() method.

A OneHotEncoder object has a constructor that will automatically initialize everything to reasonable assumptions and determines most of its parameters using the fit() method. It determines the size of the data, the different labels that exist in the data, and then creates a dynamic mapping that we can use with the transform() method.

To do a one-hot encoding of the MNIST targets, we can do this:

```
from sklearn.preprocessing import OneHotEncoder
enc = OneHotEncoder()
y = [list(v) for v in mnist.target] # reformat for sklearn
enc.fit(y)

print('Before: ', y[0])
```

```
y = enc.transform(y).toarray()
print('After: ', y[0])
print(enc.get_feature_names())
```

This will output the following:

```
Before: ['5']
After: [0. 0. 0. 0. 0. 1. 0. 0. 0. 0.]
['x0_0' 'x0_1' 'x0_2' 'x0_3' 'x0_4' 'x0_5' 'x0_6' 'x0_7' 'x0_8'
 'x0_9']
```

This code includes our classic sanity check in which we verify that label '5' was in fact converted to a row vector with 10 columns, of which number 6 is *hot*. It works, as expected. The new dimensionality of y is *n* rows and 10 columns.

This is the preferred format for the targets that use deep learning methods on MNIST. One-hot encoding targets are great for neural networks that will have exactly one neuron per class. In this case, one neuron per digit. Each neuron will need to learn to predict one-hot encoded behavior, that is, only one neuron should fire up (be "hot") while the others should be inhibited.

The preceding process can be repeated exactly to convert any other columns into one-hot encoding, provided that they contain categorical data.

Categories, labels, and specific mappings to integers or bits are very helpful when we want to classify input data into those categories, labels, or mappings. But what if we want to have input data that maps to continuous data? For example, data to predict a person's IQ by looking at their responses; or predicting the price of electricity depending on the input data about weather and the seasons. This is known as data for **regression**, which we will cover next.

Real-valued data and univariate regression

Knowing how to deal with categorical data is very important when using classification models based on deep learning; however, knowing how to prepare data for regression is as important. Data that contains continuous-like real values, such as temperature, prices, weight, speed, and others, is suitable for regression; that is, if we have a dataset with columns of different types of values, and one of those is real-valued data, we could perform regression on that column. This implies that we could use all the rest of the dataset to predict the values on that column. This is known as **univariate regression**, or regression on one variable.

Most machine learning methodologies work better if the data for regression is **normalized**. By that, we mean that the data will have special statistical properties that will make calculations more stable. This is critical for many deep learning algorithms that suffer from vanishing or exploding gradients (Hanin, B. (2018)). For example, in calculating a gradient in a neural network, an error needs to be propagated backward from the output layer to the input layer; but if the output layer has a large error and the range of values (that is their **distribution**) is also large, then the multiplications going backward can cause overflow on variables, which would ruin the training process.

To overcome these difficulties, it is desirable to normalize the distribution of variables that can be used for regression, or variables that are real-valued. The normalization process has many variants, but we will limit our discussion to two main methodologies, one that sets specific statistical properties of the data, and one that sets specific ranges on the data.

Scaling to a specific range of values

Let's go back to the heart disease dataset discussed earlier in this chapter. If you pay attention, many of those variables are real-valued and would be ideal for regression; for example, x_5 and x_{10}.

All variables are suitable for regression. This means that, technically, we can predict on any numeric data. The fact that some values are real-valued makes them more appealing for regression for a number of reasons. For example, the fact that the values in that column have a meaning that goes beyond integers and natural numbers.

Let's focus on x_5 and x_{10}, which are the variables for measuring the cholesterol level and ST depression induced by exercise relative to rest, respectively. What if we want to change the original research question the doctors intended, which was to study heart disease based on different factors? What if now we want to use all the factors, including knowing whether patients have heart disease or not, to determine or predict their cholesterol level? We can do that with regression on x_5.

So, to prepare the data on x_5 and x_{10}, we will go ahead and scale the data. For verification purposes, we will retrieve descriptive statistics on the data before and after the scaling of the data.

To reload the dataset and display descriptive statistics, we can do the following:

```
df = pd.read_csv('processed.cleveland.data', header=None)
df[[4,9]].describe()
```

In this case, index, 4 and 9 correspond to x_5 and x_{10}, and the `describe()` method outputs the following information:

```
                  4                 9
count    303.000000        303.000000
mean     246.693069          1.039604
std       51.776918          1.161075
min      126.000000          0.000000
25%      211.000000          0.000000
50%      241.000000          0.800000
75%      275.000000          1.600000
max      564.000000          6.200000
```

The most notable properties are the mean, and maximum/minimum values contained in that column. These will change once we scale the data to a different range. If we visualize the data as a scatter plot with respective histograms, it looks like *Figure 3.2*:

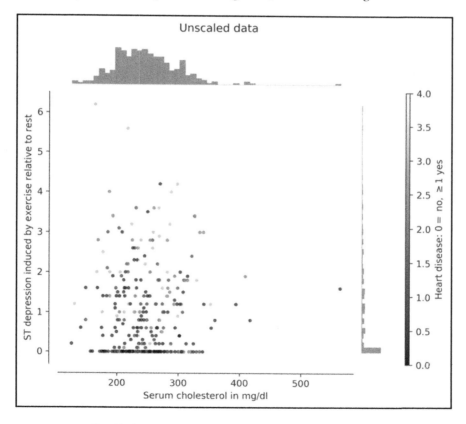

Figure 3.2 – Scatter plot of the two columns x_5 and x_{10} and their corresponding histograms

As can be seen from *Figure 3.2*, the ranges are quite different, and the distribution of the data is different as well. The new desired range here is a minimum of 0 and a maximum of 1. This range is typical when we scale the data. And it can be achieved using scikit-learn's `MinMaxScaler` object as follows:

```
from sklearn.preprocessing import MinMaxScaler
scaler = MinMaxScaler()
scaler.fit(df[[4,9]])
df[[4,9]] = scaler.transform(df[[4,9]])
df[[4,9]].describe()
```

This will output the following:

```
               4           9
count  303.000000  303.000000
mean     0.275555    0.167678
std      0.118212    0.187270
min      0.000000    0.000000
25%      0.194064    0.000000
50%      0.262557    0.129032
75%      0.340183    0.258065
max      1.000000    1.000000
```

What the `fit()` method does internally is to determine what the current min and max values are for the data. Then, the `transform()` method uses that information to remove the minimum and divide by the maximum to achieve the desired range. As can be seen, the new descriptive statistics have changed, which can be confirmed by looking at the range in the axes of *Figure 3.3*:

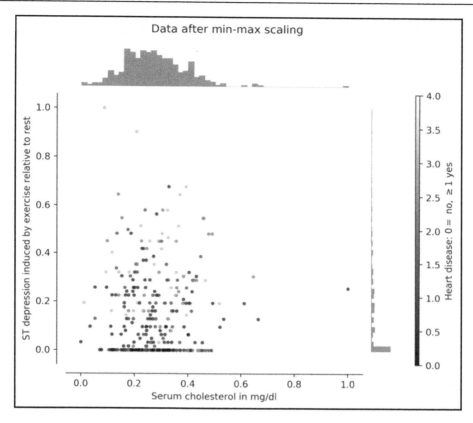

Figure 3.3 – Scatter plot of the newly scaled columns x_5 and x_{10} and their corresponding histograms

Notice, however, if you pay close attention, that the distribution of the data has not changed. That is, the histograms of the data in *Figure 3.2* and *Figure 3.3* are still the same. And this is a very important fact because, usually, you do not want to change the distribution of the data.

Standardizing to zero mean and unit variance

Another way of preprocessing real-valued data is by making it have zero mean and unit variance. This process is referred to by many names, such as normalizing, z-scoring, centering, or standardizing.

Let's say that $x=[x_5, x_{10}]$, from our features above, then we can standardize x as follows:

$$\hat{x} = \frac{(x - \mu)}{\sigma}$$

Here, μ is a vector corresponding to the means of each column on x, and σ is a vector of standard deviations of each column in x.

After the standardization of x, if we recompute the mean and standard deviation, we should get a mean of zero and a standard deviation of one. In Python, we do the following:

```
df[[4,9]] = (df[[4,9]]-df[[4,9]].mean())/df[[4,9]].std()
df[[4,9]].describe()
```

This will output the following:

	4	9
count	3.030000e+02	3.030000e+02
mean	1.700144e-16	-1.003964e-16
std	1.000000e+00	1.000000e+00
min	-2.331021e+00	-8.953805e-01
25%	-6.893626e-01	-8.953805e-01
50%	-1.099538e-01	-2.063639e-01
75%	5.467095e-01	4.826527e-01
max	6.128347e+00	4.444498e+00

Notice that after normalization, the mean is, for numerical purposes, zero. And the standard deviation is one. The same thing can be done, of course, using the scikit-learn `StandardScaler` object as follows:

```
from sklearn.preprocessing import StandardScaler
scaler = StandardScaler()
scaler.fit(df[[4,9]])
df[[4,9]] = scaler.transform(df[[4,9]])
```

This will yield the same results with negligible numerical differences. For practical purposes, both methods will achieve the same thing.

Although both ways of normalizing are appropriate, in the DataFrame directly or using a `StandardScaler` object, you should prefer using the `StandardScaler` object if you are working on a production application. Once the `StandardScaler` object uses the `fit()` method, it can be used on new, unseen, data easily by re-invoking `transform()` method; however, if we do it directly on the pandas DataFrame, we will have to manually store the mean and standard deviation somewhere and reload it every time we need to standardize new data.

Now, for comparison purposes, *Figure 3.4* depicts the new ranges after the normalization of the data. If you look at the axes closely, you will notice that the position of the zero values are where most of the data is, that is, where the mean is. Therefore, the cluster of data is centered around a mean of zero:

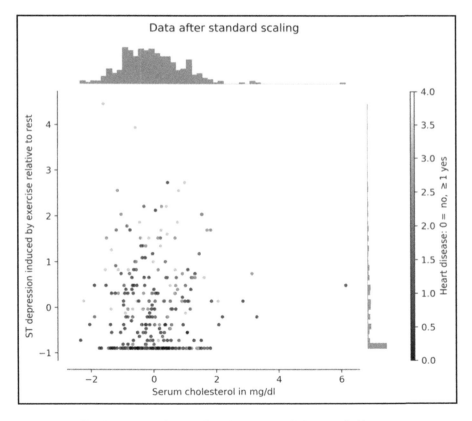

Figure 3.4 – Scatter plot of the standardized columns x_5 and x_{10} and their corresponding histograms

Notice, again, that in *Figure 3.4*, after applying the standardization process, the distribution of the data still does not change. But what if you actually want to change the distribution of the data? Keep reading on to the next section.

Altering the distribution of data

It has been demonstrated that changing the distribution of the targets, particularly in the case of regression, can have positive benefits in the performance of a learning algorithm (Andrews, D. F., et al. (1971)).

Here, we'll discuss one particularly useful transformation known as **Quantile Transformation**. This methodology aims to look at the data and manipulate it in such a way that its histogram follows either a **normal** distribution or a **uniform** distribution. It achieves this by looking at estimates of quantiles.

We can use the following commands to transform the same data as in the previous section:

```
from sklearn.preprocessing import QuantileTransformer
transformer = QuantileTransformer(output_distribution='normal')
df[[4,9]] = transformer.fit_transform(df[[4,9]])
```

This will effectively map the data into a new distribution, namely, a normal distribution.

 Here, the term **normal distribution** refers to a Gaussian-like **probability density function** (PDF). This is a classic distribution found in any statistics textbook. It is usually identified by its bell-like shape when plotted.

Note that we are also using the `fit_transform()` method, which does both `fit()` and `transform()` at the same time, which is convenient.

As can be seen in *Figure 3.5*, the variable related to cholesterol data, x_5, was easily transformed into a normal distribution with a bell shape. However, for x_{10}, the heavy presence of data in a particular region causes the distribution to have a bell shape, but with a long tail, which is not ideal:

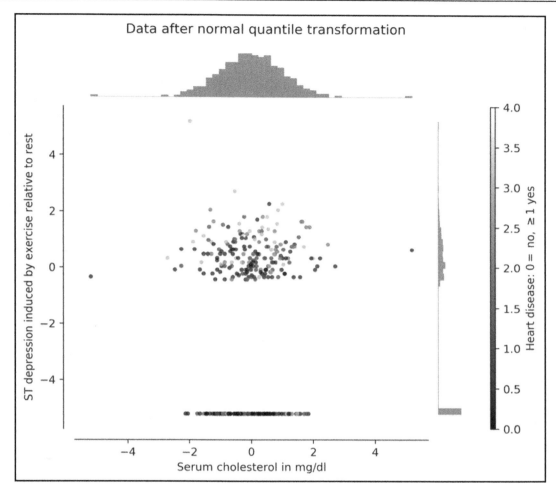

Figure 3.5 – Scatter plot of the normally transformed columns x_5 and x_{10} and their corresponding Gaussian-like histograms

The process of transforming the data for a uniform distribution is very similar. We simply need to make a small change in one line, on the QuantileTransformer() constructor, as follows:

```
transformer = QuantileTransformer(output_distribution='uniform')
```

Now, the data is transformed into a uniform distribution, as shown in *Figure 3.6*:

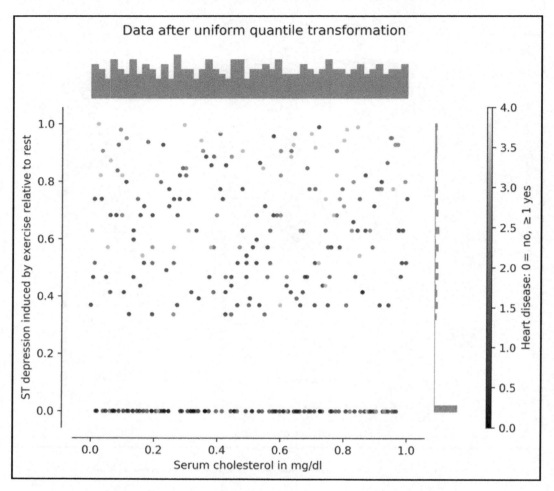

Figure 3.6 – Scatter plot of the uniformly transformed columns x_5 and x_{10} and their corresponding uniform histograms

From the figure, we can see that the data has been uniformly distributed across each variable. Once again, the clustering of data in a particular region has the effect of causing a large concentration of values in the same space, which is not ideal. This artifact also creates a gap in the distribution of the data that is usually difficult to handle, unless we use techniques to augment the data, which we'll discuss next.

Data augmentation

Now that you have learned how to process the data to have specific distributions, it is important for you to know about data augmentation, which is usually associated with missing data or high-dimensional data. Traditional machine learning algorithms may have problems dealing with data where the number of dimensions surpasses the number of samples available. The problem is not particular to all deep learning algorithms, but some algorithms have a much more difficult time learning to model a problem that has more variables to figure out than samples to work on. We have a few options to correct that: either we reduce the dimensions or variables (see the following section) or we increase the samples in our dataset (this section).

One of the tools for adding more data is known as **data augmentation** (Van Dyk, D. A., and Meng, X. L. (2001)). In this section, we will use the MNIST dataset to exemplify a few techniques for data augmentation that are particular to images but can be conceptually extended to other types of data.

We will cover the basics: adding noise, rotating, and rescaling. That is, from one original example, we will produce three new, different images of numerals. We will use the image processing library known as scikit image.

Rescaling

We begin by reloading the MNIST dataset as we have done before:

```
from sklearn.datasets import fetch_openml
mnist = fetch_openml('mnist_784')
```

Then we can simply invoke the rescale() method to create a rescaled image. The whole purpose behind resizing an image is to rescale it back to its original size because this makes the image look like a small resolution image of the original. It loses some of its characteristics in the process, but it can actually make a more robust deep learning model. That is, a model robust to the scale of objects, or in this case, the scale of numerals:

```
from skimage.transform import rescale
x = mnist.data[0].reshape(28,28)
```

Once we have x as the original image from which we will augment, we can do the scaling down and up as follows:

```
s = rescale(x, 0.5, multichannel=False)
x_= rescale(s, 2.0, multichannel=False)
```

Here, the augmented image (rescaled) is in x_. Notice that, in this case, the image is downscaled by a factor of two (50%) and then upscaled, also by a factor of two (200%). The multichannel argument is set to false since the images have only one single channel, meaning they are grayscale.

 When rescaling, be careful of rescaling by factors that give you exact divisions. For example, a 28 x 28 image that is downscaled by a factor of 0.5 goes down to 14 x 14; this is good. But if we downscale by a factor of 0.3, it will go down to 8.4 x 8.4, which goes up to 9 x 9; this is not good because it can add unnecessary complications. Keep it simple.

Besides rescaling, we can also modify the existing data slightly so as to have variations of the existing data without deviating much from the original, as we'll discuss next.

Adding noise

Similarly, we can also contaminate the original image with additive Gaussian noise. This creates random patterns all over the image to simulate a camera problem or noisy acquisition. Here, we use it to also augment our dataset and, in the end, to produce a deep learning model that is robust against noise.

For this, we use the random_noise() method as follows:

```
from skimage.util import random_noise
x_ = random_noise(x)
```

Once again, the augmented image (noisy) is in x_.

Besides noise, we can also change the perspective of an image slightly so as to preserve the original shape at a different angle, as we'll discuss next.

Rotating

We can use a plain rotation effect on the images to have even more data. The rotation of images is a crucial part of learning good features from images. Larger datasets contain, naturally, many versions of images that are slightly rotated or fully rotated. If we do not have such images in our dataset, we can manually rotate them and augment our data.

For this, we use the `rotate()` method like so:

```
from skimage.transform import rotate
x_ = rotate(x, 22)
```

In this example, the number `22` specifies the angle of rotation:

> When you are augmenting your dataset, you may want to consider having multiple rotations at random angles.

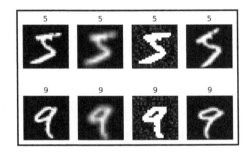

Figure 3.7 – An example of the images produced with the preceding data augmentation techniques

The first column is the original numeral of the MNIST dataset. The second column shows the effect of rescaling. The third column shows the original plus additive Gaussian noise. The last column shows a rotation of 20 degrees (top) and -20 degrees (bottom).

Other augmentation techniques

For image datasets, there are other ideas for augmenting data that include the following:

- Changing the projection of the image
- Adding compression noise (quantizing the image)
- Other types of noise besides Gaussian, such as salt and pepper, or multiplicative noise
- The translation of the image by different distances at random

But the most robust augmentation would be a combination of all of these!

Images are fun because they are highly correlated in local areas. But for general non-image datasets, such as the heart disease dataset, we can augment data in other ways, for example:

- Adding low-variance Gaussian noise
- Adding compression noise (quantization)
- Drawing new points from a calculated probability density function over the data

For other special datasets, such as text-based data, we can also do the following:

- Replace some words with synonyms
- Remove some words
- Add words that contain errors
- Remove punctuation (only if you do not care about proper language structures)

For more information on this and many other augmentation techniques, consult online resources on the latest advances pertaining to your specific type of data.

Let's now dive into some techniques for dimensionality reduction that can be used to alleviate the problem of high-dimensional and highly correlated datasets.

Data dimensionality reduction

As pointed out before, if we have the problem of having more dimensions (or variables) than samples in our data, we can either augment the data or reduce the dimensionality of the data. Now, we will address the basics of the latter.

We will look into reducing dimensions both in supervised and unsupervised ways with both small and large datasets.

Supervised algorithms

Supervised algorithms for dimensionality reduction are so called because they take the labels of the data into account to find better representations. Such methods often yield good results. Perhaps the most popular kind is called **linear discriminant analysis (LDA)**, which we'll discuss next.

Linear discriminant analysis

Scikit learn has a `LinearDiscriminantAnalysis` class that can easily perform dimensionality reduction on a desired number of components.

By **number of components**, the number of dimensions desired is understood. The name comes from **principal component analysis (PCA)**, which is a statistical approach that determines the eigenvectors and eigenvalues of the centered covariance matrix of a dataset; then, the largest eigenvalues associated with specific eigenvectors are known to be the most important, *principal*, components. When we use PCA to reduce to a specific number of components, we say that we want to keep those components that are the most important in a space induced by the eigenvalues and eigenvectors of the covariance matrix of the data.

LDA and other dimensionality reduction techniques also have a similar philosophy in which they aim to find low-dimensional spaces (based on the number of components desired) that can better represent the data based on other properties of the data.

If we use the heart disease dataset as an example, we can perform LDA to reduce the entire dataset from 13 dimensions to 2 dimensions, all the while using the labels [0, 1, 2, 3, 4] to inform the LDA algorithm how to better separate the groups represented by those labels.

To achieve this, we can follow these steps:

1. First, we reload the data and drop the missing values:

```
from sklearn.discriminant_analysis import
LinearDiscriminantAnalysis
df = pd.read_csv('processed.cleveland.data', header=None)
df = df.apply(pd.to_numeric, errors='coerce').dropna()
```

   Notice that we did not have to deal with missing values before on the heart disease dataset because pandas automatically ignores missing values. But here, because we are strictly converting data into numbers, missing values will be converted to NaN since we are specifying `errors='coerce'`, which forces any errors in the conversion to become NaN. Consequently, with `dropna()`, we ignore rows with those values from our dataset because they will cause LDA to fail.

2. Next, we prepare the X and y variables to contain the data and targets, respectively, and we perform LDA as follows:

```
X = df[[0,1,2,3,4,5,6,7,8,9,10,11,12]].values
y = df[13].values

dr = LinearDiscriminantAnalysis(n_components=2)
X_ = dr.fit_transform(X, y)
```

In this example, x_ contains the entire dataset represented in two dimensions, as given by n_components=2. The choice of two components is simply to illustrate graphically how the data looks. But you can change this to any number of components you desire.

Figure 3.8 depicts how the 13-dimensional dataset looks if compressed, or reduced, down to two dimensions:

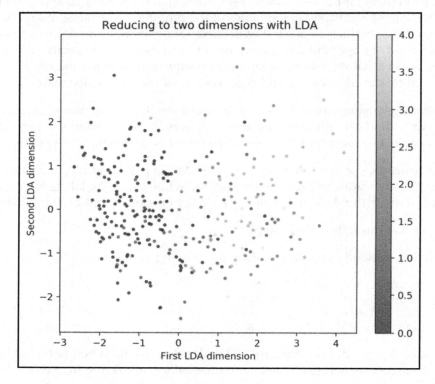

Figure 3.8 – Reducing dimensions from 13 to 2 using LDA

Notice how the values with 0 (no heart disease) are mostly clustered toward the left side, while the rest of the values (that is, 1, 2, 3, and 4, which represent heart disease) seem to cluster toward the right side. This is a nice property that was not observed in *Figures 3.2* to *3.6* when we picked two columns out of the 13.

Technically speaking, the relevant information of the 13 dimensions is still contained in the LDA-induced two dimensions. If the data seems to be separable in these low-dimensional representations, a deep learning algorithm may have a good chance of learning representations to classify or regress on the data with high performance.

While LDA can offer a very nice way to perform dimensionality reduction informed by the labels in the data, we might not always have labeled data, or we may not want to use the labels that we have. In those cases we can, and we should, explore other robust methodologies that require no label information, such as unsupervised techniques, which we'll discuss next.

Unsupervised techniques

Unsupervised techniques are the most popular methods because they need no prior information about labels. We begin with a kernelized version of PCA and then we move on to methods that operate on larger datasets.

Kernel PCA

This variant of PCA uses kernel methods to estimate distances, variances, and other parameters to determine the major components of the data (Schölkopf, B., et al. (1997)). It may take a bit more time to produce a solution than regular PCA, but it is very much worth using it over traditional PCA.

The KernelPCA class of scikit-learn can be used as follows:

```
from sklearn.decomposition import KernelPCA

dr = KernelPCA(n_components=2, kernel='linear')
X_ = dr.fit_transform(X)
```

Again, we use two dimensions as the new space, and we use a 'linear' kernel. Other popular choices for the kernel include the following:

- 'rbf' for a radial basis function kernel
- 'poly' for a polynomial kernel

Personally, I like the 'rbf' kernel in general, because it is more powerful and robust. But oftentimes, you spend valuable time trying to determine the best value for the parameter γ, which is how wide the bell of the radial basis function is. If you have the time, try 'rbf' and experiment with the parameter gamma.

The result of using kernel PCA is shown in *Figure 3.9*. The diagram again shows a clustering arrangement of the negative class (no heart disease, a value of 0) toward the bottom left of the KPCA-induced space. The positive class (heart disease, values ≥ 1) tends to cluster upward:

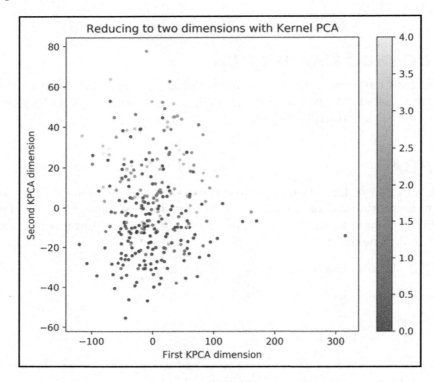

Figure 3.9 – Reducing dimensions with kernel PCA from 13 down to 2

Compared to *Figure 3.8*, LDA produces a slightly better space where the groups can be separated. However, KPCA does a good job in spite of now knowing the actual target classes. Now, LDA and KPCA might take no time on small datasets, but what if we have a lot of data? We will discuss some options next.

Large datasets

The previous examples will work well with moderate-sized datasets. However, when dealing with very large datasets, that is, with many dimensions or many samples, some algorithms may not function at their best. In the worst case, they will fail to produce a solution. The next two unsupervised algorithms are designed to function well for large datasets by using a technique called **batch training**. This technique is well known and has been applied in machine learning successfully (Hinton, G. E. (2012)).

The main idea is to divide the dataset into small (mini) batches and partially make progress toward finding a global solution to the problem at hand.

Sparse PCA

We'll first look into a sparse-coding version of PCA available in scikit-learn as `MiniBatchSparsePCA`. This algorithm will determine the best transformation into a subspace that satisfies a sparsity constraint.

> **Sparsity** is a property of matrices (or vectors) in which most of the elements are zeros. The opposite of sparsity is density. We like sparsity in deep learning because we do a lot of tensor (vector) multiplications, and if some of the elements are zeros, we do not have to perform those multiplications, thus saving time and optimizing for speed.

Follow the next steps in order to use the `MNIST` dataset and reduce its dimensions, since it has 784 dimensions and 70,000 samples. It is large enough, but even larger datasets can also be used:

1. We begin by reloading the data and preparing it for the sparse PCA encoding:

```
from sklearn.datasets import fetch_openml
mnist = fetch_openml('mnist_784')

X = mnist.data
```

2. Then we perform the dimensionality reduction as follows:

```
from sklearn.decomposition import MiniBatchSparsePCA

dr = MiniBatchSparsePCA(n_components=2, batch_size=50,
                        normalize_components=True)
X_ = dr.fit_transform(X)
```

Here, the `MiniBatchSparsePCA()` constructor takes three arguments:

- `n_components`, which we set to 2 for visualization purposes.
- `batch_size` determines how many samples the algorithm will use at a time. We set it to 50, but larger numbers may cause the algorithm to slow down.
- `normalize_components` refers to the preprocessing of the data by *centering* it, that is, making it have a zero mean and a unit variance; we recommend doing this every time, especially if you have data that is highly correlated, such as images.

The `MNIST` dataset transformed using sparse PCA looks as depicted in *Figure 3.10*:

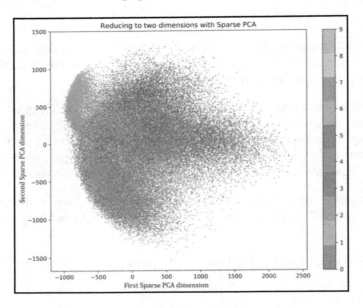

Figure 3.10 – MNIST dataset reduced to two dimensions using sparse PCA

As you can see, the separation between classes is not perfectly clear. There are some definitive clusters of digits, but it does not seem like a straightforward task due to the overlap between groups. This is caused in part by the fact that many digits may look alike. It would make sense to have the numerals 1 and 7 clustered together (the left side up and down), or 3 and 8 (the middle and up).

But let's also use another popular and useful algorithm called Dictionary Learning.

Dictionary Learning

Dictionary Learning is the process of learning the basis of transformations, called **dictionaries**, by using a process that can easily scale to very large datasets (Mairal, J., et al. (2009)).

 This was not possible with PCA-based algorithms, but this technique remains powerful and recently received the *Test of Time* award at one of the major conferences in the world, the *2019 International Conference in Machine Learning.*

The algorithm is available in scikit-learn through the `MiniBatchDictionaryLearning` class. We can use it as follows:

```
from sklearn.decomposition import MiniBatchDictionaryLearning

dr = MiniBatchDictionaryLearning(n_components=2, batch_size=50)
X_ = dr.fit_transform(X)
```

The constructor `MiniBatchDictionaryLearning()` takes on similar arguments as `MiniBatchSparsePCA()` with the same meaning. The results of the learned space are shown in *Figure 3.11*:

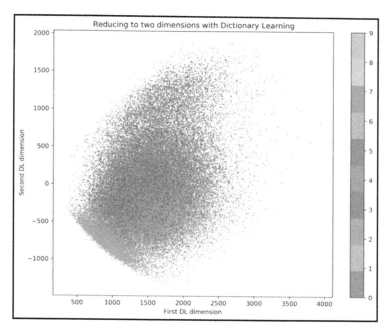

Figure 3.11 – Dimensionality reduction of MNIST data down to two dimensions using Dictionary Learning

As can be seen, there is a significant overlap among classes even if there are clearly defined clusters. This could lead to poor performance results if this data, the two-dimensional data, is used as input to train a classifier. This does not mean that algorithms are bad, necessarily. What this could mean is that, maybe, two dimensions are not the best choice of final dimensions. Continue reading to learn more about this.

Regarding the number of dimensions

Reducing dimensions is not always a necessary step. But it is highly recommended for data that is highly correlated, for example, images.

All the discussed dimensionality reduction techniques actually strive to remove redundant information in the data and preserve the important content. If we ask an algorithm to reduce the dimensions of our non-correlated, non-redundant dataset from 13 dimensions to 2, that sounds a bit risky; perhaps 8 or 9 would be a better choice.

No serious-minded machine learner would try to reduce a non-correlated, non-redundant dataset with 784 dimensions to only 2. Even if the data is highly correlated and redundant, like the MNIST dataset, asking to go from 784 down to 2 is a big stretch. It is a very risky decision that may get rid of important, discriminant, relevant information; perhaps 50 or 100 would be a better choice.

There is no general way of finding which amount of dimensions is good. It is a process that requires experimentation. If you want to become good at this, you must do your due diligence and at least try two or more experiments with different dimensions.

Ethical implications of manipulating data

There are many ethical implications and risks when manipulating data that you need to know. We live in a world where most deep learning algorithms will have to be corrected, by re-training them, because it was found that they were biased or unfair. That is very unfortunate; you want to be a person who exercises responsible AI and produces carefully thought out models.

When manipulating data, be careful about removing outliers from the data just because you think they are decreasing your model's performance. Sometimes, outliers represent information about protected groups or minorities, and removing those perpetuates unfairness and introduces bias toward the majority groups. Avoid removing outliers unless you are absolutely sure that they are errors caused by faulty sensors or human error.

Be careful of the way you transform the distribution of the data. Altering the distribution is fine in most cases, but if you are dealing with demographic data, you need to pay close attention to what you are transforming.

When dealing with demographic information such as gender, encoding female and male as 0 and 1 could be risky if we are considering proportions; we need to be careful not to promote equality (or inequality) that does not reflect the reality of the community that will use your models. The exception is when our current reality shows unlawful discrimination, exclusion, and bias. Then, our models (based on our data) should not reflect this reality, but the lawful reality that our community wants. That is, we will prepare good data to create models not to perpetuate societal problems, but models that will reflect the society we want to become.

Summary

In this chapter, we discussed many data manipulation techniques that we will come back to use all the time. It is good for you to spend time doing this now rather than later. It will make our modeling of deep learning architectures easier.

After reading this chapter, you are now able to manipulate and produce binary data for classification or for feature representation. You also know how to deal with categorical data and labels and prepare it for classification or regression. When you have real-valued data, you now know how to identify statistical properties and how to normalize such data. If you ever have the problem of data that has non-normal or non-uniform distributions, now you know how to fix that. And if you ever encounter problems of not having enough data, you learned a few data augmentation techniques. Toward the end of this chapter, you learned some of the most popular dimensionality reduction techniques. You will learn more of these along the road, for example, when we talk about autoencoders, which can be used for dimensionality reduction as well. But sit tight, we will get there in due time.

For now, we will continue our journey toward the next introductory topic about basic machine learning. Chapter 4, *Learning from Data,* introduces the most elementary concepts around the theory of deep learning, including measuring performance on regression and classification, as well as the identification of overfitting. However, before we go there, please try to quiz yourself with the following questions.

Questions and answers

1. **Which variables of the heart dataset are suitable for regression?**

   Actually, all of them. But the ideal ones are those that are real-valued.

2. **Does the scaling of the data change the distribution of the data?**

   No. The distribution remains the same. Statistical metrics such as the mean and variance may change, but the distribution remains the same.

3. **What is the main difference between supervised and unsupervised dimensionality reduction methods?**

   Supervised algorithms use the target labels, while unsupervised algorithms do not need that information.

4. **When is it better to use batch-based dimensionality reduction?**

   When you have very large datasets.

References

- Cleveland Heart Disease Dataset (1988). Principal investigators:
  a. Hungarian Institute of Cardiology. Budapest: Andras Janosi, M.D.
  b. University Hospital, Zurich, Switzerland: William Steinbrunn, M.D.
  c. University Hospital, Basel, Switzerland: Matthias Pfisterer, M.D.
  d. V.A. Medical Center, Long Beach and Cleveland Clinic Foundation: Robert Detrano, M.D., Ph.D.
- Detrano, R., Janosi, A., Steinbrunn, W., Pfisterer, M., Schmid, J.J., Sandhu, S., Guppy, K.H., Lee, S. and Froelicher, V., (1989). International application of a new probability algorithm for the diagnosis of coronary artery disease. *The American journal of cardiology*, 64(5), 304-310.
- Deng, L. (2012). The MNIST database of handwritten digit images for machine learning research (best of the web). *IEEE Signal Processing Magazine*, 29(6), 141-142.
- Sezgin, M., and Sankur, B. (2004). Survey over image thresholding techniques and quantitative performance evaluation. *Journal of Electronic imaging*, 13(1), 146-166.

- Potdar, K., Pardawala, T. S., and Pai, C. D. (2017). A comparative study of categorical variable encoding techniques for neural network classifiers. *International Journal of Computer Applications*, 175(4), 7-9.

- Hanin, B. (2018). Which neural net architectures give rise to exploding and vanishing gradients?. In *Advances in Neural Information Processing Systems* (pp. 582-591).

- Andrews, D. F., Gnanadesikan, R., and Warner, J. L. (1971). Transformations of multivariate data. *Biometrics*, 825-840.

- Van Dyk, D. A., and Meng, X. L. (2001). The art of data augmentation. *Journal of Computational and Graphical Statistics*, 10(1), 1-50.

- Schölkopf, B., Smola, A., and Müller, K. R. (1997, October). Kernel principal component analysis. In *International conference on artificial neural networks* (pp. 583-588). Springer, Berlin, Heidelberg.

- Hinton, G. E. (2012). A practical guide to training restricted Boltzmann machines. In *Neural networks: Tricks of the trade* (pp. 599-619). Springer, Berlin, Heidelberg.

- Mairal, J., Bach, F., Ponce, J., and Sapiro, G. (June, 2009). Online dictionary learning for sparse coding. In *Proceedings of the 26th annual international conference on machine learning* (pp. 689-696). ACM.

4
Learning from Data

Data preparation takes a great deal of time for complex datasets, as we saw in the previous chapter. However, time spent on data preparation is time well invested... this I can guarantee! In the same way, investing time in understanding the basic theory of learning from data is super important for any person that wants to join the field of deep learning. Understanding the fundamentals of learning theory will pay off whenever you read new algorithms or evaluate your own models. It will also make your life much easier when you get to the later chapters in this book.

More specifically, this chapter introduces the most elementary concepts around the theory of deep learning, including measuring performance on regression and classification as well as the identification of overfitting. It also offers some warnings about the sensibility of—and the need to optimize—model hyperparameters.

The outline of this chapter is as follows:

- Learning for a purpose
- Measuring success and error
- Identifying overfitting and generalization
- The art behind learning
- Ethical implications of training deep learning algorithms

Learning for a purpose

In Chapter 3, *Preparing Data*, we discussed how to prepare data for two major types of problems: **regression** and **classification**. In this section, we will cover the technical differences between classification and regression in more detail. These differences are important because they will limit the type of machine learning algorithms you can use to solve your problem.

Classification

How do you know whether your problem is classification? The answer depends on two major factors: the **problem** you are trying to solve and the **data** you have to solve your problem. There might be other factors, for sure, but these two are by far the most significant.

If your purpose is to make a model that, given some input, will determine whether the response or output of the model is to distinguish between two or more distinct categories, then you have a classification problem. Here is a non-exhaustive list of examples of classification problems:

- Given an image, indicate what number it contains (distinguish between 10 categories: 0-9 digits).
- Given an image, indicate whether it contains a cat or not (distinguish between two categories: yes or no).
- Given a sequence of readings about temperature, determine the season (distinguish between four categories: the four seasons).
- Given the text of a tweet, determine the sentiment (distinguish between two categories: positive or negative).
- Given an image of a person, determine the age group (distinguish between five categories: <18, 18-25, 26-35, 35-50, >50).
- Given an image of a dog, determine its breed (distinguish between 120 categories: those breeds that are internationally recognized).
- Given an entire document, determine whether it has been tampered with (distinguish between categories: authentic or altered).
- Given satellite readings of a spectroradiometer, determine whether the geolocation matches the spectral signature of vegetation or not (distinguish between two categories: yes or no).

As you can see from the examples in the list, there are different types of data for different types of problems. The data that we are seeing in these examples is known as **labeled data**.

Unlabeled data is very common but is rarely used for classification problems without some type of processing that allows the matching of data samples to a category. For example, unsupervised clustering can be used on unlabeled data to assign the data to specific clusters (such as groups or categories); at which point, the data technically becomes "labeled data."

The other important thing to notice from the list is that we can categorize the classification problems into two major groups:

- **Binary classification**: For classification between any two classes only
- **Multi-class classification**: For classification between more than just two classes

This distinction may seem arbitrary but it is not; in fact, the type of classification will limit the type of learning algorithm you can use and the performance you can expect. To understand this a little better, let's discuss each classification separately.

Binary classification

This type of classification is usually regarded as a much simpler problem than multiple classes. In fact, if we can solve the binary classification problem, we could, technically, solve the problem of multiple classes by deciding on a strategy to break down the problem into several binary classification problems (*Lorena, A. C. et al., 2008*).

One of the reasons why this is considered a simpler problem is because of the algorithmic and mathematical foundations behind binary classification learning algorithms. Let's say that we have a binary classification problem, such as the Cleveland dataset explained in Chapter 3, *Preparing Data*. This dataset consists of 13 medical observations for each patient—we can call that $\mathbf{x} \in \mathbb{R}^{13}$. For each of these patient records, there is an associated label that indicates whether the patient has some type of heart disease (+1) or not (-1)—we will call that $y \in \{-1, +1\}$. So, an entire dataset, $\mathcal{D}$, with N samples can be defined as a set of data and labels:

$$\mathcal{D} = \{\mathbf{x}_i, y_i\}_{i=1}^{N}$$

Then, as discussed in Chapter 1, *Introduction to Machine Learning*, the whole point of learning is to use an algorithm that will find a way to map input data, $\mathbf{x}$, to label the y correctly for all samples in $\mathcal{D}$ and to be able to further do so (hopefully) for samples outside of the known dataset, $\mathcal{D}$. Using a perceptron and a corresponding **Perceptron Learning Algorithm** (PLA), what we want is to find the parameters $(\mathbf{w}, b)$ that can satisfy the following:

$$y_i = sign(\mathbf{w}^T \mathbf{x}_i + b)$$

For all samples, i = 1, 2, ..., N. However, as we discussed in Chapter 1, *Introduction to Machine Learning*, the equation cannot be satisfied if the data is non-linearly separable. In that case, we can obtain an approximation, or a prediction, that is not necessarily the desired outcome; we will call such a prediction $\hat{y}$.

The whole point of a learning algorithm, then, becomes to reduce the differences between the desired target label, y, and the prediction, $\hat{y}$. In an ideal world, we want $\hat{y}_i = y_i$ for all cases of $i = 1, 2, ..., N$. In cases of i where $\hat{y}_i \neq y_i$, the learning algorithm must make adjustments (that is, train itself) to avoid making such mistakes in the future by finding new parameters $(\mathbf{w}, b)$ that are hopefully better.

The science behind such algorithms varies from model to model, but the ultimate goals are usually the same:

- Reduce the number of errors, $\hat{y}_i \neq y_i$, in every learning iteration.
- Learn the model parameters in as few iterations (steps) as possible.
- Learn the model parameters as fast as possible.

Since most datasets deal with non-separable problems, the PLA is disregarded in favor of other algorithms that will converge faster and in fewer iterations. Many learning algorithms like this learn to adjust the parameters $(\mathbf{w}, b)$ by taking specific steps to reduce the error, $\hat{y}_i \neq y_i$, based on derivatives with respect to the variability of the error and the choice of parameters. So, the most successful algorithms (in deep learning, at least) are those based on some type of gradient descent strategy (Hochreiter, S., et.al. 2001).

Now, let's go over the most basic iterative gradient strategy. Say that we want to learn the parameters $(\mathbf{w}, b)$ given the dataset, $\mathcal{D}$. We will have to make a small adjustment to the problem formulation to make things a little easier. What we want is for $\mathbf{w}^T \mathbf{x}_i + b$ to be implied in the expression $\mathbf{w}^T \mathbf{x}_i$. The only way this could work is if we set $\mathbf{w} = [b, w_1, w_2, \ldots, w_d]^T$ and $\mathbf{x} = [1, x_1, x_2, \ldots, x_d]^T$.

With this simplification, we can simply search for $\mathbf{w}$, which implies a search for $\mathbf{b}$ as well. Gradient descent with a fixed *learning rate* is as follows:

1. Initialize the weights to zero ($\mathbf{w} = \mathbf{0}$) and the iteration counter to zero ($t = 0$).
2. When $t \leq t_{\max}$, do the following:

    1. Calculate the gradient with respect to $\mathbf{w}_t$ and store it in $\mathbf{g}_t \leftarrow \nabla E(\mathbf{w}_t)$.
    2. Update $\mathbf{w}$ so that it looks like this: $\mathbf{w}_{t+1} = \mathbf{w}_t - \eta \mathbf{g}_t$.
    3. Increase the iteration counter and repeat.

There are a couple of things that need to be explained here:

- The gradient calculation, $\nabla E(\mathbf{w}_t)$, is not trivial. For some specific machine learning models, it can be determined analytically; but in most cases, it must be determined numerically by using some of the latest algorithms.
- We still need to define how the error, $E(\mathbf{w}_t)$, is calculated; but this will be covered in the next section of this chapter.
- A learning rate, η, needs to be specified as well, which is a problem in itself.

One way of looking at this last issue is that in order to find the parameter, $\mathbf{w}$, that minimizes the error, we need parameter η. Now, we could, when applying gradient descent, think about finding the η parameter, but we will then fall into an infinite cycle. We will not go into more detail about gradient descent and its learning rate since, nowadays, algorithms for gradient descent often include automatic calculations of it or adaptive ways of adjusting it (Ruder, S. 2016).

Multi-class classification

Classifying into multiple categories can have an important effect on the performance of learning algorithms. In a general sense, the performance of a model will decrease with the number of classes it is required to recognize. The exception is if you have plenty of data and access to lots of computing power because if you do, you can overcome the limitations of poor datasets that have class imbalance problems and you can estimate massive gradients and make large calculations and updates to the model. Computing power may not be a limitation in the future, but at the moment it is.

The multiple classes problem can be solved by using strategies such as **one versus one** or **one versus all**.

In one versus all, you essentially have an expert binary classifier that is really good at recognizing one pattern from all the others and the implementation strategy is typically cascaded. An example is shown here:

```
if classifierSummer says is Summer: you are done
else:
 if classifierFall says is Fall: you are done
 else:
   if classifierWinter says is Winter: you are done
   else:
      it must be Spring and, thus, you are done
```

Here is a graphical explanation of this strategy. Suppose we have two-dimensional data that tells us something about the four seasons of the year, as shown:

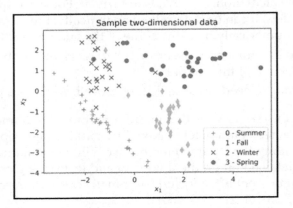

Figure 4.1 - Randomized two-dimensional data that could tell us something about the four seasons of the year

In this case of randomized two-dimensional data, we have four categories corresponding to the seasons of the year. Binary classification will not work directly. However, we could train expert binary classifiers that specialize in *one* specific category *versus all* the rest. If we train one binary classifier to determine whether data points belong to the **Summer** category, using a simple perceptron, we could get the separating hyperplane shown here:

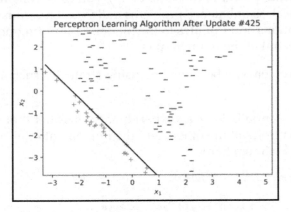

Figure 4.2: A PLA that is an expert in distinguishing from the Summer season data versus all the rest of the other seasons

Similarly, we can train the rest of the experts until we have enough to test our entire hypothesis; that is, until we are able to distinguish all the classes from each other.

Another alternative is to use classifiers that can handle multiple outputs; for example, decision trees or ensemble methods. But in the case of deep learning and neural networks, this refers to networks that can have multiple neurons in the output layer, such as the one depicted in *Figure 1.6* and *Figure 1.9* in `Chapter 1`, *Introduction to Machine Learning*.

The mathematical formulation of a multi-output neural network only changes slightly from a single-output one in that the output is no longer within a binary set of values, such as $y \in \{-1, +1\}$, but is now a vector of one-hot encoded values, such as $\mathbf{y} \in \mathbb{Z}^{|C|}$. In this case, $|C|$ denotes the size of the set C, which contains all the different class labels. For the previous example, C would contain the following: $C = \{$'*Summer*', '*Fall*', '*Winter*', '*Spring*'$\}$. Here is what each one-hot encoding would look like:

- **Summer**: $\mathbf{y} = [1, 0, 0, 0]^T$
- **Fall**: $\mathbf{y} = [0, 1, 0, 0]^T$
- **Winter**: $\mathbf{y} = [0, 0, 1, 0]^T$
- **Spring**: $\mathbf{y} = [0, 0, 0, 1]^T$

Every element in the target vector will correspond to the desired output of the four neurons. We should also point out that the dataset definition should now reflect that both the sample input data and the labels are vectors:

$$\mathcal{D} = \{\mathbf{x}_i, \mathbf{y}_i\}_{i=1}^N$$

Another way of dealing with the problem of multiple-class classification is by using **regression**.

Regression

Previously, we specified that for binary classification, the target variable could take on a set of binary values; for example, $y \in \{-1, +1\}$. We also said that for multiple classification, we could modify the target variable to be a vector whose size depends on the number of classes, $\mathbf{y} \in \mathbb{Z}^{|C|}$. Well, regression problems deal with cases where the target variable is any real value, $y \in \mathbb{R}$.

The implications here are very interesting because with a regression model and algorithm, we could *technically* do binary classification since the set of real numbers contains any binary set of numbers:

$$y \in \{-1, +1\} \subseteq \mathbb{R}.$$

Further, if we change C = {*'Summer'*, *'Fall'*, *'Winter'*, *'Spring'*} to a numerical representation instead, such as C = {0,1,2,3}, then *technically*, we would again use regression due to the same property:

$$y \in \{0, 1, 2, 3\} \subseteq \mathbb{R}.$$

 Although regression models can solve classification problems, it is recommended that you use models that are specialized in classification specifically and leave the regression models only for regression tasks.

Even if regression models can be used for classification (Tan, X., et.al. 2012), they are ideal for when the target variable is a real number. Here is a sample list of regression problems:

- When given an image, indicate how many people are in it (the output can be any integer >=0).
- When given an image, indicate the probability of it containing a cat (the output can be any real number between 0 and 1).
- When given a sequence of readings about temperature, determine what the temperature actually feels like (the output can be any integer whose range depends on the units).
- When given the text of a tweet, determine the probability of it being offensive (the output can be any real number between 0 and 1).
- When given an image of a person, determine their age (the output can be any positive integer, usually less than 100).
- When given an entire document, determine the probable compression rate (the output can be any real number between 0 and 1).
- When given satellite readings of a spectroradiometer, determine the corresponding infrared value (the output can be any real number).
- When given the headlines of some major newspapers, determine the price of oil (the output can be any real number >=0).

As you can see from this list, there are many possibilities due to the fact that the range of real numbers encompasses all integers and all positive and negative numbers, and even if the range is too broad for specific applications, the regression model can be scaled up or down to meet the range specifications.

To explain the potential of regression models, let's start with a basic **linear regression** model and in later chapters, we will cover more complex regression models based on deep learning.

The linear regression model tries to solve the following problem:

$$y_i = \mathbf{w}^T \mathbf{x}_i + b$$

The problem is solved for i = 1, 2, ..., N. We could, however, use the same trick as before and include the calculation of b in the same equation. So, we can say that we are trying to solve the following problem:

$$y_i = \mathbf{w}^T \mathbf{x}_i$$

Once again, we are trying to learn the parameters, $\mathbf{w}$, that yield $\hat{y}_i = y_i$ for all cases of i. In the case of linear regression, the prediction, $\hat{y}$, should ideally be equal to the true target value, y, if the input data, $\mathbf{x}_i$, somehow describes a perfect straight line. But because this is very unlikely, there has to be a way of learning the parameters, $\mathbf{w}$, even if $\hat{y}_i \neq y_i$. To achieve this, the linear regression learning algorithm begins by describing a low penalty for small mistakes and a larger penalty for big mistakes. This does make sense, right? It is very intuitive.

A natural way of penalizing mistakes in proportion to their size is by squaring the difference between the prediction and the target. Here is an example of when the difference is small:

$$(\hat{y}_i - y_i)^2 = (0.98 - 1)^2 = (-0.02)^2 = 0.0004$$

Here is an example of when the difference is large:

$$(\hat{y}_i - y_i)^2 = (15.8 - 1)^2 = (14.8)^2 = 219.4$$

In both of these examples, the desired target value is 1. In the first case, the predicted value of 0.98 is very close to the target and the squared difference is 0.0004, which is small compared to the second case. The second prediction is off by 14.8, which yields a squared difference of 219.4. This seems reasonable and intuitive for building up a learning algorithm; that is, one that penalizes mistakes in proportion to how big or small they are.

We can formally define the overall average error in function of the choice of parameters **w** as the averaged sum of all squared errors, which is also known as the **mean squared error (MSE)**:

$$E(\mathbf{w}) = \frac{1}{N} \sum_{i=1}^{N} (\hat{y}_i - y_i)^2 .$$

If we define the prediction in terms of the current choice of **w** as $\hat{y}_i = \mathbf{w}^T \mathbf{x}_i$, then we can rewrite the error function as follows:

$$E(\mathbf{w}) = \frac{1}{N} \sum_{i=1}^{N} (\mathbf{w}^T \mathbf{x}_i - y_i)^2 .$$

This can be simplified in terms of the ℓ_2-norm (also known as the Euclidean norm, $\|\cdot\|_2$) by first defining a matrix of data X, whose elements are data vector **x**, and a vector of corresponding targets, as follows:

$$X = \begin{bmatrix} \mathbf{x}_1^T \\ \mathbf{x}_2^T \\ \vdots \\ \mathbf{x}_N^T \end{bmatrix} \text{ and } \mathbf{y} = \begin{bmatrix} y_1 \\ y_2 \\ \vdots \\ y_N \end{bmatrix} .$$

The simplification of the error is then as follows:

$$E(\mathbf{w}) = \frac{1}{N} \|X\mathbf{w} - \mathbf{y}\|_2^2$$

This can then be expanded into the following important equation:

$$E(\mathbf{w}) = \frac{1}{N} \|\mathbf{w}^T X^T X \mathbf{w} - 2\mathbf{w}^T X^T \mathbf{y} + \mathbf{y}^T \mathbf{y}\|_2^2 .$$

This is important because it facilitates the calculation of the derivative of the error, $E(\mathbf{w})$, which is necessary for adjusting the parameters, **w**, in the direction of the derivative and in proportion to the error. Now, following the basic properties of linear algebra, we can say that the derivative of the error (which is called a gradient since it yields a matrix) is the following:

$$\nabla E(\mathbf{w}) = \frac{2}{N} (X^T X \mathbf{w} - X^T \mathbf{y}) .$$

Because we want to find the parameters that yield the smallest error, we can set the gradient to 0 and solve for **w**. By setting the gradient to 0 and ignoring constant values, we arrive at the following:

$$X^T X \mathbf{w} = X^T \mathbf{y}$$

$$\mathbf{w} = (X^T X)^{-1} X^T \mathbf{y}.$$

These are called **normal equations** (Krejn, S. G. E. 1982). Then, if we simply use the term $X^* = (X^T X)^{-1} X^T$, we arrive at the definition of a **pseudo-inverse** (Golub, G., and Kahan, W. 1965). The beauty of this is that we do not need to calculate the gradient iteratively to choose the best parameters, **w**. As a matter of fact, because the gradient is analytic and direct, we can calculate **w** in one shot, as explained in this linear regression algorithm:

1. From $\mathcal{D} = \{x_i, y_i\}_{i=1}^N$, construct the pair, (X, y).
2. Estimate the pseudo-inverse $X^* = (X^T X)^{-1} X^T$.
3. Calculate and return $\mathbf{w} = X^* \mathbf{y}$.

To show this graphically, let's say that we have a system that sends a signal that follows a linear function; however, the signal, when it is transmitted, becomes contaminated with normal noise with a 0 mean and unit variance and we are only able to observe the noisy data, as shown:

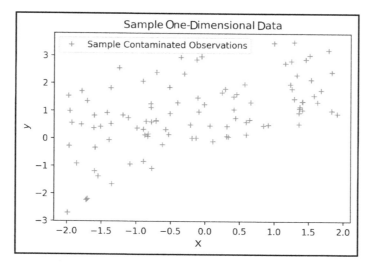

Figure 4.3 - Data readings that are contaminated with random noise

If, say, a hacker reads this data and runs linear regression to attempt to determine the true function that produced this data before it was contaminated, then the data hacker would obtain the solution shown here:

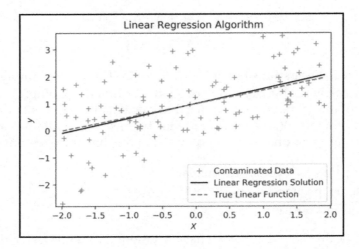

Figure 4.4 - A linear regression solution to the problem of finding the true function given noisy data readings

Clearly, as the previous figure shows, the linear regression solution is very close to the true original linear function. In this particular example, a high degree of closeness can be observed since the data was contaminated with noise that follows a pattern of **white noise**; however, for different types of noise, the model may not perform as well as in this example. Furthermore, most regression problems are not linear at all; in fact, the most interesting regression problems are highly non-linear. Nonetheless, the basic learning principle is the same:

- Reduce the number of errors, $E(\mathbf{w})$, in every learning iteration (or directly in one shot, such as in linear regression).
- Learn the model parameters in as few iterations (steps) as possible.
- Learn the model parameters as fast as possible.

The other major component that guides the learning process is the way the success or error is calculated with respect to a choice of parameters, $E(\mathbf{w})$. In the case of the PLA, it simply found a mistake and adjusted with respect to it. For multiple classes, this was through a process of gradient descent over some measure of error and in linear regression, this was through direct gradient calculation using the MSE. But now, let's dive deeper into other types of error measures and successes that can be quantitative and qualitative.

Measuring success and error

There is a wide variety of performance metrics that people use in deep learning models, such as accuracy, balanced error rate, mean squared error, and many others. To keep things organized, we will divide them into three groups: for binary classification, for multiple classes, and for regression.

Binary classification

There is one essential tool used when analyzing and measuring the success of our models. It is known as a **confusion matrix**. A confusion matrix is not only helpful in visually displaying how a model makes predictions, but we can also retrieve other interesting information from it. The following diagram shows a template of a confusion matrix:

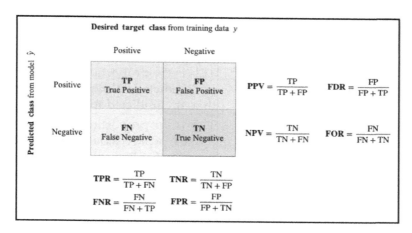

Figure 4.5 - A confusion matrix and the performance metrics derived from it

A confusion matrix and all the metrics derived from it are a very important way of conveying how good your models are. You should bookmark this page and come back to it whenever you need it.

In the preceding confusion matrix, you will notice that it has two columns in the vertical axis that indicate the true target values, while in the horizontal axis, it indicates the predicted value. The intersection of rows and columns indicates the relationship of what should have been predicted against what was actually predicted. Every entry in the matrix has a special meaning and can lead to other meaningful composite performance metrics.

Here is the list of metrics and what they mean:

Acronym	Description	Interpretation
TP	*True Positive*	This is when a data point was of the positive class and was correctly predicted to be of the positive class.
TN	*True Negative*	This is when a data point was of the negative class and was correctly predicted to be of the negative class.
FP	*False Positive*	This is when a data point was of the negative class and was incorrectly predicted to be of the positive class.
FN	*False Negative*	This is when a data point was of the positive class and was incorrectly predicted to be of the negative class.
PPV	*Positive Predictive Value* or *Precision*	This is the proportion of positive values that are predicted correctly out of all the values predicted to be positive.
NPV	*Negative Predictive Value*	This is the proportion of negative values that are predicted correctly out of all the values that are predicted to be negative.
FDR	*False Discovery Rate*	This is the proportion of incorrect predictions as false positives out of all the values that are predicted to be positive.
FOR	*False Omission Rate*	This is the proportion of incorrect predictions as false negatives out of all the values that are predicted to be negative.
TPR	*True Positive Rate, Sensitivity, Recall, Hit Rate*	This is the proportion of predicted positives that are actually positives out of all that should be positives.
FPR	*False Positive Rate* or *Fall-Out*	This is the proportion of predicted positives that are actually negatives out of all that should be negatives.
TNR	*True Negative Rate, Specificity,* or *Selectivity*	This is the proportion of predicted negatives that are actually negatives out of all that should be negatives.
FNR	*False Negative Rate* or *Miss Rate*	This is the proportion of predicted negatives that are actually positives out of all that should be positives.

Some of these can be a little bit obscure to understand; however, you don't have to memorize them now, you can always come back to this table.

There are other metrics that are a little bit complicated to calculate, such as the following:

Acronym	Description	Interpretation
ACC	*Accuracy*	This is the rate of correctly predicting the positives and the negatives out of all the samples.
F_1	*F_1-Score*	This is the average of the precision and sensitivity.
MCC	*Matthews Correlation Coefficient*	This is the correlation between the desired and the predicted classes.
BER	*Balanced Error Rate*	This is the average error rate for cases where there is a class imbalance.

I included, in this list of *complicated* calculations, acronyms such as **ACC** and **BER**, which are acronyms that have a very intuitive meaning. The main issue is, however, that these will vary when we have multiple classes. So, their calculation will be slightly different in multiple classes. The rest of the metrics remain exclusive (as defined) to binary classification.

Before we discuss metrics for multiple classes, here are the formulas for calculating the previous metrics:

$$ACC = \frac{TP + TN}{TP + TN + FP + FN} = \frac{TP + TN}{N}$$

$$F_1 = 2 \times \left(\frac{PPV \times TPR}{PPV + TPR} \right)$$

$$MCC = \frac{(TP \times TN) - (FP \times FN)}{\sqrt{(TP + FP)(TP + FN)(TN + FP)(TN + FN)}}$$

$$BER = \frac{1}{2} \times (FPR + FNR)$$

In a general sense, you want **ACC**, **F₁**, and **MCC** to be high and **BER** to be low.

Multiple classes

When we go beyond simple binary classification, we often deal with multiple classes, such as C = {'*Summer*', '*Fall*', '*Winter*', '*Spring*'} or C = {0,1,2,3}. This can limit, to a certain point, the way we measure error or success.

Consider the confusion matrix for multiple classes shown here:

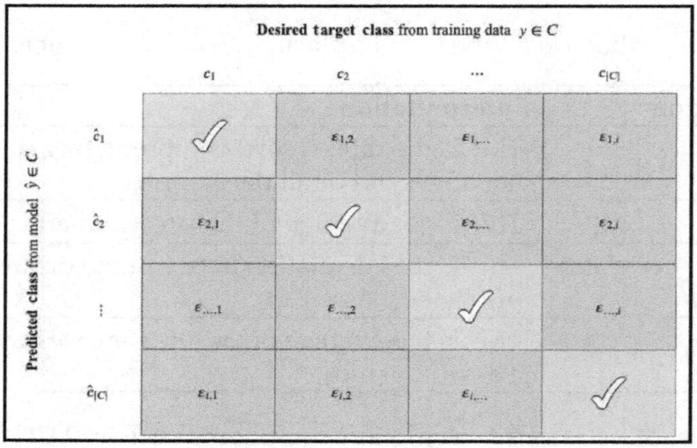

Figure 4.6 - A confusion matrix for multiple classes

From the following diagram, it is evident that the notion of true positive or negative has disappeared since we no longer have just positive and negative classes, but also sets of finite classes:

$$C = \{c_1, c_2, c_3, \ldots\}$$

Individual classes, c_i, can be strings or numbers, as long as they follow the rules of sets. That is, the set of classes, C, must be finite and unique.

To measure ACC here, we will count all the elements in the main diagonal of the confusion matrix and divide it by the total number of samples:

$$\text{ACC} = \frac{\text{tr}(E_\varepsilon)}{N}$$

In this equation, E_ε denotes the confusion matrix and $\text{tr}(\cdot)$ denotes the trace operation; that is, the sum of the elements in the main diagonal of a square matrix. Consequently, the total error is $1-\text{ACC}$, but in the case of class imbalance, the error metric or plain accuracy may be deceiving. For this, we must use the BER metric, which for multiple classes can be defined as follows:

$$\text{BER} = 1 - \frac{1}{|C|} \times \sum_{i=1}^{|C|} \frac{\varepsilon_{i,i}}{\sum_{j=1}^{|C|} \varepsilon_{j,i}}$$

In this new formula for BER, $\varepsilon_{j,i}$ refers to the element in the *j*th row and *i*th column of the confusion matrix, E_ε.

Some machine learning schools of thought use the rows of the confusion matrix to denote true labels and the columns to denote the predicted labels. The theory behind the analysis is the same and the interpretation is, too. Don't be alarmed that `sklearn` uses the flipped approach; this is irrelevant and you should not have any problems with following any discussions about this.

As an example, consider the dataset that was shown earlier in *Figure 4.1*. If we run a five-layered neural network classifier, we could obtain decision boundaries like this:

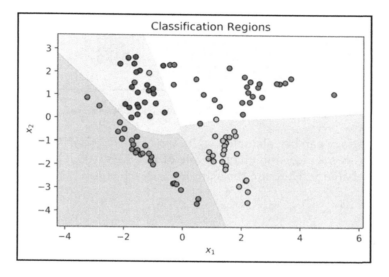

Figure 4.7 - Classification regions for a sample two-dimensional dataset with a five-layer neural net

Clearly, the dataset is not perfectly separable by a non-linear hyperplane; there are some data points that cross the boundaries for each class. In the previous graph, we can see that only the *Summer* class has no points that are incorrectly classified based on the classification boundaries.

However, this is more evident if we actually calculate and display the confusion matrix, shown here:

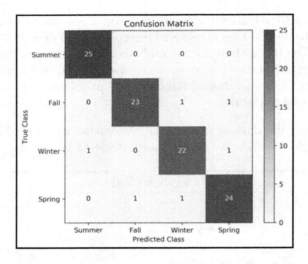

Figure 4.8 - A confusion matrix obtained from training errors on the sample two-dimensional dataset

In this case, the accuracy can be calculated as ACC=(25+23+22+24)/100, which yields an ACC of 0.94, which seems nice, and an error rate of 1-ACC = 0.06. This particular example has a slight class imbalance. Here are the samples for each class:

- **Summer**: 25
- **Fall**: 25
- **Winter**: 24
- **Spring**: 26

The **Winter** group has fewer examples than the rest and the **Spring** group has more examples than the rest. While this is a very small class imbalance, it can be enough to yield a deceivingly low error rate. We must now calculate the balanced error rate, BER.

BER can be calculated as follows:

$$\text{BER} = 1 - \frac{1}{4} \times \left(\frac{25}{25} + \frac{23}{25} + \frac{22}{24} + \frac{24}{26} \right)$$

$$\text{BER} = 1 - \frac{1 + 0.92 + 0.9166 + 0.9231}{4} = 1 - 0.9399 = 0.0601$$

Here, the difference between the error rate and BER is a 0.01% under-estimation of the error. However, for classes that are highly imbalanced, the gap can be much larger and it is our responsibility to measure carefully and report the appropriate error measure, BER.

Another interesting fact about BER is that it intuitively is the counterpart of a balanced accuracy; this means that if we remove the 1– term in the BER equation, we are left with the balanced accuracy. Further, if we examine the terms in the numerator, we can see that the fractions on it lead to class-specific accuracies; for example, the first class, **Summer**, has a 100% accuracy, the second, **Fall**, has a 92% accuracy, and so on.

In Python, the `sklearn` library has a class that can determine the confusion matrix automatically, given the true and predicted labels. The class is called `confusion_matrix` and it belongs to the `metrics` super class and we can use it as follows:

```
from sklearn.metrics import confusion_matrix
cm = confusion_matrix(y, y_pred)
print(cm)
```

If `y` contains the true labels, and `y_pred` contains the predicted labels, then the preceding instructions will output something like this:

```
[[25  0  0  0]
 [ 0 23  1  1]
 [ 1  0 22  1]
 [ 0  1  1 24]]
```

We can calculate BER by simply doing this:

```
BER = []
for i in range(len(cm)):
 BER.append(cm[i,i]/sum(cm[i,:]))
print('BER:', 1 - sum(BER)/len(BER))
```

This will output the following:

```
BER: 0.06006410256410266
```

Alternatively, `sklearn` has a built-in function to calculate the balanced accuracy score in the same super class as the confusion matrix. The class is called `balanced_accuracy_score` and we can produce BER by doing the following:

```
from sklearn.metrics import balanced_accuracy_score
print('BER', 1- balanced_accuracy_score(y, y_pred))
```

We get the following output:

```
BER: 0.06006410256410266
```

Let's now discuss the metrics for regression.

Regression

The most popular metric is **MSE**, which we discussed earlier in this chapter when explaining how linear regression works. However, we explained it as a function of the choice of hyperparameters. Here, we will redefine it in a general sense as follows:

$$\text{MSE} = \frac{1}{N} \sum_{i=1}^{N} (\hat{y}_i - y_i)^2$$

Another metric that is very similar to MSE is **mean absolute error** (**MAE**). While MSE penalizes big mistakes more (quadratically) and small errors much less, MAE penalizes everything in direct proportion to the absolute difference between what should be and what was predicted. This is a formal definition of MAE:

$$\text{MAE} = \frac{1}{N} \sum_{i=1}^{N} |\hat{y}_i - y_i|$$

Finally, out of the other measures for regression, the popular choice in deep learning is the R^2 **score**, also known as the **coefficient of determination**. This metric represents the proportion of variance, which is explained by the independent variables in the model. It measures how likely the model is to perform well on unseen data that follows the same statistical distribution as the training data. This is its definition:

$$R^2 = 1 - \frac{\sum_{i=1}^{N} (\hat{y}_i - y_i)^2}{\sum_{i=1}^{N} (y_i - \bar{y})^2}$$

The sample mean is defined as follows:

$$\bar{y} = \frac{1}{N} \sum_{i=1}^{N} y_i$$

Scikit-learn has classes available for each one of these metrics, indicated in the following table:

Regression metric	Scikit-learn class
R^2 score	sklearn.metrics.r2_score
MAE	sklearn.metrics.mean_absolute_error
MSE	sklearn.metrics.mean_squared_error

All of these classes take the true labels and predicted labels as input arguments.

As an example, if we take the data and linear regression model shown in *Figure 4.3* and *Figure 4.4* as input, we can determine the three error metrics, as follows:

```
from sklearn.metrics import mean_absolute_error
from sklearn.metrics import mean_squared_error
from sklearn.metrics import r2_score

r2 = r2_score(y,y_pred)
mae = mean_absolute_error(y,y_pred)
mse = mean_squared_error(y,y_pred)

print('R_2 score:', r2)
print('MAE:', mae)
print('MSE:', mse)
```

The output of the preceding code is as follows:

```
R_2 score: 0.9350586211501963
MAE: 0.1259473720654865
MSE: 0.022262066145814736
```

The following graph shows the sample data used, along with the performance obtained. Clearly, the performance using the three performance metrics is good:

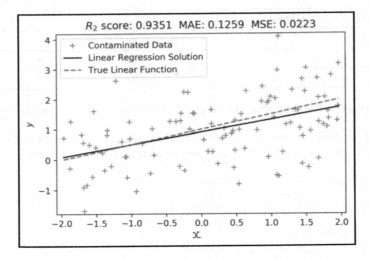

Figure 4.9 - Error metrics over a linear regression model on data contaminated with white noise

In general, you always want to have a determination coefficient that is as close to 1 as possible and all your errors (MSE and MAE) as close to 0 as possible. But while all of these are good metrics to report on our models, we need to be careful to report these metrics over **unseen validation** or **test data**. This is so that we accurately measure the generalization ability of the model and identify overfitting in our models before it becomes a catastrophic error.

Identifying overfitting and generalization

Often, when we are in a controlled machine learning setting, we are given a dataset that we can use for training and a different set that we can use for testing. The idea is that you only run the learning algorithm on the **training** data, but when it comes to seeing how good your model is, you feed your model the **test** data and observe the output. It is typical for competitions and hackathons to give out the test data but withhold the labels associated with it because the winner will be selected based on how well the model performs on the test data and you don't want them to cheat by looking at the labels of the test data and making adjustments. If this is the case, we can use a **validation** dataset, which we can create by ourselves by separating a portion of the training data to be the validation data.

The whole point of having separate sets, namely a validation or test dataset, is to measure the performance on this data, knowing that our model was not trained with it. A model's ability to perform equally, or close to equally, well on unseen validation or test data is known as **generalization.**

Generalization is the ultimate goal of most learning algorithms; all of us professionals and practitioners of deep learning dream of achieving great generalization in all of our models. Similarly, our greatest nightmare is **overfitting.**

Overfitting is the opposite of generalization. It occurs when our models perform extremely well on the training data but when presented with validation or test data, the performance decreases significantly. This indicates that our model almost memorized the intricacies of the training data and missed the big picture generalities of the sample space that lead to good models.

In this and further chapters, we will follow these rules with respect to data splits:

- If we are given test data (with labels), we will train on the training set and report the performance based on the test set.
- If we are not given test data (or if we have test data with no labels), we will split the training set, creating a validation set that we can report performance on using a cross-validation strategy.

Let's discuss each scenario separately.

If we have test data

To begin this discussion, let's say that we have a deep learning model with a set of hyper parameters, θ, which could be the weights of the model, the number of neurons, layers, the learning rate, the drop-out rate, and so on. Then, we can say that a model, H_θ, (with parameters θ) that is trained with training data, $\mathcal{D} = \{\mathbf{x}_i, y_i\}_{i=1}^{N}$, can have a training accuracy as follows:

$$ACC(H_\theta(\mathcal{D})) = \frac{\mathbf{tr}(E_\varepsilon)}{N}$$

This is the training accuracy of a trained model on the training data. Consequently, if we are given labeled test data, $\mathcal{T} = \{\mathbf{x}_i, y_i\}_{i=1}^{M}$, with M data points, we can simply estimate the **test accuracy** by calculating the following:

$$\mathrm{ACC}(H_\theta(\mathcal{T})) = \frac{\mathbf{tr}(E_\varepsilon)}{M}$$

One important property when reporting test accuracy usually holds true in most cases—all test accuracy is usually less than the training accuracy plus some noise caused by a poor selection of parameters:

$$\mathrm{ACC}(H_\theta(\mathcal{D})) \leq \mathrm{ACC}(H_\theta(\mathcal{D})) + \varepsilon_\theta$$

This usually implies that if your test accuracy is significantly larger than your training accuracy, then there could be something wrong with the trained model. Also, we could consider the possibility that the test data is drastically different from the training data in terms of its statistical distribution and the multidimensional manifold that describes it.

In summary, reporting performance on the test set is very important if we have test data that was properly chosen. Nonetheless, it would be completely normal for the performance to be less than it was in training. However, if it is significantly lower, there could be a problem of overfitting and if it is significantly greater, then there could be a problem with the code, the model, and even the choice of test data. The problem of overfitting can be solved by choosing better parameters, θ, or by choosing a different model, H_θ, which is discussed in the next section.

Now, let's briefly discuss a case where we don't have test data or we have test data with no labels.

No test data? No problem – cross-validate

Cross-validation is a technique that allows us to split the training data, $\mathcal{D} = \{\mathbf{x}_i, y_i\}_{i=1}^{N}$, into smaller groups for training purposes. The most important point to remember is that the splits are ideally made of an equal number of samples overall and that we want to rotate the choice of groups for training and validation sets.

Let's discuss the famous cross-validation strategy known as *k*-fold cross-validation (Kohavi, R. 1995). The idea here is to divide the training data into *k* groups, which are (ideally) equally large, then select *k*-1 groups for training the model and measure the performance of the group that was left out. Then, change the groups each time until all the groups have been selected for testing.

In the previous sections, we discussed measuring performance using the standard accuracy, ACC, but we could use any performance metric. To show this, we will now calculate the MSE. This is how the *k*-fold cross-validation algorithm will look:

1. Input the dataset, $\mathcal{D}$, the model, H, the parameters, θ, and the number of folds, K.
2. Divide the set of indices, $S = \{1, 2, 3, \ldots, N\}$, into K groups (ideally equal in size), $s_i \subset S$, such that $S = \{s_1, s_2, \ldots, s_K\}$.
3. For each case of $k \in \{1, 2, \ldots, K\}$, do the following:

   - Select the indices for training as $S_\mathcal{D} = \{s_1, s_2, \ldots, s_K\} - \{s_k\}$ and form the training set, $\mathcal{D} = \{\mathbf{x}_i, y_i\}_{i \in S_\mathcal{D}}$.
   - Select the indices for validation as $S_\mathcal{V} = \{s_k\}$ and form the validation set, $\mathcal{V} = \{\mathbf{x}_i, y_i\}_{i \in S_\mathcal{V}}$.
   - Train the model with a choice of parameters over the training set: $H_\theta(\mathcal{D})$.
   - Compute the error of the model, H_θ, on the validation set :
     $$\mathrm{MSE}_k(H_\theta(\mathcal{V})) = \frac{1}{|S_\mathcal{V}|} \sum_{i \in S_\mathcal{V}} (\hat{y}_i - y_i)^2$$

4. Return MSE_k for all cases of $k \in \{1, 2, \ldots, K\}$.

With this, we can calculate the cross-validation error (MSE) given by the following:

$$\bar{E}_{\mathrm{MSE}} = \frac{1}{K} \sum_{k=1}^{K} \mathrm{MSE}_k$$

We can also calculate its corresponding standard deviation:

$$\sigma_{\mathrm{MSE}} = \sqrt{\frac{1}{K-1} \sum_{i=1}^{K} \left(\mathrm{MSE}_i - \bar{E}_{\mathrm{MSE}}\right)^2}$$

It is usually a good idea to look at the standard deviation of our performance metric—regardless of the choice—since it gives an idea of how consistent our performance on the validation sets is. Ideally, we would like to have a cross-validated MSE of 0, $\bar{E}_{\mathrm{MSE}} \approx 0$, and a standard deviation of 1, $\sigma_{\mathrm{MSE}} \approx 1$.

To explain this, we can use the regression example of the sample data contaminated by white noise, shown in *Figure 4.3* and *Figure 4.4*. To keep things simple for this example, we will use a total of 100 samples, *N*=100, and we will use 3 folds. We will use scikit-learn's KFold class inside the model_selection super class and we will obtain the cross-validated MSE and its standard deviation.

To do this, we can use the following code and include other metrics as well:

```python
import numpy as np
from sklearn.metrics import mean_absolute_error
from sklearn.metrics import mean_squared_error
from sklearn.metrics import r2_score
from sklearn.model_selection import KFold

# These will be used to save the performance at each split
cv_r2 = []
cv_mae = []
cv_mse = []

# Change this for more splits
kf = KFold(n_splits=3)
k = 0

# Assuming we have pre-loaded training data X and targets y
for S_D, S_V in kf.split(X):
  X_train, X_test = X[S_D], X[S_V]
  y_train, y_test = y[S_D], y[S_V]

  # Train your model here with X_train and y_train and...
  # ... test your model on X_test saving the output on y_pred

  r2 = r2_score(y_test,y_pred)
  mae = mean_absolute_error(y_test,y_pred)
  mse = mean_squared_error(y_test,y_pred)

  cv_r2.append(r2)
  cv_mae.append(mae)
  cv_mse.append(mse)

print("R_2: {0:.6}  Std: {1:0.5}".format(np.mean(cv_r2),np.std(cv_r2)))
print("MAE: {0:.6}  Std: {1:0.5}".format(np.mean(cv_mae),np.std(cv_mae)))
print("MSE: {0:.6}  Std: {1:0.5}".format(np.mean(cv_mse),np.std(cv_mse)))
```

The result of this code will return something as follows:

```
R_2: 0.935006   Std: 0.054835
MAE: 0.106212   Std: 0.042851
MSE: 0.0184534  Std: 0.014333
```

These results are cross-validated and give a clearer picture of the generalization abilities of the model. For comparison purposes, see the results shown in *Figure 4.9*. You will notice that the results are very consistent between the performance measured before using the whole set in *Figure 4.9* and now, using only about 66% of the data (since we split it into three groups) for training and about 33% for testing, as shown:

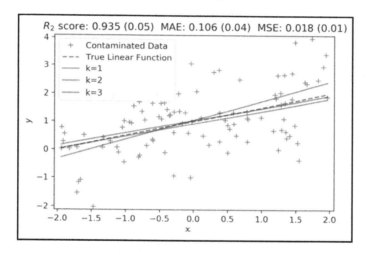

Figure 4.10 - Cross-validated performance metrics with standard deviation in parenthesis

The previous graph shows the linear regression solution found for every split of the data as well as the true original function; you can see that the solutions found are fairly close to the true model, yielding a good performance, as measured by R^2, **MAE**, and **MSE**.

Exercise

Go ahead and change the number of folds, progressively increasing it, and document your observations. What happens to the cross-validated performances? Do they stay the same, increase, or decrease? What happens to the standard deviations of the cross-validated performances? Do they stay the same, increase, or decrease? What do you think this means?

Usually, cross-validation is used on a dataset, $\mathcal{D}$, with a model, H, trained on parameters, θ. However, one of the greatest challenges in learning algorithms is finding the best set of parameters, θ, that can yield the best (test or cross-validated) performance. Many machine learning scientists believe choosing the set of parameters can be **automated** with some algorithms and others believe this is an **art** (Bergstra, J. S., et.al. 2011).

The art behind learning

For those of us who have spent decades studying machine learning, experience informs the way we choose parameters for our learning algorithms. But for those who are new to it, this is a skill that needs to be developed and this skill comes after learning how learning algorithms work. Once you have finished this book, I believe you will have enough knowledge to choose your parameters wisely. In the meantime, we can discuss some ideas for finding parameters automatically using standard and novel algorithms here.

Before we go any further, we need to make a distinction at this point and define two major sets of parameters that are important in learning algorithms. These are as follows:

- **Model parameters:** These are parameters that represent the solution that the model represents. For example, in perceptron and linear regression, this would be vector **w** and scalar b, while for a deep neural network, this would be a matrix of weights, **w**, and a vector of biases, **b**. For a convolutional network, this would be filter sets.
- **Hyperparameters:** These are parameters needed by the model to guide the learning process to search for a solution (model parameters) and are usually represented as θ. For example, in the PLA, a hyperparameter would be the maximum number of iterations; in a deep neural network, it would be the number of layers, the number of neurons, the activation function for the neurons, and the learning rate; and for a **convolutional neural network** (**CNN**), it would be the number of filters, the size of filters, the stride, the pooling size, and so on.

Put in other words, the model parameters are determined, in part, by the choice of hyperparameters. Usually, unless there is a numerical anomaly, all learning algorithms will consistently find solutions (model parameters) for the same set of hyperparameters. So, one of the main tasks when learning is finding the best set of hyperparameters that will give us the best solutions.

To observe the effects of altering the hyperparameters of a model, let's once more consider the four-class classification problem of the seasons, shown earlier in *Figure 4.7*. We will assume that we are using a fully connected network, such as the one described in `Chapter 1, Introduction to Machine Learning`, and the hyperparameter we want to determine is the best number of layers. Just for didactic purposes, let's say that the number of neurons in each layer will increase exponentially in each layer, as shown:

Layer	Neurons in each layer
1	(8)
2	(16, 8)
3	(32, 16, 8)
4	(64, 32, 16, 8)
5	(128, 64, 32, 16, 8)
6	(256, 128, 64, 32, 16, 8)
7	(512, 256, 128, 64, 32, 16, 8)

In the previous configuration, the first number in the brackets corresponds to the number of neurons closest to the input layer, while the last number in the brackets corresponds to the number of neurons closest to the output layer (which consists of 4 neurons, one per class).

So, the number of layers represents θ, in this example. If we loop through each configuration and determine the cross-validated BER, we can determine which architecture yields the best performance; that is, we are optimizing θ for performance. The results obtained will look as follows:

Layers – θ	1	2	3	4	5	6	7
BER	0.275	0.104	0.100	0.096	0.067	0.079	0.088
Standard deviation	0.22	0.10	0.08	0.10	0.05	0.04	0.08

From the results, we can easily determine that the best architecture is one with five layers since it has the lowest BER and the second smallest standard deviation. We could, indeed, gather all the data at each split for each configuration and produce the box plot shown here:

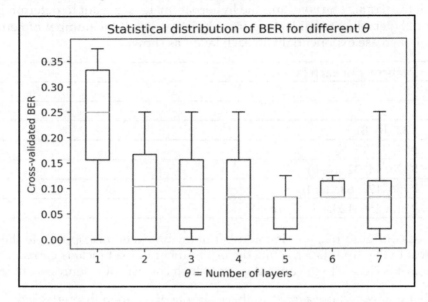

Figure 4.11 - A box plot of the cross-validated data optimizing the number of layers

This box plot illustrates a couple of important points. First, that there is a clear tendency of the model to reduce the BER as the number of layers increases up to 5, then increases after that. This is very common in machine learning and it is known as the **overfitting curve**, which is usually a *u* shape (or *n* shape, for performance metrics that are better on higher values). The lowest point, in this case, would indicate the best set of hyperparameters (at 5); anything to the left of that represents **underfitting** and anything to the right represents **overfitting**. The second thing that the box plot shows is that even if several models have a similar BER, we will choose the one that shows less variability and most consistency.

To illustrate the differences between underfitting, good fitting, and overfitting, we will show the decision boundaries produced by the worst underfit, the best fit, and the worst overfit. In this case, the worst underfit is one layer, the best fit is five layers, and the worst overfit is seven layers. Their respective decision boundaries are shown in *Figure 4.12*, *Figure 4.13*, and *Figure 4.14*, respectively:

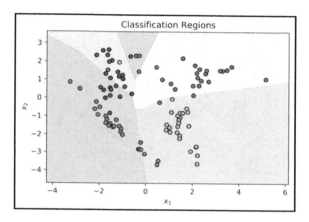

Figure 4.12 - Classification boundaries for a one-hidden-layer network that is underfitting

In the preceding graph, we can see that the underfit is clear since there are decision boundaries that prevent many datapoints from being classified correctly:

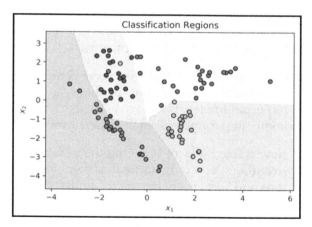

Figure 4.13 - Classification boundaries for a five-hidden-layer network that has a relatively good fit

Similarly, the previous graph shows the decision boundaries, but compared to *Figure 4.12*, these boundaries seem to provide a nicer separation of the data points for the different groups—a good fit:

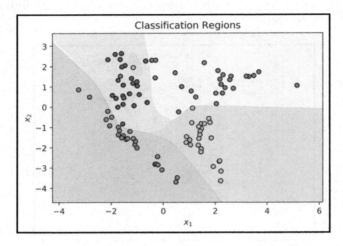

Figure 4.14 - Classification boundaries for a seven-hidden-layer network that is overfitting

If you look closely, *Figure 4.12* shows that some regions are designated very poorly, while in *figure 4.14*, the network architecture is trying *too hard* to classify all the examples perfectly, to the point where the outlier in the *Fall* class (the yellow points) that goes into the region of the *Winter* class (the blue points) has its own little region, which may have negative effects down the road. The classes in *Figure 4.13* seem to be robust against some of the outliers and have well-defined regions, for the most part.

As we progress through this book, we will deal with more complex sets of hyperparameters. Here we just dealt with one, but the theory is the same. This method of looking at the best set of hyperparameters is known as an exhaustive search. However, there are other ways of looking at parameters, such as performing a **grid search.**

Suppose that you do not have a fixed way of knowing the number of neurons in each layer (as opposed to the earlier example); you only know that you would like to have something between 4 and 1024 neurons and something between 1 and 100 layers to allow deep or shallow models. In that case, you cannot do an exhaustive search; it would take too much time! Here, grid search is used as a solution that will sample the search space in—usually—equally-spaced regions.

For example, grid search can look at a number of neurons in the [4, 1024] range on 10 equally spaced values—4, 117, 230, 344, 457, 570, 684, 797, 910, and 1024—and the number of layers that is in the [1,100] range on 10 equally spaced values—1, 12, 23, 34, 45, 56, 67, 78, 89, and 100. Rather than looking at 1020*100=102,000 searches, it will look at 10*10=100, instead.

In sklearn, there is a class, GridSearchCV, that can return the best models and hyperparameters in cross-validation; it is part of the model_selection super class. The same class group has another class, called RandomizedSearchCV, which contains a methodology based on randomly searching the space. This is called **random search.**

In **random search**, the premise is that it will look within the [4, 1024] range and the [1,100] range for neurons and layers, respectively, by randomly drawing numbers uniformly until it reaches a maximum limit of total iterations.

Typically, if you know the range and distribution of the parameter search space, try a **grid search** approach on the space you believe is likely to have a better cross-validated performance. However, if you know very little or nothing about the parameter search space, use a **random search** approach. In practice, both of these methods work well.

There are other, more sophisticated methods that work well but whose implementation in Python is not yet standard, so we will not cover them in detail here. However, you should know about them:

- Bayesian hyperparameter optimization (Feurer, M., et.al. 2015)
- Evolution theory-based hyperparameter optimization (Loshchilov, I., et.al. 2016)
- Gradient-based hyperparameter optimization (Maclaurin, D., et.al. 2015)
- Least squares-based hyperparameter optimization (Rivas-Perea, P., et.al. 2014)

Ethical implications of training deep learning algorithms

There are a few things that can be said about the ethical implications of training deep learning models. There is potential harm whenever you are handling data that represents human perceptions. But also, data about humans and human interaction has to be rigorously protected and examined carefully before creating a model that will generalize based on such data. Such thoughts are organized in the following sections.

Reporting using the appropriate performance measures

Avoid faking good performance by picking the one performance metric that makes your model look good. It is not uncommon to read articles and reports of multi-class classification models that are trained over clear, class-imbalanced datasets but report the standard accuracy. Most likely, these models will report a high standard of accuracy since the models will be biased toward the over-sampled class and against the under-sampled groups. So, these types of models must report the balanced accuracy or the balanced error rate.

Similarly, for other types of classification and regression problems, you must report the appropriate performance metric. When in doubt, report as many performance metrics as you can. Nobody has ever complained about someone reporting model performance using too many metrics.

The consequences of not reporting the appropriate metrics go from having biased models that go undetected and are deployed into production systems with disastrous consequences to having misleading information that can be detrimental to our understanding of specific problems and how models perform. We must recall that what we do may affect others and we need to be vigilant.

Being careful with outliers and verifying them

Outliers are usually seen as bad things to work around during the learning process and I agree. Models should be robust against outliers, unless they are not really outliers. If we have some data and we don't know anything about it, it is a safe assumption to interpret outliers as anomalies.

However, if we know anything about the data (because we collected it, were given all the information about it, or know the sensors that produced it), then we can verify that outliers are really outliers. We must verify that they were the product of human error when typing data or produced by a faulty sensor, data conversion error, or some other artifact because if an outlier is not the product of any of these reasons, there is no reasonable basis for us to assume that it is an outlier. In fact, data like this gives us important information about situations that may not occur frequently but will eventually happen again and the model needs to respond properly.

Consider the data shown in the following figure. If we arbitrarily decide to ignore outliers without verification (such as in the top diagram), it may be that they are in fact not really outliers and the model will create a narrow decision space that ignores the outliers. The consequence, in this example, is that one point will be incorrectly classified as belonging to another group, while another point might be left out of the majority group:

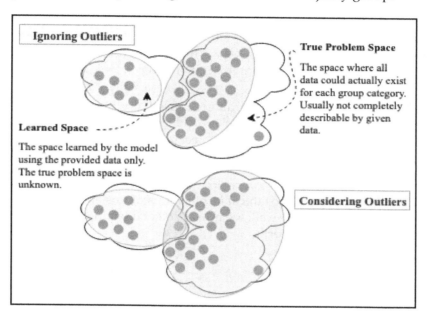

Figure 4.15 - Differences in the learned space of my models. The top diagram shows the ignoring outliers outcome. The bottom diagram shows the including outliers outcome

However, if we verify the data and discover that the outliers are completely valid input, the models might learn a better decision space that could potentially include the outliers. Nonetheless, this can yield a secondary problem where a point is classified as belonging to two different groups with different degrees of membership. While this is a problem, it is a much smaller risk than incorrectly classifying something. It is better to have, say, 60% certainty that a point belongs to one class and 40% certainty that it belongs to the other class, rather than classifying it incorrectly with 100% certainty.

If you think about it, models that were built by ignoring outliers and then deployed into government systems can cause discrimination problems. They may show bias against minority or protected population groups. If deployed into incoming school student selection, it could lead to the rejection of exceptional students. If deployed into DNA classification systems, it could incorrectly ignore the similarity of two very close DNA groups. Therefore, always verify outliers if you can.

Weight classes with undersampled groups

If you have a class imbalance, as in *Figure 4.15*, I recommend you try to balance the classes by getting more data rather than reducing it. If this is not an option, look into algorithms that allow you to weight some classes differently, so as to even out the imbalance. Here are a couple of the most common techniques:

- On small datasets, use `sklearn` and the `class_weight` option. When training a model, it penalizes mistakes based on the provided weight for that class. There are a couple of automatic alternatives that you can look into that will also help, such as `class_weight="auto"` and `class_weight="balanced"`.

- On large datasets where batch training is used, use Keras and the `BalancedBatchGenerator` class. This will prepare a selection of samples (batches) that is consistently balanced each time, thereby guiding the learning algorithm to consider all groups equally. The class is part of `imblearn.keras`.

You should try to use these strategies every time you want to have a model that is not biased toward a majority group. The ethical implications of this are similar to the previous points already mentioned. But above all, we must protect life and treat people with respect; all people have an equal, infinite worth.

Summary

In this basic-level chapter, we discussed the basics of learning algorithms and their purpose. Then, we studied the most basic way of measuring success and failure through performance analysis using accuracies, errors, and other statistical devices. We also studied the problem of overfitting and the super important concept of generalization, which is its counterpart. Then, we discussed the art behind the proper selection of hyperparameters and strategies for their automated search.

After reading this chapter, you are now able to explain the technical differences between classification and regression and how to calculate different performance metrics, such as ACC, BER, MSE, and others, as appropriate for different tasks. Now, you are capable of detecting overfitting by using train, validation, and test datasets under cross-validation strategies, you can experiment with and observe the effects of altering the hyperparameters of a learning model. You are also ready to think critically about the precautions and devices necessary to prevent human harm caused by deep learning algorithms.

The next chapter is *Chapter 5*, *Training a Single Neuron*, which revises and expands the concept of a neuron, which was introduced in *Chapter 1*, *Introduction to Machine Learning*, and shows its implementation in Python using different datasets to analyze the potential effects of different data; that is, linear and non-linearly separable data. However, before we go there, please try to quiz yourself using the following questions.

Questions and answers

1. **When you did the exercise on cross-validation, what happened to the standard deviation and what does that mean?**

   The standard deviation stabilizes and reduces on more folds. This means that the performance measurements are more reliable; it is an accurate measure of generalization or overfitting.

2. **What is the difference between hyperparameters and model parameters?**

   Model parameters are numerical solutions to a learning algorithm; hyperparameters are what the model needs to know in order to find a solution effectively.

3. **Is a grid search faster than a randomized search for hyperparameters?**

   It depends. If the choice of hyperparameters affects the computational complexity of the learning algorithm, then both could behave differently. However, in similar search spaces and in the amortized case, both should finish at about the same time.

4. **Can I use a regression-based learning algorithm for a classification problem?**

   Yes, as long as the labels, categories, or groups are mapped to a number in the set of real numbers.

5. **Can I use a classification-based learning algorithm for a regression problem?**

   No.

6. **Is the concept of a loss function the same as an error metric?**

Yes and no. Yes, in the sense that a loss function will measure performance; however, the performance may not necessarily be with respect to the accuracy of classifying or regressing the data; it may be with respect to something else, such as the quality of groups or distances in information-theoretic spaces. For example, linear regression is based on the MSE algorithm as a loss function to minimize, while the loss function of the K-means algorithm is the sum of the squared distances of the data to their means, which it aims to minimize, but this does not necessarily mean it is an error. In the latter case, it is arguably meant as a cluster quality measure.

References

- Lorena, A. C., De Carvalho, A. C., & Gama, J. M. (2008), A review on the combination of binary classifiers in multiclass problems, *Artificial Intelligence Review*, 30(1-4), 19
- Hochreiter, S., Younger, A. S., & Conwell, P. R. (2001, August), Learning to learn using gradient descent, in *International Conference on Artificial Neural Networks* (pp. 87-94), Springer: Berlin, Heidelberg
- Ruder, S. (2016), An overview of gradient descent optimization algorithms, *arXiv preprint* arXiv:1609.04747
- Tan, X., Zhang, Y., Tang, S., Shao, J., Wu, F., & Zhuang, Y. (2012, October), Logistic tensor regression for classification, in *International Conference on Intelligent Science and Intelligent Data Engineering* (pp. 573-581), Springer: Berlin, Heidelberg
- Krejn, S. G. E. (1982), *Linear Equations in Banach Spaces*, Birkhäuser: Boston
- Golub, G., & Kahan, W. (1965), Calculating the singular values and pseudo-inverse of a matrix, *Journal of the Society for Industrial and Applied Mathematics*, Series B: Numerical Analysis, 2(2), (pp. 205-224)
- Kohavi, R. (1995, August), A study of cross-validation and bootstrap for accuracy estimation and model selection, in *IJCAI*, 14(2), (pp. 1137-1145)
- Bergstra, J. S., Bardenet, R., Bengio, Y., & Kégl, B. (2011), Algorithms for hyper-parameter optimization, in *Advances in Neural Information Processing Systems*, (pp. 2546-2554)
- Feurer, M., Springenberg, J. T., & Hutter, F. (2015, February), Initializing Bayesian hyperparameter optimization via meta-learning, in *Twenty-Ninth AAAI Conference on Artificial Intelligence*

- Loshchilov, I., & Hutter, F. (2016), CMA-ES for hyperparameter optimization of deep neural networks, *arXiv preprint* arXiv:1604.07269
- Maclaurin, D., Duvenaud, D., & Adams, R. (2015, June), Gradient-based hyperparameter optimization through reversible learning, in *International Conference on Machine Learning* (pp. 2113-2122)
- Rivas-Perea, P., Cota-Ruiz, J., & Rosiles, J. G. (2014), A nonlinear least squares quasi-Newton strategy for LP-SVR hyper-parameters selection, *International Journal of Machine Learning and Cybernetics*, 5(4), (pp.579-597)

5
Training a Single Neuron

After revising the concepts around learning from data, we will now pay close attention to an algorithm that trains one of the most fundamental neural-based models: the **perceptron**. We will look at the steps required for the algorithm to function, and the stopping conditions. This chapter will present the perceptron model as the first model that represents a neuron, which aims to learn from data in a simple manner. The perceptron model is key to understanding basic and advanced neural models that learn from data. In this chapter, we will also cover the problems and considerations associated with non-linearly separable data.

Upon completion of the chapter, you should feel comfortable discussing the perceptron model, and applying its learning algorithm. You will be able to implement the algorithm over both linearly and non-linearly separable data.

Specifically, the following topics are covered in this chapter:

- The perceptron model
- The perceptron learning algorithm
- A perceptron over non-linearly separable data

The perceptron model

Back in Chapter 1, *Introduction to Machine Learning*, we briefly introduced the basic model of a neuron and the **perceptron learning algorithm (PLA)**. Here, in this chapter, we will now revisit and expand the concept and show how that is coded in Python. We will begin with the basic definition.

The visual concept

The perceptron is an analogy of a human-inspired information processing unit, originally conceived by F. Rosenblatt and depicted in *Figure 5.1* (Rosenblatt, F. (1958)). In the model, the input is represented with the vector $\mathbf{x}$, the activation of the neuron is given by the function $z(\cdot)$, and the output is y. The parameters of the neuron are $\mathbf{w}$ and b:

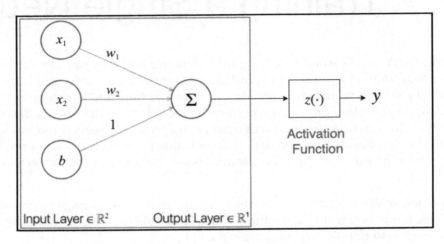

Figure 5.1 – The basic model of a perceptron

The *trainable* parameters of a perceptron are $(\mathbf{w}, b)$, and they are unknown. Thus, we can use input training data $\mathcal{D} = \{\mathbf{x}_i, y_i\}_{i=1}^{N}$ to determine these parameters using the PLA. From *Figure 5.1*, x_1 multiplies w_1, then x_2 multiplies w_2, and b is multiplied by 1; all these products are added and then passed into the *sign* activation function, which in the perceptron operates as follows:

$$sign(\mathbf{w}^T\mathbf{x} + b) = \begin{cases} +1 & \text{if } \mathbf{w}^T\mathbf{x} + b \geq 0 \\ -1 & \text{otherwise} \end{cases}$$

 The main purpose of the activation sign is to map any response of the model to a binary output: $\{-1, +1\}$.

Now let's talk about tensors in a general sense.

Tensor operations

In Python, the implementation of the perceptron requires a few simple tensor (vector) operations that can be performed through standard NumPy functionalities. First, we can assume that we are given data $\mathcal{D} = \{\mathbf{x}_i, y_i\}_{i=1}^{N}$ in the form of a vector containing multiple vectors $\mathbf{x}$ (a matrix), represented as $\mathbf{X} = \{\mathbf{x}_i\}_{i=1}^{N}$, and multiple individual targets represented as a vector $\mathbf{y} = \{y_i\}_{i=1}^{N}$. However, notice that for easier implementation of the perceptron it will be necessary to include b in $\mathbf{w}$, as suggested in *Figure 5.1*, so that the products and additions in $x_1 w_1 + x_2 w_2 + \cdots + x_d w_d + b = \mathbf{w}^T \mathbf{x} + b$ can be simplified if we modify $\mathbf{X}$ to be $\mathbf{x} = [1, x_1, x_2, \ldots, x_d]$, and $\mathbf{w}$ to be $\mathbf{w} = [b, w_1, w_2, \ldots, w_d]$. In this way, the perceptron response for an input $\mathbf{x} = [1, x_1, x_2, \ldots, x_d]$ could be simplified to be as follows:

$$sign(\mathbf{w}^T \mathbf{x}) = \begin{cases} +1 & \text{if } \mathbf{w}^T \mathbf{x} \geq 0 \\ -1 & \text{otherwise} \end{cases}$$

Notice that b is now implicit in $\mathbf{w}$.

Say that we want to have training data X, which we need to prepare for the perceptron; we can do that with a simple linearly separable dataset that can be generated through scikit-learn's dataset method called `make_classification` as follows:

```
from sklearn.datasets import make_classification

X, y = make_classification(n_samples=100, n_features=2, n_classes=2,
                           n_informative=2, n_redundant=0, n_repeated=0,
                           n_clusters_per_class=1, class_sep=1.5,
                           random_state=5)
```

Here, we use the `make_classification` constructor to produce 100 data points (`n_samples`) for two classes (`n_classes`) and with enough separation (`class_sep`) to make data that is linearly separable. However, the dataset produced binary values in y in the set $\{0, 1\}$, and we need to convert it to the values in the set $\{-1, +1\}$. This can be easily achieved by replacing the zero targets with the negative targets by simply doing the following:

```
y[y==0] = -1
```

The dataset produced looks as depicted in *Figure 5.2*:

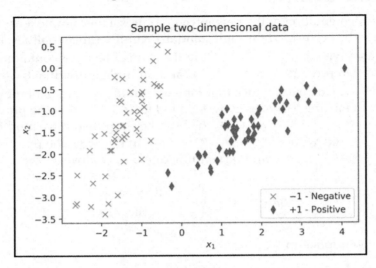

Figure 5.2– Sample two-dimensional data for perceptron testing

Next, we can add the number 1 to each input vector by adding a vector of ones to X with length N=100 as follows:

```
import numpy as np
X = np.append(np.ones((N,1)), X, 1)
```

The new data in X now contains a vector of ones. This will allow easier calculation of the tensor operation $\mathbf{w}^T \mathbf{x}_i$ for all $i \in \{1, 2, \ldots, N\}$. This common tensor operation can be performed in one single step considering the matrix $\mathbf{X} = \begin{bmatrix} 1 & \{\mathbf{x}_i\}_{i=1}^N \end{bmatrix}$ simply as $\mathbf{w}^T \mathbf{X} = \mathbf{w}^T \mathbf{x}_i \big|_{i=1}^N$. We can even combine this operation and the sign activation function in one single step as follows:

```
np.sign(w.T.dot(X[n]))
```

This is the equivalent of the mathematical tensor operation $sign(\mathbf{w}^T \mathbf{X})$. With this in mind, let's review the PLA in more detail using the dataset introduced previously, and the operations just described.

The perceptron learning algorithm

The **perceptron learning algorithm** (**PLA**) is the following:

Input: Binary class dataset $\mathcal{D} = \{\mathbf{x}_i, y_i\}_{i=1}^{N}$

- Initialize $\mathbf{w}$ to zeros, and iteration counter $t = 0$
- While there are any incorrectly classified examples:
  - Pick an incorrectly classified example, call it $\mathbf{x}^*$, whose true label is y^*
  - Update $\mathbf{w}$ as follows: $\mathbf{w}_{t+1} = \mathbf{w}_t + y^* \mathbf{x}^*$
  - Increase iteration counter, $t = t + 1$, and repeat

Return: $\mathbf{w}$

Now, let's see how this takes form in Python.

PLA in Python

Here is an implementation in Python that we will discuss part by part, while some of it has already been discussed:

```python
N = 100 # number of samples to generate
random.seed(a = 7) # add this to achieve for reproducibility

X, y = make_classification(n_samples=N, n_features=2, n_classes=2,
                           n_informative=2, n_redundant=0, n_repeated=0,
                           n_clusters_per_class=1, class_sep=1.2,
                           random_state=5)

y[y==0] = -1

X_train = np.append(np.ones((N,1)), X, 1) # add a column of ones

# initialize the weights to zeros
w = np.zeros(X_train.shape[1])
it = 0

# Iterate until all points are correctly classified
while classification_error(w, X_train, y) != 0:
    it += 1
    # Pick random misclassified point
    x, s = choose_miscl_point(w, X_train, y)
    # Update weights
    w = w + s*x
```

```
  print("Total iterations: ", it)
```

The first few lines have been discussed previously in the *Tensor operations* section of this chapter. The initialization of **w** to zeros is done with `w = np.zeros(X_train.shape[1])`. The size of this vector depends on the dimensionality of the input. Then, `it` is merely an iteration counter to keep track of the number of iterations that are performed until the PLA converges.

The `classification_error()` method is a helper method that takes as arguments the current vector of parameters `w`, the input data `X_train`, and corresponding target data `y`. The purpose of this method is to determine the number of misclassified points at the present state **w**, if there are any, and return the total count of errors. The method can be defined as follows:

```
def classification_error(w, X, y):
  err_cnt = 0
  N = len(X)
  for n in range(N):
    s = np.sign(w.T.dot(X[n]))
    if y[n] != s:
      err_cnt += 1      # we could break here on large datasets
  return err_cnt        # returns total number of errors
```

This method could be simplified as follows:

```
def classification_error(w, X, y):
  s = np.sign(X.dot(w))
  return sum(s != y)
```

However, while this is a nice optimization for small datasets, for large datasets it may not be necessary to calculate all points for error. Thus, the first (and longer) method can be used and modified according to the type of data that is expected, and if we know that we will be dealing with large datasets, we could break out of the method at the first sign of error.

The second helper method in our code is `choose_miscl_point()`. The main purpose of this method is to select, at random, one of the misclassified points, if there are any. It takes as arguments the current vector of parameters `w`, the input data `X_train`, and corresponding target data `y`. It returns a misclassified point, `x`, and what the corresponding target sign should be, `s`. The method could be implemented as follows:

```
def choose_miscl_point(w, X, y):
    mispts = []
    for n in range(len(X)):
        if np.sign(w.T.dot(X[n])) != y[n]:
            mispts.append((X[n], y[n]))
    return mispts[random.randrange(0,len(mispts))]
```

Similarly, this could be optimized for speed by randomizing a list of indices, iterating over them, and returning the first one found, as shown here:

```
def choose_miscl_point(w, X, y):
    for idx in random.permutation(len(X)):
        if np.sign(w.T.dot(X[idx])) != y[idx]:
            return X[idx], y[idx]
```

However, the first implementation can be useful for absolute beginners or for those who would like to do some additional analysis of the misclassified points, which could be conveniently available in the list `mispts`.

The crucial point, no matter the implementation, is to randomize the selection of the misclassified point.

Finally, the update happens using the current parameters, the misclassified point, and the corresponding target on the line that executes `w = w + s*x`.

If you run the complete program, it should output something like this:

```
Total iterations: 14
```

The total number of iterations may vary depending on the type of data and the random nature of the selection of the misclassified points. For the particular dataset we are using, the decision boundary could look as shown in *Figure 5.3*:

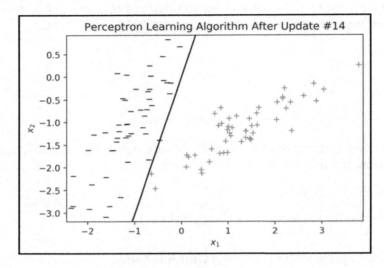

Figure 5.3 – Decision boundary found with PLA

The number of iterations will also depend on the separation or gap between data points in the feature space. The larger the gap is, the easier it is to find a solution, and the converse is also true. The worst-case scenario is when the data is non-linearly separable, which we'll address next.

A perceptron over non-linearly separable data

As we have discussed before, a perceptron will find a solution in finite time if the data is separable. However, how many iterations it will take to find a solution depends on how close the groups are to each other in the feature space.

 Convergence is when the learning algorithm finds a solution or reaches a steady state that is acceptable to the designer of the learning model.

The following paragraphs will deal with convergence on different types of data: linearly separable and non-linearly separable.

Convergence on linearly separable data

For the particular dataset that we have been studying in this chapter, the separation between the two groups of data is a parameter that can be varied (this is usually a problem with real data). The parameter is class_sep and can take on a real number; for example:

```
X, y = make_classification(..., class_sep=2.0, ...)
```

This allows us to study how many iterations it takes, on average, for the perceptron algorithm to converge if we vary the separation parameter. The experiment can be designed as follows:

- We will vary the separation coefficient from large to small, recording the number of iterations it takes to converge: 2.0, 1.9, ..., 1.2, 1.1.
- We will repeat this 1,000 times and record the average number of iterations and the corresponding standard deviation.

Notice that we decided to run this experiment down to 1.1, since 1.0 already produces a non-linearly separable dataset. If we perform the experiment, we can record the results in a table and it will look like this:

Run	2.0	1.9	1.8	1.7	1.6	1.5	1.4	1.3	1.2	1.1
1	2	2	2	2	7	10	4	15	13	86
2	5	1	2	2	4	8	6	26	62	169
3	4	4	5	6	6	10	11	29	27	293
...	...	...	...	...	...	...	...	...	...	...
998	2	5	3	1	9	3	11	9	35	198
999	2	2	4	7	6	8	2	4	14	135
1000	2	1	2	2	2	8	13	25	27	36
Avg.	2.79	3.05	3.34	3.67	4.13	4.90	6.67	10.32	24.22	184.41
Std.	1.2	1.3	1.6	1.9	2.4	3.0	4.7	7.8	15.9	75.5

This table shows that the average number of iterations taken is fairly stable when the data is nicely separated; however, as the separation gap is reduced, the number of iterations increases dramatically. To put this in a visual perspective, the same data from the table is now shown in *Figure 5.4* on a logarithmic scale:

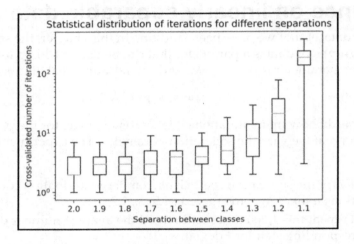

Figure 5.4 – The growth of the number of PLA iterations as the data groups are closer together

It is very clear that the number of iterations can grow exponentially as the separation gap is closing. *Figure 5.5* depicts the largest separation gap, 2.0, and indicates that the PLA found a solution after four iterations:

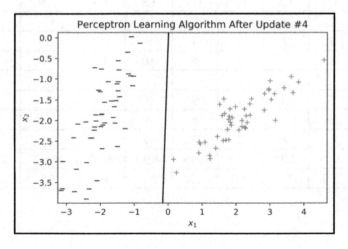

Figure 5.5 – The perceptron found a solution in four iterations for a separation gap of 2.0

Similarly, *Figure 5.6* shows that for the largest gap, 1.1, the PLA takes 183 iterations; a close inspection of the figure reveals that the solution for the latter case is difficult to find because the data groups are too close to each other:

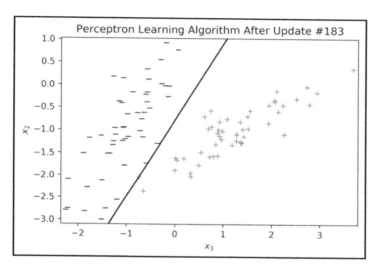

Figure 5.6 – The perceptron found a solution in 183 iterations for a separation gap of 1.1

As noted before, data that is not linearly separable can be produced with a gap of 1.0 and the PLA will run in an infinite loop since there will always be a data point that will be incorrectly classified and the `classification_error()` method will never return a zero value. For those cases, we can modify the PLA to allow finding solutions on non-linearly separable data, as we'll cover in the next section.

Convergence on non-linearly separable data

The modifications to the original PLA are rather simple, but are good enough to allow finding an acceptable solution in most cases. The main two things that we need to add to the PLA are as follows:

- A mechanism to prevent the algorithm from running forever
- A mechanism to store the best solution ever found

With respect to the first point, we can simply specify a number of iterations at which the algorithm can stop. With respect to the second point, we can simply keep a solution in storage, and compare it to the one in the current iteration.

The relevant portion of the PLA is shown here and the new changes have been marked with bold font and will be discussed in detail:

```
X, y = make_classification(n_samples=N, n_features=2, n_classes=2,
 n_informative=2, n_redundant=0, n_repeated=0,
 n_clusters_per_class=1, class_sep=1.0,
 random_state=5)

y[y==0] = -1

X_train = np.append(np.ones((N,1)), X, 1) # add a column of ones

# initialize the weights to zeros
w = np.zeros(X_train.shape[1])
it = 0
bestW = {}
bestW['err'] = N + 1 # dictionary to keep best solution
bestW['w'] = []
bestW['it'] = it

# Iterate until all points are correctly classified
#    or maximum iterations (i.e. 1000) are reached
while it < 1000:
  err = classification_error(w, X_train, y)
  if err < bestW['err']:    # enter to save a new w
    bestW['err'] = err
    bestW['it'] = it
    bestW['w'] = list(w)
  if err == 0:  # exit loop if there are no errors
    break
  it += 1
  # Pick random misclassified point
  x, s = choose_miscl_point(w, X_train, y)
  # Update weights
  w += s*x

print("Best found at iteration: ", bestW['it'])
print("Number of misclassified points: ", bestW['err'])
```

In this code, `bestW` is a dictionary for keeping track of the best results so far, and it is initialized to reasonable values. Notice first that the loop is now bounded by the number 1,000, which is the maximum number of iterations you currently allow and you can change it to anything you desire to be the maximum number of allowed iterations. It would be reasonable to reduce this number for large datasets or high-dimensional datasets where every iteration is costly.

The next changes are the inclusion of the conditional statement, `if err < bestW['err']`, which determines whether we should store a new set of parameters. Every time the error, as determined by the total number of misclassified examples, is lower than the error of the stored parameters, then an update is made. And just for completion, we have to still check that there are no errors, which indicates that the data is linearly separable, a solution has been found, and the loop needs to terminate.

The last few `print` statements will simply inform the iteration and error obtained when the best solution was recorded. The output may look as follows:

```
Best found at iteration: 95
Number of misclassified points: 1
```

This output was produced by running the updated PLA over the dataset with a separation of 1.0, which is depicted in *Figure 5.7*:

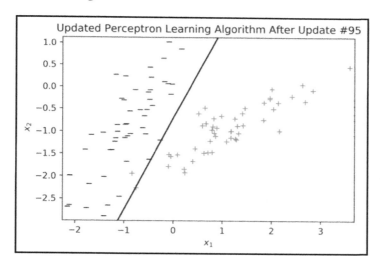

Figure 5.7 – The updated PLA finds a solution with only one misclassified point after 95 iterations

From the figure, it can be seen that there is one sample from the positive class that is incorrectly classified. Knowing that in this example there is a total of 100 data points, we can determine that the accuracy is 99/100.

This type of algorithm, which stores the *best solution so far*, is usually known as a **pocket algorithm** (Muselli, M. 1997). And the idea of the early termination of a learning algorithm is inspired by well-known numerical optimization methods.

One of the general limitations is that the perceptron can only produce solutions that are based on a line in two dimensions, or a linear hyperplane in multiple dimensions. However, this limitation can be easily solved by putting several perceptrons together and in multiple layers to produce highly complex non-linear solutions for separable and non-separable problems. This will be the topic of the next chapter.

Summary

This chapter presented an overview of the classic perceptron model. We covered the theoretical model and its implementation in Python for both linearly and non-linearly separable datasets. At this point, you should feel confident that you know enough about the perceptron that you can implement it yourself. You should be able to recognize the perceptron model in the context of a neuron. Also, you should now be able to implement a pocket algorithm and early termination strategies in a perceptron, or any other learning algorithm in general.

Since the perceptron is the most essential element that paved the way for deep neural networks, after we have covered it here, the next step is to go to Chapter 6, *Training Multiple Layers of Neurons*. In that chapter, you will be exposed to the challenges of deep learning using the multi-layer perceptron algorithm, such as gradient descent techniques for error minimization, and hyperparameter optimization to achieve generalization. But before you go there, please try to quiz yourself with the following questions.

Questions and answers

1. **What is the relationship between the separability of the data and the number of iterations of the PLA?**

    The number of iterations can grow exponentially as the data groups get close to one another.

2. **Will the PLA always converge?**

    Not always, only for linearly separable data.

3. **Can the PLA converge on non-linearly separable data?**

    No. However, you can find an acceptable solution by modifying it with the pocket algorithm, for example.

4. **Why is the perceptron important?**

Because it is one of the most fundamental learning strategies that has helped conceive the possibility of learning. Without the perceptron, it could have taken longer for the scientific community to realize the potential of computer-based automatic learning algorithms.

References

- Rosenblatt, F. (1958). The perceptron: a probabilistic model for information storage and organization in the brain. *Psychological review*, 65(6), 386.
- Muselli, M. (1997). On convergence properties of the pocket algorithm. *IEEE Transactions on Neural Networks*, 8(3), 623-629.

6
Training Multiple Layers of Neurons

Previously, in Chapter 6, *Training a Single Neuron*, we explored a model involving a single neuron and the concept of the perceptron. A limitation of the perceptron model is that, at best, it can only produce linear solutions on a multi-dimensional hyperplane. However, this limitation can be easily solved by using multiple neurons and multiple layers of neurons in order to produce highly complex non-linear solutions for separable and non-separable problems. This chapter introduces you to the first challenges of deep learning using the **Multi-Layer Perceptron (MLP)** algorithm, such as a gradient descent technique for error minimization, followed by hyperparameter optimization experiments to determine trustworthy accuracy.

The following topics will be covered in this chapter:

- The MLP model
- Minimizing the error
- Finding the best hyperparameters

The MLP model

We have previously seen, in `Chapter 5`, *Training a Single Neuron*, that Rosenblatt's perceptron model is simple and powerful for some problems (Rosenblatt, F. 1958). However, for more complicated and highly non-linear problems, Rosenblatt did not give enough attention to his models that connected many more neurons in different architectures, including deeper models (Tappert, C. 2019).

Years later, in the 1990s, Prof. Geoffrey Hinton, the 2019 Turing Award winner, continued working to connect more neurons together since this is more brain-like than simple neurons (Hinton, G. 1990). Most people today know this type of approach as *connectionist*. The main idea is to connect neurons in different ways that will resemble brain connections. One of the first successful models was the MLP, which uses a supervised gradient descent-based learning algorithm that learns to approximate a function, $f(\mathbf{x})$, using labeled data, $\mathcal{D} = \{\mathbf{x}_i, y_i\}_{i=1}^{N}$.

Figure 6.1 depicts an MLP with one layer of multiple neurons that indicate how the input connects to all neurons through weights, which stimulate a neuron to produce a large (non-zero) numerical response, depending on the variable weights that need to be *learned*:

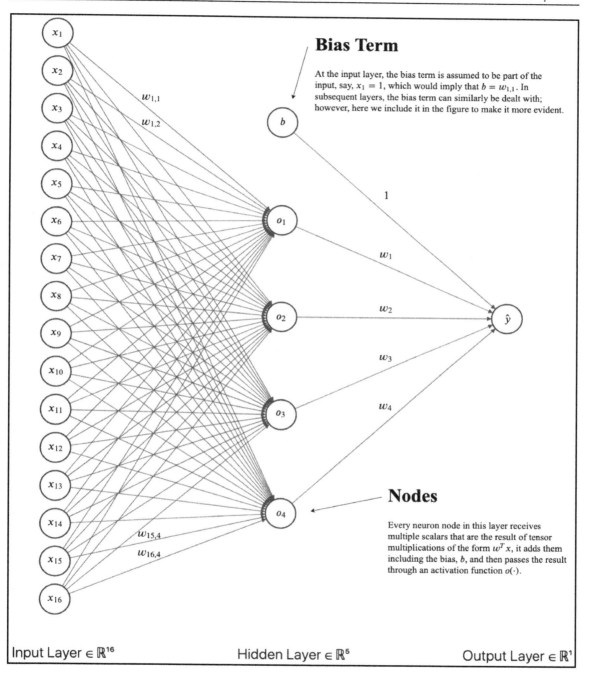

Bias Term

At the input layer, the bias term is assumed to be part of the input, say, $x_1 = 1$, which would imply that $b = w_{1,1}$. In subsequent layers, the bias term can similarly be dealt with; however, here we include it in the figure to make it more evident.

Nodes

Every neuron node in this layer receives multiple scalars that are the result of tensor multiplications of the form $w^T x$, it adds them including the bias, b, and then passes the result through an activation function $o(\cdot)$.

Input Layer $\in \mathbb{R}^{16}$ · · · Hidden Layer $\in \mathbb{R}^5$ · · · Output Layer $\in \mathbb{R}^1$

Figure 6.1 – Multiple perceptrons in one hidden layer

For completeness, *Figure 6.2* depicts the same architecture but vertically; it also shows positive weights in light gray and negative weights in darker gray. *Figure 6.2* aims to show that some features might stimulate some neurons more than others:

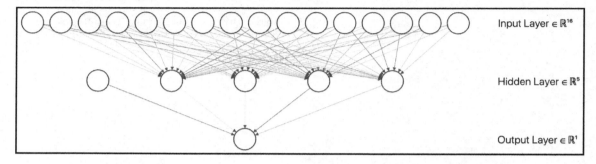

Figure 6.2 – MLP with weights that are grayscale-coded: lighter grays denote positive weights, darker grays denote negative weights

Based on *Figure 6.2*, the layer of neurons at the top is known as the **input layer**. These features are connected to different neurons in a layer known as a **hidden layer**. This layer usually consists of at least one layer of neurons, but in deep learning, it may contain many more.

On the interpretation of the weights close to the input layer: One of the key differences between the MLP and the perceptron is that the interpretation of the weights in the input layer is lost in the MLP unless the hidden layer contains only one neuron. Usually, in a perceptron, you can argue that the importance of certain features is directly correlated to the value (weight) directly associated with those features. For example, the feature associated with the most negative weight is said to negatively influence the outcome, and the feature associated with the most positive weight is also influencing the outcome in a significant manner. Therefore, looking into the absolute value of the weights in a perceptron (and in linear regression) can inform us about feature importance. Not so much in the MLP; the more neurons are involved and the more layers are involved, the chances of interpreting weights and feature importance is reduced significantly. You must not rely heavily on the first-layer weights to deduce feature importance. Be careful.

From *Figure 6.1*, we can see that neurons, $o(\mathbf{w}^T\mathbf{x})$, are simplified to imply that there is some non-linear activation function, $o(\cdot)$, over the scalar, resulting from adding the products of the features and the weights associated with those features and that neuron, $\mathbf{w}^T\mathbf{x}$. In deeper MLP layers, the input is no longer data from the input layer, $\mathbf{X}$, but are rather outputs from previous layers: $\mathbf{w}^T o(\mathbf{w}^T\mathbf{x})$. We will make some changes to the notation in the next section to describe this process more formally.

For now, what you need to know is that the MLP is a lot better than the perceptron in that is has the ability to learn highly complex non-linear models. The perceptron is only able to provide linear models. But with this power comes great responsibility. The MLP has a non-convex and non-smooth loss function that limits how the learning process is achieved, and although there has been much progress, their problems still persist. Another disadvantage is that the learning algorithms may need other hyperparameters to assure the success (convergence) of the algorithm. Finally, it is worth noting that the MLP requires preprocessing of the input features (normalization) to mitigate neurons overfitting on specific features.

Now, let's examine how the learning process actually happens.

Minimizing the error

Learning from data using an MLP was one of the major problems since its conception. As we pointed out before, one of the major problems with neural networks was the computational tractability of deeper models, and the other was stable learning algorithms that would converge to a reasonable minimum. One of the major breakthroughs in machine learning, and what paved the way for deep learning, was the development of the learning algorithm based on backpropagation. Many scientists independently derived and applied forms of backpropagation in the 1960s; however, most of the credit has been given to Prof. G. E. Hinton and his group (Rumelhart, D. E., et.al. 1986). In the next few paragraphs, we will go over this algorithm, whose sole purpose is to **minimize the error** caused by incorrect predictions made during training.

To begin, we will describe the dataset, which is called **spirals**. This is a widely known benchmark dataset that has two classes that are separable, yet highly non-linear. The positive and negative classes go around each other on opposite sides of a two-dimensional space as they grow from the center outward, as shown in *Figure 6.3*:

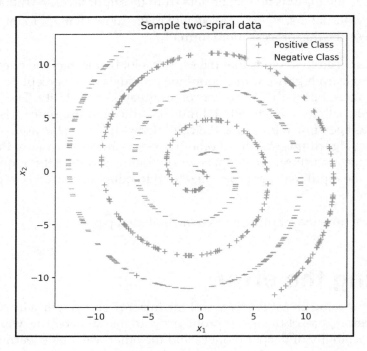

Figure 6.3 – Sample data from the two-spiral benchmark

The dataset can be produced using the following function in Python:

```python
def twoSpirals(N):
  np.random.seed(1)
  n = np.sqrt(np.random.rand(N,1)) * 780 * (2*np.pi)/360
  x = -np.cos(n)*n
  y = np.sin(n)*n
  return (np.vstack((np.hstack((x,y)),np.hstack((-x,-y)))),
          np.hstack((np.ones(N)*-1,np.ones(N))))

X, y = twoSpirals(300)   #Produce 300 samples
```

In this code fragment, we will receive in x a two-column matrix whose rows are samples of the spiral dataset, and y contains the corresponding target class in the $\{+1, -1\}$ set. *Figure 6.3* was produced based on the preceding code fragment, which contains 300 samples.

We will also use a very simple MLP architecture with only three neurons in a single hidden layer; this is only to explain *backpropagation* as clearly as possible. The proposed MLP is shown in *Figure 6.4*:

 Backpropagation is known among the professionals today as **backprop**. If you read any recent online discussions about it, it will most likely be referred to as backprop, for short.

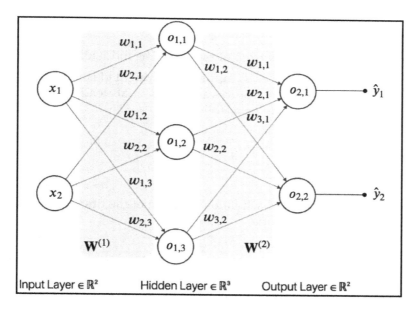

Figure 6.4 - Simple MLP architecture for backpropagation-based learning on the spiral dataset

The architecture of the network shown in *Figure 6.4* assumes that there is a well-defined input vector containing multiple vectors, $\mathbf{x}$ (a matrix), represented as $\mathbf{X} = \{\mathbf{x}_i\}_{i=1}^{N}$, and multiple individual targets represented as a vector, $\mathbf{y} = \{y_i\}_{i=1}^{N}$. Also, each $l = \{1, 2\}$ layer, , has a matrix of weights, $\mathbf{w}^{(l)}$, which is the case with the first layer. For example, from *Figure 6.4*, the weight matrices would be as follows:

$$\mathbf{W}^{(1)} = \begin{bmatrix} w_{1,1} & w_{1,2} & w_{1,2} \\ w_{2,1} & w_{2,2} & w_{2,3} \end{bmatrix}$$

$$\mathbf{W}^{(2)} = \begin{bmatrix} w_{1,1} & w_{1,2} \\ w_{2,1} & w_{2,2} \\ w_{3,1} & w_{3,2} \end{bmatrix}.$$

These matrices have real values initialized at random. The hidden layer, $l = 1$, consists of three neurons. Each neuron in receives as input, $z_i^{(1)}$, a weighted sum of observations consisting of the inner product of the features and the weights leading to the ith neuron; for example, for the first neuron it would be as follows:

$$z_1^{(1)} = \begin{bmatrix} x_1 & x_2 \end{bmatrix} \begin{bmatrix} w_{1,1} \\ w_{2,1} \end{bmatrix}$$

Here, $o\left(z_1^{(1)}\right)$ denotes the output of the activation function of the first neuron in the first layer, which in this case would be a sigmoid.

 The sigmoid activation function is denoted as $o(z) = \frac{1}{1 + e^{-z}}$. This function is interesting because it squashes whatever value it receives as input and maps it to values between 0 and 1. It is also a nice function to use in gradient calculation since its derivative is well known and easy to compute: $\frac{d}{dz} o(z) = o(z)(1 - o(z))$.

In Python, we could easily code the sigmoid as follows:

```
def sigmoid(z, grad=False):
  if grad:
    return z * (1. - z)
  return 1. / (1. + np.exp(-z))
```

Finally, the output layer consists of two neurons that, in this case, we will use to model each of the target classes, the positive spiral, and the negative spiral.

With this in mind, we can do backprop to correct the weights based on the direction of the gradient that minimizes the error for a given set of labeled samples; for more details, refer to this tutorial (Florez, O. U. 2017). We will be following the steps outlined in the following sections.

Step 1 – Initialization

We will perform an initial step in which we *randomly initialize* the network weights. In our example, we will use the following values:

$$\mathbf{W}^{(1)} = \begin{bmatrix} w_{1,1} & w_{1,2} & w_{1,2} \\ w_{2,1} & w_{2,2} & w_{2,3} \end{bmatrix} = \begin{bmatrix} -0.16595599 & 0.44064899 & -0.99977125 \\ -0.39533485 & -0.70648822 & -0.81532281 \end{bmatrix}$$

$$\mathbf{W}^{(2)} = \begin{bmatrix} w_{1,1} & w_{1,2} \\ w_{2,1} & w_{2,2} \\ w_{3,1} & w_{3,2} \end{bmatrix} = \begin{bmatrix} -0.62747958 & -0.30887855 \\ -0.20646505 & 0.07763347 \\ -0.16161097 & 0.370439 \end{bmatrix}$$

In Python, we can generate these weights between -1 and 1 by using the following:

```
w1 = 2.0*np.random.random((2, 3))-1.0
w2 = 2.0*np.random.random((3, 2))-1.0
```

Step 2 – The forward pass

The next step would be the **forward pass**. In this step, the input, $\mathbf{X} = \{\mathbf{x}_i\}_{i=1}^{N}$, is presented at the input layer and propagated forward into the network until we observe the resulting vector in the output layer. The forward pass in our small example would be as follows. We first begin with a linear transformation of a single sample, $\mathbf{x}_i$, using weight $\mathbf{W}^{(1)}$ in the first layer:

$$\mathbf{z}^{(1)} = \mathbf{x}_i \mathbf{W}^{(1)} = \begin{bmatrix} x_1 & x_2 \end{bmatrix} \begin{bmatrix} w_{1,1} & w_{1,2} & w_{1,2} \\ w_{2,1} & w_{2,2} & w_{2,3} \end{bmatrix}$$

Thus, for some cases of $\mathbf{x}_1 = [7.08535569 \quad 5.20423916]$, we calculate the following:

$$\mathbf{z}^{(1)} = \mathbf{x}_i \mathbf{W}^{(1)} = [7.08535569 \quad 5.20423916] \begin{bmatrix} -0.16595599 & 0.44064899 & -0.99977125 \\ -0.39533485 & -0.70648822 & -0.81532281 \end{bmatrix}$$

This would result in the following:

$$\mathbf{z}^{(1)} = [-3.23327435 \quad -0.55457885 \quad -11.32686981]$$

Then, we pass $\mathbf{z}^{(1)}$ through the sigmoid function and obtain $o_1(\cdot)$, which is the output of the three neurons in the first hidden layer. This results in the following:

$$o_1(\mathbf{z}^{(1)}) = \text{sigmoid}([-3.23327435 \quad -0.55457885 \quad -11.32686981])$$

$$o_1(\mathbf{z}^{(1)}) = [0.03793257 \quad 0.36480273 \quad 0.00001204]$$

This could be implemented as follows:

```
o1 = sigmoid(np.matmul(X, w1))
```

One interesting way to look at what we have accomplished so far in the first layer is that we have mapped the input data, which was in two dimensions, into three dimensions, which will be now processed to observe the output back in two dimensions.

The same process is repeated for any subsequent layers in the group of hidden layers. In our example, we will do this only one more time for the output layer. We calculate the following:

$$\mathbf{z}^{(2)} = o_1(\mathbf{z}^{(1)})\mathbf{W}^{(2)} = \begin{bmatrix} o_{1,1} & o_{1,2} & o_{1,3} \end{bmatrix} \begin{bmatrix} w_{1,1} & w_{1,2} \\ w_{2,1} & w_{2,2} \\ w_{3,1} & w_{3,2} \end{bmatrix}$$

This results in the following calculation:

$$z^{(2)} = \begin{bmatrix} 0.03793257 & 0.36480273 & 0.00001204 \end{bmatrix} \begin{bmatrix} -0.62747958 & -0.30887855 \\ -0.20646505 & 0.07763347 \\ -0.16161097 & 0.370439 \end{bmatrix}$$

This leads to the following:

$$\mathbf{z}^{(2)} = \begin{bmatrix} -0.09912288 & 0.01660881 \end{bmatrix}$$

Again, we pass $\mathbf{z}^{(2)}$ through the sigmoid function and obtain $o_2(\cdot)$, which is the output of the two neurons in the output layer. This results in the following:

$$o_2(\mathbf{z}^{(2)}) = \text{sigmoid}(\begin{bmatrix} -0.09912288 & 0.01660881 \end{bmatrix})$$

$$o_2(\mathbf{z}^{(2)}) = \begin{bmatrix} 0.47523955 & 0.50415211 \end{bmatrix}$$

We implement this as follows:

```
o2 = sigmoid(np.matmul(o1, w2))
```

At this point, we need to give some meaning to this output so that we can determine the next step. What we would like to model in these two last neurons is the probability of the input data, $\mathbf{x}_i$, belonging to the positive class in $o_{2,1}$, and the probability of it belonging to the negative class in $o_{2,2}$. The next step is to establish an error metric in order to learn.

Error metrics, or error functions, are also known as **loss** functions.

Step 3 – Calculating loss

The next step is to define and **calculate the total loss**. In Chapter 4, *Learning from Data*, we discussed some error metrics (or losses), such as the **Mean Squared Error (MSE)**:

$$L = \frac{1}{N} \sum_{i=1}^{N} (\mathbf{y}_i - \hat{\mathbf{y}}_i)^2$$

It is important to think about this loss in terms of its derivative since we want to adjust the weights of the network in terms of the gradient as given by this loss function. Thus, we can do small changes that do not affect at all the overall result of the learning process but can result in nice derivatives. For example, if we take the derivative of L, the square will imply a multiplication by a factor of 2, but we could nullify the effect of that by slightly modifying the MSE, introducing a division by 2, as follows:

$$L = \frac{1}{2N} \sum_{i=1}^{N} (\mathbf{y}_i - \hat{\mathbf{y}}_i)^2$$

This loss, therefore, can be used to determine how "wrong" the predictions are from the actual target outcome. In the preceding example, the desired outcome was as follows:

$$\mathbf{y}_1 = \begin{bmatrix} 1 & 0 \end{bmatrix}$$

The predicted response was as follows:

$$\hat{\mathbf{y}}_1 = \begin{bmatrix} 0.47523955 & 0.50415211 \end{bmatrix}$$

This is normal since the weights were initialized at random; thus, it is expected from the model to perform poorly. The network can be further improved by using a modern approach that penalizes weights from taking on very large values. In neural networks, there is always a risk of having *exploding* or *vanishing* gradients, and a simple technique to reduce the effects of large gradients is to put a limit on the scale of the numbers that the weights can take. This is widely known as **regularization**. It leads to other nice properties, such as *sparse* models. We can achieve this regularization by modifying the loss as follows:

$$L = \frac{1}{2N} \sum_{i=1}^{N} (\mathbf{y}_i - \hat{\mathbf{y}}_i)^2 + \frac{\lambda}{2L} \sum_{j=1}^{L} \left\| \mathbf{W}^{(j)} \right\|_2^2$$

This loss can be implemented as follows:

```
L = np.square(y-o2).sum()/(2*N)  +
lambda*(np.square(w1).sum()+np.square(w2).sum())/(2*N)
```

The added regularization term adds up all the weights in each layer and large weights are penalized according to the λ parameter. This is a hyperparameter that needs to be fine-tuned by ourselves. A large λ value penalizes heavily any large weights, and a small λ value ignores any effects of the weights in the learning process. This is the loss function we will use in this model, and note that the regularization term is also easily differentiable.

Step 4 – The backward pass

The next step is to perform the **backward pass**. The goal is to adjust the weights in proportion to the loss and in a direction that reduces it. We start by calculating the partial derivative of L with respect to the weights in the output layer, $\frac{\partial L}{\partial \mathbf{w}^{(2)}}$, and then with respect to the first layer, $\frac{\partial L}{\partial \mathbf{w}^{(1)}}$.

Let's begin the *backward pass* by solving the first partial derivative. We can do so by using the well-known chain rule that allows us to decompose the main derivative in pieces that represent the same process; we do that as follows:

$$\frac{\partial L}{\partial \mathbf{W}^{(2)}} = \frac{\partial L}{\partial \mathbf{o}_2} \frac{\partial \mathbf{o}_2}{\partial \mathbf{z}^{(2)}} \frac{\partial \mathbf{z}^{(2)}}{\partial \mathbf{W}^{(2)}}$$

Here, $\mathbf{o}_l = o_l(\mathbf{z}^{(l)})$ for all cases of $l \in \{1,2\}$. If we define each piece of these partial derivatives independently, we arrive at the following:

$$\frac{\partial L}{\partial \mathbf{o}_2} = -(\mathbf{y} - \mathbf{o}_2)$$

$$\frac{\partial \mathbf{o}_2}{\partial \mathbf{z}^{(2)}} = \mathbf{o}_2 \left(1 - \mathbf{z}^{(2)}\right)$$

$$\frac{\partial \mathbf{z}^{(2)}}{\partial \mathbf{W}^{(2)}} = \mathbf{o}_1$$

These three partial derivatives have an exact solution every time. In our example, their values would be as follows:

$$\frac{\partial L}{\partial \mathbf{o}_2} = -([1 \quad 0] - [0.47523955 \quad 0.50415211]) = [-0.52476045 \quad 0.50415211]$$

$$\frac{\partial \mathbf{o}_2}{\partial \mathbf{z}^{(2)}} = [0.47523955 \quad 0.50415211](1 - [-0.09912288 \quad 0.01660881])$$
$$= [-0.10894822 \quad 0.01633295]$$

$$\frac{\partial \mathbf{z}^{(2)}}{\partial \mathbf{W}^{(2)}} = [0.03793257 \quad 0.36480273 \quad 0.00001204]$$

Now, since we need to update the weights, $\mathbf{W}^{(2)} \in \mathbb{R}^{3 \times 2}$, we need a 3 x 2 matrix, and, therefore, we can get this update by multiplying the vectors of the partial derivatives, as follows:

$$\frac{\partial \mathbf{L}}{\partial \mathbf{W}^2} = \begin{bmatrix} 0.03793257 \\ 0.36480273 \\ 0.00001204 \end{bmatrix} [-0.10894822 \quad 0.01633295][-0.52476045 \quad 0.50415211]$$

$$= \begin{bmatrix} 0.00216867 & 0.0031235 \\ 0.0208564 & 0.00300389 \\ 0.00000069 & 0.0000001 \end{bmatrix}$$

To get this result, we first need to perform an element-wise multiplication of the two small vectors on the right, and then perform an ordinary multiplication by the left transposed vector. In Python, we could do this:

```
dL_do2 = -(y - o2)
do2_dz2 = sigmoid(o2, grad=True)
dz2_dw2 = o1
dL_dw2 = dz2_dw2.T.dot(dL_do2*do2_dz2) + lambda*np.square(w2).sum()
```

Now that we have calculated the derivative, we can perform an update of the weights using a traditional scaling factor on the gradient known as the **learning rate**. We calculate the new $\mathbf{w}^{(2)}_*$ value, as follows:

$$\mathbf{W}^{(2)}_* = \mathbf{W}^{(2)} - \alpha \frac{\partial L}{\partial \mathbf{W}^{(2)}}$$

$$\mathbf{w}^{(2)}_* = \begin{bmatrix} -0.62747958 & -0.30887855 \\ -0.20646505 & 0.07763347 \\ -0.16161097 & 0.370439 \end{bmatrix} - 0.001 \begin{bmatrix} 0.00216867 & 0.00031235 \\ 0.0208564 & 0.00300389 \\ 0.000000069 & 0.0000001 \end{bmatrix}$$

$$= \begin{bmatrix} -0.62748175 & -0.30887886 \\ -0.20648591 & 0.07763046 \\ -0.16161097 & 0.370439 \end{bmatrix}$$

The **learning rate** is a mechanism that we use in machine learning to limit the influence of the derivatives in the update process. Remember that the derivative is interpreted as the rate of change of the weights given some input data. A *large* learning rate values too much the direction and magnitude of the derivatives and has the risk of skipping a good local minimum. A *small* learning rate only partially considers the information of the derivative at the risk of making very slow progress toward a local minimum. The learning rate is another hyperparameter that needs to be tuned.

Now, we proceed to calculate the next derivative, $\frac{\partial L}{\partial \mathbf{w}^{(1)}}$, which will allow us to calculate the update on $\mathbf{w}^{(1)}$. We begin by defining the partial derivative and attempt to simplify its calculation, as follows:

$$\frac{\partial L}{\partial \mathbf{w}^{(1)}} = \frac{\partial L}{\partial \mathbf{o}_1} \frac{\partial \mathbf{o}_1}{\partial \mathbf{z}^{(1)}} \frac{\partial \mathbf{z}^{(1)}}{\partial \mathbf{w}^{(1)}}$$

If we pay close attention to the first partial derivative, $\frac{\partial L}{\partial \mathbf{o}_1}$, we can notice that its derivative is defined as follows:

$$\frac{\partial L}{\partial \mathbf{o}_1} = \underline{\frac{\partial L}{\partial \mathbf{z}^{(2)}}} \frac{\partial \mathbf{z}^{(2)}}{\partial \mathbf{o}_1}$$

But the underlined term has already been calculated before! Notice that the underlined term is equivalent to the underlined term in the previously defined equation:

$$\frac{\partial L}{\partial \mathbf{w}^{(2)}} = \underline{\frac{\partial L}{\partial \mathbf{o}_2} \frac{\partial \mathbf{o}_2}{\partial \mathbf{z}^{(2)}}} \frac{\partial \mathbf{z}^{(2)}}{\partial \mathbf{w}^{(2)}}$$

This is a nice property that is possible due to the chain rule in differentiation and allows us to *recycle* computations and have a much more efficient learning algorithm. This nice property also tells us that we are indeed incorporating information of deeper layers into layers closer to the input. Let's now proceed to the individual calculation of each partial derivative knowing that we have done some of the work already.

Since $\frac{\partial \mathbf{z}^{(2)}}{\partial \mathbf{o}_1} = \mathbf{W}^{(2)}$, then the first term can be expressed as follows:

$$\frac{\partial L}{\partial \mathbf{o}_1} = \frac{\partial L}{\partial \mathbf{o}_2} \frac{\partial \mathbf{o}_2}{\partial \mathbf{z}^{(2)}} \frac{\partial \mathbf{z}^{(2)}}{\partial \mathbf{o}_1} = (-\mathbf{y} - \mathbf{o}_2) \mathbf{o}_2 \left(1 - \mathbf{z}^{(2)}\right) \mathbf{W}^{(2)}$$

In our example, this leads to the following result:

$$\frac{\partial L}{\partial \mathbf{o}_1} = [-0.10894822 \quad 0.01633295][-0.52476045 \quad 0.50415211] \begin{bmatrix} -0.62747958 & -0.30887855 \\ -0.206446505 & 0.07769947 \\ -0.16161097 & 0.370439 \end{bmatrix}^T$$

$$= [-0.03841748 \quad -0.0111647 \quad -0.0061892]$$

Now, the second term in the partial derivative can be calculated as follows:

$$\frac{\partial \mathbf{o}_1}{\partial \mathbf{z}^{(1)}} = \mathbf{o}(1 - \mathbf{z}^{(1)})$$

$$= [0.03793257 \quad 0.36480273 \quad 0.00001204][1 - [-3.23327435 \quad -0.55457885 \quad -11.32686981]]$$

This leads to the following vector:

$$\frac{\partial \mathbf{o}_1}{\partial \mathbf{z}^{(1)}} = [0.16057899 \quad 0.56711462 \quad 0.00014847]$$

After this, we are now able to calculate the last term, which can be directly computed as follows:

$$\frac{\partial \mathbf{z}^{(1)}}{\partial \mathbf{W}^{(1)}} = \mathbf{x}_1 = [7.08535569 \quad 5.20423916]$$

Finally, we can replace the results of the individual partial derivatives into the products of the chain rule:

$$\frac{\partial L}{\partial \mathbf{W}^{(1)}} = \frac{\partial L}{\partial \mathbf{o}_1} \frac{\partial \mathbf{o}_1}{\partial \mathbf{z}^{(1)}} \frac{\partial \mathbf{z}^{(1)}}{\partial \mathbf{W}^{(1)}}$$

$$= \begin{bmatrix} 7.08535569 \\ 5.20423916 \end{bmatrix} \begin{bmatrix} -0.03841748 & -0.0111647 & -0.0061892 \end{bmatrix} \begin{bmatrix} 0.16057899 & 0.56711462 & 0.00014847 \end{bmatrix}$$

This is obtained by rearranging the vectors to obtain a resulting matrix consistent with the weight matrix dimensions, $\mathbf{W}^{(1)} \in \mathbb{R}^{2 \times 3}$. The multiplications lead to the following:

$$\frac{\partial L}{\partial \mathbf{W}^{(1)}} = \begin{bmatrix} -0.04370984 & -0.04486212 & -0.00000651 \\ -0.03210516 & -0.03295151 & -0.00000478 \end{bmatrix}$$

In Python, we do this like so:

```
dL_dz2 = dL_do2 * do2_dz2
dz2_do1 = w2
dL_do1 = dL_dz2.dot(dz2_do1.T)
do1_dz1 = sigmoid(o1, grad=True)
dz1_dw1 = X
dL_dw1 = dz1_dw1.T.dot(dL_do1*do1_dz1) + lambda*np.square(w1).sum()
```

Lastly, the corresponding $\mathbf{w}_*^{(1)}$ update is calculated as follows:

$$\mathbf{W}_*^{(1)} = \mathbf{W}^{(1)} - \alpha \frac{\partial L}{\partial \mathbf{W}^{(1)}}$$

$$\mathbf{W}_*^{(1)} = \begin{bmatrix} -0.16595599 & 0.44064899 & -0.99977125 \\ -0.39533485 & -0.70648822 & -0.81532281 \end{bmatrix} - 0.001 \begin{bmatrix} -0.04370984 & -0.04486212 & -0.00000651 \\ -0.03210516 & -0.03295151 & -0.00000478 \end{bmatrix}$$

$$= \begin{bmatrix} -0.16591228 & 0.44069385 & -0.99977124 \\ -0.39530275 & -0.70645527 & -0.81532281 \end{bmatrix}$$

This concludes the backprop algorithm by assigning $\mathbf{W}_{t+1}^{(1)} = \mathbf{W}_*^{(1)}, \mathbf{W}_{t+1}^{(2)} = \mathbf{W}_*^{(2)}$ at iteration t (or *epoch*), which we implement as follows:

```
w1 += -alpha*dL_dw1
w2 += -alpha*dL_dw2
```

The process repeats for as many epochs as we wish. We could let the algorithm run with the following parameters:

$$t = 100000$$
$$\lambda = 0.00001$$
$$\alpha = 0.001$$

Then, the resulting separating hyperplane would look like that in the following figure:

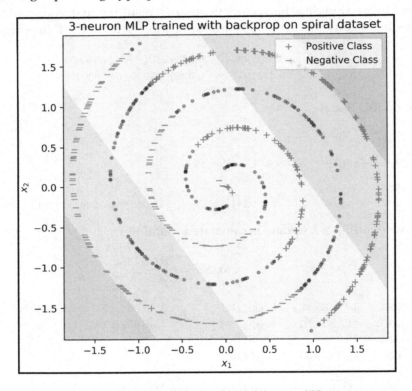

Figure 6.5 - Separating the hyperplane of the sample three-neuron MLP

This figure shows that there are many samples that are misclassified, which are depicted as black dots. The total accuracy is 62%. Clearly, three neurons are good enough to produce a classifier better than random chance; however, this is not the best possible outcome. What we must do now is tune-up the classifier by changing the hyperparameters and the number of neurons or layers. This is what we will discuss next.

Finding the best hyperparameters

There is a simpler way of coding what we coded in the previous section using Keras. We can rely on the fact that the backprop is coded correctly and is improved for stability and there is a richer set of other features and algorithms that can improve the learning process. Before we begin the process of optimizing the set of hyperparameters of the MLP, we should indicate what would be the equivalent implementation using Keras. The following code should reproduce the same model, almost the same loss function, and almost the same backprop methodology:

```
from tensorflow.keras.models import Sequential
from tensorflow.keras.layers import Dense

mlp = Sequential()
mlp.add(Dense(3, input_dim=2, activation='sigmoid'))
mlp.add(Dense(2, activation='sigmoid'))

mlp.compile(loss='mean_squared_error',
            optimizer='sgd',
            metrics=['accuracy'])

# This assumes that you still have X, y from earlier
# when we called X, y = twoSpirals(300)
mlp.fit(X, y, epochs=1000, batch_size=60)
```

This would produce an error of 62.3% and a decision boundary like the one shown in *Figure 6.7*:

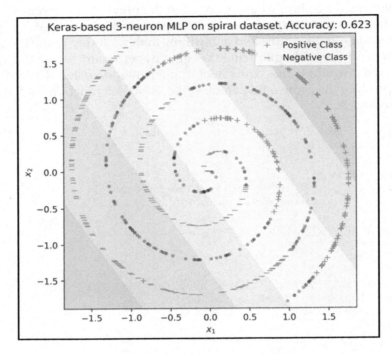

Figure 6.6 – Keras-based MLP for the same model as in *Figure 6.5*

The figure is very similar to *Figure 6.6*, which is expected since they are the same model. But let's review briefly the meaning of the model described in the code.

As explained before, `from tensorflow.keras.models import Sequential` imports the Sequential library, which allows us to create a *sequential* model as opposed to a *functional* approach to model creation, `mlp = Sequential()`, and it also allows us to add elements to the model, `mlp.add()`, such as multiple layers of neurons (dense layers): `Dense(...)`.

The first layer of the sequential model must specify the dimension of the input (input layer size), which in this case is 2, and the activation function, which is a sigmoid: `mlp.add(Dense(3, input_dim=2, activation='sigmoid'))`. In this case, the number 3 indicates how many neurons this model will have in the first hidden layer.

The second (and last) layer is similar but denotes the two neurons in the output layer: `mlp.add(Dense(2, activation='sigmoid'))`.

Once the sequential model has been specified, we must compile it, `mlp.compile(...)`, defining the loss to be minimized, `loss='mean_squared_error'`, the optimization (backprop) algorithm to be used, `optimizer='sgd'`, and also a list of what metrics to report after each training epoch, `metrics=['accuracy']`. The mean squared loss defined here does not include the regularization term described before, but this should not have a greater impact here; the loss is, therefore, something we have seen before:

$$L = \frac{1}{N} \sum_{i=1}^{N} (\mathbf{y}_i - \hat{\mathbf{y}}_i)^2$$

The `sgd` optimizer defines an algorithm known as **stochastic gradient descent**. This is a robust way of calculating the gradient and updating the weights accordingly and has been around since the 1950s [Amari, S. I. 1993]. In Keras, it has a default *learning rate* of $\alpha = 0.01$; however, this rate has a decay strategy that allows the learning rate to adapt to the learning process.

With this in mind, what we will do is vary the following hyperparameters:

- The learning rate, $\alpha \geq 1$, is adaptive.
- The number of layers, between 2, 3, and 4, with 16 neurons each (except the output layer).
- The activation function, either ReLU or sigmoid.

This can be achieved by running several experiments with cross-validation, as explained before in `Chapter 4`, *Learning from Data*. The following table shows a comprehensive list of the experiments performed under five-fold cross-validation and the corresponding results:

Exp.	Hyperparameters	Mean Accuracy	Std.
a	(16-Sigmoid, 2-Sigmoid)	0.6088	0.004
b	(16-ReLU, 2-Sigmoid)	0.7125	0.038
c	(16-Sigmoid, 16-Sigmoid, 2-Sigmoid)	0.6128	0.010
d	(16-ReLU, 16-Sigmoid, 2-Sigmoid)	0.7040	0.067
e	(16-Sigmoid, 16-Sigmoid, 16-Sigmoid, 2-Sigmoid)	0.6188	0.010
f	(16-ReLU, 16-Sigmoid, 16-ReLU, 2-Sigmoid)	0.7895	0.113
g	(16-ReLU, 16-ReLU, 16-Sigmoid, 2-Sigmoid)	**0.9175**	0.143
h	(16-ReLU, 16-ReLU, 16-ReLU, 2-Sigmoid)	0.9050	0.094
i	(16-ReLU, 16-Sigmoid, 16-Sigmoid, 2-Sigmoid)	0.6608	0.073

Note that other experiments were performed with an additional fifth layer, but the results were not much better in terms of average performance and variability. It appears that four layers with as little as 16 neurons in each layer (except the output layer, with 2) are sufficient to produce adequate class separation. *Figure 6.8* shows a sample run from experiment g, which achieved the highest performance with 99% accuracy:

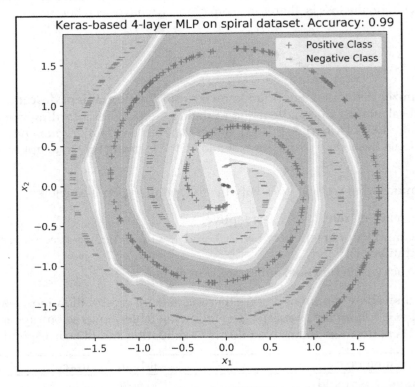

Figure 6.7 – Classification boundaries for the two-spirals dataset using a four-layered (16,16,16,2) neural network. Corresponds to experiment g in Table 1

A visual inspection of *Figure 6.8* reveals that the largest margin of confusion is in the center area where the spirals originate and are very close to each other. Notice also that the separating hyperplane seems to be non-smooth in some areas, which is typical of the MLP. Some suggest that this phenomenon is due to the fact that neurons in the input layer are using a linear function to approximate a function, and deeper layers are mixtures of linear functions that produce non-linear functions based on such linear functions. Of course, it is much more complicated than that, but it is interesting to note here.

Before we conclude this chapter, note that there are other hyperparameters that we could have optimized empirically. We could have chosen different optimizers, such as `adam` or `rmsprop`; we could have tried other activation functions such as `tanh`, or `softmax`; we could have tried more layers; or we could have tried more (or less) and different numbers of neurons in increasing, decreasing, or mixed order. However, for now, these experiments are sufficient to make the point that experimentation with different things is key in finding what works best for us in our particular application or the problem we are trying to solve.

This concludes our introductory chapters, and the coming ones will look at specific types of architecture that have a specific purpose, as opposed to the MLP, which is usually considered a multipurpose, fundamental neural network. Our next chapter will deal with autoencoders; they can be seen as a special type of neural network aiming to encode input data into a smaller dimensional space and then reconstructing it back to the original input space, minimizing the loss of information in the reconstructed data. An autoencoder allows us to compress data, and learn from the data without the label associated with it. The latter makes the autoencoder a special kind of neural network that learns using what is categorized as **unsupervised learning**.

Summary

This intermediate-introductory chapter showed the design of an MLP and the paradigms surrounding its functionality. We covered the theoretical framework behind its elements and we had a full discussion and treatment of the widely known backprop mechanism to perform gradient descent on a loss function. Understanding the backprop algorithm is key for further chapters since some models are designed specifically to overcome some potential difficulties with backprop. You should feel confident that what you have learned about backprop will serve you well in knowing what deep learning is all about. This backprop algorithm, among other things, is what makes deep learning an exciting area. Now, you should be able to understand and design your own MLP with different layers and different neurons. Furthermore, you should feel confident in changing some of its parameters, although we will cover more of this in the further reading.

Chapter 7, *Autoencoders*, will continue with an architecture very similar to the MLP that is widely used today for many different learning tasks associated with learning representations of data. This chapter begins a new part that is dedicated to *unsupervised learning* algorithms and models based on the type of learning where you can learn from data even if it is not labeled.

Questions and answers

1. **Why is the MLP better than the perceptron model?**

   The larger number and layers of neurons give the MLP the advantage over the perceptron to model non-linear problems and solve much more complicated pattern recognition problems.

2. **Why is backpropagation so important to know about?**

   Because it is what makes neural networks learn in the era of big data.

3. **Does the MLP always converge?**

   Yes and no. It does always converge to a local minimum in terms of the loss function; however, it is not guaranteed to converge to a global minimum since, usually, most loss functions are non-convex and non-smooth.

4. **Why should we try to optimize the hyperparameters of our models?**

   Because anyone can train a simple neural network; however, not everyone knows what things to change to make it better. The success of your model depends heavily on you trying different things and proving to yourself (and others) that your model is the best that it can be. This is what will make you a better learner and a better deep learning professional.

References

- Rosenblatt, F. (1958). The perceptron: a probabilistic model for information storage and organization in the brain. *Psychological Review*, 65(6), 386.
- Tappert, C. C. (2019). Who is the Father of Deep Learning? *Symposium on Artificial Intelligence.*
- Hinton, G. E. (1990). Connectionist learning procedures. *Machine learning.* Morgan Kaufmann, 555-610.
- Rumelhart, D. E., Hinton, G. E., & Williams, R. J. (1986). Learning representations by back-propagating errors. *Nature*, 323(6088), 533-536.
- Florez, O. U. (2017). One LEGO at a time: Explaining the Math of How Neural Networks Learn. *Online*: https://omar-florez.github.io/scratch_mlp/.
- Amari, S. I. (1993). Backpropagation and stochastic gradient descent method. *Neurocomputing*, 5(4-5), 185-196.

Section 2: Unsupervised Deep Learning

2

After looking at the MLP as the first supervised approach, this section focuses on the learning algorithms known as unsupervised algorithms. It begins with simple autoencoders and moves on to deeper and larger neural models.

This section consists of the following chapters:

- Chapter 7, *Autoencoders*
- Chapter 8, *Deep Autoencoders*
- Chapter 9, *Variational Autoencoders*
- Chapter 10, *Restricted Boltzmann Machines*

7
Autoencoders

This chapter introduces the autoencoder model by explaining the relationship between encoding and decoding layers. We will be showcasing a model that belongs to the unsupervised learning family. This chapter also introduces a loss function commonly associated with the autoencoder model, and it also applies it to the dimensionality reduction of MNIST data and its visualization in an autoencoder-induced latent space.

The following topics will be covered in this chapter:

- Introduction to unsupervised learning
- Encoding and decoding layers
- Applications in dimensionality reduction and visualization
- Ethical implications of unsupervised learning

Introduction to unsupervised learning

As machine learning has progressed over the last few years, I have come across many ways to categorize the different types of learning. Recently, at the NeurIPS 2018 conference in Montreal, Canada, Dr. Alex Graves shared information about the different types of learning, shown in *Figure 7.1*:

	Labeled Data	**No Labels**
Active	Reinforcement Learning	Existing Motivation
	Active Learning	Defined Exploration
Passive	Supervised Learning	Unsupervised Learning

Figure 7.1 – Different types of learning

Such efforts at categorization are very useful today when there are many learning algorithms being studied and improved. The first row depicts *active* learning, which means that there is a sense of interaction between the learning algorithm and the data. For example, in reinforcement learning and active learning operating over *labeled data*, the reward policies can inform what type of data the model will read in the following iterations. However, traditional supervised learning, which is what we have studied so far, involves no interaction with the data source and instead assumes that the dataset is fixed and that its dimensionality and shape will not change; these non-interactive approaches are known as *passive* learning.

The second column in the table in the *Figure 7.1* represents a special kind of learning algorithm that requires *no labels* to learn from data. Other algorithms require you to have a dataset that has data $\mathbf{x}$ that is associated with a label y; that is: $\mathcal{D} = \{\mathbf{x}_i, y_i\}_{i=1}^{N}$. However, unsupervised algorithms have no need for labels to "do things" with data.

You can think of labels as a **teacher**. A teacher tells the learner that x corresponds to y and the learner attempts to learn the relationship between $\mathbf{x}$ and y iteratively by trial and error, adjusting its *beliefs* (parameters) until it gets it right. However, if there is no teacher, the learner does not know anything about the label y and therefore learns *something* about $\mathbf{x}$ by itself, provided some boundaries, and it forms its own beliefs about $\mathbf{x}$ without ever knowing anything about y.

In the following chapters, we will study **unsupervised learning**, which is the type of learning that assumes that the data we have will not change in its shape or form and will remain consistent during the learning process and also during its deployment. These algorithms are guided by something other than labels, for example, a unique loss function for data compression. On the other hand, there are other algorithms that have an exploration mechanism or a specific motivation to learn from data in an interactive way, and these algorithms are **active learning** algorithms. We will not discuss these algorithms in this book since this book is intended to be introductory and for absolute beginners. However, we will discuss at length some of the most robust *unsupervised* deep learning models.

We will begin by learning about **autoencoders**. An autoencoder has the sole purpose of taking input data into a neural network that is composed of two parts: an **encoder** and a **decoder**. The encoder portion has the mission of encoding the input data, usually into a lower-dimensional space, thereby compressing or encoding the input data. The decoder portion of the model is in charge of taking the encoded (or compressed) latent representation of the input data and then reconstructing it back to its original shape and to its original values without losing any data. That is, in an ideal autoencoder, the input is equal to the output. Let's discuss this in more detail in the following sections.

Encoding and decoding layers

The autoencoder can be broken down into two major components that serve specific purposes during an unsupervised learning process. The left side of *Figure 7.2* shows an autoencoder that is implemented using fully connected (dense) layers. It receives as input some vector $\mathbf{x} \in \mathbb{R}^8$ and then it goes into six hidden layers; the first three, with 6, 4, and 2 neurons, respectively, are meant to compress the input data down to two dimensions, since the output of two neurons is two scalar values. This first set of layers is known as the **encoder**:

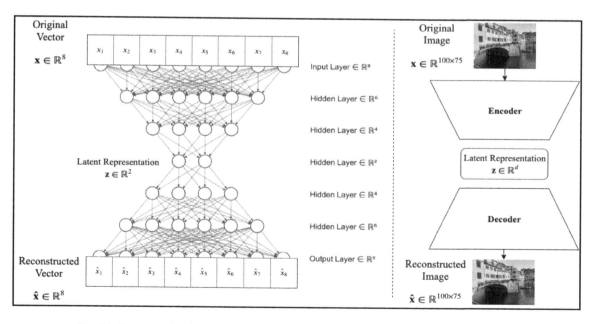

Figure 7.2 – Two representations of an autoencoder. Left: full and descriptive model. Right: compact and abstracted model representation

The second set of neurons is meant to reconstruct the input data back to its original dimensionality and values $\hat{x} \in \mathbb{R}^8$ using three layers with 4, 6, and 8 neurons, respectively; this group of layers is known as the **decoder**.

 Note that the last layer of the autoencoder *must have* the same number of neurons as the number of dimensions of the input vector. Otherwise, the reconstruction would not match the input data.

In this case, the autoencoder shown on the left in *Figure 7.2* acts as a compression network, in the sense that after training the model to achieve good reconstruction, if we disconnect the decoder, we end up with a neural network that encodes the input data into two dimensions (or any dimensions we choose, for that matter). This presents a unique advantage over supervised models: in a supervised model, we teach a network to look for a pattern that will permit an association with a given target label; however, in unsupervised learning (or in this autoencoder, for example), the network does not look for a specific pattern but rather learns to use the input space in any way that preserves the most representative and most important information of the input data, so as to allow good reconstruction in the decoder.

Think of a neural network and an autoencoder that takes input images of cats and dogs; a traditional neural network can be trained to distinguish between dogs and cats and it is tasked with finding important patterns in the images of dogs and cats so as to tell the difference between them; however, an autoencoder will train to learn the most important patterns, the most representative of all patterns, so as to preserve that information and allow good reconstruction regardless of the label. In a way, the traditional supervised neural network is biased to see the world in terms of cats and dogs, while the autoencoder is free to learn from the world regardless of cats or dogs.

The diagram on the right of *Figure 7.2* depicts an alternative representation of an autoencoder that is more abstract and compact. This type of representation is useful when describing a relatively deep autoencoder, when the number of layers is large to the point of it being difficult to represent all the neurons and all the layers one by one (as in the left side of the *Figure 7.2*). We will use those trapezoidal shapes to denote that there is an encoder/decoder; we note also that this abstraction will allow us the freedom to use other types of layers and not only dense (fully connected) layers. The diagram on the right of *Figure 7.2* depicts an autoencoder that takes an image as input, then encodes the input into a d-dimensional space, and then reconstructs the *latent* vector back to the input (image) space.

A **latent space** is a space where the learned lower-dimensional patterns are mapped. It is also known as the *learned representation space*. Ideally, this latent space is rich in important information about the input data and has fewer dimensions than the input data without any loss of information.

Let's now go ahead and implement each of the autoencoder parts based on the simple model on the left in *Figure 7.2*.

Encoding layers

The TensorFlow and Keras libraries that we will be using are `Input` and `Dense` from `tensorflow.keras.layers` and `Model` from `tensorflow.keras.models`. We will be using the `keras` functional approach as opposed to *sequential* modeling. Import the following:

```
from tensorflow.keras.layers import Input, Dense
from tensorflow.keras.models import Model
```

The `Input` layer will be used to describe the dimensionality of the input vector, which in our case will be `8`:

```
inpt_dim = 8
ltnt_dim = 2

inpt_vec = Input(shape=(inpt_dim,))
```

Then, considering all of our activation functions as `sigmoid` just for the sake of this example, we can define the pipeline of the encoder layers as follows:

```
elayer1 = Dense(6, activation='sigmoid')(inpt_vec)
elayer2 = Dense(4, activation='sigmoid') (elayer1)
encoder = Dense(ltnt_dim, activation='sigmoid') (elayer2)
```

The `Dense` class constructor receives the number of neurons and the activation function as parameters and at the end of the definition (on the right side), we must include what the input to the layer is, and this is assigned a name on the left side. Thus, in the line `elayer1 = Dense(6, activation='sigmoid')(inpt_vec)`, the name assigned to the layer is `elayer1`, then 6 is the number of neurons, `activation='sigmoid'` assigns a `sigmoid` activation function to the dense layer, and `inpt_vec` is the input to this layer in the pipeline.

In the preceding three lines of code, we have defined the layers of the encoder, and the `encoder` variable points to the object that can output the latent variable if we make it a model and call `predict()` on it:

```
latent_ncdr = Model(inpt_vec, encoder)
```

In this line of code, `latent_ncdr` contains the model that can map the input data to the latent space once it is trained. But before we do that, let's go ahead and define the layers of the decoder in a similar way.

Decoding layers

We can define the decoder layers as follows:

```
dlayer1 = Dense(4, activation='sigmoid')(encoder)
dlayer2 = Dense(6, activation='sigmoid') (dlayer1)
decoder = Dense(inpt_dim, activation='sigmoid') (dlayer2)
```

Note that in the preceding code, the number of neurons usually goes in increasing order until the last layer that matches the input dimension. In this case, 4, 6, and 8 are defined as `inpt_dim`. Similarly, the `decoder` variable points to the object that can output the reconstructed input if we make it a model and call `predict()` on it.

We have separated the encoder and decoder intentionally here, simply to show that we could have the ability to access the different components of the network if we choose to do so. However, we should probably also define the autoencoder as a whole, from input to output, by using the `Model` class as follows:

```
autoencoder = Model(inpt_vec, decoder)
```

This is exactly what we meant earlier when we said "if we make it a model and call `predict()` on it." This declaration is making a model that takes as input the input vector defined in `inpt_vec` and retrieves the output from the `decoder` layer. Then, we can use this as a model object that has a few nice functions in Keras that will allow us to pass input, read output, train, and do other things that we will discuss in the upcoming sections. For now, since we have defined our model, and before we can train it, we should define what the objective of the training will be, that is, what our loss function will be.

Loss function

Our loss function has to be in terms of the goal of the autoencoder. This goal is to reconstruct the input perfectly. That means that our input $\mathbf{x} \in \mathbb{R}^8$ and our reconstruction $\hat{\mathbf{x}} \in \mathbb{R}^8$ have to be identical in an ideal autoencoder. This implies that the absolute difference must be zero:

$$|\mathbf{x} - \hat{\mathbf{x}}| = 0$$

However, this may not be realistic, and it is not in terms of a function that we can easily differentiate. For this, we can come back to the classic mean squared error function, which is defined as follows:

$$L = \frac{1}{N} \sum_{i=1}^{N} (\mathbf{x}_i - \hat{\mathbf{x}}_i)^2$$

We want to make $L = 0$, ideally, or at best minimize it as much as possible. We interpret this loss function as minimizing the average of the squared differences between the input and its reconstruction. If we use a standard backprop strategy, say, some type of standard gradient descent technique, we can compile the model and prepare it for training as follows:

```
autoencoder.compile(loss='mean_squared_error', optimizer='sgd')
```

The `compile()` method prepares the model for training. The loss function defined previously is given as a parameter, `loss='mean_squared_error'`, and the optimization technique chosen here is known as **stochastic gradient descent (SGD)**, `optimizer='sgd'`. For more information on SGD, please see Amari, S. I. (1993).

Learning and testing

Since this is an introductory example of a simple autoencoder, we will train only with one data point and begin the learning process. We also want to show the encoded version and the reconstructed version.

We will use the number 39 in binary as eight digits, which corresponds to 00100111. We will declare this as our input vector as follows:

```
import numpy as np
x = np.array([[0., 0., 1., 0., 0., 1., 1., 1.]])
```

We can then perform the training as follows:

```
hist = autoencoder.fit(x, x, epochs=10000, verbose=0)

encdd = latent_ncdr.predict(x)
x_hat = autoencoder.predict(x)
```

The `fit()` method performs the training. Its first two arguments are the input data and the desired target output; in the case of the autoencoder, they are both x. The number of epochs is specified as `epochs=10000`, since the model can produce a decent output at this point, and we set the verbosity to zero since we do not need to visualize every epoch, using `verbose=0`.

In Google Colab or Jupyter Notebook, it is not a good idea to visualize more than 1,000 epochs on the screen at a time. The web browser might become unresponsive to the JavaScript code in charge of displaying all these epochs. Beware.

The `predict()` method in the latent encoder model, `latent_ncdr`, and in the `autoencoder` model produce the output at the specified layers. If we retrieve `encdd`, we can see the latent representation of the input, and if we retrieve `x_hat`, we can see the reconstruction. We can even calculate the mean squared error manually as follows:

```
print(encdd)
print(x_hat)
print(np.mean(np.square(x-x_hat)))   # MSE
```

This produces the following output:

```
[[0.54846555 0.4299447 ]]
[[0.07678119 0.07935049 0.91219556 0.07693048 0.07255505 0.9112366
0.9168126 0.9168152 ]]
0.0066003498745448655
```

The numbers here will vary due to the unsupervised nature of the learning algorithm. The first output vector can be any real numbers. The second output vector will likely have real numbers close to zero and close to one, resembling the original binary vector, but the exact values will vary every single time.

The first vector of two elements is the latent representation, [0.55, 0.43]; this may not mean much to us at this point, but it will be very important to us in terms of data compression. It means that we are able to represent eight digits using two.

Although this is a toy example and representing a binary number with two digits is not very exciting, the theory behind this is that we could take any eight floating-point digits in the range [0, 1] and compress them down to two digits in the same range.

The second vector displayed shows evidence of a good reconstruction: something that should be a zero is a 0.08 and something that should be a one is a 0.91. The **mean squared error (MSE)** as calculated manually yields a 0.007, which, although not zero, is small enough to be good.

We can visualize the decay of the MSE throughout the training phase using the information stored in the `hist` object defined during the invocation of `fit()`. This object contains the information of the loss function value across epochs and allows us to visualize the process with the following code:

```
import matplotlib.pyplot as plt

plt.plot(hist.history['loss'])
plt.title('Model reconstruction loss')
plt.ylabel('MSE')
plt.xlabel('Epoch')
plt.show()
```

This produces what you see in *Figure 7.3*:

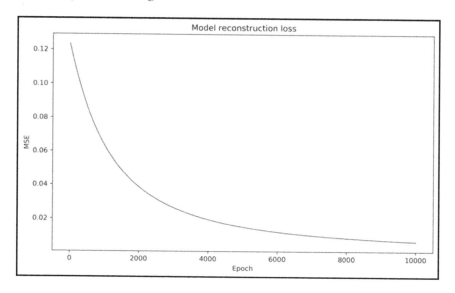

Figure 7.3 – Reconstruction loss across epochs of training of an autoencoder as described in terms of the MSE

Okay, once again, this was a toy example with one data point. We would never do this in *real life*. To show how bad an idea this is, we can take the binary string we used to train the model and invert every single bit, which gives 11011000 (or 216 in decimal). If we gave this to the autoencoder, we would expect a *good* reconstruction, but let's see what happens if we try to do that:

```
x = np.array([[1., 1., 0., 1., 1., 0., 0., 0.]])   #216

encdd = latent_ncdr.predict(x)
x_hat = autoencoder.predict(x)

print(encdd)
print(x_hat)
print(np.mean(np.square(x-x_hat)))
```

We get the following output:

```
[[0.51493704 0.43615338]]
[[0.07677279 0.07933337 0.9122421 0.07690183 0.07254466 0.9112378 0.9167745
0.91684484]]
0.8444848864148122
```

 Once again, the numbers here will vary due to the unsupervised nature of the learning algorithm. If your results are different from what you see here (I'm sure they are), that is not a problem.

If you compare these results with the ones from before, you will notice that the latent representation is not that different, and the reconstructed output does not at all match the given input. It is evident that the model **memorized** the input on which it was trained. This is evident when we calculate the MSE and we obtain a value of 0.84, which is large compared to the one previously obtained.

The solution to this is, of course, adding more data. But this concludes the toy example of building an autoencoder. What really changes after this is the type and amount of data, the number of layers, and the types of layers. In the next section, we will look at the application of a simple autoencoder in dimensionality reduction problems.

Applications in dimensionality reduction and visualization

Among some of the most interesting applications of autoencoders is dimensionality reduction [Wang, Y., et al. (2016)]. Given that we live in a time where data storage is easily accessible and affordable, large amounts of data are currently stored everywhere. However, not everything is relevant information. Consider, for example, a database of video recordings of a home security camera that always faces one direction. Chances are that there is a lot of repeated data in every video frame or image and very little of the data gathered will be useful. We would need a strategy to look at what is really important in those images. Images, by their nature, have a lot of redundant information, and there is usually correlation among image regions, which makes autoencoders very useful in compressing the information in images (Petscharnig, S., et al. (2017)).

To demonstrate the applicability of autoencoders in dimensionality reduction for images, we will use the well-known MNIST dataset.

MNIST data preparation

For details about MNIST, please go to Chapter 3, *Preparing Data*. Here we will only mention that the MNIST data will be scaled to the range [0, 1]. We also need to convert all images into vectors by reshaping the 28 by 28 digit images into a 784-dimensional vector. This can be achieved as follows:

```
from tensorflow.keras.datasets import mnist

(x_train, y_train), (x_test, y_test) = mnist.load_data()

x_train = x_train.astype('float32') / 255.
x_test = x_test.astype('float32') / 255.

x_train = x_train.reshape((len(x_train), 28*28))
x_test = x_test.reshape((len(x_test), 28*28))
```

We will use x_train to train the autoencoder and x_test to test the generalization capability of the autoencoder to both encode and decode MNIST digits. For visualization purposes, we will need y_test, but y_train can be ignored since we do not need labels in unsupervised machine learning.

Figure 7.4 depicts the first eight samples in x_test. These samples will be used across a few experiments to show the capabilities of different autoencoder models:

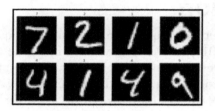

Figure 7.4 – Test MNIST digits to be used for comparison

Autoencoders for MNIST

We can design a few experiments with different numbers of layers to see how the autoencoder changes its performance for MNIST. We can start with an autoencoder with four layers, always using a latent dimension of two. This is done to facilitate visualizing the MNIST digits in a two-dimensional space induced by the autoencoders.

Based on the previously defined autoencoder, we can propose the following four-layer base autoencoder:

```
inpt_dim = 28*28
ltnt_dim = 2

inpt_vec = Input(shape=(inpt_dim,))

elayer1 = Dense(392, activation='sigmoid')(inpt_vec)
elayer2 = Dense(28, activation='sigmoid') (elayer1)
elayer3 = Dense(10, activation='sigmoid') (elayer2)
encoder = Dense(ltnt_dim, activation='tanh')(elayer3)

dlayer1 = Dense(10, activation='sigmoid')(encoder)
dlayer2 = Dense(28, activation='sigmoid')(dlayer1)
dlayer3 = Dense(392, activation='sigmoid')(dlayer2)
decoder = Dense(inpt_dim, activation='sigmoid')(dlayer3)

latent_ncdr = Model(inpt_vec, encoder)
autoencoder = Model(inpt_vec, decoder)

autoencoder.compile(loss='binary_crossentropy', optimizer='adam')

hist = autoencoder.fit(x_train, x_train, epochs=100, batch_size=256,
                    shuffle=True, validation_data=(x_test, x_test))
```

This will be the base of the subsequent models. There are a few things that are highlighted that are new and need to be introduced properly. The first important thing is a new activation function called the **hyperbolic tangent**. This activation function is defined as follows:

$$\tanh(z) = \frac{\sinh(z)}{\cosh(z)} = \frac{e^z - e^{-z}}{e^z + e^{-z}}$$

The corresponding first derivative is relatively simple:

$$\frac{d}{dz}\tanh(z) = \frac{d}{dz}\frac{\sinh(z)}{\cosh(z)} = 1 - \frac{\sinh^2(z)}{\cosh^2(z)} = 1 - \tanh^2(z)$$

Besides having a nice and easily calculable derivative, the hyperbolic tangent activation function has a nice output range of [-1, 1]. This allows a neutral range that is not necessarily constrained to the sigmoid range [0, 1]. For visualization purposes, sometimes it is interesting to visualize in the hyperbolic tangent range, but it is not necessary to do so.

Another new element we have introduced is the loss function called **binary cross-entropy**:

$$L = -\frac{1}{N}\sum_{i=1}^{N} \mathbf{x}_i \cdot \log(p(\hat{\mathbf{x}}_i)) + (1 - \mathbf{x}_i) \cdot \log(1 - p(\hat{\mathbf{x}}_i))$$

In general, binary cross-entropy uses information, which are theoretical ideas to calculate the error between the target data **x** and the reconstructed (or predicted) data $\hat{\mathbf{x}}$. In a way, it measures the amount of entropy, or surprise, between the target and the prediction. For example, in an ideal autoencoder, it is not surprising that the target **x** is equal to its reconstruction $\hat{\mathbf{x}}$, and the loss should be zero. However, if the target **x** is not equal to $\hat{\mathbf{x}}$, that would be surprising and would yield a high loss.

For a more complete discussion on autoencoders using cross-entropy loss, see (Creswell, A., et. al. (2017)).

A new optimizer called **Adam** has also been introduced (Kingma, D. P., et. al. (2014)). It is an algorithm for stochastic optimization that uses an adaptive learning rate that has proven to be very fast in some deep learning applications. Speed is a nice property when we are dealing with deep learning models and large datasets. Time is of the essence, and Adam provides a nice approach that has become popular.

Finally, the last new thing we added was on the `fit()` method. You should have noticed that there are two new parameters: `shuffle=True`, which allows the shuffling of data during the training process; and `validation_data=( , )`, which specifies a tuple of data that is used to monitor the loss using validation data, or data that the model has never seen, and will never use, for training.

That is all the new things we have introduced. The next step is to explain the autoencoder architectures we will try in our experiments. Please see *Figure 7.5* for a reference regarding the experiments we will perform:

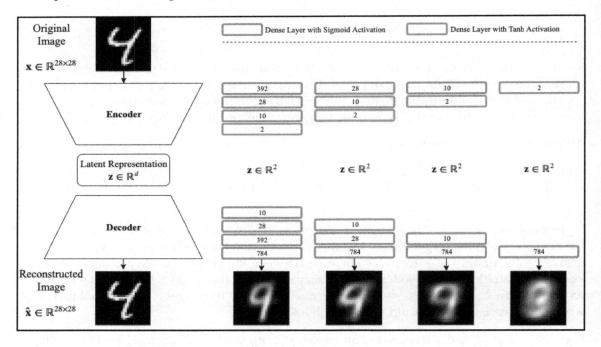

Figure 7.5 – Different autoencoder configurations to demonstrate the difference in the quality of the latent representations

In the figure, you will notice that we are using the abstracted representation of an autoencoder, and on the right side of the *Figure 7.5* are the different layers that each autoencoder architecture will use. The first architecture shown corresponds to the code shown in this section. That is, the code shows an autoencoder with encoding layers of 392, 28, 10, and 2 neurons, respectively; while the decoding layers contain 10, 28, 392, and 784 neurons, respectively. The next model on the right contains the same layers except for removing the pair of layers corresponding to 392 neurons, and so on.

The last autoencoder model only contains two layers, one encoding (two neurons) and one decoding (784 neurons). At this point, you should be able to modify the Python code to remove the necessary layers and replicate the models depicted in *Figure 7.5*. The next step is to train the models in *Figure 7.5* and visualize the quality of the output.

Training and visualization

The execution of `autoencoder.fit()` for 100 epochs produces a viable model that can easily encode into two dimensions as specified. Looking closely into the loss function during training, we can observe that it converges properly:

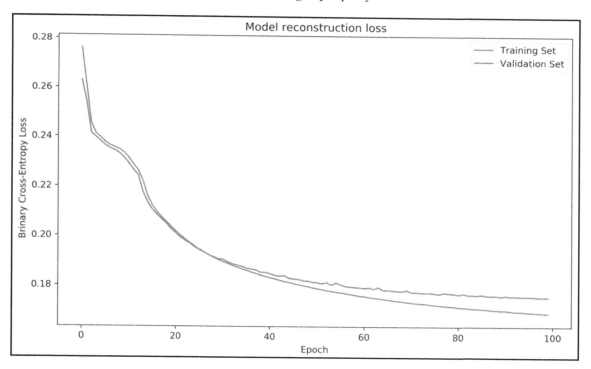

Figure 7.6 – Loss function monitoring during the training of a four-layer autoencoder

Once the model has been trained successfully, we can retrieve the encoded representation using the following:

```
encdd = latent_ncdr.predict(x_test)
```

We are using the test set, x_test. This encoding will encode into two dimensions, as specified, and will produce a latent representation in the range [-1, 1], as specified. Similarly, we can always take the test set and use the autoencoder to compress it and reconstruct it to see how similar the input is to the reconstruction. We do so with this:

```
x_hat = autoencoder.predict(x_test)
```

Before we look into the latent representations learned from MNIST, we can look into the reconstruction quality as a way of assessing the quality of the learned model. *Figure 7.7* shows the reconstruction results (in x_hat) using *Figure 7.4* as a reference to the input provided to each model. The figure is broken down into four parts, each part corresponding to the models described in *Figure 7.5*: a) the model with eight layers, b) the model with six layers, c) the model with four layers, and d) the model with two layers:

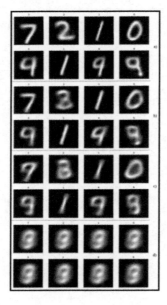

Figure 7.7 – Autoencoder reconstruction for the models in Figure 7.5: a) the model with eight layers, b) the model with six layers, c) the model with four layers, and d) the model with two layers

From *Figure 7.7.a*, we can see that the model with eight layers (392, 28, 10, 2, 10, 28, 392, 784) is capable of producing generally good reconstructions with the exception of the numbers 4 and 9. It is evident that both digits are closely related (visually) and the autoencoder has some difficulty distinguishing clearly between the two digits. To further explore this observation, we can visualize test data in the latent space (in encdd), which is depicted in *Figure 7.8*:

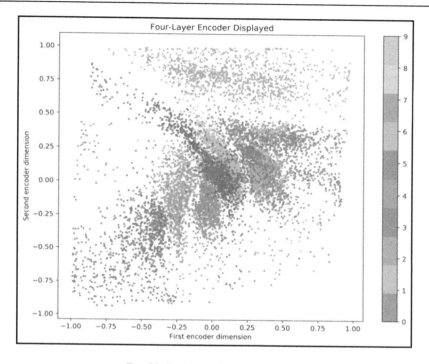

Figure 7.8 – Four-layer encoder using MNIST test data

The overlap between digits four and nine is evident in the latent space produced by the autoencoder. However, most of the other groups of digits have relatively clear separate clusters. *Figure 7.8* also explains the natural closeness of other numbers that look like each other; for example, one and seven appear to be close to each other, as well as zero and six, and so do three and eight. However, numbers that do not look alike are in opposite sections of the latent space – for example, zero and one.

Figure 7.9 depicts the three-layer autoencoder that removed the layer with 392 neurons and left a 28, 10, 2 neuron architecture. Clearly, the quality of the latent space is significantly reduced, although some of the major structure is consistent. That is, zero and one are on opposite sides, and other numbers that look alike are closer together; the overlap is greater in comparison to *Figure 7.8*. The quality of this three-layer autoencoder is consistently lower, as shown in *Figure 7.7.b*:

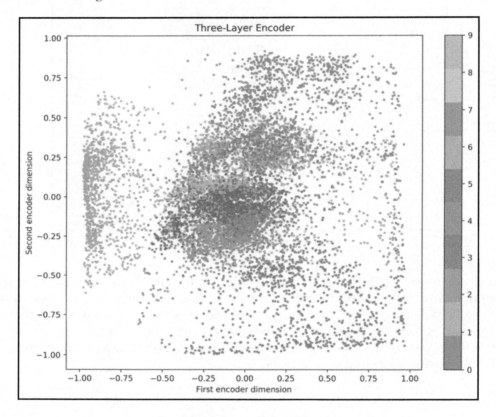

Figure 7.9 – Three-layer encoder using MNIST test data

In *Figure 7.10*, we can observe the results of the two-layer autoencoder with 10 and 2 neurons, which again has a greater digit overlap than the previous autoencoders; this is also evident in the poor reconstruction shown in *Figure 7.7.c*:

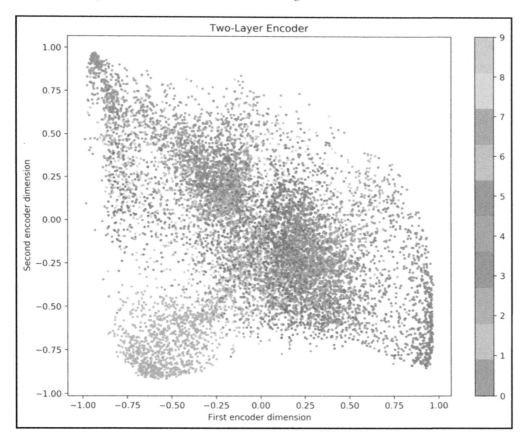

Figure 7.10 – Two-layer encoder using MNIST test data

Finally, *Figure 7.11* shows the latent space of the one-layer autoencoder. Clearly, this is a terrible idea. Just consider what we are asking the autoencoder to do: we are asking just two neurons to find a way to look at an entire image of a digit and find a way (learning weights **W**) to map all images to two dimensions. It is just not possible to do that. Logically, if we only have one layer, we would want at least 10 neurons to adequately model each of the 10 digits in MNIST:

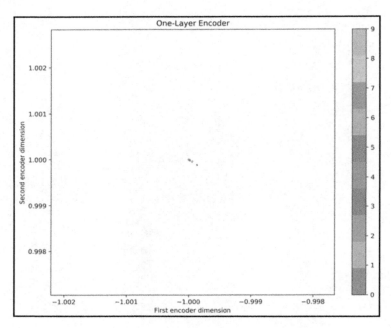

Figure 7.11 – One-layer encoder using MNIST test data – a bad idea

Close observation of *Figure 7.11* also makes it clear that the scale of the axes varies just slightly; this can be interpreted as the encoder not being able to separate into different regions of the latent space all the digits of MNIST. In practice, please do not use autoencoders with a few layers with a few neurons, unless the dimensionality of the input space is already very low. Autoencoders might be more successful in deep configurations, as shown in this experiment. Learn more about deep autoencoders in the next chapter.

Ethical implications of unsupervised learning

Unsupervised learning, such as what we see happening in the autoencoder we have been exploring so far, is not magical. It is well established and has very rigorous boundaries that are known and pre-defined. It does not have the capability of learning new things outside the limitations given by the data. Remember, unsupervised learning is **passive** learning as explained in the introductory section of this chapter.

However, even the most robust of unsupervised learning models have ethical risks associated with them. One of the major problems is that they create difficulties when dealing with outliers or data that may contain edge cases. For example, say that there is a large amount of data for IT recruitment, which includes years of experience, current salary, and programming languages that a candidate knows. If the data mostly contains data about candidates with the same programming language experience, and only a few know Python, then those candidates that know the Python language might be placed into a boundary or a region that might be difficult to visualize clearly, because the model has learned that since Python is an infrequent language, it may not be relevant in terms of data compression, dimensionality reduction, or data visualization. Furthermore, consider what would happen if 5 years later, you used that same model despite there being newer programming languages that were not known about during training 5 years ago. The model may or may not map such information properly for visualization or data compression applications.

You must be very careful about what data is used to train an autoencoder, and having a variety of cases is important for the reliability of any model. If there is not enough diversity in the data, the autoencoder will be biased toward learning only from one input space. Imagine that you train an autoencoder on images of the 10 MNIST digits from earlier – you would not expect the autoencoder to perform properly on images of cats; that would be a mistake and would likely produce unwanted results. When using, for example, images of people, you must make sure that there is enough variety and diversity in the training data to produce proper training and a robust model that does not perform incorrectly for images of people that were not considered part of the training data.

Summary

This chapter showed that autoencoders are very simple models that can be used to encode and decode data for different purposes, such as data compression, data visualization, and simply finding latent spaces where only important features are preserved. We showed that the number of neurons and the number of layers in the autoencoder are important for the success of the model. Deeper (more layers) and wider (more neurons) traits are often ingredients for good models, even if that leads to slower training times.

At this point, you should know the difference between supervised and unsupervised learning in terms of passive learning. You should also feel comfortable implementing the two basic components of an autoencoder: the encoder and the decoder. Similarly, you should be able to modify the architecture of an autoencoder to fine-tune it to achieve better performance. Taking the example we discussed in this chapter, you should be able to apply an autoencoder to a dimensionality reduction problem or to a data visualization problem. Also, you should be considering the risks and responsibilities associated with unsupervised learning algorithms when it comes to the data used to train them.

Chapter 8, *Deep Autoencoders*, will continue with deeper and wider autoencoder architectures that go beyond the introduction we covered in this chapter. The next chapter will introduce the idea of deep belief networks and the significance of this type of deep unsupervised learning. It will explain such concepts by introducing deep autoencoders and contrasting them with shallow autoencoders. The chapter will also give important advice on optimizing the number of neurons and layers to maximize performance.

Questions and answers

1. **Is overfitting a bad thing for an autoencoder?**

   Actually, no. You want the autoencoder to overfit! That is, you want it to exactly replicate the input data in the output. However, there is a caveat. Your dataset must be really large in comparison to the size of the model; otherwise, the memorization of the data will prevent the model from generalizing to unseen data.

2. **Why did we use two neurons in the encoder's last layer?**

   For visualization purposes only. The two-dimensional latent space produced by the two neurons allows us to easily visualize the data in the latent space. In the next chapter, we will use other configurations that do not necessarily have a two-dimensional latent space.

3. **What is so cool about autoencoders again?**

They are simple neural models that learn without a teacher (unsupervised). They are not biased toward learning specific labels (classes). They learn about the world of data through iterative observations, aiming to learn the most representative and relevant features. They can be used as feature extraction models, but we will discuss more about that in future chapters.

References

- Amari, S. I. (1993). Backpropagation and stochastic gradient descent method. *Neurocomputing*, 5(4-5), 185-196.
- Wang, Y., Yao, H., & Zhao, S. (2016). Auto-encoder based dimensionality reduction. *Neurocomputing*, 184, 232-242.
- Petscharnig, S., Lux, M., & Chatzichristofis, S. (2017). Dimensionality reduction for image features using deep learning and autoencoders. In *Proceedings of the 15th International Workshop on Content-Based Multimedia Indexing* (p. 23). ACM.
- Creswell, A., Arulkumaran, K., & Bharath, A. A. (2017). On denoising autoencoders trained to minimize binary cross-entropy. *arXiv preprint* arXiv:1708.08487.
- Kingma, D. P., & Ba, J. (2014). Adam: A method for stochastic optimization. arXiv preprint arXiv:1412.6980.

8
Deep Autoencoders

This chapter introduces the concept of deep belief networks and the significance of this type of deep unsupervised learning. It explains such concepts by introducing deep autoencoders along with two regularization techniques that can help create robust models. These regularization techniques, batch normalization and dropout, have been known to facilitate the learning of deep models and have been widely adopted. We will demonstrate the power of a deep autoencoder on MNIST and on a much harder dataset known as CIFAR-10, which contains color images.

By the end of this chapter, you will appreciate the benefits of making deep belief networks by observing the ease of modeling and quality of the output that they provide. You will be able to implement your own deep autoencoder and prove to yourself that deeper models are better than shallow models for most tasks. You will become familiar with batch normalization and dropout strategies for optimizing models and maximizing performance.

This chapter is organized as follows:

- Introducing deep belief networks
- Making deep autoencoders
- Exploring latent spaces with deep autoencoders

Introducing deep belief networks

In machine learning, there is a field that is often discussed when talking about **deep learning (DL)**, called **deep belief networks (DBNs)** (Sutskever, I., and Hinton, G. E. (2008)). Generally speaking, this term is used also for a type of machine learning model based on graphs, such as the well-known **Restricted Boltzmann Machine**. However, DBNs are usually regarded as part of the DL family, with deep autoencoders as one of the most notable members of that family.

Deep autoencoders are considered DBNs in the sense that there are latent variables that are only visible to single layers in the forward direction. These layers are usually many in number compared to autoencoders with a single pair of layers. One of the main tenets of DL and DBNs in general is that during the learning process, there is different knowledge represented across different sets of layers. This knowledge representation is learned by *feature learning* without a bias toward a specific class or label. Furthermore, it has been demonstrated that such knowledge appears to be hierarchical. Consider images, for example; usually, layers closer to the input layer learn features that are of low order (that is, edges), while deeper layers learn higher-order features, that is, well-defined shapes, patterns, or objects (Sainath, T. N., et.al. (2012)).

In DBNs, as in most DL models, the interpretability of the feature space can be difficult. Usually, looking at the weights of the first layer can offer information about the features learned and or the looks of the feature maps; however, due to high non-linearities in the deeper layers, interpretability of the feature maps has been a problem and careful considerations need to be made (Wu, K., et.al. (2016)). Nonetheless, despite this, DBNs are showing excellent results in feature learning. In the next few sections, we will cover deeper versions of autoencoders on highly complex datasets. We will be introducing a couple of new types of layers into the mix to demonstrate how deep a model can be.

Making deep autoencoders

An autoencoder can be called *deep* so long as it has more than one pair of layers (an encoding one and a decoding one). Stacking layers on top of each other in an autoencoder is a good strategy to improve its power for feature learning in finding unique latent spaces that can be highly discriminatory in classification or regression applications. However, in `Chapter 7`, *Autoencoders*, we covered how to stack layers onto an autoencoder, and we will do that again, but this time we will use a couple of new types of layers that are beyond the dense layers we have been using. These are the **batch normalization** and **dropout** layers.

There are no neurons in these layers; however, they act as mechanisms that have very specific purposes during the learning process that can lead to more successful outcomes by means of preventing overfitting or reducing numerical instabilities. Let's talk about each of these and then we will continue to experiment with both of these on a couple of important datasets.

Batch normalization

Batch normalization has been an integral part of DL since it was introduced in 2015 (Ioffe, S., and Szegedy, C. (2015)). It has been a major game-changer because it has a couple of nice properties:

- It can prevent the problem known as **vanishing gradient** or **exploding gradient**, which is very common in recurrent networks (Hochreiter, S. (1998)).
- It can lead to faster training by acting as a regularizer to the learning model (Van Laarhoven, T. (2017)).

A summary of these properties and the block image we will use to denote batch normalization are shown in *Figure 8.1*:

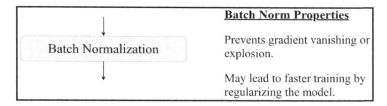

Figure 8.1 – Batch normalization layer main properties

The authors of *batch norm*, as it is often called by data scientists, introduced this simple mechanism to accelerate training or model convergence by providing stability to the calculation of gradients and how they affect the update of the weights across different layers of neurons. This is because they can prevent gradient vanishing or explosion, which is a natural consequence of gradient-based optimization operating on DL models. That is, the deeper the model is, the way the gradient affects the layers and individual units in deeper layers can have the effect of large updates or very small updates that can lead to variable overflow or numerical-zero values.

As illustrated at the top of *Figure 8.2*, batch normalization has the ability to regulate the boundaries of the input data by normalizing the data that goes in so that the output follows a normal distribution. The bottom of the figure illustrates where batch normalization is applied, that is, within the neuron right before sending the output to the next layer:

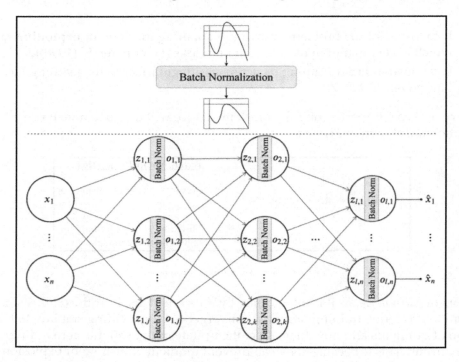

Figure 8.2 – Batch normalization on a simple autoencoder

Consider having a (mini-)batch of data, B, of size n, which allows us to define the following equations. First, the mean of the batch, at layer l, can be calculated as follows:

$$\mu_l = \frac{1}{n} \sum_{i=1}^{n} z_{l,i}$$

The corresponding standard deviation is calculated as follows:

$$\sigma_l^2 = \frac{1}{n} \sum_{i=1}^{n} \left(z_{l,i} - \mu_l \right)^2 .$$

Then, we can normalize every unit i in layer l as follows:

$$\hat{z}_{l,i} = \frac{z_{l,i} - \mu_l}{\sqrt{\sigma_l^2 + \epsilon}}$$

Here, $\epsilon = 0.001$ is a constant introduced merely for numerical stability, but can be altered as needed. Finally, the normalized neural output of every unit i in layer l, $\tilde{z}_{l,i}$, can be calculated before it goes into the activation function as follows:

$$\tilde{z}_{l,i} = \gamma_{l,i} * \hat{z}_{l,i} + \beta_{l,i}$$

Here, γ and β are parameters that need to be learned for each neural unit. After this, any choice of activation function at unit i in layer l will receive the normalized input, $o_{l,i}(\tilde{z}_{l,i})$, and produce an output that is optimally normalized to minimize the loss function.

One easy way to look at the benefits is to imagine the normalization process: although it occurs at each unit, the learning process itself determines the best normalization that is required to maximize the performance of the model (loss minimization). Therefore, it has the capability to nullify the effects of the normalization if it is not necessary for some feature or latent spaces, or it can also use the normalization effects. The important point to remember is that, when batch normalization is used, the learning algorithm will learn to use normalization optimally.

We can use `tensorflow.keras.layers.BatchNormalization` to create a batch normalization layer as follows:

```
from tensorflow.keras.layers import BatchNormalization
...
bn_layer = BatchNormalization()(prev_layer)
...
```

This is obviously done using the functional paradigm. Consider the following example of a dataset corresponding to movie reviews, called *IMDb* (Maas, A. L., et al. (2011)), which we will explain in more detail in Chapter 13, *Recurrent Neural Networks*. In this example, we are simply trying to prove the effects of adding a batch normalization layer as opposed to not having one. Take a close look at the following code fragment:

```
from tensorflow.keras.models import Model
from tensorflow.keras.layers import Dense, Activation, Input
from tensorflow.keras.layers import BatchNormalization
from keras.datasets import imdb
```

```
from keras.preprocessing import sequence
import numpy as np

inpt_dim = 512      #input dimensions
ltnt_dim = 256      #latent dimensions

# -- the explanation for this will come later --
(x_train, y_train), (x_test, y_test) = imdb.load_data()
x_train = sequence.pad_sequences(x_train, maxlen=inpt_dim)
x_test = sequence.pad_sequences(x_test, maxlen=inpt_dim)
# ---------------------------------------------
```

And we proceed with building the model:

```
x_train = x_train.astype('float32')
x_test = x_test.astype('float32')

# model with batch norm
inpt_vec = Input(shape=(inpt_dim,))
el1 = Dense(ltnt_dim)(inpt_vec)          #dense layer followed by
el2 = BatchNormalization()(el1)          #batch norm
encoder = Activation('sigmoid')(el2)
decoder = Dense(inpt_dim, activation='sigmoid')(encoder)
autoencoder = Model(inpt_vec, decoder)

# compile and train model with bn
autoencoder.compile(loss='binary_crossentropy', optimizer='adam')
autoencoder.fit(x_train, x_train, epochs=20, batch_size=64,
                shuffle=True, validation_data=(x_test, x_test))
```

In this code fragment, batch normalization is placed right before the activation layer. This will, therefore, normalize the input to the activation function, which in this case is a `sigmoid`. Similarly, we can build the same model without a batch normalization layer as follows:

```
# model without batch normalization
inpt_vec = Input(shape=(inpt_dim,))
el1 = Dense(ltnt_dim)(inpt_vec) #no batch norm after this
encoder = Activation('sigmoid')(el1)
latent_ncdr = Model(inpt_vec, encoder)
decoder = Dense(inpt_dim, activation='sigmoid')(encoder)
autoencoder = Model(inpt_vec, decoder)

# compile and train model with bn
autoencoder.compile(loss='binary_crossentropy', optimizer='adam')
autoencoder.fit(x_train, x_train, epochs=20, batch_size=64,
                shuffle=True, validation_data=(x_test, x_test))
```

If we train both models and plot their performance as they minimize the loss function, we will notice quickly that having batch normalization pays off, as shown in *Figure 8.3*:

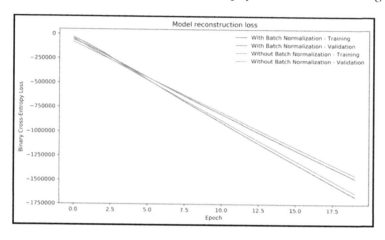

Figure 8.3 – Comparison of learning progress with and without batch normalization

The figure indicates that having batch normalization has the effect of reducing the loss function both in training and in validation sets of data. These results are consistent with many other experiments that you can try on your own! However, as we said before, it is not necessarily a guarantee that this will happen all the time. This is a relatively modern technique that has proven to function properly so far, but this does not mean that it works for everything that we know of.

We highly recommend that in all your models, you first try to solve the problem with a model that has no batch normalization, and then once you feel comfortable with the performance you have, come back and use batch normalization to see if you can get a slight boost in **performance** and **training speed**.

Let's say that you tried batch normalization and you were rewarded with a boost in performance, speed, or both, but you have now discovered that your model was overfitting all this time. Fear not! There is another interesting and novel technique, known as **dropout**. This can offer a model an alternative to reduce overfitting, as we will discuss in the following section.

Dropout

Dropout is a technique published in 2014 that became popular shortly after that year (Srivastava, N., Hinton, G., et.al. (2014)). It came as an alternative to combat overfitting, which is one of its major properties, and can be summarized as follows:

- It can reduce the chances of overfitting.
- It can lead to better generalization.
- It can reduce the effect of dominating neurons.
- It can promote neuron diversity.
- It can promote better neuron teamwork.

The block image we will use for dropout, along with its main properties, is shown in *Figure 8.4*:

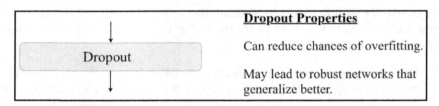

Figure 8.4 – Dropout layer properties

A dropout strategy works because it enables the network to search for an alternative hypothesis to solve the problem by disconnecting a particular number of neurons that represent certain hypotheses (or models) within a network itself. One easy way to look at this strategy is by thinking about the following: Imagine that you have a number of experts that are tasked with passing judgment on whether an image contains a cat or a chair. There might be a large number of experts that moderately believe that there is a chair in the image, but it only takes one expert to be particularly loud and fully convinced that there is a cat to persuade the decision-maker into listening to this particularly loud expert and ignoring the rest. In this analogy, experts are neurons.

There might be some neurons that are particularly convinced (sometimes incorrectly, due to overfitting on irrelevant features) of a certain fact about the information, and their output values are particularly high compared to the rest of the neurons in that layer, so much so that the deeper layers learn to listen more to that particular layer, thus perpetuating overfitting on deeper layers. **Dropout** is the mechanism that will select a number of neurons in a layer and completely disconnect them from the layer so that no input flows into those neurons nor is there output coming out of those neurons, as shown in *Figure 8.5*:

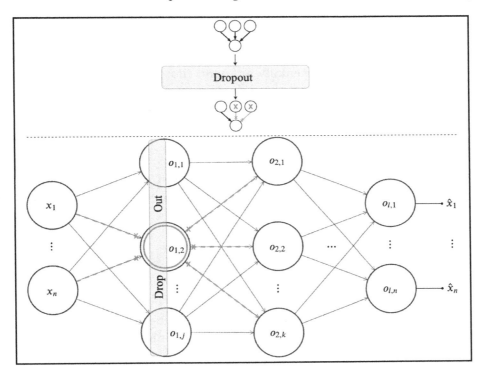

Figure 8.5 – Dropout mechanism over the first hidden layer. Dropout here disconnects one neuron from the layer

In the preceding diagram, the first hidden layer has a dropout rate of one third. This means that, completely at random, one third of the neurons will be disconnected. *Figure 8.5* shows an example of when the second neuron in the first hidden layer is disconnected: no input from the input layer goes in, and no output comes out of it. The model is completely oblivious to its existence; for all practical purposes, this is a different neural network!

However, the neurons that are disconnected are only disconnected for one training step: their weights are unchanged for one training step, while all other weights are updated. This has a few interesting implications:

- Due to the random selection of neurons, those *troublemakers* that tend to dominate (overfit) on particular features are bound to be selected out at some point, and the rest of the neurons will learn to process feature spaces without those *troublemakers*. This leads to the prevention and reduction of overfitting, while promoting collaboration among diverse neurons that are experts in different things.
- Due to the constant ignorance/disconnection of neurons, the network has the potential of being fundamentally different – it is almost as if we are training multiple neural networks in every single step without actually having to make many different models. It all happens because of dropout.

It is usually recommended to use dropout in deeper networks to ameliorate the traditional problem of overfitting that is common in DL.

To show the difference in performance when using dropout, we will use the exact same dataset as in the previous section, but we will add an additional layer in the autoencoder as follows:

```
from tensorflow.keras.layers import Dropout
...
# encoder with dropout
inpt_vec = Input(shape=(inpt_dim,))
el1 = Dense(inpt_dim/2)(inpt_vec)
```

In this code, the dropout rate is 10%, meaning that 10% of the neurons in the dense layer el4 are disconnected multiple times at random during training.

```
el2 = Activation('relu')(el1)
el3 = Dropout(0.1)(el2)
el4 = Dense(ltnt_dim)(el3)
encoder = Activation('relu')(el4)
```

The decoder is left exactly the same as before, and the baseline model simply does not contain a dropout layer:

```
# without dropout
inpt_vec = Input(shape=(inpt_dim,))
el1 = Dense(inpt_dim/2)(inpt_vec)
el2 = Activation('relu')(el1)
el3 = Dense(ltnt_dim)(el2)
encoder = Activation('relu')(el3)
```

If we choose `'adagrad'` and we perform training over 100 epochs and compare the performance results, we can obtain the performance shown in *Figure 8.6*:

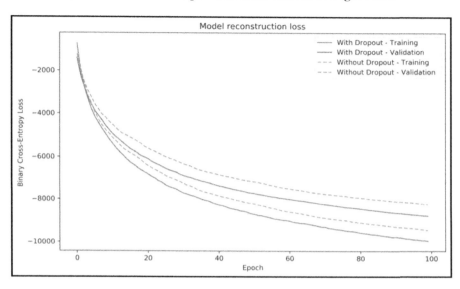

Figure 8.6 – Autoencoder reconstruction loss comparing models with dropout and without

Here is the full code:

```
from tensorflow.keras.models import Model
from tensorflow.keras.layers import Dense, Activation, Input
from tensorflow.keras.layers import Dropout
from keras.datasets import imdb
from keras.preprocessing import sequence
import numpy as np
import matplotlib.pyplot as plt

inpt_dim = 512
ltnt_dim = 128

(x_train, y_train), (x_test, y_test) = imdb.load_data()
x_train = sequence.pad_sequences(x_train, maxlen=inpt_dim)
x_test = sequence.pad_sequences(x_test, maxlen=inpt_dim)

x_train = x_train.astype('float32')
x_test = x_test.astype('float32')
```

Then we define the model with dropout like so:

```
# with dropout
inpt_vec = Input(shape=(inpt_dim,))
el1 = Dense(inpt_dim/2)(inpt_vec)
el2 = Activation('relu')(el1)
el3 = Dropout(0.1)(el2)
el4 = Dense(ltnt_dim)(el3)
encoder = Activation('relu')(el4)

# model that takes input and encodes it into the latent space
latent_ncdr = Model(inpt_vec, encoder)

decoder = Dense(inpt_dim, activation='relu') (encoder)

# model that takes input, encodes it, and decodes it
autoencoder = Model(inpt_vec, decoder)
```

Then we compile it, train it, store the training history, and clear the variables to re-use them as follows:

```
autoencoder.compile(loss='binary_crossentropy', optimizer='adagrad')

hist = autoencoder.fit(x_train, x_train, epochs=100, batch_size=64,
                       shuffle=True, validation_data=(x_test, x_test))

bn_loss = hist.history['loss']
bn_val_loss = hist.history['val_loss']

del autoencoder
del hist
```

And then we do the same for a model without dropout:

```
# now without dropout
inpt_vec = Input(shape=(inpt_dim,))
el1 = Dense(inpt_dim/2)(inpt_vec)
el2 = Activation('relu')(el1)
el3 = Dense(ltnt_dim)(el2)
encoder = Activation('relu')(el3)

# model that takes input and encodes it into the latent space
latent_ncdr = Model(inpt_vec, encoder)

decoder = Dense(inpt_dim, activation='relu') (encoder)

# model that takes input, encodes it, and decodes it
autoencoder = Model(inpt_vec, decoder)
```

```
autoencoder.compile(loss='binary_crossentropy', optimizer='adagrad')

hist = autoencoder.fit(x_train, x_train, epochs=100, batch_size=64,
                       shuffle=True, validation_data=(x_test, x_test))
```

Next we gather the training data and plot it like so:

```
loss = hist.history['loss']
val_loss = hist.history['val_loss']

fig = plt.figure(figsize=(10,6))
plt.plot(bn_loss, color='#785ef0')
plt.plot(bn_val_loss, color='#dc267f')
plt.plot(loss, '--', color='#648fff')
plt.plot(val_loss, '--', color='#fe6100')
plt.title('Model reconstruction loss')
plt.ylabel('Binary Cross-Entropy Loss')
plt.xlabel('Epoch')
plt.legend(['With Drop Out - Training',
            'With Drop Out - Validation',
            'Without Drop Out - Training',
            'Without Drop Out - Validation'], loc='upper right')
plt.show()
```

From *Figure 8.6* we can see that the performance of the model with dropout is superior than without. This suggests that training without dropout has a higher chance of overfitting, the reason being that the learning curve is worse on the validation set when dropout is not used.

As mentioned earlier, the `adagrad` optimizer has been chosen for this particular task. We made this decision because it is important for you to learn more optimizers, one at a time. Adagrad is an adaptive algorithm; it performs updates with respect to the frequency of features (Duchi, J., et al. (2011)). If features occur frequently, the updates are small, while larger updates are done for features that are out of the ordinary.

It is recommended to use Adagrad when the **dataset is sparse**. For example, in word embedding cases such as the one in this example, frequent words will cause small updates, while rare words will require larger updates.

Finally, it is important to mention that `Dropout(rate)` belongs to the `tf.keras.layers.Dropout` class. The rate that is taken as a parameter corresponds to the rate at which neurons will be disconnected at random at every single training step for the particular layer on which dropout is used.

 It is recommended that you use a dropout rate between **0.1 and 0.5** to achieve significant changes to your network's performance. And it is recommended to use dropout **only in deep networks**. However, these are empirical findings and your own experimentation is necessary.

Now that we have explained these two relatively new concepts, dropout and batch normalization, we will create a deep autoencoder network that is relatively simple and yet powerful in finding latent representations that are not biased toward particular labels.

Exploring latent spaces with deep autoencoders

Latent spaces, as we defined them in Chapter 7, *Autoencoders*, are very important in DL because they can lead to powerful decision-making systems that are based on assumed rich latent representations. And, once again, what makes the latent spaces produced by autoencoders (and other unsupervised models) rich in their representations is that they are not biased toward particular labels.

In Chapter 7, *Autoencoders*, we explored the MNIST dataset, which is a standard dataset in DL, and showed that we can easily find very good latent representations with as few as four dense layers in the encoder and eight layers for the entire autoencoder model. In the next section, we will take on a much more difficult dataset known as CIFAR-10, and then we will come back to explore the latent representation of the IMDB dataset, which we have already explored briefly in the previous sections of this chapter.

CIFAR-10

In 2009, the *Canadian Institute for Advanced Research (CIFAR)* released a very large collection of images that can be used to train DL models to recognize a variety of objects. The one we will use in this example is widely known as CIFAR-10, since it has only 10 classes and a total of 60,000 images; *Figure 8.7* depicts samples of each class:

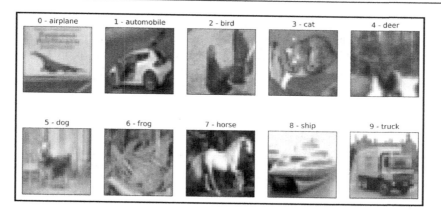

Figure 8.7 – Sample images from the CIFAR-10 dataset. The number indicates the numeric value assigned to each class for convenience

Every image in the dataset is 32 by 32 pixels using 3 dimensions to keep track of the color details. As can be seen from the figure, these small images contain other objects beyond those labeled, such as text, background, structures, landscapes, and other partially occluded objects, while preserving the main object of interest in the foreground. This makes it more challenging than MNIST, where the background is always black, images are grayscale, and there is only one number in every image. If you have never worked in computer vision applications, you may not know that it is exponentially more complicated to deal with CIFAR-10 compared to MNIST. Therefore, our models need to be more robust and deep in comparison to MNIST ones.

In TensorFlow and Keras, we can easily load and prepare our dataset with the following code:

```
import numpy as np
from tensorflow.keras.datasets import cifar10

(x_train, y_train), (x_test, y_test) = cifar10.load_data()
x_train = x_train.astype('float32') / 255.
x_test = x_test.astype('float32') / 255.
x_train = x_train.reshape((len(x_train), np.prod(x_train.shape[1:])))
x_test = x_test.reshape((len(x_test), np.prod(x_test.shape[1:])))

print('x_train shape is:', x_train.shape)
print('x_test shape is:', x_test.shape)
```

The preceding code outputs the following:

```
x_train shape is: (50000, 3072)
x_test shape is: (10000, 3072)
```

This says that we have one-sixth of the dataset (~16%) separated for test purposes, while the rest is used for training. The 3,072 dimensions come from the number of pixels and channels: $32 \times 32 \times 3 = 3072$. The preceding code also normalizes the data from the range [0, 255] down to [0.0, 1.0] in floating-point numbers.

To move on with our example, we will propose a deep autoencoder with the architecture shown in *Figure 8.8*, which will take a 3,072-dimensional input and will encode it down to 64 dimensions:

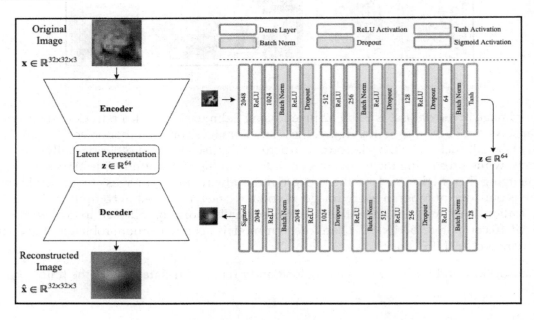

Figure 8.8 – Architecture of a deep autoencoder on the CIFAR-10 dataset

This architecture uses 17 layers in the encoder and 15 layers in the decoder. Dense layers in the diagram have the number of neurons written in their corresponding block. As can be seen, this model implements a series of strategic batch normalization and dropout strategies throughout the process of encoding the input data. In this example, all dropout layers have a 20% dropout rate.

If we train the model for 200 epochs using the standard `adam` optimizer and the standard binary cross-entropy loss, we could obtain the training performance shown in *Figure 8.9*:

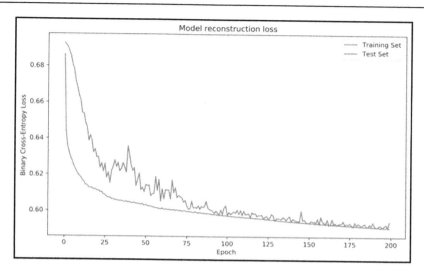

Figure 8.9 – Reconstruction of the loss of the deep autoencoder model on CIFAR-10

Here is the full code:

```
from tensorflow import keras
from tensorflow.keras.datasets import cifar10
from tensorflow.keras.models import Model
from tensorflow.keras.layers import Dense, Dropout, Activation, Input
from tensorflow.keras.layers import BatchNormalization
import matplotlib.pyplot as plt
import numpy as np

inpt_dim = 32*32*3
ltnt_dim = 64

# The data, split between train and test sets:
(x_train, y_train), (x_test, y_test) = cifar10.load_data()
x_train = x_train.astype('float32') / 255.
x_test = x_test.astype('float32') / 255.
x_train = x_train.reshape((len(x_train), np.prod(x_train.shape[1:])))
x_test = x_test.reshape((len(x_test), np.prod(x_test.shape[1:])))
print('x_train shape:', x_train.shape)
print('x_test shape:', x_test.shape)
```

We define the model as follows:

```
inpt_vec = Input(shape=(inpt_dim,))
el1 = Dense(2048)(inpt_vec)
el2 = Activation('relu')(el1)
el3 = Dense(1024)(el2)
```

```
el4 = BatchNormalization()(el3)
el5 = Activation('relu')(el4)
el6 = Dropout(0.2)(el5)

el7 = Dense(512)(el6)
el8 = Activation('relu')(el7)
el9 = Dense(256)(el8)
el10 = BatchNormalization()(el9)
el11 = Activation('relu')(el10)
el12 = Dropout(0.2)(el11)

el13 = Dense(128)(el12)
el14 = Activation('relu')(el13)
el15 = Dropout(0.2)(el14)
el16 = Dense(ltnt_dim)(el15)
el17 = BatchNormalization()(el16)
encoder = Activation('tanh')(el17)

# model that takes input and encodes it into the latent space
latent_ncdr = Model(inpt_vec, encoder)
```

Next we define the decoder portion of the model like this:

```
dl1 = Dense(128)(encoder)
dl2 = BatchNormalization()(dl1)
dl3 = Activation('relu')(dl2)

dl4 = Dropout(0.2)(dl3)
dl5 = Dense(256)(dl4)
dl6 = Activation('relu')(dl5)
dl7 = Dense(512)(dl6)
dl8 = BatchNormalization()(dl7)
dl9 = Activation('relu')(dl8)

dl10 = Dropout(0.2)(dl9)
dl11 = Dense(1024)(dl10)
dl12 = Activation('relu')(dl11)
dl13 = Dense(2048)(dl12)
dl14 = BatchNormalization()(dl13)
dl15 = Activation('relu')(dl14)
decoder = Dense(inpt_dim, activation='sigmoid') (dl15)
```

We put it together in an autoencoder model, compile it and train it like so:

```
# model that takes input, encodes it, and decodes it
autoencoder = Model(inpt_vec, decoder)

# setup RMSprop optimizer
```

```
opt = keras.optimizers.RMSprop(learning_rate=0.0001, decay=1e-6, )

autoencoder.compile(loss='binary_crossentropy', optimizer=opt)

hist = autoencoder.fit(x_train, x_train, epochs=200, batch_size=10000,
                       shuffle=True, validation_data=(x_test, x_test))

# and now se visualize the results
fig = plt.figure(figsize=(10,6))
plt.plot(hist.history['loss'], color='#785ef0')
plt.plot(hist.history['val_loss'], color='#dc267f')
plt.title('Model reconstruction loss')
plt.ylabel('Binary Cross-Entropy Loss')
plt.xlabel('Epoch')
plt.legend(['Training Set', 'Test Set'], loc='upper right')
plt.show()
```

The model performance shown in *Figure 8.9* converges nicely and loss decays both on the training and test sets, which implies that the model is not overfitting and continues to adjust the weights properly over time. To visualize the model's performance on unseen data (the test set), we can simply pick samples from the test set at random, such as the ones in *Figure 8.10*, which produce the output shown in *Figure 8.11*:

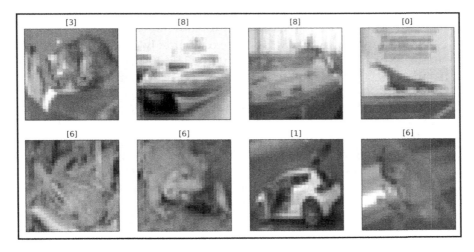

Figure 8.10 – Sample input from the test set of CIFAR-10

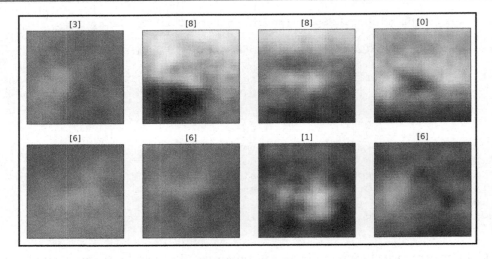

Figure 8.11 – Sample output (reconstructions) from the samples given in Figure 8.10

You can see from *Figure 8.11* that the reconstructions correctly address the color spectrum of the input data. However, it is clear that the problem is much harder in reconstruction terms than MNIST. Shapes are blurry although they seem to be in the correct spatial position. A level of detail is evidently missing in the reconstructions. We can make the autoencoder deeper, or train for longer, but the problem might not be properly solved. We can justify this performance with the fact that we deliberately chose to find a latent representation of size 64, which is smaller than a tiny 5 by 5 image: $5 \times 5 \times 3 = 75$. If you think about it and reflect on this, then it is clear that it is nearly impossible, as 3,072 to 64 represents a 2.08% compression!

A solution to this would be not to make the model larger, but to acknowledge that the latent representation size might not be large enough to capture relevant details of the input to have a good reconstruction. The current model might be too aggressive in reducing the dimensionality of the feature space. If we use UMAP to visualize the 64-dimensional latent vectors in 2 dimensions, we will obtain the plot shown in *Figure 8.12*:

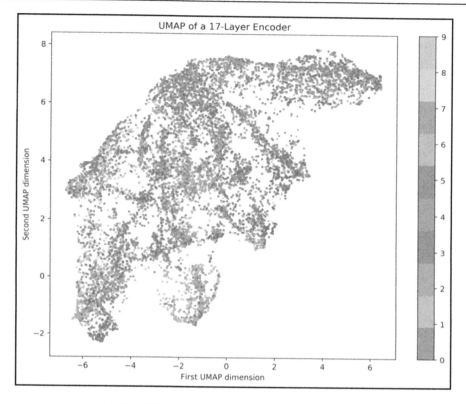

Figure 8.12 – UMAP two-dimensional representation of the latent vectors in the test set

We have not spoken about UMAP before, but we will briefly state that this a ground-breaking data visualization tool that has been proposed recently and is starting to gain attention (McInnes, L., et al. (2018)). In our case, we simply used UMAP to visualize the data distribution since we are not using the autoencoder to encode all the way down to two dimensions. *Figure 8.12* indicates that the distribution of the classes is not sufficiently clearly defined so as to enable us to observe separation or well-defined clusters. This confirms that the deep autoencoder has not captured sufficient information for class separation; however, there are still clearly defined groups in some parts of the latent space, such as the clusters on the bottom middle and left, one of which is associated with a group of airplane images, for example. This **deep belief network** has acquired knowledge about the input space well enough to make out some different aspects of the input; for example, it knows that airplanes are quite different from frogs, or at least that they might appear in different conditions, that is, a frog will appear against green backgrounds while an airplane is likely to have blue skies in the background.

Convolutional neural networks (CNNs) are a much better alternative for most computer vision and image analysis problems such as this one. We will get there in due time in Chapter 12, *Convolutional Neural Networks*. Be patient for now as we gently introduce different models one by one. You will see how we can make a convolutional autoencoder that can achieve much better performance than an autoencoder that uses fully connected layers. For now, we will continue with autoencoders for a little longer.

The model introduced in *Figure 8.8* can be produced using the functional approach; the encoder can be defined as follows:

```python
from tensorflow.keras.models import Model
from tensorflow.keras.layers import Dense, Dropout, Activation, Input
from tensorflow.keras.layers import BatchNormalization, MaxPooling1D
import numpy as np

inpt_dim = 32*32*3
ltnt_dim = 64

inpt_vec = Input(shape=(inpt_dim,))
el1 = Dense(2048)(inpt_vec)
el2 = Activation('relu')(el1)
el3 = Dense(1024)(el2)
el4 = BatchNormalization()(el3)
el5 = Activation('relu')(el4)
el6 = Dropout(0.2)(el5)

el7 = Dense(512)(el6)
el8 = Activation('relu')(el7)
el9 = Dense(256)(el8)
el10 = BatchNormalization()(el9)
el11 = Activation('relu')(el10)
el12 = Dropout(0.2)(el11)

el13 = Dense(128)(el12)
el14 = Activation('relu')(el13)
el15 = Dropout(0.2)(el14)
el16 = Dense(ltnt_dim)(el15)
el17 = BatchNormalization()(el16)
encoder = Activation('tanh')(el17)

# model that takes input and encodes it into the latent space
latent_ncdr = Model(inpt_vec, encoder)
```

Notice that all the dropout layers have a 20% rate every time. The 17 layers go from mapping an input of `inpt_dim=3072` dimensions down to `ltnt_dim = 64` dimensions. The last activation function of the encoder is the hyperbolic tangent `tanh`, which provides an output in the range [-1,1]; this choice is only made for convenience in visualizing the latent space.

Next, the definition of the decoder is as follows:

```
dl1 = Dense(128)(encoder)
dl2 = BatchNormalization()(dl1)
dl3 = Activation('relu')(dl2)

dl4 = Dropout(0.2)(dl3)
dl5 = Dense(256)(dl4)
dl6 = Activation('relu')(dl5)
dl7 = Dense(512)(dl6)
dl8 = BatchNormalization()(dl7)
dl9 = Activation('relu')(dl8)

dl10 = Dropout(0.2)(dl9)
dl11 = Dense(1024)(dl10)
dl12 = Activation('relu')(dl11)
dl13 = Dense(2048)(dl12)
dl14 = BatchNormalization()(dl13)
dl15 = Activation('relu')(dl14)
decoder = Dense(inpt_dim, activation='sigmoid') (dl15)

# model that takes input, encodes it, and decodes it
autoencoder = Model(inpt_vec, decoder)
```

The last layer of the decoder has a `sigmoid` activation function that maps back to the input space range, that is, [0.0, 1.0]. Finally, we can train the `autoencoder` model as previously defined using the `binary_crossentropy` loss and `adam` optimizer for 200 epochs like so:

```
autoencoder.compile(loss='binary_crossentropy', optimizer='adam')

hist = autoencoder.fit(x_train, x_train, epochs=200, batch_size=5000,
                       shuffle=True, validation_data=(x_test, x_test))
```

The results have been previously shown in *Figures 8.9* to *8.11*. However, it is interesting to revisit MNIST, but this time using a deep autoencoder, as we will discuss next.

MNIST

The `MNIST` dataset is a good example of a dataset that is less complex than CIFAR-10, and that can be approached with a deep autoencoder. Previously, in `Chapter 7`, *Autoencoders*, we discussed shallow autoencoders and showed that adding layers was beneficial. In this section, we go a step further to show that a deep autoencoder with dropout and batch normalization layers can perform better at producing rich latent representations. *Figure 8.13* shows the proposed architecture:

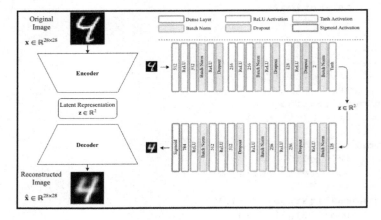

Figure 8.13 – Deep autoencoder for MNIST

The number of layers and the sequence of layers is the same as in *Figure 8.8*; however, the number of neurons in the dense layers and the latent representation dimensions have changed. The compression rate is from 784 to 2, or 0.25%:

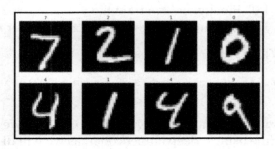

Figure 8.14 – MNIST original sample digits of the test set

And yet, the reconstructions are very good, as shown in *Figure 8.14* and in *Figure 8.15*:

Figure 8.15 – Reconstructed MNIST digits from the original test set shown in *Figure 8.14*

The reconstructions shown in the figure show a level of detail that is very good, although it seems blurry around the edges. The general shape of the digits seems to be captured well by the model. The corresponding latent representations of the test set are shown in *Figure 8.16*:

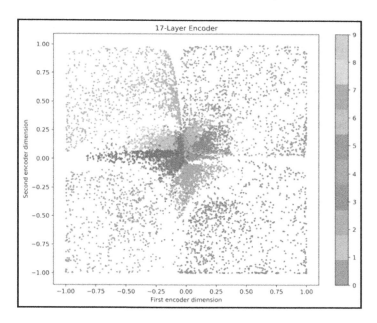

Figure 8.16 – Latent representation of MNIST digits in the test set, partially shown in *Figure 8.14*

From the preceding plot, we can see that there are well-defined clusters; however, it is important to point out that the autoencoder knows nothing about labels and that these clusters have been learned from the data alone. This is the power of autoencoders at their best. If the encoder model is taken apart and re-trained with labels, the model is likely to perform even better. However, for now, we will leave it here and continue with a type of *generative* model in Chapter 9, *Variational Autoencoders*, which comes next.

Summary

This intermediate chapter showed the power of deep autoencoders when combined with regularization strategies such as dropout and batch normalization. We implemented an autoencoder that has more than 30 layers! That's *deep*! We saw that in difficult problems a deep autoencoder can offer an unbiased latent representation of highly complex data, as most deep belief networks do. We looked at how dropout can reduce the risk of overfitting by ignoring (disconnecting) a fraction of the neurons at random in every learning step. Furthermore, we learned that batch normalization can offer stability to the learning algorithm by gradually adjusting the response of some neurons so that activation functions and other connected neurons don't saturate or overflow numerically.

At this point, you should feel confident applying batch normalization and dropout strategies in a deep autoencoder model. You should be able to create your own deep autoencoders and apply them to different tasks where a rich latent representation is required for data visualization purposes, data compression or dimensionality reduction problems, and other types of data embeddings where a low-dimensional representation is required.

Chapter 9, *Variational Autoencoders*, will continue with autoencoders but from a *generative modeling* perspective. Generative models have the ability to generate data by sampling a probability density function, which is quite interesting. We will specifically discuss the variational autoencoder model as a better alternative to a deep autoencoder in the presence of noisy data.

Questions and answers

1. **Which regularization strategy discussed in this chapter alleviates overfitting in deep models?**

   Dropout.

2. **Does adding a batch normalization layer make the learning algorithm have to learn more parameters?**

   Actually, no. For every layer in which dropout is used, there will be only two parameters for every neuron to learn: σ, μ. If you do the math, the addition of new parameters is rather small.

3. **What other deep belief networks are out there?**

   Restricted Boltzmann machines, for example, are another very popular example of deep belief networks. Chapter 10, *Restricted Boltzmann Machines*, will cover these in more detail.

4. **How come deep autoencoders perform better on MNIST than on CIFAR-10?**

   Actually, we do not have an objective way of saying that deep autoencoders are better on these datasets. We are biased in thinking about it in terms of clustering and data labels. Our bias in thinking about the latent representations in *Figure 8.12* and *Figure 8.16* in terms of labels is precluding us from thinking about other possibilities. Consider the following for CIFAR-10: what if the autoencoder is learning to represent data according to textures? Or color palettes? Or geometric properties? Answering these questions is key to understanding what is going on inside the autoencoder and why it is learning to represent the data in the way it does, but requires more advanced skills and time. In summary, we don't know for sure whether it is underperforming or not until we answer these questions; otherwise, if we put on our lenses of classes, groups, and labels, then it might just seem that way.

References

- Sutskever, I., & Hinton, G. E. (2008). Deep, narrow sigmoid belief networks are universal approximators. *Neural computation*, 20(11), 2629-2636.
- Sainath, T. N., Kingsbury, B., & Ramabhadran, B. (2012, March). Auto-encoder bottleneck features using deep belief networks. In 2012 *IEEE international conference on acoustics, speech and signal processing (ICASSP)* (pp. 4153-4156). IEEE.
- Wu, K., & Magdon-Ismail, M. (2016). Node-by-node greedy deep learning for interpretable features. *arXiv preprint* arXiv:1602.06183.
- Ioffe, S., & Szegedy, C. (2015, June). Batch Normalization: Accelerating Deep Network Training by Reducing Internal Covariate Shift. In *International Conference on Machine Learning (ICML)* (pp. 448-456).
- Srivastava, N., Hinton, G., Krizhevsky, A., Sutskever, I., & Salakhutdinov, R. (2014). Dropout: a simple way to prevent neural networks from overfitting. *The journal of machine learning research*, 15(1), 1929-1958.
- Duchi, J., Hazan, E., & Singer, Y. (2011). Adaptive subgradient methods for online learning and stochastic optimization. *Journal of machine learning research*, 12(Jul), 2121-2159.
- McInnes, L., Healy, J., & Umap, J. M. (2018). Uniform manifold approximation and projection for dimension reduction. *arXiv preprint* arXiv:1802.03426.
- Maas, A. L., Daly, R. E., Pham, P. T., Huang, D., Ng, A. Y., & Potts, C. (2011, June). Learning word vectors for sentiment analysis. In *Proceedings of the 49th annual meeting of the association for computational linguistics*: *Human language technologies*-volume 1 (pp. 142-150). Association for Computational Linguistics.
- Hochreiter, S. (1998). The vanishing gradient problem during learning recurrent neural nets and problem solutions. International Journal of Uncertainty, *Fuzziness and Knowledge-Based Systems*, 6(02), 107-116.
- Van Laarhoven, T. (2017). L2 regularization versus batch and weight normalization. *arXiv preprint* arXiv:1706.05350.

Variational Autoencoders 9

Autoencoders can be really powerful in finding rich latent spaces. They are almost magical, right? What if we told you that **variational autoencoders** (**VAEs**) are even more impressive? Well, they are. They have inherited all the nice things about traditional autoencoders and added the ability to generate data from a parametric distribution.

In this chapter, we will introduce the philosophy behind generative models in the unsupervised deep learning field and their importance in the production of new data. We will present the VAE as a better alternative to a deep autoencoder. At the end of this chapter, you will know where VAEs come from and what their purpose is. You will be able to see the difference between deep and shallow VAE models and you will be able to appreciate the generative property of VAEs.

The chapter is organized as follows:

- Introducing deep generative models
- Examining the VAE model
- Comparing deep and shallow VAEs on MNIST
- Thinking about the ethical implications of generative models

Introducing deep generative models

Deep learning has very interesting contributions to the general machine learning community, particularly when it comes to deep discriminative and generative models. We are familiar with what a discriminative model is—for example, a **Multilayer Perceptron (MLP)** is one. In a discriminative model, we are tasked with guessing, predicting, or approximating a desired target, y, given input data x. In statistical theory terms, we are modeling the conditional probability density function, $p(y|x)$. On the other hand, by a generative model, this is what most people mean:

A model that can generate data x that follows a particular distribution based on an input or stimulus z.

In deep learning, we can build a neural network that can model this generative process very well. In statistical terms, the neural model approximates the conditional probability density function, $p(x|z)$. While there are several generative models today, in this book, we will talk about three in particular.

First, we will talk about VAEs, which are discussed in the next section. Second, Chapter 10, *Restricted Boltzmann Machines*, will introduce a graphical approach and its properties (Salakhutdinov, R., et al. (2007)). The last approach will be covered in Chapter 14, *Generative Adversarial Networks*. These networks are changing the way we think about model robustness and data generation (Goodfellow, I., *et al.* (2014)).

Examining the VAE model

The VAE is a particular type of autoencoder (Kingma, D. P., & Welling, M. (2013)). It learns specific statistical properties of the dataset derived from a Bayesian approach. First, let's define $p_\theta(\mathbf{z})$ as the prior probability density function of a random latent variable, $\mathbf{z} \in \mathbb{R}^d$. Then, we can describe a conditional probability density function, $p_\theta(\mathbf{x}|\mathbf{z})$, which can be interpreted as a model that can produce data—say, $\mathbf{X} = \{\mathbf{x}_i\}_{i=1}^N$. It follows that we can approximate the posterior probability density function in terms of the conditional and prior distributions, as follows:

$$p_\theta(\mathbf{z}|\mathbf{x}) \propto p_\theta(\mathbf{x}|\mathbf{z})\, p_\theta \mathbf{z}$$

It turns out that an exact posterior is intractable, but this problem can be solved, approximately, by making a few assumptions and using an interesting idea to compute gradients. To begin with, the prior can be assumed to follow an isotropic Gaussian distribution, $p_\theta(\mathbf{z}) \sim \mathcal{N}(0, \mathbf{I}\sigma^2)$. We can also assume that the conditional distribution, $p_\theta(\mathbf{x}|\mathbf{z})$, can be parametrized and modeled using a neural network; that is, given a latent vector $\mathbf{z}$, we use a neural network to *generate* $\mathbf{x}$. The weights of the network, in this case, are denoted as θ, and the network would be the equivalent of the *decoder* network. The choice of the parametric distribution could be Gaussian, for outputs where $\mathbf{x}$ can take on a wide variety of values, or Bernoulli, if the output $\mathbf{x}$ is likely to be binary (or Boolean) values. Next, we must go back again to another neural network to approximate the posterior, using $q_\phi(\mathbf{z}|\mathbf{x})$ with separate parameters, ϕ. This network can be interpreted as the *encoder* network that takes $\mathbf{x}$ as input and generates the latent variable $\mathbf{z}$.

Under this assumption, we can define a loss function as follows:

$$L = \underbrace{-D_{KL}\left(q_\phi\left(\mathbf{z}|\mathbf{x}_i\right)\|p_\theta(\mathbf{z})\right)}_{\text{encoder}} + \underbrace{\mathbb{E}_{q_\phi(\mathbf{z}|\mathbf{x}_i)}\left[\log p_\theta\left(\mathbf{x}_i|\mathbf{z}\right)\right]}_{\text{decoder}}$$

The full derivation can be followed in Kingma, D. P., & Welling, M. (2013). However, in short, we can say that in the first term, $D_{KL}(\cdot)$ is the Kullback–Leibler divergence function, which aims to measure how different the distribution of the prior is, $p_\theta(\mathbf{z})$, with respect to the distribution of the posterior, $q_\phi(\mathbf{z}|\mathbf{x})$. This happens in the *encoder*, and we want to make sure that the prior and posterior of $\mathbf{z}$ are a close match. The second term is related to the decoder network, which aims to minimize the reconstruction loss based on the negative log likelihood of the conditional distribution, $p_\theta(\mathbf{x}|\mathbf{z})$, with respect to the expectation of the posterior, $q_\phi(\mathbf{z}|\mathbf{x})$.

One last trick to make the VAE learn through gradient descent is to use an idea called **re-parameterization**. This trick is necessary because it is impossible to encode one sample, $\mathbf{x}$, to approximate an isotropic Gaussian with 0 mean and some variance, and draw a sample $\mathbf{z}$ from that distribution, pause there, and then go on to decode that and calculate the gradients, and then go back and make updates. The re-parametrization trick is simply a method for generating samples from $q_\phi(\mathbf{z}|\mathbf{x})$, while at the same time, it allows gradient calculation. If we say that $\mathbf{z} \sim q_\phi(\mathbf{z}|\mathbf{x})$, we can express the random variable $\mathbf{z}$ in terms of an auxiliary variable, ϵ, with marginal probability density function, $p(\epsilon)$, such that, $\mathbf{z} = g_\phi(\epsilon, \mathbf{x})$ and $g_\phi(\cdot)$ is a function parameterized by ϕ and returns a vector. This allows gradient calculations on parameters θ (generator or decoder) and updates on both ϕ and θ using any available gradient descent method.

 The *tilde* sign (~) in the $\mathbf{z} \sim q_\phi(\mathbf{z}|\mathbf{x})$ equation can be interpreted as *follows the distribution of*. Thus, the equation can be read as $\mathbf{z}$ follows the distribution of the posterior, $q_\phi(\mathbf{z}|\mathbf{x})$.

Figure 9.1 depicts the VAE architecture, explicitly showing the pieces involved in the *bottlenecks* and how the pieces of the network are interpreted:

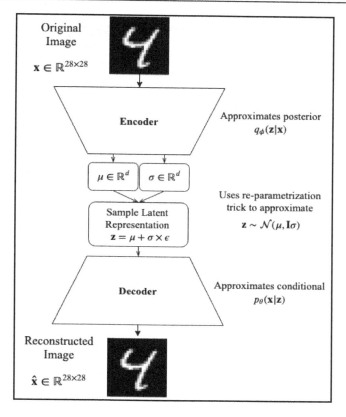

Figure 9.1 – VAE architecture

The preceding figure shows that in an ideal VAE, the parameters of the distributions are learned precisely and perfectly to achieve exact reconstruction. However, this is just an illustration, and in practice, perfect reconstruction can be difficult to achieve.

 Bottlenecks are the latent representations or parameters that are found in neural networks that go from layers with large numbers of neural units to layers with a decreasing number of neural units. These bottlenecks are known to produce interesting feature spaces (Zhang, Y., *et al.* (2014)).

Now, let's prepare to make our first VAE piece by piece. We will begin by describing the dataset we will use.

The heart disease dataset revisited

In `Chapter 3`, *Preparing Data*, we described in full the properties of a dataset called the **Cleveland Heart Disease** dataset. A screenshot of two columns from this dataset is depicted in *Figure 9.2*. Here, we will revisit this dataset with the purpose of reducing the original 13 dimensions of the data down to only two dimensions. Not only that, but we will also try to produce new data from the generator—that is, the decoder:

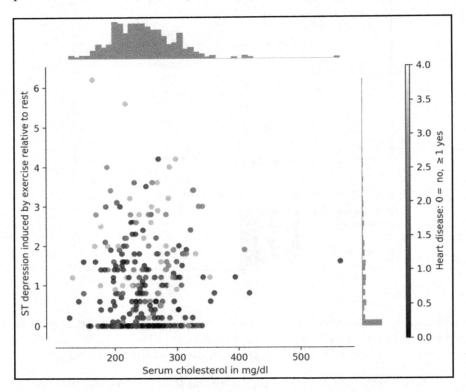

Figure 9.2 – The Cleveland Heart Disease dataset samples on two columns

Our attempts to perform dimensionality reduction can be easily justified by looking at *Figures 3.8* and *3.9* in `Chapter 3`, *Preparing Data*, and noticing that the data can possibly be processed so as to see whether a neural network can cause the data associated with hearts with no disease to cluster separately from the rest. Similarly, we can justify the generation of new data given that the dataset itself only contains 303 samples.

To download the data, we can simply run the following code:

```
#download data
!wget
https://archive.ics.uci.edu/ml/machine-learning-databases/heart-disease/pro
cessed.cleveland.data
```

Then, to load the data into a data frame and separate the training data and the targets, we can execute the following code:

```
import pandas as pd
df = pd.read_csv('processed.cleveland.data', header=None)
# this next line deals with possible numeric errors
df = df.apply(pd.to_numeric, errors='coerce').dropna()
X = df[[0, 1, 2, 3, 4, 5, 6, 7, 8, 9, 10, 11, 12]].values
y = df[13].values
```

The next thing we will need to do is to code the re-parametrization trick so that we can sample random noise during training.

The re-parametrization trick and sampling

Remember that the re-parametrization trick aims to sample from $p(\epsilon)$ instead of $q_\phi(\mathbf{z}|\mathbf{x})$. Also, recall the distribution $p(\epsilon) \sim \mathcal{N}(\mathbf{0}, \mathbf{I})$. This will allow us to make the learning algorithm learn the parameters of $q_\phi(\mathbf{z}|\mathbf{x})$—that is, μ, σ—and we simply produce a sample from $\mathbf{z} = \mu + \sigma \times \epsilon$.

To achieve this, we can generate the following method:

```
from tensorflow.keras import backend as K

def sampling(z_params):
  z_mean, z_log_var = z_params
  batch = K.shape(z_mean)[0]
  dims = K.int_shape(z_mean)[1]
  epsilon = K.random_normal(shape=(batch, dims))
  return z_mean + K.exp(0.5 * z_log_var) * epsilon
```

The `sampling()` method receives the mean and log variance of $q_\phi(\mathbf{z}|\mathbf{x})$ (which are to be learned), and returns a vector that is sampled from this parametrized distribution; ϵ is just random noise from a Gaussian (`random_normal`) distribution with 0 mean and unit variance. To make this method fully compatible with mini-batch training, the samples are generated according to the size of the mini-batch.

Learning the posterior's parameters in the encoder

The posterior distribution, $q_\phi(\mathbf{z}|\mathbf{x})$, is intractable by itself, but since we are using the re-parametrization trick, we can actually perform sampling based on ϵ. We will now make a simple encoder to learn these parameters.

For numerical stability, we need to scale the input to make it have 0 mean and unit variance. For this, we can invoke the methodology learned in Chapter 3, *Preparing Data*:

```
from sklearn.preprocessing import StandardScaler
scaler = StandardScaler()
scaler.fit(X)
x_train = scaler.transform(X)
original_dim = x_train.shape[1]
```

The `x_train` matrix contains the scaled training data. The following variables will also be useful for designing the encoder of the VAE:

```
input_shape = (original_dim, )
intermediate_dim = 13
batch_size = 18 # comes from ceil(sqrt(x_train.shape[0]))
latent_dim = 2 # useful for visualization
epochs = 500
```

These variables are straightforward, except that the batch size is in terms of the square root of the number of samples. This is an empirical value found to be a good start, but on larger datasets, it is not guaranteed to be the best.

Next, we can build the encoder portion, as follows:

```
from tensorflow.keras.layers import Lambda, Input, Dense, Dropout,
BatchNormalization
from tensorflow.keras.models import Model

inputs = Input(shape=input_shape)
bn = BatchNormalization()(inputs)
dp = Dropout(0.2)(bn)
```

```
x = Dense(intermediate_dim, activation='sigmoid')(dp)
x = Dropout(0.2)(x)
z_mean = Dense(latent_dim)(x)
z_log_var = Dense(latent_dim)(x)
z_params = [z_mean, z_log_var]
z = Lambda(sampling, output_shape=(latent_dim,))(z_params)
encoder = Model(inputs, [z_mean, z_log_var, z])
```

This approach of encoder utilizes the `Lambda` class, which is part of the `tensorflow.keras.layers` collection. This allows us to use the previously defined `sampling()` method (or any arbitrary expression, really) as a layer object. *Figure 9.3* illustrates the architecture of the full VAE, including the layers of the encoder described in the preceding code block:

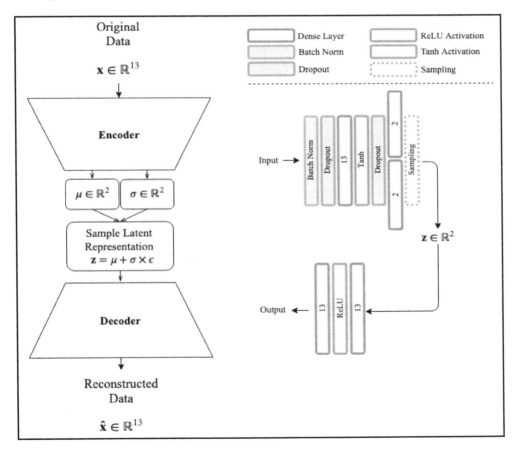

Figure 9.3 – VAE architecture for the Cleveland Heart Disease dataset

The encoder uses batch normalization, followed by **dropout** at the input layers, followed by a dense layer that has **Tanh activation** and **dropout**. From the **dropout**, two dense layers are in charge of modeling the parameters of the distribution of the latent variable, and a sample is drawn from this parametrized distribution. The decoder network is discussed next.

Modeling the decoder

The decoder portion of the VAE is very much standard with respect to what you already know about an autoencoder. The decoder takes the latent variable, which in the VAE was produced by a parametric distribution, and then it should reconstruct the input exactly. The decoder can be specified as follows:

```
latent_inputs = Input(shape=(latent_dim,))
x = Dense(intermediate_dim, activation='relu')(latent_inputs)
r_outputs = Dense(original_dim)(x)     # reconstruction outputs
decoder = Model(latent_inputs, r_outputs)
```

In the preceding code, we simply connect two dense layers—the first contains a ReLU activation, while the second has linear activations in order to map back to the input space. Finally, we can define the complete VAE in terms of inputs and outputs as defined in the encoder and decoder:

```
outputs = decoder(encoder(inputs)[2])   # it is index 2 since we want z
vae = Model(inputs, outputs)
```

The VAE model is completed as described here and depicted in *Figure 9.3*. The next steps leading to the training of this model include the definition of a loss function, which we will discuss next.

Minimizing the loss

We explained earlier that the loss function needs to be in terms of the encoder and decoder; this is the equation we discussed:

$$L = \underbrace{-D_{KL}\left(q_\phi\left(\mathbf{z}|\mathbf{x}_i\right)\|p_\theta(\mathbf{z})\right)}_{\text{encoder}} + \underbrace{\mathbb{E}_{q_\phi(\mathbf{z}|\mathbf{x}_i)}\left[\log p_\theta\left(\mathbf{x}_i|\mathbf{z}\right)\right]}_{\text{decoder}}$$

If we want to code this loss, we will need to code it in terms of something more practical. Applying all the previous assumptions made on the problem, including the re-parametrization trick, allows us to rewrite an approximation of the loss in simpler terms, as follows:

$$L \simeq \underbrace{\frac{1}{2} \sum_{j=1}^{J} (1 + log(\sigma_j^2) - (\mu_j)^2 - (\sigma_j)^2}_{encoder} + \underbrace{\frac{1}{L} \sum_{l=1}^{L} log\, p_\theta(\mathbf{x}|\mathbf{z}_l)}_{decoder}$$

This is for all samples of $\mathbf{x}$ where $\mathbf{z}_l = \mu + \sigma\epsilon$ and $\epsilon \sim \mathcal{N}(\mathbf{0}, \mathbf{I})$. Furthermore, the decoder loss portion can be approximated using any of your favorite reconstruction losses—for example, the **mean squared error** (**MSE**) loss or the binary cross-entropy loss. It has been proven that minimizing any of these losses will also minimize the posterior.

We can define the reconstruction loss in terms of the MSE, as follows:

```
from tensorflow.keras.losses import mse
r_loss = mse(inputs, outputs)
```

Alternatively, we could do so with the binary cross-entropy loss, like so:

```
from tensorflow.keras.losses import binary_crossentropy
r_loss = binary_crossentropy(inputs, outputs)
```

One additional thing we could do, which is optional, is to monitor how important the reconstruction loss is in comparison to the KL-divergence loss (the term related to the encoder). One typical thing to do is to make the reconstruction loss be multiplied by either the latent dimension or by the input dimension. This effectively makes the loss larger by that factor. If we do the latter, we can penalize the reconstruction loss, as follows:

```
r_loss = original_dim * r_loss
```

The KL-divergence loss for the encoder term can now be expressed in terms of the mean and variance, as follows:

```
kl_loss = 1 + z_log_var - K.square(z_mean) - K.exp(z_log_var)
kl_loss = 0.5 * K.sum(kl_loss, axis=-1)
```

Therefore, we can simply add the overall loss to the model, which becomes the following:

```
vae_loss = K.mean(r_loss + kl_loss)
vae.add_loss(vae_loss)
```

With this, we are good to go ahead and compile the model and train it, as explained next.

Training a VAE

The finishing touch is to compile the VAE model, which will put all the pieces together. During the compilation, we will choose an optimizer (the gradient descent method). In this case, we will choose *Adam* (Kingma, D. P., *et al.* (2014)).

 Fun fact: the creator of the VAE is the same person who soon after created Adam. His name is **Diederik P. Kingma** and he is currently a research scientist at Google Brain.

To compile the model and choose the optimizer, we do the following:

```
vae.compile(optimizer='adam')
```

Finally, we train with training data for 500 epochs, using a batch size of 18, like so:

```
hist = vae.fit(x_train, epochs=epochs,
               batch_size=batch_size,
               validation_data=(x_train, None))
```

Notice that we are using the training set as the validation set. This is not recommended in most settings, but here, it works because the chance of selecting identical mini-batches for training and validation is very low. Furthermore, it would usually be considered cheating to do that; however, the latent representation used in the reconstruction does not directly come from the input; rather, it comes from a distribution similar to the input data. To demonstrate that the training and validation sets yield different results, we plot the training progress across epochs, as shown in *Figure 9.4*:

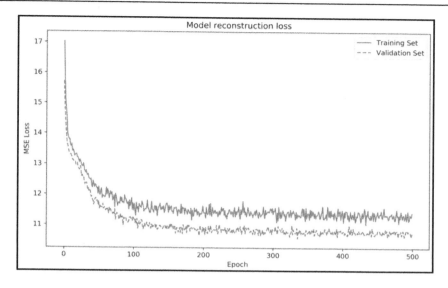

Figure 9.4 – VAE training performance across epochs

The preceding figure not only indicates that the model converges quickly, but it also shows that the model does not overfit on the input data. This is a nice property to have, usually.

Figure 9.4 can be produced with the following code:

```
import matplotlib.pyplot as plt

fig = plt.figure(figsize=(10,6))
plt.plot(hist.history['loss'], color='#785ef0')
plt.plot(hist.history['val_loss'], '--', color='#dc267f')
plt.title('Model reconstruction loss')
plt.ylabel('MSE Loss')
plt.xlabel('Epoch')
plt.legend(['Training Set', 'Validation Set'], loc='upper right')
plt.show()
```

However, note that the results may vary due to the unsupervised nature of the VAE.

Next, if we take a look at the latent representation that is produced by sampling from a random distribution using the parameters that were learned during training, we can see what the data looks like. *Figure 9.5* depicts the latent representations obtained:

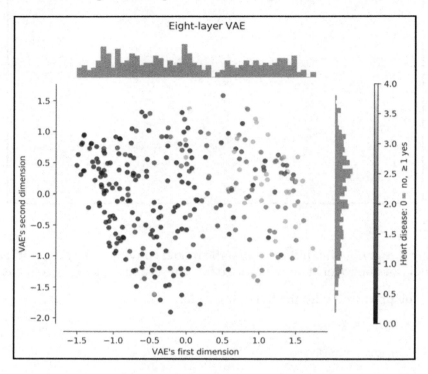

Figure 9.5 – VAE's sampled latent representation in two dimensions

The figure clearly suggests that the data corresponding to no indication of heart disease is clustered on the left quadrants, while the samples corresponding to heart disease are clustered on the right quadrant of the latent space. The histogram shown on the top of the figure suggests the presence of two well-defined clusters. This is great! Also, recall that the VAE does not know anything about labels: we can't stress this enough! Compare *Figure 9.5* here with *Figure 3.9* in Chapter 3, *Preparing Data*, and you will notice that the performance of the VAE is superior to KPCA. Furthermore, compare this figure with *Figure 3.8* in Chapter 3, *Preparing Data*, and notice that the performance of the VAE is comparable (if not better) than **Linear Discriminant Analysis (LDA)**, which uses label information to produce low-dimensional representations. In other words, LDA cheats a little bit.

One of the most interesting properties of the VAE is that we can generate data; let's go ahead and see how this is done.

Generating data from the VAE

Since the VAE learns the parameters of a parametric distribution over the latent space, which is sampled to reconstruct the input data back, we can use those parameters to draw more samples and reconstruct them. The idea is to generate data for whatever purposes we have in mind.

Let's start by encoding the original dataset and see how close the reconstruction is to the original. Then, generating data should be straightforward. To encode the input data into the latent space and decode it, we do the following:

```
encdd = encoder.predict(x_train)
x_hat = decoder.predict(encdd[0])
```

Recall that x_train is x and x_hat is the reconstruction, $\hat{x}$. Notice that we are using encdd[0] as the input for the decoder. The reason for this is that the encoder yields a list of three vectors, [z_mean, z_log_var, z]. Therefore, to use the 0 element in the list is to refer to the mean of the distribution corresponding to the samples. In fact, encdd[0][10] would yield a two-dimensional vector corresponding to the mean parameter of the distribution that can produce the 10th sample in the dataset—that is, x_train[10]. If you think about it, the mean could be the best latent representation that we can find since it would be the most likely to reconstruct the input in the decoder.

With this in mind, we can take a look at how good the reconstruction is by running something like this:

```
import numpy as np
print(np.around(scaler.inverse_transform(x_train[0]), decimals=1))
print(np.around(scaler.inverse_transform(x_hat[0]), decimals=1))
```

This gives the following output:

```
[ 63.0   1.0   1.0  145.0  233.0   1.0   2.0  150.0   0.0   2.3   3.0   0.0   6.0 ]
[ 61.2   0.5   3.1  144.1  265.1   0.5   1.4  146.3   0.2   1.4   1.8   1.2   4.8 ]
```

> If the output shows scientific notation that is difficult to read, try disabling it temporarily like this:
> ```
> import numpy as np
> np.set_printoptions(suppress=True)
> print(np.around(scaler.inverse_transform(x_train[0]),
> decimals=1))
> print(np.around(scaler.inverse_transform(x_hat[0]),
> decimals=1))
> np.set_printoptions(suppress=False)
> ```

In this example, we are focusing on the first data point in the training set—that is, x_train[0]—in the top row; its reconstruction is the bottom row. Close examination reveals that there are differences between both; however, these differences might be relatively small in terms of the MSE.

Another important aspect to point out here is that the data needs to be scaled back to its original input space since it was scaled prior to its use in training the model. Fortunately, the StandardScaler() class has an inverse_transform() method that can help in mapping any reconstruction back to the range of values of each dimension in input space.

In order to generate more data at will, we can define a method to do so. The following method produces random noise, uniformly, in the range [-2, +2], which comes from an examination of *Figure 9.5*, which shows the range of the latent space to be within such range:

```
def generate_samples(N = 10, latent_dim = 2):
    noise = np.random.uniform(-2.0, 2.0, (N,latent_dim))
    gen = decoder.predict(noise)
    return gen
```

This function would need to be adjusted according to the range of values in the latent space; also, it can be adjusted by looking at the distribution of the data in the latent space. For example, if the latent space seems to be normally distributed, then a normal distribution can be used like this: noise = np.random.normal(0.0, 1.0, (N,latent_dim)), assuming 0 mean and unit variance.

We can call the function to generate *fake* data by doing the following:

```
gen = generate_samples(10, latent_dim)
print(np.around(scaler.inverse_transform(gen), decimals=1))
```

This gives the following output:

```
[[ 43.0  0.7  2.7  122.2  223.8  0.0  0.4  172.2  0.0  0.3  1.2  0.1  3.6]
 [ 57.4  0.9  3.9  133.1  247.6  0.1  1.2  129.0  0.8  2.1  2.0  1.2  6.4]
 [ 60.8  0.7  3.5  142.5  265.7  0.3  1.4  136.4  0.5  1.9  2.0  1.4  5.6]
 [ 59.3  0.6  3.2  137.2  261.4  0.2  1.2  146.2  0.3  1.2  1.7  0.9  4.7]
 [ 51.5  0.9  3.2  125.1  229.9  0.1  0.7  149.5  0.4  0.9  1.6  0.4  5.1]
 [ 60.5  0.5  3.2  139.9  268.4  0.3  1.3  146.1  0.3  1.2  1.7  1.0  4.7]
 [ 48.6  0.5  2.6  126.8  243.6  0.1  0.7  167.3  0.0  0.2  1.1  0.1  3.0]
 [ 43.7  0.8  2.9  121.2  219.7  0.0  0.5  163.8  0.1  0.5  1.4  0.1  4.4]
 [ 54.0  0.3  2.5  135.1  264.2  0.2  1.0  163.4  0.0  0.3  1.1  0.3  2.7]
 [ 52.5  1.0  3.6  123.3  227.8  0.0  0.8  137.7  0.7  1.6  1.8  0.6  6.2]]
```

Recall that this data is generated from random noise. You can see how this is a major breakthrough in the deep learning community. You can use this data to augment your dataset and produce as many samples as you wish. We can look at the quality of the generated samples and decide for ourselves whether the quality is good enough for our purposes.

Now, granted that since you and I may not be medical doctors specializing in heart disease, we might not be qualified to determine with certainty that the data generated makes sense; but if we did this correctly, it generally does make sense. To make this clear, the next section uses MNIST images to prove that the generated samples are good since we can all make a visual assessment of numeral images.

Comparing a deep and shallow VAE on MNIST

Comparing shallow and deep models is part of the experimentation process that leads to finding the best models. In this comparison over MNIST images, we will be implementing the architecture shown in *Figure 9.6* as the shallow model, while the deep model architecture is shown in *Figure 9.7*:

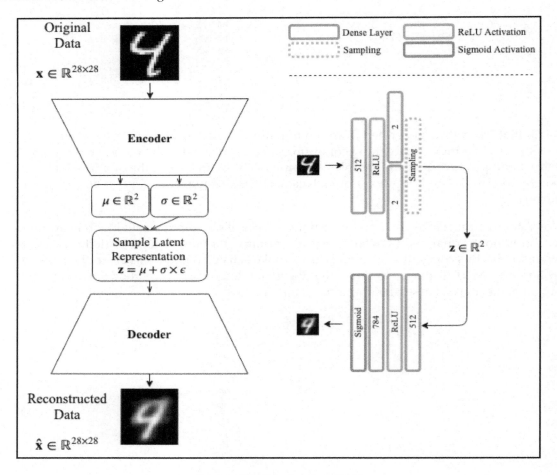

Figure 9.6 – VAE shallow architecture over MNIST

As you can appreciate, both models are substantially different when it comes to the number of layers involved in each one. The quality of the reconstruction will be different as a consequence:

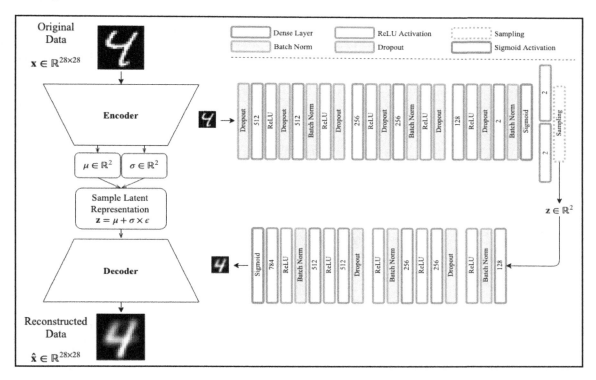

Figure 9.7 – VAE deep architecture over MNIST

These models will be trained using a small number of epochs for the shallow VAE and a much larger number of epochs for the deeper model.

The code to reproduce the shallow encoder can be easily inferred from the example used in the Cleveland Heart Disease dataset; however, the code for the deep VAE will be discussed in the sections that follow.

Shallow VAE

One of the first things that we can use to compare the VAE is its learned representations. *Figure 9.8* depicts the latent space projections of the training set:

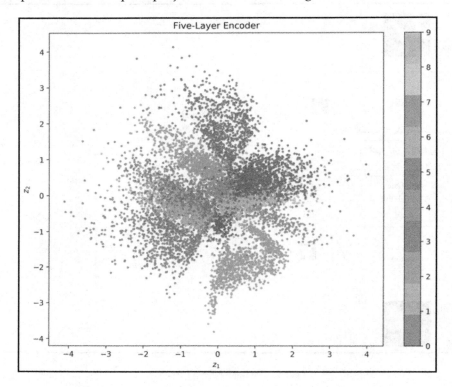

Figure 9.8 – Shallow VAE latent space projections of the training dataset

From the preceding figure, we can observe clusters of data points that are spreading out from the center coordinates. What we would like to see are well-defined clusters that are ideally separated enough so as to facilitate classification, for example. In this case, we see a little bit of overlap among certain groups, particularly number **4** and number **9**, which makes a lot of sense.

The next thing to look into is the reconstruction ability of the models. *Figure 9.9* shows a sample of the input, and *Figure 9.10* shows the corresponding reconstructions after the model has been trained:

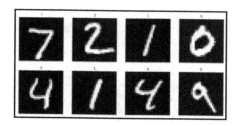

Figure 9.9 – Sample input to the VAE

The expectation for the shallow model is to perform in a manner that is directly related to the size of the model:

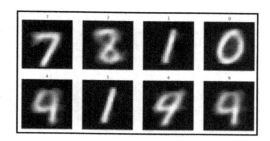

Figure 9.10 – Shallow VAE reconstructions with respect to the input in Figure 9.9

Clearly, there seem to be some issues with the reconstruction of the number 2 and number 8, which is confirmed by observing the great deal of overlap shown between these two numerals in *Figure 9.8*.

Another thing we can do is to visualize the data generated by the VAE if we draw numbers from the range of the latent space. *Figure 9.11* shows the latent space as it changes across the two dimensions:

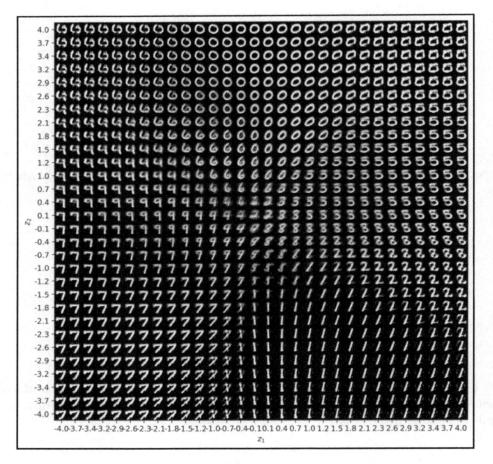

Figure 9.11 – Shallow VAE latent space exploration in the range [-4,4] in both dimensions

What we find really interesting in *Figure 9.11* is that we can see how numerals are transformed into others progressively as the latent space is traversed. If we take the center line going from top to bottom, we can see how we can go from the number 0 to the number 6, then to the number 2, then to the number 8, down to the number 1. We could do the same by tracing a diagonal path, or other directions. Making this type of visualization also allows us to see some artifacts that were not seen in the training dataset that could cause potential problems if we generate data without care.

To see whether the deeper model is any better than this, we will implement it in the next section.

Deep VAE

Figure 9.7 depicts a deep VAE architecture that can be implemented in parts—first the encoder, and then the decoder.

Encoder

The encoder can be implemented using the functional paradigm, as follows:

```
from tensorflow.keras.layers import Lambda, Input, Dense, Dropout
from tensorflow.keras.layers import Activation, BatchNormalization
from tensorflow.keras.models import Model

inpt_dim = 28*28
ltnt_dim = 2

inpt_vec = Input(shape=(inpt_dim,))
```

Here, `inpt_dim` corresponds to the 784 dimensions of a 28*28 MNIST image. Continuing with the rest, we have the following:

```
el1 = Dropout(0.1)(inpt_vec)
el2 = Dense(512)(el1)
el3 = Activation('relu')(el2)
el4 = Dropout(0.1)(el3)
el5 = Dense(512)(el4)
el6 = BatchNormalization()(el5)
el7 = Activation('relu')(el6)
el8 = Dropout(0.1)(el7)

el9 = Dense(256)(el8)
el10 = Activation('relu')(el9)
el11 = Dropout(0.1)(el10)
el12 = Dense(256)(el11)
el13 = BatchNormalization()(el12)
el14 = Activation('relu')(el13)
el15 = Dropout(0.1)(el14)

el16 = Dense(128)(el15)
el17 = Activation('relu')(el16)
el18 = Dropout(0.1)(el17)
el19 = Dense(ltnt_dim)(el18)
```

```
el20 = BatchNormalization()(el19)
el21 = Activation('sigmoid')(el20)

z_mean = Dense(ltnt_dim)(el21)
z_log_var = Dense(ltnt_dim)(el21)
z = Lambda(sampling)([z_mean, z_log_var])
encoder = Model(inpt_vec, [z_mean, z_log_var, z])
```

Note that the encoder model uses dropout layers with a 10% dropout rate. The rest of the layers are all things we have seen before, including batch normalization. The only new thing here is the `Lambda` function, which is exactly as defined earlier in this chapter.

Next, we will define the decoder.

Decoder

The decoder is a few layers shorter than the encoder. This choice of layers is simply to show that as long as the number of dense layers is almost equivalent in the encoder and decoder, some of the other layers can be omitted as part of the experiment to look for performance boosts.

This is the design of the decoder:

```
ltnt_vec = Input(shape=(ltnt_dim,))
dl1 = Dense(128)(ltnt_vec)
dl2 = BatchNormalization()(dl1)
dl3 = Activation('relu')(dl2)

dl4 = Dropout(0.1)(dl3)
dl5 = Dense(256)(dl4)
dl6 = Activation('relu')(dl5)
dl7 = Dense(256)(dl6)
dl8 = BatchNormalization()(dl7)
dl9 = Activation('relu')(dl8)

dl10 = Dropout(0.1)(dl9)
dl11 = Dense(512)(dl10)
dl12 = Activation('relu')(dl11)
dl13 = Dense(512)(dl12)
dl14 = BatchNormalization()(dl13)
dl15 = Activation('relu')(dl14)
dl16 = Dense(inpt_dim, activation='sigmoid')(dl15)

decoder = Model(ltnt_vec, dl16)
```

Once again, there is nothing new here that we have not seen before. It is all layers after more layers. Then, we can put all this together in the model, as follows:

```
outputs = decoder(encoder(inpt_vec)[2])
vae = Model(inpt_vec, outputs)
```

That is it! After this, we can compile the model, choose our optimizer, and train the model in the exact same way that we did in earlier sections.

If we want to visualize the latent space of the deep VAE in order to compare it with *Figure 9.8*, we could look at the space shown in *Figure 9.12*:

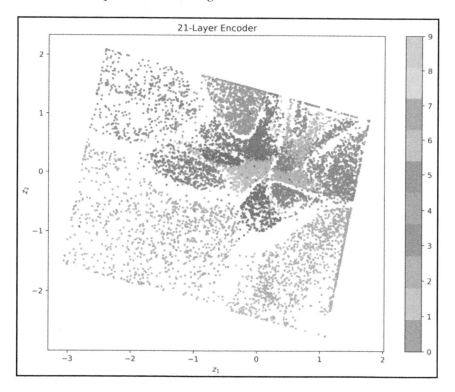

Figure 9.12 – Deep VAE latent space projections of the training dataset

As you can see, the latent space appears to be different in the way the geometry of it looks. This is most likely the effect of activation functions delimiting the latent space range for specific manifolds. One of the most interesting things to observe is the separation of groups of samples even if there still exists some overlap–for example, with numerals **9** and **4**. However, the overlaps in this case are less severe in comparison to *Figure 9.8*.

Figure 9.13 shows the reconstruction of the same input shown in *Figure 9.9*, but now using the deeper VAE:

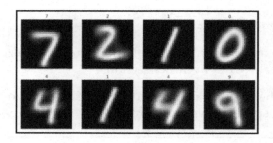

Figure 9.13 – Deep VAE reconstructions with respect to the input in Figure 9.9. Compare to Figure 9.10

Clearly, the reconstruction is much more better and robust in comparison to the shallow VAE. To make things even clearer, we can also explore the generator by traversing the latent space by producing random noise in the same range as the latent space. This is shown in *Figure 9.14*:

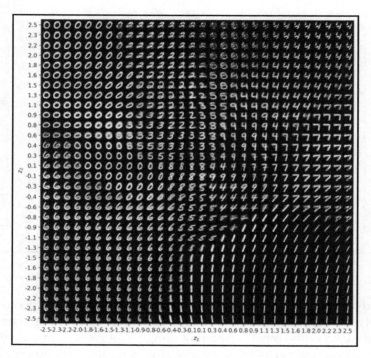

Figure 9.14 – Deep VAE latent space exploration in the range [-4,4] in both dimensions. Compare to Figure 9.11

The latent space of the deeper VAE clearly seems to be richer in diversity and more interesting from a visual perspective. If we pick the rightmost line and traverse the space from bottom to top, we can see how numeral 1 becomes a 7 and then a 4 with smaller and progressive changes.

Denoising VAEs

VAEs are also known to be good in image denoising applications (Im, D. I. J., *et al.* (2017)). This property is achieved by injecting noise as part of the learning process. To find out more about this, you can search the web for denoising VAEs and you will find resources on that particular topic. We just want you to be aware of them and know that they exist if you need them.

Thinking about the ethical implications of generative models

Generative models are one of the most exciting topics in deep learning nowadays. But with great power comes great responsibility. We can use the power of generative models for many good things, such as the following:

- Augmenting your dataset to make it more complete
- Training your model with unseen data to make it more stable
- Finding adversarial examples to re-train your model and make it more robust
- Creating new images of things that look like other things, such as images of art or vehicles
- Creating new sequences of sounds that sound like other sounds, such as people speaking or birds singing
- Generating new security codes for data encryption

We can go on as our imagination permits. What we must always remember is that these generative models, if not modeled properly, can lead to many problems, such as bias, causing trustworthiness issues on your models. It can be easy to use these models to generate a fake sequence of audio of a person saying something that they did not really say, or producing an image of the face of a person doing something they did not really do, or with a body that does not belong to the face.

Some of the most notable wrongdoings include deepfakes. It is not worth our time going through the ways of achieving such a thing, but suffice to say, our generative models should not be used for malicious purposes. Soon enough, international law will be established to punish those who commit crimes through malicious generative modeling.

But until international laws are set and countries adopt new policies, you must follow the best practices when developing your models:

- Test your models for the most common types of bias: historical, societal, algorithmic, and so on (Mehrabi, N., *et al.* (2019)).
- Train your models using reasonable training and test sets.
- Be mindful of data preprocessing techniques; see `Chapter 3`, *Preparing Data*, for more details.
- Make sure your models produce output that always respects the dignity and worth of all human beings.
- Have your model architectures validated by a peer.

With this in mind, go on and be as responsible and creative as you can with this new tool that you now have at your disposal: VAEs.

Summary

This advanced chapter has shown you one of the most interesting and simpler models that is able to generate data from a learned distribution using the configuration of an autoencoder and by applying variational Bayes principles leading to a VAE. We looked at the pieces of the model itself and explained them in terms of input data from the Cleveland dataset. Then, we generated data from the learned parametric distribution, showing that VAEs can easily be used for this purpose. To prove the robustness of VAEs on shallow and deep configurations, we implemented a model over the MNIST dataset. The experiment proved that deeper architectures produce well-defined regions of data distributions as opposed to fuzzy groups in shallow architectures; however, both shallow and deep models are particularly good for the task of learning representations.

By this point, you should feel confident in identifying the pieces of a VAE and being able to tell the main differences between a traditional autoencoder and a VAE in terms of its motivation, architecture, and capabilities. You should appreciate the generative power of VAEs and feel ready to implement them. After reading this chapter, you should be able to code both basic and deep VAE models and be able to use them for dimensionality reduction and data visualization, as well as to generate data while being mindful of the potential risks. Finally, you should now be familiarized with the usage of the `Lambda` functions for general-purpose use in TensorFlow and Keras.

If you have liked learning about unsupervised models so far, stay with me and continue to `Chapter 10`, *Restricted Boltzmann Machines*, which will present a unique model that is rooted in what is known as graphical models. Graphical models use graph theory mixed with learning theory to perform machine learning. An interesting aspect of restricted Boltzmann machines is that the algorithm can go forward and backward during learning to satisfy connection constraints. Stay tuned!

Questions and answers

1. **How is data generation possible from random noise?**

   Since the VAE learns the parameters of a parametric random distribution, we can simply use those parameters to sample from such a distribution. Since random noise usually follows a normal distribution with certain parameters, we can say that we are sampling random noise. The nice thing is that the decoder knows what to do with the noise that follows a particular distribution.

2. **What is the advantage of having a deeper VAE?**

   It is hard to say what the advantage is (if there is any) without having the data or knowing the application. For the Cleveland Heart Disease dataset, for example, a deeper VAE might not be necessary; while for MNIST or CIFAR, a moderately large model might be beneficial. It depends.

3. **Is there a way to make changes to the loss function?**

   Of course, you can change the loss function, but be careful to preserve the principles on which it is constructed. Let's say that a year from now we found a simpler way of minimizing the negative log likelihood function, then we could (and should) come back and edit the loss to adopt the new ideas.

References

- Kingma, D. P., & Welling, M. (2013). Auto-encoding variational Bayes. *arXiv preprint* arXiv:1312.6114.
- Salakhutdinov, R., Mnih, A., & Hinton, G. (2007, June). Restricted Boltzmann machines for collaborative filtering. In *Proceedings of the 24th International Conference on Machine Learning* (pp. 791-798).
- Goodfellow, I., Pouget-Abadie, J., Mirza, M., Xu, B., Warde-Farley, D., Ozair, S., Courville, A. and Bengio, Y. (2014). Generative adversarial nets. In *Advances in Neural Information Processing Systems* (pp. 2672-2680).
- Zhang, Y., Chuangsuwanich, E., & Glass, J. (2014, May). Extracting deep neural network bottleneck features using low-rank matrix factorization. In *2014 IEEE International Conference on Acoustics, Speech and Signal Processing (ICASSP)* (pp. 185-189). IEEE.
- Kingma, D. P., & Ba, J. (2014). Adam: A method for stochastic optimization. *arXiv preprint* arXiv:1412.6980.
- Mehrabi, N., Morstatter, F., Saxena, N., Lerman, K., & Galstyan, A. (2019). A survey on bias and fairness in machine learning. *arXiv preprint* arXiv:1908.09635.
- Im, D. I. J., Ahn, S., Memisevic, R., & Bengio, Y. (2017, February). Denoising criterion for variational auto-encoding framework. In *Thirty-First AAAI Conference on Artificial Intelligence*.

Restricted Boltzmann Machines

10

Together, we have seen the power of unsupervised learning and hopefully convinced ourselves that it can be applied to different problems. We will finish the topic of unsupervised learning with an exciting approach known as **Restricted Boltzmann Machines (RBMs)**. When we do not care about having a large number of layers, we can use RBMs to learn from the data and find ways to satisfy an energy function that will produce a model that is robust at representing input data.

This chapter complements Chapter 8, *Deep Autoencoders*, by introducing the backward-forward nature of RBMs, while contrasting it with the forward-only nature of **Autoencoders (AEs)**. This chapter compares RBMs and AEs in the problem of dimensionality reduction, using MNIST as the case study. Once you are finished with this chapter, you should be able to use an RBM using scikit-learn and implement a solution using a Bernoulli RBM. You will be able to perform a visual comparison of the latent spaces of an RBM and an AE, and also visualize the learned weights for an inspection of the inner workings of an RBM and an AE.

This chapter is organized as follows:

- Introduction to RBMs
- Learning data representations with RBMs
- Comparing RBMs and AEs

Introduction to RBMs

RBMs are unsupervised models that can be used in different applications that require rich latent representations. They are usually used in a pipeline with a classification model with the purpose of extracting features from the data. They are based on **Boltzmann Machines (BMs)**, which we discuss next (Hinton, G. E., and Sejnowski, T. J. (1983)).

BMs

A BM can be thought of as an undirected dense graph, as depicted in *Figure 10.1*:

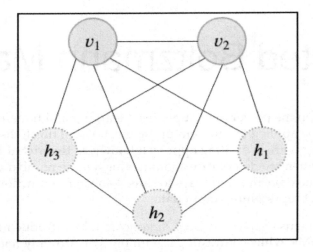

Figure 10.1 – A BM model

This undirected graph has some neural units that are modeled to be **visible**, $\{v_1, v_2\}$, and a set of neural units that are **hidden**, $\{h_1, h_2, h_3\}$. Of course, there could be many more than these. But the point of this model is that all neurons are connected to each other: they all *talk* among themselves. The training of this model will not be covered here, but essentially it is an iterative process where the input is presented in the visible layers, and every neuron (one at a time) adjusts its connections with other neurons to satisfy a loss function (usually based on an energy function), and the process repeats until the learning process is considered to be satisfactory.

While the RB model was quite interesting and powerful, it took a very long time to train! Take into consideration that this was around in the early 1980s and performing computations on larger graphs than this and with larger datasets could have a significant impact on the training time. However, in 1983, G. E. Hinton and his collaborators proposed a simplification of the BM model by restricting the communication between neurons, as we will discuss next.

RBMs

The *restriction* of traditional BMs lies in the communication between neurons; that is, visible neurons can only talk to hidden neurons and hidden neurons can only talk to visible neurons, as depicted in *Figure 10.2*:

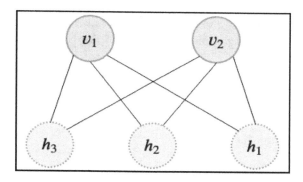

Figure 10.2 – An RBM model. Compare to the BM model in Figure 10.1

The graph shown in *Figure 10.2* is known as a **dense bipartite graph**. Perhaps you are thinking that it looks a lot like the typical dense neural networks that we have been using so far; however, it is not quite the same. The main difference is that all the neural networks that we have used only communicate information going forward from input (visible) to hidden layers, while an RBM can go both ways! The rest of the elements are familiar: we have weights and biases that need to be learned.

If we stick to the simple model shown in *Figure 10.2*, we could explain the learning theory behind an RBM in simpler terms.

Let's interpret every single neural unit as a random variable whose current state depends on the state of other neural units.

 This interpretation allows us to use sampling techniques related to **Markov Chain Monte Carlo (MCMC)** (Brooks, S., et al. (2011)); however, we will not go into the details of these in this book.

Using this interpretation, we can define an energy function for the model as follows:

$$E(v, h) = -\sum_{i=1}^{2}\sum_{j=1}^{3} w_{ij} v_i h_j - \sum_{i=1}^{2} b_i^{(v)} v_i - \sum_{j=1}^{3} b_j^{(h)} h_j$$

where $b^{(v)}, b^{(h)}$ denote the biases on a visible neural unit and a hidden neural unit, respectively. It turns out that we can also express the joint probability density function of neural an hidden units as follows:

$$P(v, h) = \frac{e^{-E(v,h)}}{Z}$$

which has a simple marginal distribution:

$$P(v) = \sum_h P(v, h) \equiv \frac{\sum_h e^{-E(v,h)}}{Z}$$

The denominator in the conditional and marginal is known as a normalizing factor that has only the effect of ensuring that probability values add up to one, and can be defined as follows:

$$Z = \sum_{v,h} e^{-E(v,h)}$$

These formulations allow us to quickly find MCMC techniques for training; most notably, you will find in the literature that Contrastive Divergence involving Gibbs sampling is the most common approach (Tieleman, T. (2008)).

There are only a handful of RBMs implemented that are readily available for a learner to get started; one of them is a Bernoulli RBM that is available in scikit-learn, which we discuss next.

Bernoulli RBMs

While the generalized RBM model does not make any assumptions about the data that it uses, a Bernoulli RBM does make the assumption that the input data represents values in the range [0,1] that can be interpreted as probability values. In the ideal case, values are in the set {0,1}, which is closely related to Bernoulli trials. If you are interested, there are other approaches that assume that the inputs follow a Gaussian distribution. You can find out more by reading Yamashita, T. et al. (2014).

There are only a few datasets that we can use for this type of RBM; MNIST is an example that can be interpreted as binary inputs where the data is 0 when there are no digit traces and 1 where there is digit information. In scikit-learn, the `BernoulliRBM` model can be found in the neural network collection: `sklearn.neural_network`.

Under the assumption of Bernoulli-like input distribution, this RBM model *approximately* optimizes the log likelihood using a method called **Persistent Contrastive Divergence (PCD)** (Tieleman, T., and Hinton, G. (2009)). It turned out that PCD was much faster than any other algorithm at the time and fostered discussions and much excitement that was soon overshadowed by the popularization of **backpropagation** compared to dense networks.

In the next section, we will implement a Bernoulli RBM on MNIST with the purpose of learning the representations of the dataset.

Learning data representations with RBMs

Now that you know the basic idea behind RBMs, we will use the `BernoulliRBM` model to learn data representations in an unsupervised manner. As before, we will do this with the MNIST dataset to facilitate comparisons.

For some people, the task of **learning representations** can be thought of as **feature engineering**. The latter has an explicability component to the term, while the former does not necessarily require us to prescribe meaning to the learned representations.

In scikit-learn, we can create an instance of the RBM by invoking the following instructions:

```
from sklearn.neural_network import BernoulliRBM
rbm = BernoulliRBM()
```

The default parameters in the constructor of the RBM are the following:

- n_components=256, which is the number of hidden units, h_i, while the number of visible units, v_i, is inferred from the dimensionality of the input.
- learning_rate=0.1 controls the strength of the learning algorithm with respect to updates, and it is recommended to explore it with values in the set {*1, 0.1, 0.01, 0.001*}.
- batch_size=10 controls how many samples are used in the batch-learning algorithm.
- n_iter=10 controls the number of iterations that are run before we stop the learning algorithm. The nature of the algorithm allows it to keep going as much as we want; however, the algorithm usually finds good solutions in a few iterations.

We will only change the default number of components to make it 100. Since the original number of dimensions in the MNIST dataset is 784 (because it consists of 28 x 28 images), having 100 dimensions does not seem like a bad idea.

To train the RBM with 100 components over MNIST training data loaded into x_train, we can do the following:

```
from sklearn.neural_network import BernoulliRBM
from tensorflow.keras.datasets import mnist
import numpy as np

(x_train, y_train), (x_test, y_test) = mnist.load_data()

image_size = x_train.shape[1]
original_dim = image_size * image_size
x_train = np.reshape(x_train, [-1, original_dim])
x_test = np.reshape(x_test, [-1, original_dim])
x_train = x_train.astype('float32') / 255
x_test = x_test.astype('float32') / 255

rbm = BernoulliRBM(verbose=True)

rbm.n_components = 100
rbm.fit(x_train)
```

The output during training might look like this:

```
[BernoulliRBM] Iteration 1, pseudo-likelihood = -104.67, time = 12.84s
[BernoulliRBM] Iteration 2, pseudo-likelihood = -102.20, time = 13.70s
[BernoulliRBM] Iteration 3, pseudo-likelihood = -97.95, time = 13.99s
[BernoulliRBM] Iteration 4, pseudo-likelihood = -99.79, time = 13.86s
```

```
[BernoulliRBM] Iteration 5, pseudo-likelihood = -96.06, time = 14.03s
[BernoulliRBM] Iteration 6, pseudo-likelihood = -97.08, time = 14.06s
[BernoulliRBM] Iteration 7, pseudo-likelihood = -95.78, time = 14.02s
[BernoulliRBM] Iteration 8, pseudo-likelihood = -99.94, time = 13.92s
[BernoulliRBM] Iteration 9, pseudo-likelihood = -93.65, time = 14.10s
[BernoulliRBM] Iteration 10, pseudo-likelihood = -96.97, time = 14.02s
```

We can look into the representations learned by invoking the `transform()` method on the MNIST test data, `x_test`, as follows:

```
r = rbm.transform(x_test)
```

In this case, there are 784 input dimensions, but the `r` variable will have 100 dimensions. To visualize the test set in the latent space induced by the RBM, we can use UMAPs as we did before, which will produce the two-dimensional plot shown in *Figure 10.3*:

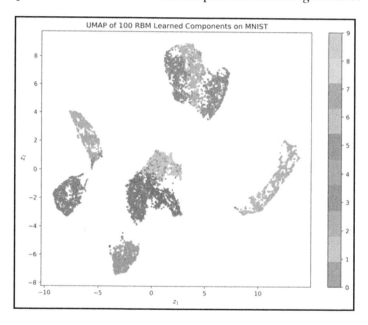

Figure 10.3 – UMAP representation of the learned representations by the RBM on MNIST test data

The full code to produce this plot from the RBM feature space using UMAP is as follows:

```
import matplotlib.pyplot as plt
import umap

y_ = list(map(int, y_test))
X_ = rbm.transform(x_test)

X_ = umap.UMAP().fit_transform(X_)

plt.figure(figsize=(10,8))
plt.title('UMAP of 100 RBM Learned Components on MNIST')
plt.scatter(X_[:,0], X_[:,1], s=5.0, c=y_, alpha=0.75, cmap='tab10')
plt.xlabel('$z_1$')
plt.ylabel('$z_2$')
plt.colorbar()
```

Compare *Figure 10.3* with the representations shown in previous chapters. From the figure, we can appreciate that there are clear class separations and clustering, while at the same time there are slight overlaps between classes. For example, there is some overlap between the numerals 3 and 8, which is to be expected since these numbers look alike. This plot also shows that the RBM generalizes very well since the data in *Figure 10.3* is coming from data that is unseen by the model.

We can further inspect the weights (or *components*) learned by the RBM; that is, we can retrieve the weights associated with the visible layers as follows:

```
v = rbm.components_
```

In this case, the v variable will be a 784 x 100 matrix describing the learned weights. We can visualize every single one of the neurons and reconstruct the weights associated with those neurons, which will look like the components in *Figure 10.4*:

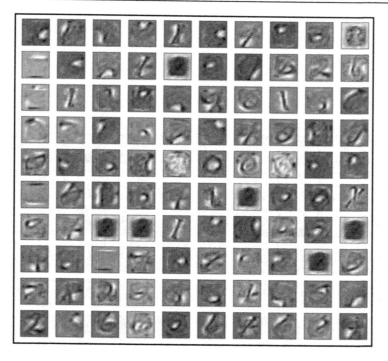

Figure 10.4 – Learned weights of the RBM

A close examination of *Figure 10.4* informs us that there are weights that pay attention to diagonal features, or circular features, or features that are very specific to specific digits and edges in general. The bottom row, for example, has features that appear to be associated with the numbers 2 and 6.

The weights shown in *Figure 10.4* can be used to transform the input space into richer representations that can later be used for classification in a pipeline that allows for this task.

To satisfy our learning curiosity, we could also look into the RBM and its states by sampling the network using the gibbs() method. This means that we could visualize what happens when we present the input to the visible layer and then what the response is from the hidden layer, and then use that as input again and repeat to see how the stimulus of the model changes. For example, run the following code:

```
import matplotlib.pyplot as plt
plt.figure()
cnt = 1
for i in range(10):      #we look into the first ten digits of test set
    x = x_test[i]
    for j in range(10):  #we project and reuse as input ten times
```

```
        plt.subplot(10, 10, cnt)
        plt.imshow(x.reshape((28, 28)), cmap='gray')
        x = rbm.gibbs(x)    #here use current as input and use as input again
        cnt += 1
    plt.show()
```

This will effectively produce a plot like the one shown in *Figure 5*:

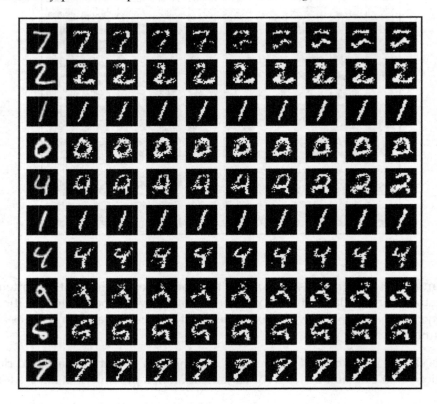

Figure 10.5 – Gibbs sampling on an MNIST-based RBM

Figure 10.5 shows the input in the first column, and the remaining 10 columns are successive sampling calls. Clearly, as the input is propagated back and forth within the RBM, it suffers from some slight deformations. Take row number five, corresponding to the digit 4; we can see how the input is being deformed until it looks like a number 2. This information has no immediate effect on the learned features unless a strong deformation is observed at the first sampling call.

In the next section, we will use an AE to make a comparison with an RBM.

Comparing RBMs and AEs

Now that we have seen how RBMs perform, a comparison with AEs is in order. To make this comparison fair, we can propose the closest configuration to an RBM that an AE can have; that is, we will have the same number of hidden units (neurons in the encoder layer) and the same number of neurons in the visible layer (the decoder layer), as shown in *Figure 10.6*:

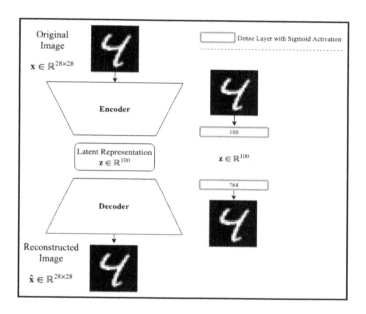

Figure 10.6 – AE configuration that's comparable to RBM

We can model and train our AE using the tools we covered in Chapter 7, *Autoencoders,* as follows:

```
from tensorflow.keras.layers import Input, Dense
from tensorflow.keras.models import Model

inpt_dim = 28*28    # 784 dimensions
ltnt_dim = 100      # 100 components

inpt_vec = Input(shape=(inpt_dim,))
encoder = Dense(ltnt_dim, activation='sigmoid')(inpt_vec)
latent_ncdr = Model(inpt_vec, encoder)
decoder = Dense(inpt_dim, activation='sigmoid')(encoder)
autoencoder = Model(inpt_vec, decoder)
```

```
autoencoder.compile(loss='binary_crossentropy', optimizer='adam')
autoencoder.fit(x_train, x_train, epochs=200, batch_size=1000)
```

There is nothing new here, except that we are training with only two dense layers that are large enough to provide nice representations. *Figure 10.7* depicts the UMAP visualization of the learned representations on the test set:

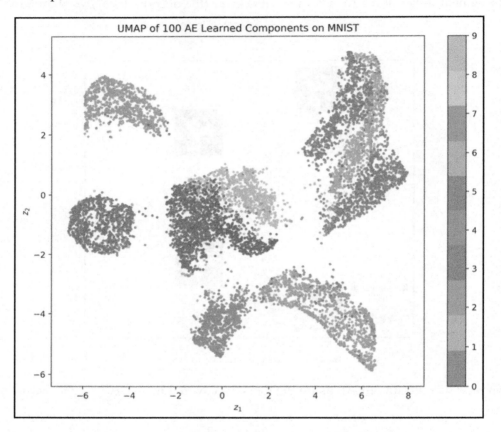

Figure 10.7 – AE-induced representations using a UMAP visualization

The preceding figure is produced with the following code:

```
import matplotlib.pyplot as plt
import umap

y_ = list(map(int, y_test))
X_ = latent_ncdr.predict(x_test)

X_ = umap.UMAP().fit_transform(X_)

plt.figure(figsize=(10,8))
plt.title('UMAP of 100 AE Learned Components on MNIST')
plt.scatter(X_[:,0], X_[:,1], s=5.0, c=y_, alpha=0.75, cmap='tab10')
plt.xlabel('$z_1$')
plt.ylabel('$z_2$')
plt.colorbar()
```

From *Figure 10.7*, you can see that the data is nicely clustered; although the clusters are closer together than in *Figure 10.3*, the within-cluster separations seems to be better. Similarly to the RBM, we can visualize the weights that were learned.

Every Model object in tensorflow.keras has a method called get_weights() that can retrieve a list with all the weights at every layer. Let's run this:

```
latent_ncdr.get_weights()[0]
```

It gives us access to the weights of the first layer and allows us to visualize them in the same way we did for the RBM weights. *Figure 10.8* shows the learned weights:

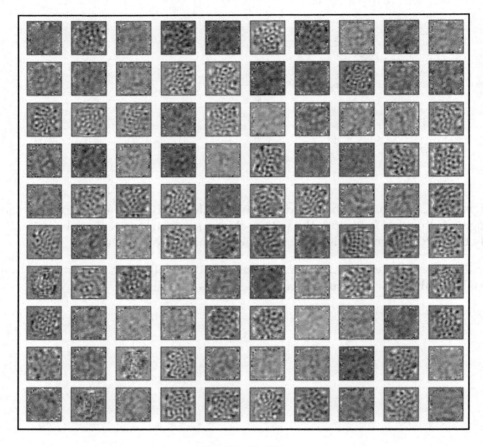

Figure 10.8 – AE weights

The weights shown in *Figure 10.8*, in comparison with those of the RBM in *Figure 10.4*, have no noticeable digit-specific features. These features seem to be oriented to textures and edges in very unique regions. This is very interesting to see because it suggests that fundamentally different models will produce fundamentally different latent spaces.

 If both RBMs and AEs produce interesting latent spaces, imagine what we could achieve if we use both of them in our deep learning projects! Try it!

Finally, to prove that the AE achieves high-quality reconstructions as modeled, we can look at *Figure 10.9*:

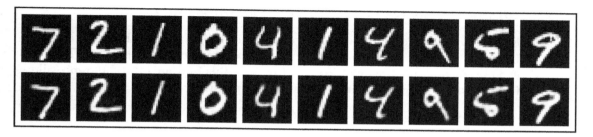

Figure 10.9 – AE inputs (top row) and reconstructions (bottom row)

The reconstructions using 100 components seem to have high quality, as shown in *Figure 10.9*. This is, however, not possible for RBMs since their purpose is not to reconstruct data, necessarily, as we have explained in this chapter.

Summary

This intermediate-level chapter has shown you the basic theory behind how RBMs work and their applications. We paid special attention to a Bernoulli RBM that operates on input data that may follow a Bernoulli-like distribution in order to achieve fast learning and efficient computations. We used the MNIST dataset to showcase how interesting the learned representations are for an RBM, and we visualized the learned weights as well. We concluded by comparing the RBM with a very simple AE and showed that both learned high-quality latent spaces while being fundamentally different models.

At this point, you should be able to implement your own RBM model, visualize its learned components, and see the learned latent space by projecting (transforming) the input data and looking at the hidden layer projections. You should feel confident in using an RBM on large datasets, such as MNIST, and even perform a comparison with an AE.

The next chapter is the beginning of a new group of chapters about supervised deep learning. Chapter 11, *Deep and Wide Neural Networks*, will get us started in a series of exciting and new topics surrounding supervised deep learning. The chapter will explain the differences in performance and the complexities of deep versus wide neural networks in supervised settings. It will introduce the concept of dense networks and sparse networks in terms of the connections between neurons. You can't miss it!

Questions and answers

1. **Why can't we perform data reconstructions with an RBM?**

   RBMs are fundamentally different to AEs. An RBM aims to optimize an energy function, while an AE aims to optimize a data reconstruction function. Thus, we can't do reconstructions with RBMs. However, this fundamental difference allows for new latent spaces that are interesting and robust.

2. **Can we add more layers to an RBM?**

   No. Not in the current model presented here. The concept of stacked layers of neurons fits the concept of deep AEs better.

3. **What is so cool about RBMs then?**

   They are simple. They are fast. They provide rich latent spaces. They have no equal at this point. The closest competitors are AEs.

References

- Hinton, G. E., and Sejnowski, T. J. (1983, June). Optimal perceptual inference. In Proceedings of the *IEEE conference on Computer Vision and Pattern Recognition* (Vol. 448). IEEE New York.
- Brooks, S., Gelman, A., Jones, G., and Meng, X. L. (Eds.). (2011). *Handbook of Markov Chain Monte Carlo*. CRC press.
- Tieleman, T. (2008, July). Training restricted Boltzmann machines using approximations to the likelihood gradient. In Proceedings of the 25th *International Conference on Machine Learning* (pp. 1064-1071).
- Yamashita, T., Tanaka, M., Yoshida, E., Yamauchi, Y., and Fujiyoshii, H. (2014, August). To be Bernoulli or to be Gaussian, for a restricted Boltzmann machine. In 2014 22nd *International Conference on Pattern Recognition* (pp. 1520-1525). IEEE.
- Tieleman, T., and Hinton, G. (2009, June). Using fast weights to improve persistent contrastive divergence. In Proceedings of the 26th Annual *International Conference on Machine Learning* (pp. 1033-1040).

Section 3: Supervised Deep Learning

3

Upon completion of this section, you will know how to implement basic and advanced deep learning models for classification, regression, and generating data based on learned latent spaces.

This section consists of the following chapters:

- Chapter 11, *Deep and Wide Neural Networks*
- Chapter 12, *Convolutional Neural Networks*
- Chapter 13, *Recurrent Neural Networks*
- Chapter 14, *Generative Adversarial Networks*
- Chapter 15, *Final Remarks on the Future of Deep Learning*

11
Deep and Wide Neural Networks

So far, we have covered a variety of unsupervised deep learning methodologies that can lead to many interesting applications, such as feature extraction, information compression, and data augmentation. However, as we move toward supervised deep learning methodologies that can perform classification or regression, for example, we have to begin by addressing an important question related to neural networks that might be in your mind already: *what is the difference between wide and deep neural networks?*

In this chapter, you will implement deep and wide neural networks to see the difference in the performance and complexities of both. As a bonus, we will cover the concepts of dense networks and sparse networks in terms of the connections between neurons. We will also optimize the dropout rates in our networks to maximize the generalization ability of the network, which is a critical skill to have today.

This chapter is organized as follows:

- Wide neural networks
- Dense deep neural networks
- Sparse deep neural networks
- Hyperparameter optimization

Wide neural networks

Before we discuss the types of neural networks covered in this chapter, it might be appropriate to revisit the definition of deep learning and then continue addressing all these types.

Deep learning revisited

Recently, on February 9, 2020, Turing Award winner Yann LeCun gave an interesting talk at the AAAI-20 conference in New York City. In his talk, he provided clarity with respect to what deep learning is, and before we give this definition here, let me remind you that LeCun (along with J. Bengio, and G. Hinton) is considered one of the fathers of deep learning, and received the Turing Award for precisely his achievements in the area. Therefore, what he has to say is important. Secondly, throughout this book, we have not given a strong definition of what deep learning is; people might be thinking that it refers to deep neural networks, but that is not factually correct – it is much more than that, so let's set the record straight once and for all.

> *"It is not just supervised learning, it is not just neural networks, **Deep Learning** is the idea of building a system by assembling parametrized modules into a (possibly dynamic) computation graph, and training it to perform a task by optimizing the parameters using a gradient-based method." - Yann LeCun*

Most of the models we have covered so far fit this definition, with the exception of the simple introductory models that we used to explain the more complex ones. The only reason why those introductory models are not included as deep learning is that they are not necessarily part of a computation graph; we are referring specifically to the perceptron (Rosenblatt, F. (1958)*)*, and the corresponding **Perceptron Learning Algorithm (PLA)** (Muselli, M. (1997)*)*. However, from the **Multilayer Perceptron (MLP)** and forward, all algorithms presented so far are, in fact, deep learning algorithms.

This is an important distinction to make at this point since this is a deep learning book, and you are *learning* about deep learning. We are about to learn some of the most interesting topics in deep learning and we need to keep a focus on what deep learning is. We will talk about deep networks and wide networks; however, both are deep learning. In fact, all the models we will be discussing here are deep learning models.

With this clarification in mind, let's define what a wide network is.

Wide layers

What makes a neural network **wide** is a relatively large number of neurons in a relatively small number of hidden layers. Recent developments in deep learning have even made possible the computational treatment of wide networks with an infinite amount of neural units (Novak, R., et al. (2019)*). Although this is a very nice advance in the field, we will limit our layers to have a reasonable number of units. To make our comparison with a *less wide* network, we will create a wide network for the CIFAR-10 dataset. We will create the architecture shown in the following figure:

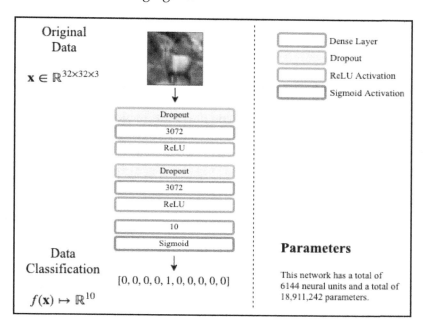

Figure 11.1 – Network architecture of a wide network for CIFAR-10

One important aspect of neural networks that we will consider from now on is the number of **parameters**.

In deep learning, the number of **parameters** is defined as the number of variables that the learning algorithm needs to estimate through gradient descent techniques in order to minimize the loss function. The great majority of parameters are, usually, the weights of a network; however, other parameters might include biases, mean and standard deviation for *batch normalization*, filters for convolutional networks, memory vectors for recurrent networks, and many others.

Knowing the number of parameters has been of particular importance because, in an ideal world, you want to have more data samples than variables you want to learn. In other words, an ideal learning scenario includes more data than parameters. If you think about it, it is intuitive; imagine having a matrix with two rows and three columns. The three columns describe the color representation in red, green, and blue of a fruit. The two rows correspond to one sample for an orange and another one for an apple. If you want to build a linear regression system to determine the probability of the data being from an orange, you certainly would like to have a lot more data! Especially since there are many apples that may have a color that is close to the color of an orange. More data is better! But if you have more parameters, like in linear regression where you have as many parameters as columns, then your problem is usually described as an *ill-posed* problem. In deep learning, this phenomenon is known as **over-parametrization**.

Only in deep learning do over-parametrized models work really well. There is research that has shown that in the particular case of neural networks, given the redundancy of data as it flows in non-linear relationships, the loss functions can produce smooth landscapes (Soltanolkotabi, M., et al. (2018)). This is particularly interesting because then we could prove that over-parametrized deep learning models will converge to very good solutions using gradient descent (Du, S. S., et al. (2018)).

Summaries

In Keras, there is a function called `summary()` that, called from a `Model` object, can give the total number of parameters to be estimated. For example, let's create the wide network in *Figure 11.1*:

```
from tensorflow.keras.layers import Input, Dense, Dropout
from tensorflow.keras.models import Model

inpt_dim = 32*32*3    # this corresponds to the dataset
                      # to be explained shortly
inpt_vec = Input(shape=(inpt_dim,), name='inpt_vec')
d1 = Dropout(0.5, name='d1')(inpt_vec)
l1 = Dense(inpt_dim, activation='relu', name='l1')(d1)
d2 = Dropout(0.2, name='d2')(l1)
l2 = Dense(inpt_dim, activation='relu', name='l2') (d2)
output = Dense(10, activation='sigmoid', name='output') (l2)

widenet = Model(inpt_vec, output, name='widenet')

widenet.compile(loss='binary_crossentropy', optimizer='adam')
widenet.summary()
```

This code produces the following output:

```
Model: "widenet"

Layer (type)              Output Shape       Param #
=================================================================
inpt_vec (InputLayer)     [(None, 3072)]     0

d1 (Dropout)              (None, 3072)       0

l1 (Dense)                (None, 3072)       9440256

d2 (Dropout)              (None, 3072)       0

l2 (Dense)                (None, 3072)       9440256

output (Dense)            (None, 10)         30730
=================================================================
Total params: 18,911,242
Trainable params: 18,911,242
Non-trainable params: 0
```

The summary produced here indicates that the total number of parameters in the model is 18,911,242. This is to show that a simple wide network can have nearly 19 million parameters for a problem with 3,072 features. This is clearly an over-parametrized model on which we will perform gradient descent to learn those parameters; in other words, this is a deep learning model.

Names

Another new thing that we will introduce in this chapter is the use of **names** for individual pieces of the Keras models. You should have noticed that in the preceding code, the script contains a new argument with a string assigned to it; for example, `Dropout(0.5, name='d1')`. This is used internally to keep track of the names of pieces in the model. This can be good practice; however, it is not required. If you do not provide names, Keras will automatically assign generic names to each individual piece. Assigning names to elements can be helpful when saving or restoring models (we will do that soon enough – be patient), or can be useful when printing summaries, like the preceding one.

Now, let's look at the dataset that we will load. Precisely, the data mentioned earlier that has 3,072 dimensions, called CIFAR-10.

The CIFAR-10 dataset

The dataset we will work with in this chapter is called **CIFAR-10**. It comes from the acronym **Canadian Institute For Advanced Research (CIFAR)**. The number 10 comes from the number of classes with which the dataset is organized. It is a dataset of color images that also has an alternative database with 100 different objects, known as CIFAR-100; however, we will focus on CIFAR-10 for now. Each color image is 32×32 pixels. Its total dimensions, considering the color channels, is $32 \times 32 \times 3 = 3072$.

The diagram in *Figure 11.1* has one image sample and *Figure 11.2* has an example for each class within the test set:

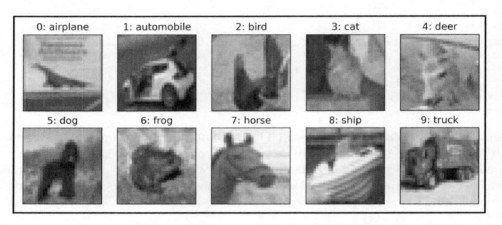

Figure 11.2 – Sample color images for each class in the CIFAR-10 dataset

This dataset can be loaded by executing the following commands:

```
from tensorflow.keras.datasets import cifar10
from tensorflow.keras.utils import to_categorical
import NumPy as np

(x_train, y_train), (x_test, y_test) = cifar10.load_data()

# Makes images floats between [0,1]
x_train = x_train.astype('float32') / 255.
x_test = x_test.astype('float32') / 255.

# Reshapes images to make them vectors of 3072-dimensions
x_train = x_train.reshape((len(x_train), np.prod(x_train.shape[1:])))
x_test = x_test.reshape((len(x_test), np.prod(x_test.shape[1:])))

# Converts list of numbers into one-hot encoded vectors of 10-dim
```

```
y_train = to_categorical(y_train, 10)
y_test = to_categorical(y_test, 10)

print('x_train shape:', x_train.shape)
print('x_test shape:', x_test.shape)
```

This downloads the data automatically and produces the following output:

```
x_train shape: (50000, 3072)
x_test shape: (10000, 3072)
```

These things are nothing new except for the dataset. For more information about how this dataset was prepared, please check Chapter 3, *Preparing Data*, where we go over how to convert data into usable data by normalizing it and converting targets to one-hot encoding.

The output we receive by printing the shape of the dataset, using the .shape attribute of NumPy arrays, tells us that we have 50,000 samples to train with, and 10,000 samples on which to test our training performance. This is the standard split in the deep learning community and helps the comparison among methodologies.

New training tools

With the code we have so far, we can easily begin the training process by invoking the fit() method as follows:

```
widenet.fit(x_train, y_train, epochs=100, batch_size=1000,
            shuffle=True, validation_data=(x_test, y_test))
```

This is nothing new; we covered all these details in Chapter 9, *Variational Autoencoders*. However, we want to introduce new important tools into the mix that will help us train a better model, much more efficiently, and preserve our best-trained model.

Saving or loading models

Saving our trained model is important if we want to sell a product, or distribute a working architecture, or to control versions of models. These models can be saved by calling on either of the following methods:

- save(), used to save the whole model, including optimizer states such as the gradient descent algorithm, the number of epochs, the learning rate, and others.
- save_weights(), used to save only the parameters of the model.

For example, we can save our model's weights as follows:

```
widenet.save_weights("widenet.hdf5")
```

This will create a file in your local disk called `widenet.hdf5`. This type of file extension is for a standard file format called **Hierarchical Data Format (HDF)**, which enables consistency across common platforms, and, therefore, the easy sharing of data.

You can re-load a saved model later on by simply executing the following:

```
widenet.load_weights("widenet.hdf5")
```

Note that doing this relies on you building the model first, that is, creating **exactly** all the layers of the model in the exact same order and with the exact same names. An alternative, to save all the effort of reconstructing the model exactly, is to use the `save()` method.

```
widenet.save("widenet.hdf5")
```

However, the downside of using the `save()` method is that to load the model you will need to import an additional library, as follows:

```
from tensorflow.keras.models import load_model

widenet = load_model("widenet.hdf5")
```

This essentially removes the need to re-create the model. Throughout this chapter, we will be saving our model weights simply so that you get used to it. Now let's take a look at how to use **callbacks**, which are interesting ways to monitor the learning process. We will start with a **callback** for reducing the learning rate.

Reducing the learning rate on the fly

Keras has a superclass for **callbacks**, found in `tensorflow.keras.callbacks`, where we have, among other nice things, a class for reducing the learning rate of the learning algorithm. If you don't remember what the **learning rate** is, feel free to go back to Chapter 6, *Training Multiple Layers of Neurons*, to review the concept. But, as a quick recap, the learning rate controls how big the steps that are taken to update the parameters of the model in the direction of the gradient are.

The problem is that, many times, you will encounter that certain types of deep learning models *get stuck* in the learning process. By *getting stuck* we mean that there is no progress being made toward reducing the loss function either on the training or validation set. The technical term the *professionals* use is that the learning looks like a **plateau**. It is a problem that is evident when you look at how the loss function is minimized across epochs because it looks like a *plateau*, that is, a flat line. Ideally, we want to see the loss decreasing at every epoch, and it is usually the case for the first few epochs, but there can be a time when reducing the learning rate can help the learning algorithm to *focus* by making small changes to the existing acquired knowledge, that is, the learned parameters.

The class we are discussing here is called `ReduceLROnPlateau`. You can load it as follows:

```
from tensorflow.keras.callbacks import ReduceLROnPlateau
```

To use this library, you will have to use the `callbacks` argument in the `fit()` function after defining it like this:

```
reduce_lr = ReduceLROnPlateau(monitor='val_loss', factor=0.1, patience=20)

widenet.fit(x_train, y_train, batch_size=128, epochs=100,
            callbacks=reduce_lr, shuffle=True,
            validation_data=(x_test, y_test))
```

In this code fragment, we call `ReduceLROnPlateau` with the following arguments:

- `monitor='val_loss'`, this is the default value, but you can change it to look for a plateau in the `'loss'` curve.
- `factor=0.1`, this is the default value, and it is the rate by which the learning rate will be reduced. For example, the default learning rate for the Adam optimizer is 0.001, but when a plateau is detected, it will be multiplied by 0.1, leading to a new updated learning rate of 0.0001.
- `patience=20`, the default value is 10, and is the number of epochs with no improvement in the monitored loss, which will be considered a plateau.

There are other arguments that you can use in this method, but these are the most popular, in my opinion.

Next, let's look at another important callback: *early stopping*.

Stopping the learning process early

This next callback is interesting because it allows you to stop the training if there is no progress being made and **it allows you to keep the best version of the model** during the learning process. It is found in the same class as the preceding one and is called `EarlyStopping()`, and you can load it as follows:

```
from tensorflow.keras.callbacks import EarlyStopping
```

The early stopping callback essentially lets you stop the training process if there has been no progress in the last few epochs, as specified in the `patience` parameter. You can define and use the early stopping callback as follows:

```
stop_alg = EarlyStopping(monitor='val_loss', patience=100,
restore_best_weights=True)

widenet.fit(x_train, y_train, batch_size=128, epochs=1000,
            callbacks=stop_alg, shuffle=True,
            validation_data=(x_test, y_test))
```

Here is a short explanation of each of the arguments used in `EarlyStopping()`:

- `monitor='val_loss'`, this is the default value, but you can change it to look for changes in the `'loss'` curve.
- `patience=100`, the default value is 10 and is the number of epochs with no improvement in the monitored loss. I personally like to set this to a larger number than the patience in `ReduceLROnPlateau`, because I like to let the learning rate produce an improvement in the learning process (hopefully) before I terminate the learning process because there was no improvement.
- `restore_best_weights=True`, the default value is `False`. If `False`, the model weights obtained at the last epoch are preserved. However, if set to `True`, it will preserve and return the best weights at the end of the learning process.

This last argument is my personal favorite because I can set the number of epochs to a large number, within reason, and let the training go for as long as it needs. In the preceding example, if we set the number of epochs to 1,000, it does not necessarily mean that the learning process will go for 1,000 epochs, but if there is no progress within 50 epochs, the process can stop early. If the process gets to a point at which it has learned good parameters, it can get to a point at which there is no progress, then stop after 50 epochs and still return the best model that was ever recorded during the learning process.

We can combine all the preceding callbacks and the saving methodology as follows:

```
from tensorflow.keras.callbacks import ReduceLROnPlateau, EarlyStopping

reduce_lr = ReduceLROnPlateau(monitor='val_loss', factor=0.5, patience=20)
stop_alg = EarlyStopping(monitor='val_loss', patience=100,
                         restore_best_weights=True)

hist = widenet.fit(x_train, y_train, batch_size=1000, epochs=1000,
                   callbacks=[stop_alg, reduce_lr], shuffle=True,
                   validation_data=(x_test, y_test))

widenet.save_weights("widenet.hdf5")
```

Notice that the callbacks have been combined into a list of callbacks that will monitor the learning process, looking for plateaus to decrease the learning rate, or looking to stop the process if there has been no improvement in a few epochs. Also, notice that we created a new variable, `hist`. This variable contains a dictionary with logs of the learning process, such as the losses across epochs. We can plot such losses to see how the training takes place as follows:

```
import matplotlib.pyplot as plt

plt.plot(hist.history['loss'], color='#785ef0')
plt.plot(hist.history['val_loss'], color='#dc267f')
plt.title('Model reconstruction loss')
plt.ylabel('Binary Cross-Entropy Loss')
plt.xlabel('Epoch')
plt.legend(['Training Set', 'Test Set'], loc='upper right')
plt.show()
```

This produces the curves in *Figure 11.3*:

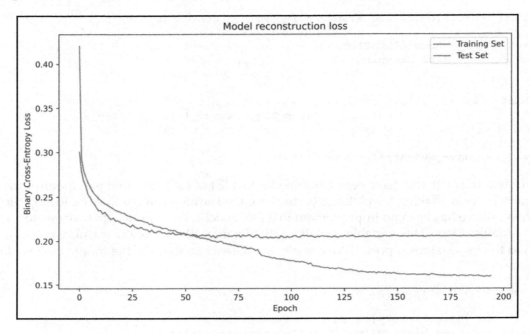

Figure 11.3 – Model loss of widenet across epochs using callbacks

From the figure, we can clearly see the evidence of the learning rate reduction around epoch 85 where the learning is adjusted after the plateau in the validation loss (that is, the loss over the test set); however, this has little effect on the validation loss, and therefore training is terminated early around epoch 190 since there was no improvement in the validation loss.

In the next section, we will analyze the performance of the `widenet` model in a quantitative manner that will allow comparison later on.

Results

Here, we want to simply explain the performance of the network in terms that are easy to understand and to communicate to others. We will be focusing on analyzing the confusion matrix of the model, precision, recall, F1-score, accuracy, and balanced error rate. If you do not recall what these terms mean, please go back and quickly review Chapter 4, *Learning from Data*.

One of the nice things about scikit-learn is that it has a nice automated process for calculating a report for classification performance that includes most of the terms mentioned above. It is simply called a **classification report**. This and the other libraries that we will need can be found in the sklearn.metrics class and can be imported as follows:

```
from sklearn.metrics import classification_report
from sklearn.metrics import confusion_matrix
from sklearn.metrics import balanced_accuracy_score
```

These three libraries operate in a similar way – they take the ground truth and the predictions to evaluate performance:

```
from sklearn.metrics import classification_report
from sklearn.metrics import confusion_matrix
from sklearn.metrics import balanced_accuracy_score
import NumPy as np

y_hat = widenet.predict(x_test)      # we take the neuron with maximum
y_pred = np.argmax(y_hat, axis=1)    # output as our prediction

y_true = np.argmax(y_test, axis=1)    # this is the ground truth
labels=[0, 1, 2, 3, 4, 5, 6, 7, 8, 9]

print(classification_report(y_true, y_pred, labels=labels))

cm = confusion_matrix(y_true, y_pred, labels=labels)
print(cm)

ber = 1- balanced_accuracy_score(y_true, y_pred)
print('BER:', ber)
```

This code outputs something like this:

```
        precision   recall   f1-score   support
0       0.65        0.59     0.61       1000
1       0.65        0.68     0.67       1000
2       0.42        0.47     0.44       1000
3       0.39        0.37     0.38       1000
4       0.45        0.44     0.44       1000
5       0.53        0.35     0.42       1000
6       0.50        0.66     0.57       1000
7       0.66        0.58     0.62       1000
8       0.62        0.71     0.67       1000
9       0.60        0.57     0.58       1000
accuracy                     0.54       10000
```

```
[[587  26  86  20  39   7  26  20 147  42]
 [ 23 683  10  21  11  10  22  17  68 135]
 [ 63  21 472  71 141  34 115  41  24  18]
 [ 19  22  90 370  71 143 160  43  30  52]
 [ 38  15 173  50 442  36 136  66  32  12]
 [ 18  10 102 224  66 352 120  58  29  21]
 [  2  21  90  65  99  21 661   9  14  18]
 [ 36  15  73  67  90  45  42 582  13  37]
 [ 77  70  18  24  17   3  20   9 713  49]
 [ 46 167  20  28  14  14  30  36  74 571]]
```

```
BER: 0.4567
```

The part on the top indicates the output of `classification_report()`. It gives the precision, recall, f1-score, and accuracy of the model. Ideally, we want to have all of those numbers as close to 1.0 as possible. Intuitively, the accuracy needs to be 100% (or 1.0); however, the rest of the numbers require careful study. From this report, we can observe that the total accuracy is 54%. From the rest of the report, we can determine that the classes that are more accurately classified are 1 and 8, corresponding to *automobile* and *ship*. Similarly, we can see that the two classes most poorly classified are 3 and 5, corresponding to *cats* and *dogs*, respectively.

While these numbers are informative, we could look into what is the source of the confusion, by looking at the confusion matrix, which is the group of numbers produced by `confusion_matrix()`. If we inspect the confusion matrix on row number four (corresponding to label 3, *cats*), we see that it correctly classifies 370 cats as cats, but 143 cats were classified as dogs, and 160 cats were classified as frogs, just to name the most serious areas of confusions. Another way to look at it is visually, as shown in the following figure:

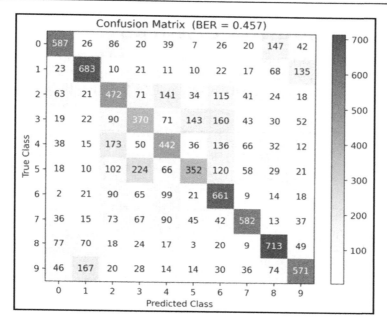

Figure 11.4 – Confusion matrix visualization for the widenet model

Ideally, we want to see a confusion matrix that is diagonal; however, in this case, we don't see that effect. After visual inspection, from *Figure 11.4*, we can observe which classes have the lowest correct predictions and confirm, visually, where the confusion is.

Finally, it is important to note that while **classification accuracy (ACC)** is 54%, we still need to verify the **balanced error rate (BER)** to complement what we know about the accuracy. This is particularly important when the classes are not evenly distributed, that is, when there are more samples for some classes compared to others. As explained in `Chapter 4`, *Learning from Data*, we can simply calculate the balanced accuracy and subtract it from one. This reveals that the BER is 0.4567, or 45.67%. In an ideal world, we want to lower the BER to zero, and definitely stay away from a BER of 50%, which would imply that the model is no better than random chance.

In this case, the accuracy of the model is not impressive; however, this is a very challenging classification problem for fully connected networks, thus, this performance is not surprising. Now, we will try to do a similar experiment, changing from a relatively wide network, to a deep network, and compare the results.

Dense deep neural networks

It is widely known that deeper networks can offer good performance in classification tasks (Liao, Q., et al. (2018)). In this section, we want to build a deep dense neural network and see how it performs in the CIFAR-10 dataset. We will be building the model shown in the following figure:

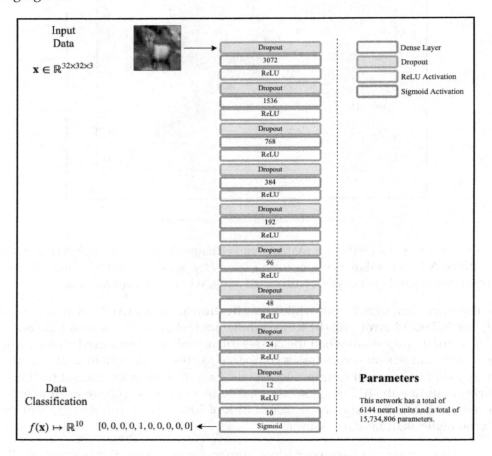

Figure 11.5 – Network architecture of a deep dense network for CIFAR-10

One of the aims of this model is to have the same number of neural units as the model in *Figure 11.1*, for the wide network. This model has a bottleneck architecture, where the number of neurons decreases as the network gets deeper. This can be coded programmatically using the Keras functional approach, as we discuss next.

Building and training the model

One interesting fact about Keras' functional approach is that we can **recycle** variable names as we build the model and that we can even build a model using a loop. For example, let's say that I would like to create dense layers with dropout rates that exponentially decrease along with the number of neurons by a factor of 1.5 and 2, respectively.

We could achieve this by having a cycle that uses an initial dropout rate, dr, and an initial number of neural units, units, and decreases both by a factor of 1.5 and 2, respectively, every time, as long as the number of neural units is always greater than 10; we stop at 10 because the last layer will contain 10 neurons, one for each class. It looks something like this:

```
while units > 10:
  dl = Dropout(dr)(dl)
  dl = Dense(units, activation='relu')(dl)
  units = units//2
  dr = dr/1.5
```

The preceding code snippet illustrates that we can reuse variables without confusing Python since TensorFlow operates over a computational graph that has no problem in resolving parts of the graph in the correct sequence. The code also shows that we can create a bottleneck-type of network very easily with an exponentially decaying number of units and dropout rate.

The full code to build this model looks like this:

```
# Dimensionality of input for CIFAR-10
inpt_dim = 32*32*3

inpt_vec = Input(shape=(inpt_dim,))

units = inpt_dim    # Initial number of neurons
dr = 0.5    # Initial drop out rate

dl = Dropout(dr)(inpt_vec)
dl = Dense(units, activation='relu')(dl)

# Iterative creation of bottleneck layers
units = units//2
dr = dr/2
while units>10:
  dl = Dropout(dr)(dl)
  dl = Dense(units, activation='relu')(dl)
  units = units//2
  dr = dr/1.5
```

```
# Output layer
output = Dense(10, activation='sigmoid')(dl)

deepnet = Model(inpt_vec, output)
```

Compiling and training the model goes like this:

```
deepnet.compile(loss='binary_crossentropy', optimizer='adam')
deepnet.summary()

reduce_lr = ReduceLROnPlateau(monitor='val_loss', factor=0.5, patience=20,
                              min_delta=1e-4, mode='min')
stop_alg = EarlyStopping(monitor='val_loss', patience=100,
                         restore_best_weights=True)
hist = deepnet.fit(x_train, y_train, batch_size=1000, epochs=1000,
                   callbacks=[stop_alg, reduce_lr], shuffle=True,
                   validation_data=(x_test, y_test))

deepnet.save_weights("deepnet.hdf5")
```

This produces the following output, caused by deepnet.summary() in the preceding code:

```
Model: "model"
```

Layer (type)	Output Shape	Param #
input_1 (InputLayer)	[(None, 3072)]	0
dropout (Dropout)	(None, 3072)	0
dense (Dense)	(None, 3072)	9440256
. . .		
dense_8 (Dense)	(None, 12)	300
dense_9 (Dense)	(None, 10)	130

```
Total params: 15,734,806
Trainable params: 15,734,806
Non-trainable params: 0
```

As shown in the preceding summary, and also in *Figure 11.5*, the total number of parameters of this model is **15,734,806**. This confirms that this is an over-parametrized model. The printed summary also depicts how each part of the model is named when no specific name is provided; that is, they all receive a generic name based on the name of the class and a consecutive number.

The fit() method trains the deep model and when we plot the training logged in the hist variable, as we did earlier for *Figure 11.3*, we obtain the following figure:

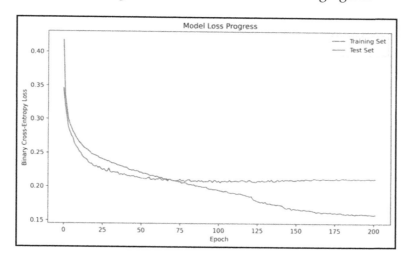

Figure 11.6 – Model loss of deepnet across epochs using callbacks

From *Figure 11.6*, we see that the deep network stops training after about 200 epochs and the training and test sets cross paths around epoch 70, after which, the model begins to overfit the training set. If we compare this result to the one in *Figure 11.3* for the wide network, we can see that the model starts overfitting around epoch 55.

Let's now discuss the quantitative results of this model.

Results

If we generate a classification report in the same manner as we did for the wide network, we obtain the results shown here:

```
           precision    recall   f1-score   support

    0        0.58         0.63      0.60       1000
    1        0.66         0.68      0.67       1000
    2        0.41         0.42      0.41       1000
    3        0.38         0.35      0.36       1000
    4        0.41         0.50      0.45       1000
    5        0.51         0.36      0.42       1000
    6        0.50         0.63      0.56       1000
    7        0.67         0.56      0.61       1000
    8        0.65         0.67      0.66       1000
    9        0.62         0.56      0.59       1000

    accuracy                       0.53      10000


[[627  22  62  19  45  10  25  18 132  40]
 [ 38 677  18  36  13  10  20  13  55 120]
 [ 85  12 418  82 182  45  99  38  23  16]
 [ 34  14 105 347  89 147 161  50  17  36]
 [ 58  12 158  34 496  29 126  55  23   9]
 [ 25   7 108 213  91 358 100  54  23  21]
 [  9  15  84  68 124  26 631   7  11  25]
 [ 42  23  48  58 114  57  61 555  10  32]
 [110  75  16  22  30  11   8   5 671  52]
 [ 51 171  14  34  16   9  36  36  69 564]]

BER 0.4656
```

This suggests comparable results to the wide model, in which we obtained a 0.4567 BER, which represents a difference of 0.0089 in favor of the wide model, which does not represent a significant difference in this case. We can verify that the models are also comparable with respect to their classification performance on particular classes by looking at the preceding results or at the confusion matrix shown in the following figure:

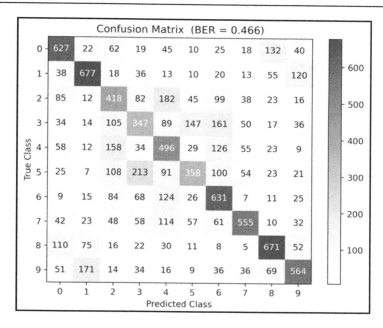

Figure 11.7 – Confusion matrix visualization for the deepnet model

From the preceding results, we can confirm that the toughest class to classify is number 3, *cats*, which are often confused with dogs. Similarly, the easiest to classify is number 1, *ships*, which are often confused with airplanes. But once again, this is consistent with the results from the wide network.

One more type of deep network that we can experiment with is one that promotes sparsity among the weights of the network, which we'll discuss next.

Sparse deep neural networks

A sparse network can be defined as *sparse* in different aspects of its architecture (Gripon, V., and Berrou, C., 2011). However, the specific type of sparseness we'll look into in this section is the sparseness obtained with respect to the weights of the network, that is, its parameters. We will be looking at each specific parameter to see if it is relatively close to zero (computationally speaking).

Currently, there are three ways of imposing weight sparseness in Keras over Tensorflow, and they are related to the concept of a vector norm. If we look at the Manhattan norm, ℓ_1, or the Euclidean norm, ℓ_2, they are defined as follows:

$$\|\mathbf{w}\|_1 = \sum_{i=1}^{n} |w_i|$$
,

$$\|\mathbf{w}\|_2 = \sum_{i=1}^{n} w_i^2$$

Here, n is the number of elements in the vector $\mathbf{w}$. As you can see, in simple terms, the ℓ_1-norm adds up all elements in terms of their absolute value, while the ℓ_2-norm does it in terms of their squared values. It is evident that if both norms are close to zero, $\ell_1, \ell_2 \approx 0$, the chances are that most of its elements are zero or close to zero. As a matter of personal choice here, we will use the ℓ_2-norm because, as opposed to ℓ_1, very large vectors are quadratically penalized so as to avoid specific neurons dominating specific terms.

Keras contains these tools in the `regularizers` class: `tf.keras.regularizers`. We can import them as follows:

- ℓ_1-norm: `tf.keras.regularizers.l1(l=0.01)`
- ℓ_2-norm: `tf.keras.regularizers.l2(l=0.01)`

These regularizers are applied to the loss function of the network in order to minimize the norm of the weights.

A **regularizer** is a term that is used in machine learning to denote a term or function that provides elements to an objective (loss) function, or to a general optimization problem (such as gradient descent), in order to provide numerical stability or promote the feasibility of the problem. In this case, the regularizer promotes the stability of the weights by preventing the explosion of some weight values, while at the same time promoting general sparsity.

The parameter `l=0.01` is a penalty factor that directly determines the importance of minimizing weight norms. In other words, the penalty is applied as follows:

$$\ell_2 = l \sum_{i=1}^{n} w_i^2$$

Therefore, using a very small value, such as `l=0.0000001` will pay little attention to the norm, and `l=0.01` will pay a lot of attention to the norm during the minimization of the loss function. Here's the catch: this parameter needs to be tuned up because if the network is too big, there might be several millions of parameters, which can make the norm look very large, and so a small penalty is in order; whereas if the network is relatively small, a larger penalty is recommended. Since this exercise is on a very deep network with 15+ million parameters, we will use a value of `l=0.0001`.

Let's go ahead and build a sparse network.

Building a sparse network and training it

To build this network, we will use the exact same architecture shown in *Figure 11.5*, except that the declaration of each individual dense layer will contain a specification that we want to consider the minimization of the norm of the weights associated with that layer. Please look at the code of the previous section and compare it to the following code, where we highlight the differences:

```
# Dimensionality of input for CIFAR-10
inpt_dim = 32*32*3

inpt_vec = Input(shape=(inpt_dim,))

units = inpt_dim     # Initial number of neurons
dr = 0.5     # Initial drop out rate

dl = Dropout(dr)(inpt_vec)
dl = Dense(units, activation='relu',
           kernel_regularizer=regularizers.l2(0.0001))(dl)

# Iterative creation of bottleneck layers
units = units//2
dr = dr/2
while units>10:
  dl = Dropout(dr)(dl)
  dl = Dense(units, activation='relu',
```

```
                        kernel_regularizer=regularizers.l2(0.0001))(dl)
    units = units//2
    dr = dr/1.5

# Output layer
output = Dense(10, activation='sigmoid',
                    kernel_regularizer=regularizers.l2(0.0001))(dl)

sparsenet = Model(inpt_vec, output)
```

Compiling and training the model goes the same, like this:

```
sparsenet.compile(loss='binary_crossentropy', optimizer='adam')
sparsenet.summary()

reduce_lr = ReduceLROnPlateau(monitor='val_loss', factor=0.5, patience=20,
                              min_delta=1e-4, mode='min')
stop_alg = EarlyStopping(monitor='val_loss', patience=100,
                         restore_best_weights=True)
hist = sparsenet.fit(x_train, y_train, batch_size=1000, epochs=1000,
                     callbacks=[stop_alg, reduce_lr], shuffle=True,
                     validation_data=(x_test, y_test))

sparsenet.save_weights("sparsenet.hdf5")
```

The output of `sparsenet.summary()` is identical to the one shown in the previous section for `deepnet.summary()`, so we will not repeat it here. However, we can look at the training curve as the loss is minimized – see the following figure:

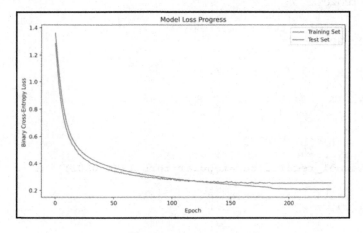

Figure 11.8 – Loss function optimization across epochs for the sparsenet model

From the figure, we can see that both curves, the training and test set, are minimized closely together up to around epoch 120, where both start to digress, and the model begins to overfit after that. In comparison to previous models in *Figure 11.3* and *Figure 11.6*, we can see that this model can be trained a bit more slowly and still achieve relative convergence. Note, however, that while the loss function still remains the binary cross-entropy, the model is also minimizing the ℓ_2-norm, making this particular loss not directly comparable to the previous ones.

Let's now discuss the quantitative results of this model.

Results

When we look at a quantitative analysis of performance, we can tell that the model is comparable to the previous models. There is a slight gain in terms of a BER; however, it is not enough to declare victory and the problem solved by any means – see the following analysis:

```
       precision  recall  f1-score  support

0       0.63       0.64    0.64      1000
1       0.71       0.66    0.68      1000
2       0.39       0.43    0.41      1000
3       0.37       0.23    0.29      1000
4       0.46       0.45    0.45      1000
5       0.47       0.50    0.49      1000
6       0.49       0.71    0.58      1000
7       0.70       0.61    0.65      1000
8       0.63       0.76    0.69      1000
9       0.69       0.54    0.60      1000

accuracy                   0.55      10000

[[638  17  99   7  27  13  27  10 137  25]
 [ 40 658  11  32  11   7  21  12 110  98]
 [ 78  11 431  34 169  93 126  31  19   8]
 [ 18  15  96 233  52 282 220  46  14  24]
 [ 47   3 191  23 448  36 162  57  28   5]
 [ 17   6 124 138  38 502 101  47  16  11]
 [  0   9  59  51 111  28 715   8  13   6]
 [ 40   1  66  50  85  68  42 608  12  28]
 [ 76  45  18  16  25   8  22   5 755  30]
 [ 51 165  12  38   6  23  29  43  98 535]]

BER  0.4477
```

What we can clearly conclude is that the model is not worse in terms of performance when compared to other models discussed in this chapter. In fact, close inspection of the confusion matrix shown in the following figure indicates that similar errors are made with this network as well in terms of objects that are similar in nature:

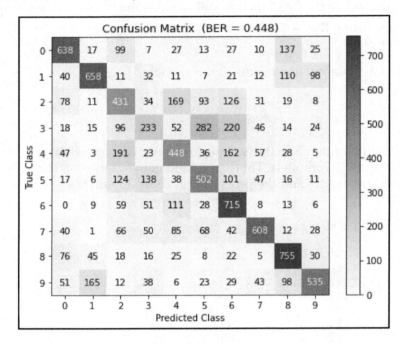

Figure 11.9 – Confusion matrix for the sparsenet model

Now, since it is difficult to appreciate the differences between the models we have discussed so far – wide, deep, and sparse – we can calculate and plot the norm of the weights of each trained model, as shown in the following figure:

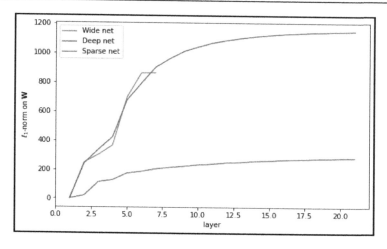

Figure 11.10 – Cumulative norm weights of the trained models

This figure shows the calculation in terms of the ℓ_1-norm so as to have values close enough to appreciate them; on the horizontal axis we have the number of layers, and on the vertical axis, we have the cumulative norm as we progress in the layers of the networks. This is where we can appreciate how different the networks are with respect to their parameters. In a sparse network, the cumulative norm is much smaller (about four to five times) in comparison to the other networks. This can be an interesting and important characteristic for those networks that might be implemented on a chip or other applications in which zero-weights can lead to efficient computations in production (Wang, P., et al. 2018).

While the level at which the network weights are affected by the norm can be determined experimentally through hyperparameter optimization techniques, it is often more common to determine other parameters such as the dropout rate, the number of neural units, and others we discuss in the next section.

Hyperparameter optimization

There are a few methodologies out there for optimizing parameters; for example, some are gradient-based (Rivas, P., et al. 2014; Maclaurin, D., et al. 2015), others are Bayesian (Feurer, M., et al. 2015). However, it has been difficult to have a generalized method that works extremely well and that is efficient at the same time – usually, you get one or the other. You can read more about other algorithms here (Bergstra, J. S., et al. 2011).

For any beginner in this field, it might be better to get started with something simple and easy to remember, such as random search (Bergstra, J., & Bengio, Y. 2012) or grid search. These two methods are very similar and while we will focus here on **grid search**, the implementations of both are very similar.

Libraries and parameters

We will need to use two major libraries that we have not covered before: GridSearchCV, for executing the grid search with cross-validation, and KerasClassifier, to create a Keras classifier that can communicate with scikit-learn.

Both libraries can be imported as follows:

```
from sklearn.model_selection import GridSearchCV
from tensorflow.keras.wrappers.scikit_learn import KerasClassifier
```

The hyperparameters that we will optimize (and their possible values) are the following:

- **Dropout rate**: 0.2, 0.5
- **Optimizer**: rmsprop, adam
- **Learning rate**: 0.01, 0.0001
- **Neurons in hidden layers**: 1024, 512, 256

In total, the possible combination of hyperparameters is 2x2x2x3=24. This is the total number of options in the four-dimensional grid. The number of alternatives can be much larger and more comprehensive but remember: we want to keep things simple for this example. Furthermore, since we will be applying cross-validation, you will multiply the possible combinations by the number of splits in cross-validation and that would be how many complete, end-to-end training sessions will be executed to determine the best combination of hyperparameters.

Be mindful of the number of options you will try in the grid search, since all of them will be tested, and this can take a lot of time for larger networks and for larger datasets. When you gain more experience, you will be able to choose a smaller set of parameters just by thinking about the architecture that you define.

The full implementation is discussed next.

Implementation and results

The complete code for the grid search is shown here, but consider that most of these things are repetitive since this is modeled on the wide network model discussed earlier in this chapter:

```
from sklearn.model_selection import GridSearchCV
from tensorflow.keras.wrappers.scikit_learn import KerasClassifier
from tensorflow.keras.layers import Input, Dense, Dropout
from tensorflow.keras.models import Model
from tensorflow.keras.optimizers import Adam, RMSprop
from tensorflow.keras.datasets import cifar10
from tensorflow.keras.utils import to_categorical
from tensorflow.keras.callbacks import ReduceLROnPlateau, EarlyStopping
import NumPy as np

# load and prepare data (same as before)
(x_train, y_train), (x_test, y_test) = cifar10.load_data()
x_train = x_train.astype('float32') / 255.0
x_test = x_test.astype('float32') / 255.0
x_train = x_train.reshape((len(x_train), np.prod(x_train.shape[1:])))
x_test = x_test.reshape((len(x_test), np.prod(x_test.shape[1:])))
y_train = to_categorical(y_train, 10)
y_test = to_categorical(y_test, 10)
```

We declare a method to build a model and return it like so:

```
# A KerasClassifier will use this to create a model on the fly
def make_widenet(dr=0.0, optimizer='adam', lr=0.001, units=128):
  # This is a wide architecture
  inpt_dim = 32*32*3
  inpt_vec = Input(shape=(inpt_dim,))
  dl = Dropout(dr)(inpt_vec)
  l1 = Dense(units, activation='relu')(dl)
  dl = Dropout(dr)(l1)
  l2 = Dense(units, activation='relu') (dl)
  output = Dense(10, activation='sigmoid') (l2)

  widenet = Model(inpt_vec, output)

  # Our loss and lr depends on the choice
  if optimizer == 'adam':
    optmzr = Adam(learning_rate=lr)
  else:
```

```
        optmzr = RMSprop(learning_rate=lr)

    widenet.compile(loss='binary_crossentropy', optimizer=optmzr,
                    metrics=['accuracy'])

    return widenet
```

Then we put the pieces together, searching for parameters, and training as follows:

```
# This defines the model architecture
kc = KerasClassifier(build_fn=make_widenet, epochs=100, batch_size=1000,
                    verbose=0)

# This sets the grid search parameters
grid_space = dict(dr=[0.2, 0.5],        # Dropout rates
                optimizer=['adam', 'rmsprop'],
                lr=[0.01, 0.0001],   # Learning rates
                units=[1024, 512, 256])

gscv = GridSearchCV(estimator=kc, param_grid=grid_space, n_jobs=1, cv=3,
verbose=2)
gscv_res = gscv.fit(x_train, y_train, validation_split=0.3,
                callbacks=[EarlyStopping(monitor='val_loss',
                                        patience=20,
                                        restore_best_weights=True),
                        ReduceLROnPlateau(monitor='val_loss',
                                        factor=0.5, patience=10)])

# Print the dictionary with the best parameters found:
print(gscv_res.best_params_)
```

This will print out several lines, one for each time the cross-validation runs. We will omit a lot of the output here, just to show you what it looks like, but you can tune the level of verbosity manually if you want:

```
Fitting 3 folds for each of 24 candidates, totalling 72 fits
[CV] dr=0.2, lr=0.01, optimizer=adam, units=1024 ...................
[Parallel(n_jobs=1)]: Using backend SequentialBackend with 1 concurrent
workers.
[CV] ...... dr=0.2, lr=0.01, optimizer=adam, units=1024, total= 21.1s
[CV] dr=0.2, lr=0.01, optimizer=adam, units=1024 ...................
[Parallel(n_jobs=1)]: Done 1 out of 1 | elapsed: 21.1s remaining: 0.0s
[CV] ...... dr=0.2, lr=0.01, optimizer=adam, units=1024, total= 21.8s
[CV] dr=0.2, lr=0.01, optimizer=adam, units=1024 ...................
[CV] ...... dr=0.2, lr=0.01, optimizer=adam, units=1024, total= 12.6s
[CV] dr=0.2, lr=0.01, optimizer=adam, units=512 ...................
[CV] ....... dr=0.2, lr=0.01, optimizer=adam, units=512, total= 25.4s
.
```

.
.
.

```
[CV] .. dr=0.5, lr=0.0001, optimizer=rmsprop, units=256, total= 9.4s
[CV] dr=0.5, lr=0.0001, optimizer=rmsprop, units=256 ................
[CV] .. dr=0.5, lr=0.0001, optimizer=rmsprop, units=256, total= 27.2s
[Parallel(n_jobs=1)]: Done 72 out of 72 | elapsed: 28.0min finished
```

{'dr': 0.2, 'lr': 0.0001, 'optimizer': 'adam', 'units': 1024}

This last line is the most precious information you need since it is the best combination of parameters that give the best results. Now you can go ahead and change your original implementation of the wide network with these **optimized** parameters and see how the performance changes. You should receive a boost in the average accuracy of around 5%, which is not bad!

Alternatively, you can try out a larger set of parameters or increase the number of splits for cross-validation. The possibilities are endless. You should always try to optimize the number of parameters in your models for the following reasons:

- It gives you confidence in your model.
- It gives your clients confidence in you.
- It tells the world that you are a professional.

Good work! It is time to wrap up.

Summary

This chapter discussed different implementations of neural networks, namely, wide, deep, and sparse implementations. After reading this chapter, you should appreciate the differences in design and how they may affect performance or training time. At this point, you should be able to appreciate the simplicity of these architectures and how they present new alternatives to other things we've discussed so far. In this chapter, you also learned to optimize the hyperparameters of your models, for example, the dropout rates, aiming to maximize the generalization ability of the network.

I am sure you noticed that these models achieved accuracies beyond random chance, that is, > 50%; however, the problem we discussed is a very difficult problem to solve, and you might not be surprised that a general neural architecture, like the ones we studied here, does not perform extraordinarily well. In order to achieve better performance, we can use a more specialized type of architecture designed to solve problems with a high spatial correlation of the input, such as image processing. One type of specialized architecture is known as a **Convolutional Neural Network (CNN)**.

Our next station, `Chapter 12`, *Convolutional Neural Networks*, will discuss precisely that. You will be able to see how much a difference can make when you move from a general-purpose model to a more field-specific model. You cannot miss this upcoming chapter. But before you go, please try to quiz yourself with the following questions.

Questions and answers

1. **Was there a significant difference in performance between a wide or deep network?**

   Not much in the case, we studied here. However, one thing you must remember is that both networks learned fundamentally different things or aspects of the input. Therefore, in other applications, the performance might vary.

2. **Is deep learning the same as a deep neural network?**

   No. Deep learning is the area of machine learning focused on all algorithms that train over-parametrized models using novel gradient descent techniques. Deep neural networks are networks with many hidden layers. Therefore, a deep network is deep learning. But deep learning is not uniquely specific to deep networks.

3. **Could you give an example of when sparse networks are desired?**

   Let's think about robotics. In this field, most things run on microchips that have memory constraints and storage constraints and computational power constraints; finding neural architectures whose weights are mostly zero would mean you do not have to calculate those products. This implies having weights that can be stored in less space, loaded quickly, and computed faster. Other possibilities include IoT devices, smartphones, smart vehicles, smart cities, law enforcement, and so on.

4. **How can we make these models perform better?**

   We can further optimize the hyperparameters by including more options. We can use autoencoders to preprocess the input. But the most effective thing would be to switch to CNNs to solve this problem since CNNs are particularly good at the classification of images. See the next chapter.

References

- Rosenblatt, F. (1958). The perceptron: a probabilistic model for information storage and organization in the brain. *Psychological review*, 65(6), 386.
- Muselli, M. (1997). On convergence properties of the pocket algorithm. *IEEE Transactions on Neural Networks*, 8(3), 623-629.
- Novak, R., Xiao, L., Hron, J., Lee, J., Alemi, A. A., Sohl-Dickstein, J., & Schoenholz, S. S. (2019). Neural Tangents: Fast and Easy Infinite Neural Networks in Python. *arXiv preprint* arXiv:1912.02803.
- Soltanolkotabi, M., Javanmard, A., & Lee, J. D. (2018). Theoretical insights into the optimization landscape of over-parameterized shallow neural networks. *IEEE Transactions on Information Theory*, 65(2), 742-769.
- Du, S. S., Zhai, X., Poczos, B., & Singh, A. (2018). Gradient descent provably optimizes over-parameterized neural networks. *arXiv preprint* arXiv:1810.02054.
- Liao, Q., Miranda, B., Banburski, A., Hidary, J., & Poggio, T. (2018). A surprising linear relationship predicts test performance in deep networks. *arXiv preprint* arXiv:1807.09659.
- Gripon, V., & Berrou, C. (2011). Sparse neural networks with large learning diversity. *IEEE transactions on neural networks*, 22(7), 1087-1096.
- Wang, P., Ji, Y., Hong, C., Lyu, Y., Wang, D., & Xie, Y. (2018, June). SNrram: an efficient sparse neural network computation architecture based on resistive random-access memory. In *2018 55th ACM/ESDA/IEEE Design Automation Conference* (DAC) (pp. 1-6). IEEE.
- Rivas-Perea, P., Cota-Ruiz, J., & Rosiles, J. G. (2014). A nonlinear least squares quasi-newton strategy for lp-svr hyper-parameters selection. *International Journal of Machine Learning and Cybernetics*, 5(4), 579-597.
- Maclaurin, D., Duvenaud, D., & Adams, R. (2015, June). Gradient-based hyperparameter optimization through reversible learning. In *International Conference on Machine Learning* (pp. 2113-2122).
- Feurer, M., Springenberg, J. T., & Hutter, F. (2015, February). Initializing Bayesian hyperparameter optimization via meta-learning. In *Twenty-Ninth AAAI Conference on Artificial Intelligence*.
- Bergstra, J., & Bengio, Y. (2012). Random search for hyper-parameter optimization. The *Journal of Machine Learning Research*, 13(1), 281-305.
- Bergstra, J. S., Bardenet, R., Bengio, Y., & Kégl, B. (2011). Algorithms for hyper-parameter optimization. In *Advances in neural information processing systems* (pp. 2546-2554).

Convolutional Neural Networks 12

This chapter introduces convolutional neural networks, starting with the convolution operation and moving forward to ensemble layers of convolutional operations, with the aim of learning about filters that operate over datasets. The pooling strategy is then introduced to show how such changes can improve the training and performance of a model. The chapter concludes by showing how to visualize the filters learned.

By the end of this chapter, you will be familiar with the motivation behind convolutional neural networks and will know how the convolution operation works in one and two dimensions. When you finish this chapter, you will know how to implement convolution in layers so as to learn filters through gradient descent. Finally, you will have a chance to use many tools that you learned previously, including dropout and batch normalization, but now you will know how to use pooling as an alternative to reduce the dimensionality of the problem and create levels of information abstraction.

This chapter is organized as follows:

- Introduction to convolutional neural networks
- Convolution in *n*-dimensions
- Convolutional layers
- Pooling strategies
- Visualization of filters

Introduction to convolutional neural networks

Previously, in Chapter 11, *Deep and Wide Neural Networks*, we used a dataset that was very challenging for a general-purpose network. However, **convolutional neural networks (CNNs)** will prove to be more effective, as you will see. CNNs have been around since the late 80s (LeCun, Y., et al. (1989)). They have transformed the world of computer vision and audio processing (Li, Y. D., et al. (2016)). If you have some kind of AI-based object recognition capability in your smartphone, chances are it is using some kind of CNN architecture; for example:

- The recognition of objects in images
- The recognition of a digital fingerprint
- The recognition of voice commands

CNNs are interesting because they have solved some of the most challenging problems in computer vision, including beating a human being at an image recognition problem called ImageNet (Krizhevsky, A., et al. (2012)). If you can think of the most complex object recognition tasks, CNNs should be your first choice for experimentation: they will never disappoint!

The key to the success of CNNs is their unique ability to **encode spatial relationships**. If we contrast two different datasets, one about student school records that includes current and past grades, attendance, online activity, and so on, and a second dataset about images of cats and dogs, if we aim to classify students or cats and dogs, the data is different. In one we have student features that have no spatial relationships.

For example, if grades are the first feature, attendance does not have to be next to it, so their positions can be interchanged and the classification performance should not be affected, right? However, with images of cats and dogs, features (pixels) of eyes have to be adjacent to a nose or an ear; when you change the spatial features and observe an ear in the middle of two eyes (strange), the performance of the classifier should be affected because there is usually no cat or dog that has an ear in between its eyes. This is the type of spatial relationship that CNNs are good at encoding. You can also think of audio or speech processing. You know that some sounds must come after others in certain words. If the dataset allows for spatial relationships, CNNs have the potential to perform well.

Convolution in n-dimensions

The name of CNNs comes from their signature operation: **convolution**. This operation is a mathematical operation that is very common in the signal processing area. Let's go ahead and discuss the convolution operation.

1-dimension

Let's start with the discrete-time convolution function in one dimension. Suppose that we have input data, $\mathbf{x} \in \mathbb{R}^n$, and some weights, $\mathbf{w} \in \mathbb{R}^m$, we can define the discrete-time convolution operation between the two as follows:

$$(x * w)[n] \equiv h[n] = \sum_{m=-\infty}^{\infty} x[m]w[n - m]$$

.

In this equation, the convolution operation is denoted by a * symbol. Without complicating things too much, we can say that $\mathbf{w}$ is inverted, $w[-m]$, and then shifted, $w[n - m]$. The resulting vector is $\mathbf{h} \in \mathbb{R}^{n+m-1}$, which can be interpreted as the *filtered* version of the input when the filter $\mathbf{w}$ is applied.

If we define the two vectors as follows, $\mathbf{x} = [2, 3, 2]$ and $\mathbf{w} = [-1, 2, -1]$, then the convolution operation yields $\mathbf{h} = [-2, 1, 2, 1, -2]$.

Figure 12.1 shows every single step involved in obtaining this result by inverting and shifting the filter and multiplying across the input data:

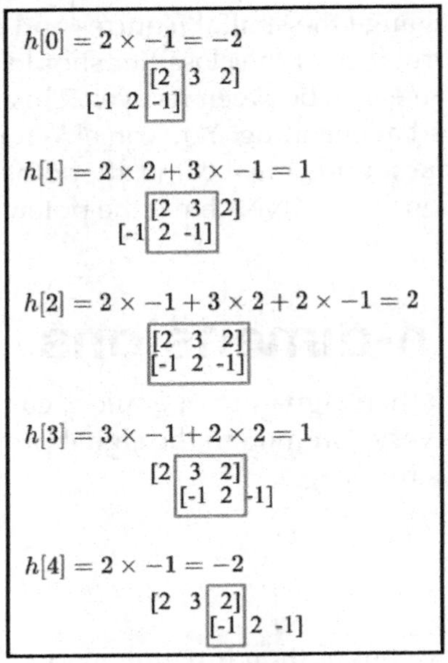

$$h[0] = 2 \times -1 = -2$$
$$[2\ 3\ 2]$$
$$[-1\ 2\ -1]$$

$$h[1] = 2 \times 2 + 3 \times -1 = 1$$
$$[2\ 3\ 2]$$
$$[-1\ 2\ -1]$$

$$h[2] = 2 \times -1 + 3 \times 2 + 2 \times -1 = 2$$
$$[2\ 3\ 2]$$
$$[-1\ 2\ -1]$$

$$h[3] = 3 \times -1 + 2 \times 2 = 1$$
$$[2\ 3\ 2]$$
$$[-1\ 2\ -1]$$

$$h[4] = 2 \times -1 = -2$$
$$[2\ 3\ 2]$$
$$[-1\ 2\ -1]$$

Figure 12.1 - Example of a convolution operation involving two vectors

In NumPy, we can achieve this by using the `convolve()` method as follows:

```
import numpy as np
h = np.convolve([2, 3, 2], [-1, 2, -1])
print(h)
```

This outputs the following:

```
[-2, 1, 2, 1, -2]
```

Now, if you think about it, the most "complete" information is when the filter fully overlaps with the input data, and that is for $h[2] = 2$. In Python, you can get that by using the `'valid'` argument as follows:

```
import numpy as np
h = np.convolve([2, 3, 2], [-1, 2, -1], 'valid')
print(h)
```

This simply gives the following:

```
2
```

Once again, this is only to maximize the *relevant* information because the convolution operation is more *uncertain* around the edges of the vector, that is, at the beginning and the end where the vectors do not fully overlap. Furthermore, for convenience, we could obtain an output vector of the same size as the input by using the `'same'` argument as follows:

```
import numpy as np
h = np.convolve([2, 3, 2], [-1, 2, -1], 'same')
print(h)
```

This prints the following:

```
[1 2 1]
```

Here are some practical reasons for each of the three ways of using convolution:

- Use `'valid'` when you need all the *good* information without any of the noise caused by the partial overlaps of the filter.
- Use `'same'` when you want to make it easier for the computations to work. This will make it easy in the sense that you will have the same dimensions in the input and the output.
- Otherwise, use nothing to obtain the full analytical solution to the convolution operation for any purposes that you want.

 Convolution became very popular with the surge of microprocessors specialized in multiplying and adding numbers extremely quickly and with the development of the **fast Fourier transform** (**FFT**) algorithm. The FFT exploits the mathematical property that convolution in the discrete time domain is equivalent to multiplication in the Fourier domain and vice versa.

Now, let's move on to the next dimension.

2-dimensions

A two-dimensional convolution is very similar to the one-dimensional convolution. However, rather than having a vector, we will have a matrix, and that's why images are directly applicable here.

Let's say that we have two matrices: one represents some input data, and the other is a filter, like so:

$$\mathbf{x} = \begin{bmatrix} 2 & 2 & 2 \\ 2 & 3 & 2 \\ 2 & 2 & 2 \end{bmatrix}, \quad \mathbf{w} = \begin{bmatrix} -1 & -1 & -1 \\ -1 & 8 & -1 \\ -1 & -1 & -1 \end{bmatrix}.$$

We can calculate the two-dimensional discrete convolution by inverting (in both dimensions) and shifting (also in both dimensions) the filter. The equation is as follows:

$$(x * w)\,[n_1, n_2] = h\,[n_1, n_2] = \sum_{m_1 = -\infty}^{\infty} \sum_{m_2 = -\infty}^{\infty} x\,[n_1, n_2]\, w\,[n_1 - m_1, n_2 - m_2]$$

This is very similar to the one-dimensional version. The following diagram illustrates the first two steps and the last one, to save space and avoid repetition:

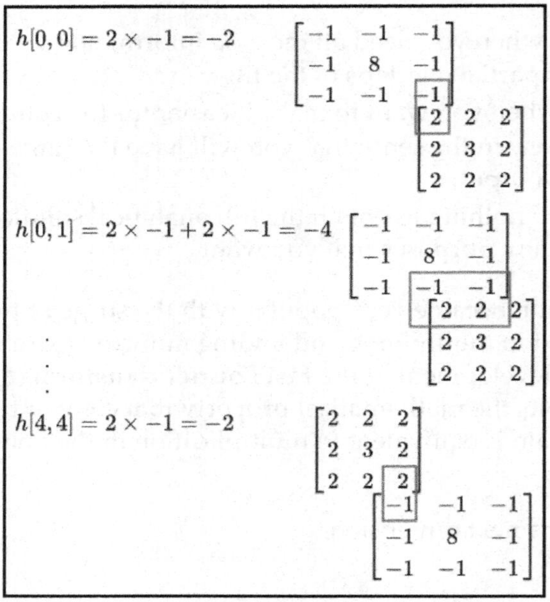

Figure 12.2 - Two-dimensional discrete convolution example

In Python, we can calculate the two-dimensional convolution using SciPy's
`convolve2d` method, as follows:

```
import numpy as np
from scipy.signal import convolve2d
x = np.array([[2,2,2],[2,3,2],[2,2,2]])
w = np.array([[-1,-1,-1],[-1,8,-1],[-1,-1,-1]])
h = convolve2d(x,w)
print(h)
```

This outputs the following:

```
[[-2 -4 -6 -4 -2]
 [-4  9  5  9 -4]
 [-6  5  8  5 -6]
 [-4  9  5  9 -4]
 [-2 -4 -6 -4 -2]]
```

The results shown here are the full analytical result. However, similar to the one-dimensional implementation, if you only want results that fully overlap, you can invoke a `'valid'` result, or if you want a result of the same size as the input, you can invoke the `'same'` alternative as follows:

```
import numpy as np
from scipy.signal import convolve2d
x = np.array([[2,2,2],[2,3,2],[2,2,2]])
w = np.array([[-1,-1,-1],[-1,8,-1],[-1,-1,-1]])
h = convolve2d(x,w,mode='valid')
print(h)
h = convolve2d(x,w,mode='same')
print(h)
```

This would yield the following:

```
[[8]]

[[9 5 9]
 [5 8 5]
 [9 5 9]]
```

Now, let's move on to n-dimensional convolutions.

n-dimensions

Once you have understood convolution in one and two dimensions, you have understood the basic concept behind it. However, you might still need to perform convolutions in larger dimensions, for example, in multispectral datasets. For this, we can simply prepare NumPy arrays of any number of dimensions and then use SciPy's `convolve()` functionality. Consider the following example:

```
import numpy as np
from scipy.signal import convolve
x = np.array([[[1,1],[1,1]],[[2,2],[2,2]]])
w = np.array([[[1,-1],[1,-1]],[[1,-1],[1,-1]]])
h = convolve(x,w)
print(h)
```

Here, vectors $x, w \in \mathbb{R}^{2 \times 2 \times 2}$ are three-dimensional arrays, and can be convolved successfully, producing the following output:

```
[[[ 1  0 -1]
  [ 2  0 -2]
  [ 1  0 -1]]

 [[ 3  0 -3]
  [ 6  0 -6]
  [ 3  0 -3]]

 [[ 2  0 -2]
  [ 4  0 -4]
  [ 2  0 -2]]]
```

The only difficult part about n-dimensional convolutions could be visualizing them or imagining them in your mind. We humans can easily understand one, two, and three dimensions, but larger dimensional spaces are tricky to illustrate. But remember, if you understand how convolution works in one and two dimensions, you can trust that the math works and the algorithms work in any dimensions.

Next, let's look at how to *learn* such convolutional filters by defining Keras layers and adding them to a model.

Convolutional layers

Convolution has a number of properties that are very interesting in the field of deep learning:

- It can successfully encode and decode spatial properties of the data.
- It can be calculated relatively quickly with the latest developments.
- It can be used to address several computer vision problems.
- It can be combined with other types of layers for maximum performance.

Keras has wrapper functions for TensorFlow that involve the most popular dimensions, that is, one, two, and three dimensions: `Conv1D`, `Conv2D`, and `Conv3D`. In this chapter, we will continue to focus on two-dimensional convolutions, but be sure that if you have understood the concept, you can easily go ahead and use the others.

Conv2D

The two-dimensional convolution method has the following signature: `tensorflow.keras.layers.Conv2D`. The most common arguments used in a convolutional layer are the following:

- `filters` refers to the number of filters to be learned in this particular layer and affects the dimension of the output of the layer.
- `kernel_size` refers to the size of the filters; for example, in the case of *Figure 12.2*, it would be size (3,3).
- `strides=(1, 1)` is new for us. Strides is defined as the size of the steps that are taken when the filters are sliding across the input. All the examples we have shown so far assume that we follow the original definition of convolution and take unit steps. However, in convolutional layers, you can take larger steps, which will lead to smaller outputs but also the loss of information.
- `padding='valid'` refers to the way of dealing with the information in the edges of the convolution result. Note that the options here are only `'valid'` or `'same'`, and that there is no way of obtaining the full analytical result. The meaning is the same as we have seen before in this chapter.
- `activation=None` gives the option to include an activation function in the layer if you need one; for example, `activation='relu'`.

To exemplify this, consider a convolutional layer such as the one shown in the following diagram, where the first layer is convolutional (in 2D) with 64 filters of size 9x9 and a stride of 2, 2 (that is, two in each direction). We will explain the rest of the model in the following diagram as we proceed:

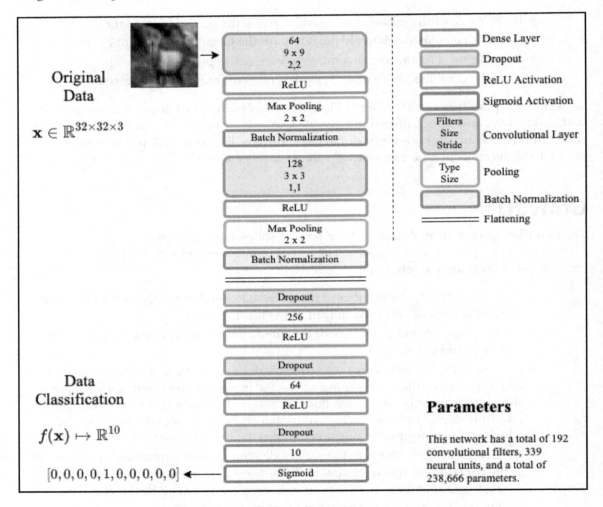

Figure 12.3 - Architecture of a convolutional neural network for CIFAR 10

The first convolutional layer in the diagram can be defined as follows:

```
import tensorflow as tf
from tensorflow.keras.layers import Conv2D
input_shape = (1, 32, 32, 3)
```

```
x = tf.random.normal(input_shape)
l = Conv2D(64, (9,9), strides=(2,2), activation='relu',
           input_shape=input_shape)(l)
print(l.shape)
```

This essentially will create a convolutional layer with the given specifications. The print statement will effectively produce the following:

```
(1, 12, 12, 64)
```

If you do the math, each and every single filter out of the 64 will produce a 23x23 `'valid'` output, but since a (2,2) stride is being used, an 11.5x11.5 output should be obtained. However, since we cannot have fractions, TensorFlow will round up to 12x12. Therefore, we end up with the preceding shape as the output.

The layer+activation combo

As mentioned previously, the Conv2D class has the ability to include an activation function of your choice. This is much appreciated because it will save some lines of code for all who want to learn to code efficiently. However, we have to be careful not to forget to document somewhere the type of activation used.

Figure 12.3 shows the activation in a separate block. This is a good idea to keep track of what activations are used throughout. The most common activation function for a convolutional layer is a ReLU, or any of the activations of the ReLU family, for example, leaky ReLU and ELU. The next *new* element is a pooling layer. Let's talk about this.

Pooling strategies

You will usually find pooling accompanying convolutional layers. Pooling is an idea that is intended to reduce the number of computations by reducing the dimensionality of the problem. We have a few pooling strategies available to us in Keras, but the most important and popular ones are the following two:

- AveragePooling2D
- MaxPooling2D

These also exist for other dimensions, such as 1D. However, in order to understand pooling, we can simply look at the example in the following diagram:

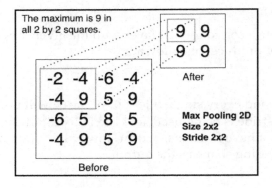

Figure 12.4 - Max pooling example in 2D

In the diagram, you can observe how max pooling would look at individual 2x2 squares moving two spaces at a time, which leads to a 2x2 result. The whole point of pooling is to **find a smaller summary of the data** in question. When it comes to neural networks, we often look at neurons that are *excited* the most, and so it makes sense to look at the maximum values as good representatives of larger portions of data. However, remember that you can also look at the average of the data (`AveragePooling2D`), which is also good in all senses.

There is a slight difference in time performance in favor of max pooling, but this is very small.

In Keras, we can implement pooling very easily. In the case of max pooling in 2D, for example, we can simply do the following:

```
import tensorflow as tf
from tensorflow.keras.layers import MaxPooling2D
x = tf.constant([[-2, -4, -6, -4],
                 [-4, 9, 5, 9],
                 [-6, 5, 8, 5],
                 [-4, 9, 5, 9]])
x = tf.reshape(x, [1, 4, 4, 1])
y = MaxPooling2D(pool_size=(2, 2), strides=(2, 2), padding='valid')
print(tf.reshape(y(x), [2, 2]))
```

This produces the same output as in *Figure 12.4*:

```
tf.Tensor(
[[9 9]
 [9 9]], shape=(2, 2), dtype=int32)
```

We can also do the same for average pooling as follows:

```
import tensorflow as tf
from tensorflow.keras.layers import AveragePooling2D
x = tf.constant([[[-2., -4., -6., -4],
                  [-4., 9., 5., 9.],
                  [-6., 5., 8., 5.],
                  [-4., 9., 5., 9.]]])
x = tf.reshape(x, [1, 4, 4, 1])
y = AveragePooling2D(pool_size=(2, 2), strides=(2, 2), padding='valid')
print(tf.reshape(y(x), [2, 2]))
```

This gives the following output:

```
tf.Tensor(
[[-0.25 1.  ]
 [ 1.  6.75]], shape=(2, 2), dtype=float32)
```

Both pooling strategies work perfectly fine in terms of summarizing the data. You will be safe in choosing either one.

Now for the big reveal. We will put all of this together in a CNN next.

Convolutional neural network for CIFAR-10

We have reached the point where we can actually implement a fully functional CNN after looking at the individual pieces: understanding the convolution operation, understanding pooling, and understanding how to implement convolutional layers and pooling. Now we will be implementing the CNN architecture shown in *Figure 12.3*.

Implementation

We will be implementing the network in *Figure 12.3* step by step, broken down into sub-sections.

Loading data

Let's load the CIFAR-10 dataset as follows:

```
from tensorflow.keras.datasets import cifar10
from tensorflow.keras.utils import to_categorical
import numpy as np

# The data, split between train and test sets:
(x_train, y_train), (x_test, y_test) = cifar10.load_data()
x_train = x_train.astype('float32') / 255.
x_test = x_test.astype('float32') / 255.

y_train = to_categorical(y_train, 10)
y_test = to_categorical(y_test, 10)
print('x_train shape:', x_train.shape)
print('x_test shape:', x_test.shape)
```

This should effectively load the dataset and print its shape, which is as follows:

```
x_train shape: (50000, 32, 32, 3)
x_test shape: (10000, 32, 32, 3)
```

This is very straightforward, but we can go further and verify that the data is loaded correctly by loading and plotting the first image of every class in the x_train set as follows:

```
import matplotlib.pyplot as plt
import numpy as np

(_, _), (_, labels) = cifar10.load_data()
idx = [3, 6, 25, 46, 58, 85, 93, 99, 108, 133]

clsmap = {0: 'airplane',
          1: 'automobile',
          2: 'bird',
          3: 'cat',
          4: 'deer',
          5: 'dog',
          6: 'frog',
          7: 'horse',
          8: 'ship',
          9: 'truck'}

plt.figure(figsize=(10,4))
for i, (img, y) in enumerate(zip(x_test[idx].reshape(10, 32, 32, 3),
labels[idx])):
  plt.subplot(2, 5, i+1)
```

```
    plt.imshow(img, cmap='gray')
    plt.xticks([])
    plt.yticks([])
    plt.title(str(y[0]) + ": " + clsmap[y[0]])
plt.show()
```

This will produce the output shown in the following screenshot:

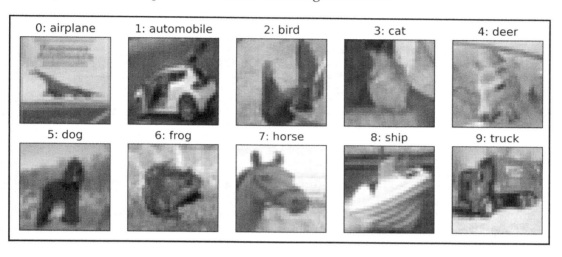

Figure 12.5 - Samples of CIFAR-10

Next, we will implement the layers of the network.

Compiling the model

Again, recall the model in *Figure 12.3*, and how we can implement it as shown here. Everything you are about to see is something we have looked at in this and previous chapters:

```
# Importing the Keras libraries and packages
from tensorflow.keras.layers import Conv2D, MaxPooling2D, Flatten
from tensorflow.keras.layers import Input, Dense, Dropout,
BatchNormalization
from tensorflow.keras.models import Model
from tensorflow.keras.optimizers import RMSprop

# dimensionality of input and latent encoded representations
inpt_dim = (32, 32, 3)

inpt_img = Input(shape=inpt_dim)
```

```
# Convolutional layer
cl1 = Conv2D(64, (9, 9), strides=(2, 2), input_shape = inpt_dim,
            activation = 'relu')(inpt_img)

# Pooling and BatchNorm
pl2 = MaxPooling2D(pool_size = (2, 2))(cl1)
bnl3 = BatchNormalization()(pl2)
```

We continue adding more convolutional layers like so:

```
# Add a second convolutional layer
cl4 = Conv2D(128, (3, 3), strides=(1, 1), activation = 'relu')(bnl3)
pl5 = MaxPooling2D(pool_size = (2, 2))(cl4)
bnl6 = BatchNormalization()(pl5)

# Flattening for compatibility
fl7 = Flatten()(bnl6)

# Dense layers + Dropout
dol8 = Dropout(0.5)(fl7)
dl9 = Dense(units = 256, activation = 'relu')(dol8)
dol10 = Dropout(0.2)(dl9)
dl11 = Dense(units = 64, activation = 'relu')(dol10)
dol12 = Dropout(0.1)(dl11)
output = Dense(units = 10, activation = 'sigmoid')(dol12)

classifier = Model(inpt_img, output)
```

Then we can compile the model and print a summary as follows:

```
# Compiling the CNN with RMSprop optimizer
opt = RMSprop(learning_rate=0.001)

classifier.compile(optimizer = opt, loss = 'binary_crossentropy',
                metrics = ['accuracy'])

print(classifier.summary())
```

This will output a summary of the network that will look like this:

```
Model: "model"
```

Layer (type)	Output Shape	Param #
input_1 (InputLayer)	[(None, 32, 32, 3)]	0
conv2d (Conv2D)	(None, 12, 12, 64)	15616
max_pooling2d_4 (MaxPooling2	(None, 6, 6, 64)	0

```
batch_normalization (BatchNo    (None, 6, 6, 64)         256


    .

    .

    .


dropout_2 (Dropout)             (None, 64)               0

dense_2 (Dense)                 (None, 10)               650
================================================================
Total params: 238,666
Trainable params: 238,282
Non-trainable params: 384
```

One thing that must be very obvious to you at this point is the number of parameters of this network. If you recall from the previous chapter, you will be surprised that this network has nearly a quarter of a million parameters, while the wide or deep network had a few million parameters. Furthermore, you will see shortly that this relatively small network, while still *overparameterized*, is going to perform better than the networks in the previous chapter that had more parameters.

Next, let's train the network.

Training the CNN

We can train the CNN using the *callbacks* that we studied in Chapter 11, *Deep and Wide Neural Networks*, to stop the network early if there is no progress, and to reduce the learning rate to focus the efforts of the gradient descent algorithm if it reaches a *plateau*.

We will train it as follows:

```python
# Fitting the CNN to the images
from tensorflow.keras.callbacks import ReduceLROnPlateau, EarlyStopping

reduce_lr = ReduceLROnPlateau(monitor='val_loss', factor=0.5, patience=10,
                              min_delta=1e-4, mode='min', verbose=1)

stop_alg = EarlyStopping(monitor='val_loss', patience=35,
                         restore_best_weights=True, verbose=1)

hist = classifier.fit(x_train, y_train, batch_size=100, epochs=1000,
                      callbacks=[stop_alg, reduce_lr], shuffle=True,
                      validation_data=(x_test, y_test))

classifier.save_weights("cnn.hdf5")
```

The results of this will vary from computer to computer. For example, it may take fewer or more epochs, or the gradient might take a different direction if the mini-batches (which are selected at random) contain several edge cases. However, for the most part, you should get a similar result to this:

```
Epoch 1/1000
500/500 [==============================] - 3s 5ms/step - loss: 0.2733 -
accuracy: 0.3613 - val_loss: 0.2494 - val_accuracy: 0.4078 - lr: 0.0010
Epoch 2/1000
500/500 [==============================] - 2s 5ms/step - loss: 0.2263 -
accuracy: 0.4814 - val_loss: 0.2703 - val_accuracy: 0.4037 - lr: 0.0010
.
.
.
Epoch 151/1000
492/500 [=============================>.] - ETA: 0s - loss: 0.0866 -
accuracy: 0.8278
Epoch 00151: ReduceLROnPlateau reducing learning rate to
3.906250185536919e-06.
500/500 [==============================] - 2s 4ms/step - loss: 0.0866 -
accuracy: 0.8275 - val_loss: 0.1153 - val_accuracy: 0.7714 - lr: 7.8125e-06
Epoch 152/1000
500/500 [==============================] - 2s 4ms/step - loss: 0.0864 -
accuracy: 0.8285 - val_loss: 0.1154 - val_accuracy: 0.7707 - lr: 3.9063e-06
Epoch 153/1000
500/500 [==============================] - 2s 4ms/step - loss: 0.0861 -
accuracy: 0.8305 - val_loss: 0.1153 - val_accuracy: 0.7709 - lr: 3.9063e-06
Epoch 154/1000
500/500 [==============================] - 2s 4ms/step - loss: 0.0860 -
accuracy: 0.8306 - val_loss: 0.1153 - val_accuracy: 0.7709 - lr: 3.9063e-06
Epoch 155/1000
500/500 [==============================] - 2s 4ms/step - loss: 0.0866 -
accuracy: 0.8295 - val_loss: 0.1153 - val_accuracy: 0.7715 - lr: 3.9063e-06
Epoch 156/1000
496/500 [=============================>.] - ETA: 0s - loss: 0.0857 -
accuracy: 0.8315Restoring model weights from the end of the best epoch.
500/500 [==============================] - 2s 4ms/step - loss: 0.0857 -
accuracy: 0.8315 - val_loss: 0.1153 - val_accuracy: 0.7713 - lr: 3.9063e-06
Epoch 00156: early stopping
```

At this point, when the training is finished, you can get an estimate of the accuracy of 83.15%. Be careful, this is not a **balanced** accuracy. For that, we will take a look at the **Balanced Error Rate** (**BER**) metric in the next section. But before we do that, we can look at the training curve to see how the loss was minimized.

The following code will produce what we want:

```
import matplotlib.pyplot as plt

fig = plt.figure(figsize=(10,6))
plt.plot(hist.history['loss'], color='#785ef0')
plt.plot(hist.history['val_loss'], color='#dc267f')
plt.title('Model Loss Progress')
plt.ylabel('Brinary Cross-Entropy Loss')
plt.xlabel('Epoch')
plt.legend(['Training Set', 'Test Set'], loc='upper right')
plt.show()
```

This gives the plot shown in *Figure 12.6*:

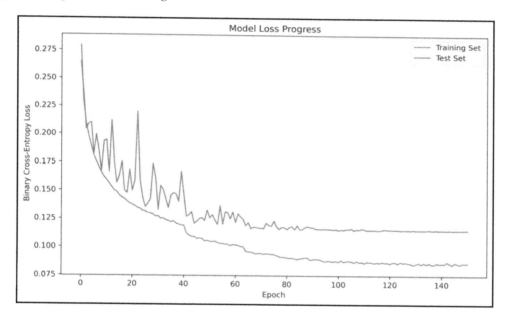

Figure 12.6 - Loss minimization for a CNN on CIFAR-10

From this diagram, you can appreciate the bumps that the learning curve has, particularly visible on the training set curve, which are due to the reduction in the learning rate through the callback function, `ReduceLROnPlateau`. The training stops after the loss no longer improves on the test set, thanks to the `EarlyStopping` callback.

Results

Now, let's look at objective, numerical results:

```
from sklearn.metrics import classification_report
from sklearn.metrics import confusion_matrix
from sklearn.metrics import balanced_accuracy_score
import matplotlib.pyplot as plt
import numpy as np

(_, _), (_, labels) = cifar10.load_data()

y_ = labels
y_hat = classifier.predict(x_test)
y_pred = np.argmax(y_hat, axis=1)

print(classification_report(np.argmax(y_test, axis=1),
                            np.argmax(y_hat, axis=1),
                            labels=[0, 1, 2, 3, 4, 5, 6, 7, 8, 9]))
cm = confusion_matrix(np.argmax(y_test, axis=1),
                      np.argmax(y_hat, axis=1),
                      labels=[0, 1, 2, 3, 4, 5, 6, 7, 8, 9])
print(cm)
ber = 1- balanced_accuracy_score(np.argmax(y_test, axis=1),
                                 np.argmax(y_hat, axis=1))
print('BER', ber)
```

This will give us the following numerical results, which we can compare with the results from the previous chapter:

```
   precision  recall  f1-score  support

0     0.80     0.82     0.81      1000
1     0.89     0.86     0.87      1000
2     0.73     0.66     0.69      1000
3     0.57     0.63     0.60      1000
4     0.74     0.74     0.74      1000
5     0.67     0.66     0.66      1000
6     0.84     0.82     0.83      1000
7     0.82     0.81     0.81      1000
8     0.86     0.88     0.87      1000
9     0.81     0.85     0.83      1000

             accuracy  0.77     10000

[[821  12  36  18  12   8   4   4  51  34]
 [ 17 860   3   7   2   6   8   1  22  74]
 [ 61   2 656  67  72  53  43  24  11  11]
```

```
[ 11    7   47  631   55  148   38   36   10   17]
[ 21    2   48   63  736   28   31   54   12    5]
[ 12    3   35  179   39  658   16   41    4   13]
[  2    4   32   67   34   20  820    8    8    5]
[ 12    3   18   41   42   52    5  809    3   15]
[ 43   22   12   12    2    5    3    0  875   26]
[ 29   51   10   19    2    3    5    9   26  846]]
```

BER 0.2288

Accuracy for specific classes can be as high as 87%, while the lowest accuracy is 66%. This is much better than the previous models in the previous chapter. The BER is of 0.2288, which can all be interpreted as a balanced accuracy of 77.12%. This matches the accuracy reported in the test set during training, which indicates that the model was trained properly. For comparison purposes, the following diagram shows a visual representation of the confusion matrix:

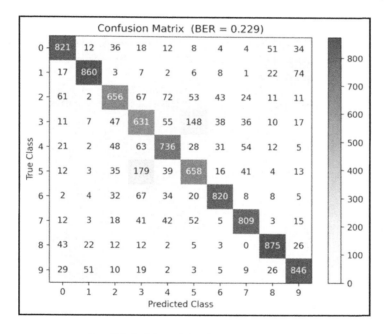

Figure 12.7 - Confusion matrix for a CNN trained over CIFAR-10

It might be a bit clearer from the visual confusion matrix that classes 3 and 5 can be confused between themselves more than other classes. Classes 3 and 5 correspond to cats and dogs, respectively.

That's it. As you can see, this is a nice result already, but you could perform more experiments on your own. You can edit and add more convolutional layers to your model and make it better. If you are curious, there are other larger CNNs that have been very successful. Here are the two most famous ones:

- VGG-19: This contains 12 convolutional layers and 3 dense layers (Simonyan, K., et al. (2014)).
- ResNet: This contains 110 convolutional layers and 1 dense layer (He, K., et al. (2016)). This particular configuration can achieve an error rate as low as 6.61% (±0.16%) on CIFAR-10.

Let's discuss next how to visualize the filters learned.

Visualization of filters

This last piece in this chapter deals with the visualization of the learned filters. This may be useful to you if you want to do research on what the network is learning. It may help with the *explainability* of the network. However, note that the deeper the network is, the more complicated it gets to understand it.

The following code will help you visualize the filters of the first convolutional layer of the network:

```
from sklearn.preprocessing import MinMaxScaler

cnn1 = classifier.layers[1].name    # get the name of the first conv layer
W = classifier.get_layer(name=cnn1).get_weights()[0]   #get the filters
wshape = W.shape  #save the original shape

# this part will scale to [0, 1] for visualization purposes
scaler = MinMaxScaler()
scaler.fit(W.reshape(-1,1))
W = scaler.transform(W.reshape(-1,1))
W = W.reshape(wshape)

# since there are 64 filters, we will display them 8x8
fig, axs = plt.subplots(8,8, figsize=(24,24))
fig.subplots_adjust(hspace = .25, wspace=.001)
axs = axs.ravel()
for i in range(W.shape[-1]):
  # we reshape to a 3D (RGB) image shape and display
  h = np.reshape(W[:,:,:,i], (9,9,3))
  axs[i].imshow(h)
  axs[i].set_title('Filter ' + str(i))
```

This code depends heavily on knowing which layer you want to visualize, the number of filters you want to visualize, and the size of the filters themselves. In this case, we want to visualize the first convolutional layer. It has 64 filters (displayed in an 8x8 grid), and each filter is 9x9x3 because the input is color images. *Figure 12.8* shows the resulting plot of the code shown previously:

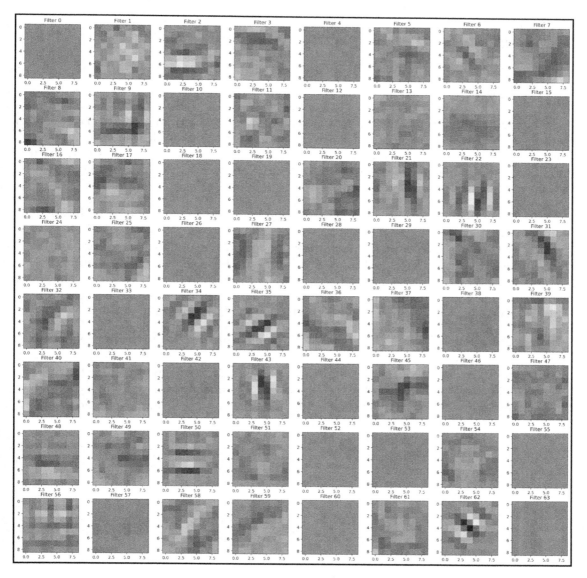

Figure 12.8 - Filters learned in the first convolutional layer

If you are an expert in image processing, you may recognize some of these patterns as they resemble Gabor filters (Jain, A. K., et al. (1991)). Some of these filters are designed to look for edges, textures, or specific shapes. The literature suggests that in convolutional networks, deeper layers usually encode highly complex information, while the first layers are used to detect features such as edges.

Feel free to go ahead and try to display another layer by making the necessary modifications.

Summary

This intermediate chapter showed how to create CNNs. You learned about the convolution operation, which is the fundamental concept behind them. You also learned how to create convolutional layers and aggregated pooling strategies. You designed a network to learn filters to recognize objects based on CIFAR-10 and learned how to display the learned filters.

At this point, you should feel confident explaining the motivation behind convolutional neural networks rooted in computer vision and signal processing. You should feel comfortable coding the convolution operation in one and two dimensions using NumPy, SciPy, and Keras/TensorFlow. Furthermore, you should feel confident implementing convolution operations in layers and learning filters through gradient descent techniques. If you are asked to show what the network has learned, you should feel prepared to implement a simple visualization method to display the filters learned.

CNNs are great at encoding highly correlated spatial information, such as images, audio, or text. However, there is an interesting type of network that is meant to encode information that is sequential in nature. Chapter 13, *Recurrent Neural Networks*, will present the most fundamental concepts of recurrent networks, leading to long short-term memory models. We will explore multiple variants of sequential models with applications in image classification and natural language processing.

Questions and answers

1. **What data summarization strategy discussed in this chapter can reduce the dimensionality of a convolutional model?**

   Pooling.

2. **Does adding more convolutional layers make the network better?**

   Not always. It has been shown that more layers has a positive effect on networks, but there are certain occasions when there is no gain. You should determine the number of layers, filter sizes, and pooling experimentally.

3. **What other applications are there for CNNs?**

   Audio processing and classification; image denoising; image super-resolution; text summarization and other text-processing and classification tasks; the encryption of data.

References

- LeCun, Y., Boser, B., Denker, J. S., Henderson, D., Howard, R. E., Hubbard, W., and Jackel, L. D. (1989). *Backpropagation applied to handwritten zip code recognition. Neural computation*, 1(4), 541-551.

- Li, Y. D., Hao, Z. B., and Lei, H. (2016). *Survey of convolutional neural networks. Journal of Computer Applications*, 36(9), 2508-2515.

- Krizhevsky, A., Sutskever, I., and Hinton, G. E. (2012). *Imagenet classification with deep convolutional neural networks.* In *Advances in neural information processing systems* (pp. 1097-1105).

- Simonyan, K., and Zisserman, A. (2014). *Very deep convolutional networks for large-scale image recognition.* arXiv preprint arXiv:1409.1556.

- He, K., Zhang, X., Ren, S., and Sun, J. (2016). *Deep residual learning for image recognition.* In *Proceedings of the IEEE conference on computer vision and pattern recognition* (pp. 770-778).

- Jain, A. K., and Farrokhnia, F. (1991). *Unsupervised texture segmentation using Gabor filters. Pattern recognition*, 24(12), 1167-1186.

13
Recurrent Neural Networks

This chapter introduces recurrent neural networks, starting with the basic model and moving on to *newer* recurrent layers that are able to handle internal memory learning to remember, or forget, certain patterns found in datasets. We will begin by showing that recurrent networks are powerful in the case of inferring patterns that are temporal or sequential, and then we will introduce an improvement on the traditional paradigm for a model that has internal memory, which can be applied in both directions in the temporal space.

We will approach the learning task by looking at a sentiment analysis problem as a sequence-to-vector application, and then we will focus on an autoencoder as a vector-to-sequence and sequence-to-sequence model at the same time. By the end of this chapter, you will be able to explain why a long short-term memory model is better than the traditional dense approach. You will be able to describe how a bi-directional long short-term memory model might represent an advantage over the single directional approach. You will be able to implement your own recurrent networks and apply them to NLP problems or to image-related applications, including sequence-to-vector, vector-to-sequence, and sequence-to-sequence modeling.

This chapter is organized as follows:

- Introduction to recurrent neural networks
- Long short-term memory models
- Sequence-to-vector models
- Vector-to-sequence models
- Sequence-to-sequence models
- Ethical implications

Introduction to recurrent neural networks

Recurrent neural networks (**RNNs**) are based on the early work of Rumelhart (Rumelhart, D. E., et al. (1986)), who was a psychologist who worked closely with Hinton, whom we have already mentioned here several times. The concept is simple, but revolutionary in the area of pattern recognition that uses sequences of data.

 A **sequence of data** is any piece of data that has high correlation in either time or space. Examples include audio sequences and images.

The concept of recurrence in RNNs can be illustrated as shown in the following diagram. If you think of a dense layer of neural units, these can be stimulated using some input at different time steps, t. *Figures 13.1 (b)* and *(c)* show an RNN with five time steps, $t = 5$. We can see in *Figures 13.1 (b)* and *(c)* how the input is accessible to the different time steps, but more importantly, the output of the neural units is also available to the next layer of neurons:

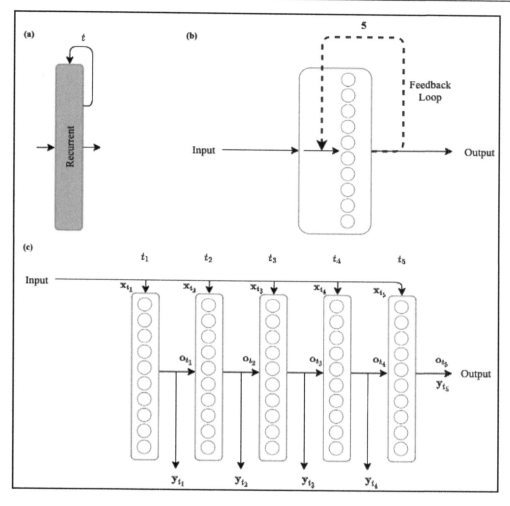

Figure 13.1. Different representations of recurrent layers: (a) will be the preferred use in this book; (b) depicts the neural units and the feedback loop; and (c) is the expanded version of (b), showing what really happens during training

The ability of an RNN to see how the previous layer of neurons is stimulated helps the network to interpret sequences much better than without that additional piece of information. However, this comes at a cost: there will be more parameters to be calculated in comparison to a traditional dense layer due to the fact that there are weights associated with the input x_t and the previous output o_{t-1}.

Simple RNNs

In Keras, we can create a simple RNN with **five time steps** and **10 neural units** (see *Figure 13.1*) as follows:

```
from tensorflow.keras import Sequential
from tensorflow.keras.layers import SimpleRNN

n_units = 10
t_steps = 5
inpt_ftrs=2
model = Sequential()
model.add(SimpleRNN(n_units, input_shape=(t_steps, inpt_ftrs)))
model.summary()
```

This gives the following summary:

```
Model: "sequential"
_____
Layer (type)                 Output Shape   Param #
=================================================================
simple_rnn (SimpleRNN)       (None, 10)       130
=================================================================
Total params: 130
Trainable params: 130
Non-trainable params: 0
```

The preceding sample code assumes that the number of **features in the input** would be just **two**; for example, we can have sequential data in two dimensions. These types of RNNs are called *simple* because they resemble the simplicity of dense networks with `tanh` activations and a recurrence aspect to it.

RNNs are usually tied to embedding layers, which we discuss next.

Embedding layers

An embedding layer is usually paired with RNNs when there are sequences that require additional processing in order to make RNNs more robust. Consider the case when you have the sentence *"This is a small vector"*, and you want to train an RNN to detect when sentences are correctly written or poorly written. You can train an RNN with all the sentences of length five that you can think of, including *"This is a small vector"*. For this, you will have to figure out a way to transform a sentence into something that the RNN can understand. Embedding layers come to the rescue.

There is a technique called **word embedding**, which is tasked with converting a word into a vector. There are several successful approaches out there, such as Word2Vec (Mikolov, T., et al. (2013)) or GloVe (Pennington, J., et al. (2014)). However, we will focus on a simple technique that is readily available. We will do this in steps:

1. Determine the length of the sentences you want to work on. This will become the dimensionality of the input for the RNN layer. This step is not necessary for the design of the embedding layer, but you will need it for the RNN layer very soon, and it is important that you decide this early on.
2. Determine the number of different words in your dataset and assign a number to them, creating a dictionary: word-to-index. This is known as a vocabulary.

> Most people will determine the vocabulary and then calculate the frequency of each word to rank the words in the vocabulary so as to have the index 0 corresponding to the most common word in the dataset, and the last index corresponding to the most uncommon word. This can be helpful if you want to ignore the most common words or the most uncommon words, for example.

3. Substitute the words in all the sentences of the dataset with their corresponding index.
4. Determine the dimensionality of the word embedding and train an embedding layer to map from the numerical index into a real-valued vector with the desired dimensions.

Look at the example in *Figure 13.2*. If we take the word *This*, whose given index is 7, some trained embedding layer can map that number into a vector of size 10, as you can see in *Figure 13.2 (b)*. That is the word embedding process.

You can repeat this process for the complete sentence *"This is a small vector"*, which can be mapped to a **sequence** of indices [7, 0, 6, 1, 28], and it will produce for you a **sequence** of vectors; see *Figure 13.2 (c)*. In other words, it will produce a **sequence of word embeddings**. The RNN can easily process these sequences and determine whether the sentence that these sequences represent is a correct sentence.

However, we must say that determining whether a sentence is correct is a challenging and interesting problem (Rivas, P. et al. (2019)):

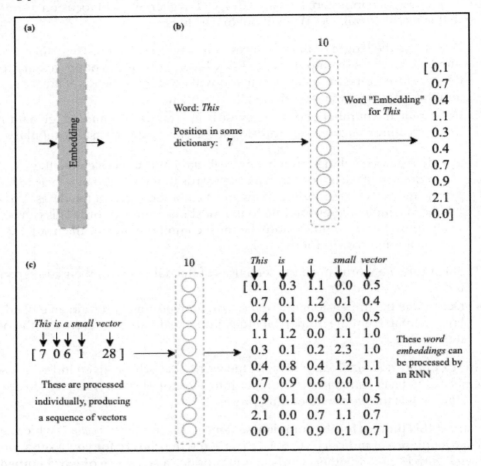

Figure 13.2. Embedding layer: (a) will be the preferred use in this book; (b) shows an example of a word embedding; and (c) shows a sequence of words and its corresponding matrix of word embeddings

Based on the model shown in *Figure 13.2*, an embedding layer in Keras can be created as follows:

```
from tensorflow.keras import Sequential
from tensorflow.keras.layers import Embedding

vocab_size = 30
embddng_dim = 10
seqnc_lngth = 5
```

```
model = Sequential()
model.add(Embedding(vocab_size, embddng_dim, input_length=seqnc_lngth))
model.summary()
```

This produces the following summary:

```
Model: "sequential"

Layer (type)              Output Shape       Param #
=================================================================
embedding (Embedding)     (None, 5, 10)      300
=================================================================
Total params: 300
Trainable params: 300
Non-trainable params: 0
```

Note, however, that the vocabulary size is usually in the order of thousands for typical NLP tasks in most common languages. Just think of your good old-fashioned dictionary ... How many entries does it have? Several thousand, usually.

Similarly, sentences are usually longer than five words, so you should expect to have longer sequences than in the preceding example.

Finally, the embedding dimension depends on how rich you want your model to be in the embedding space, or on your model space constraints. If you want a smaller model, consider having embeddings of 50 dimensions for example. But if space is not a problem and you have an excellent dataset with millions of entries, and you have unlimited GPU power, you should try embedding dimensions of 500, 700, or even 1000+ dimensions.

Now, let's try to put the pieces together with a real-life example.

Word embedding and RNNs on IMDb

The IMDb dataset was explained in previous chapters, but to keep things brief, we will say that it has movie reviews based on text and a positive (1) or negative (0) review associated with every entry.

Keras lets you have access to this dataset and gives a couple of nice features to optimize time when designing a model. For example, the dataset is already processed according to the frequency of each word such that the smallest index is associated with frequent words and vice versa. With this in mind, you can also exclude the most common words in the English language, say 10 or 20. And you can even limit the size of the vocabulary to, say, 5,000 or 10,000 words.

Before we go further, we will have to justify some things you are about see:

- A vocabulary size of 10,000. We can make an argument in favor of keeping a vocabulary size of 10,000 since the task here is to determine whether a review is positive or negative. That is, we do not need an overly complex vocabulary to determine this.
- Eliminating the top 20 words. The most common words in English include words such as "a" or "the"; words like these are probably not very important in determining whether a movie review is positive or negative. So, eliminating the 20 most common should be OK.
- Sentence length of 128 words. Having smaller sentences, such as 5-word sentences, might be lacking enough content, and it would not make a lot of sense having longer sentences, such as 300-word sentences, since we can probably sense the tone of a review in fewer words than that. The choice of 128 words is completely arbitrary, but justified in the sense explained.

With such considerations, we can easily load the dataset as follows:

```
from keras.datasets import imdb
from keras.preprocessing import sequence

inpt_dim = 128
index_from = 3

(x_train, y_train),(x_test, y_test)=imdb.load_data(num_words=10000,
                                            start_char=1,
                                            oov_char=2,
                                            index_from=index_from,
                                            skip_top=20)
x_train = sequence.pad_sequences(x_train,
                            maxlen=inpt_dim).astype('float32')
x_test = sequence.pad_sequences(x_test, maxlen=inpt_dim).astype('float32')

# let's print the shapes
print('x_train shape:', x_train.shape)
print('x_test shape:', x_test.shape)
```

We can also print some data for verification purposes like this:

```
# let's print the indices of sample #7
print(' '.join(str(int(id)) for id in x_train[7]))

# let's print the actual words of sample #7
wrd2id = imdb.get_word_index()
wrd2id = {k:(v+index_from) for k,v in wrd2id.items()}
wrd2id["<PAD>"] = 0
wrd2id["<START>"] = 1
wrd2id["<UNK>"] = 2
wrd2id["<UNUSED>"] = 3

id2wrd = {value:key for key,value in wrd2id.items()}
print(' '.join(id2wrd[id] for id in x_train[7] ))
```

This will output the following:

```
x_train shape: (25000, 128)
x_test shape: (25000, 128)

 55   655    707    6371    956    225    1456    841    42 1310    225
2 ...
very middle class suburban setting there's zero atmosphere or mood there's
<UNK> ...
```

The first part of the preceding code shows how to load the dataset split into training and test sets, x_train and y_train, x_test and y_test, respectively. The remaining part is simply to display the shape of the dataset (dimensionality) for purposes of verification, and also for verification, we can print out sample #7 in its original form (the indices) and also its corresponding word. Such a portion of the code is a little bit strange if you have not used IMDb before. But the major points are that we need to reserve certain indices for special tokens: beginning of the sentence <START>, unused index <UNUSED>, unknown word index <UNK>, and zero padding index <PAD>. One we have made a special allocation for these tokens, we can easily map from the indices back to words. These indices will be learned by the RNN, and it will learn how to handle them, either by ignoring those, or by giving specific weights to them.

Now, let's implement the architecture shown in the following diagram, which uses all the layers explained previously:

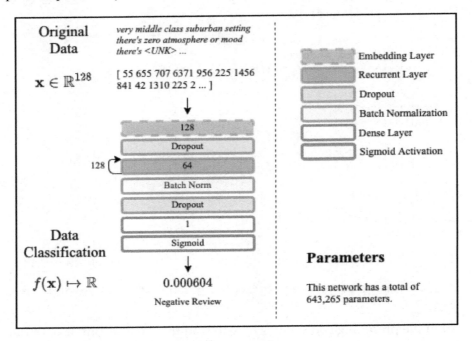

Figure 13.3. An RNN architecture for the IMDb dataset

The diagram shows the same example (#7 from the training set) that is associated with a negative review. The architecture depicted in the diagram along with the code that loads the data is the following:

```
from keras.datasets import imdb
from keras.preprocessing import sequence
from tensorflow.keras.models import Model
from tensorflow.keras.layers import SimpleRNN, Embedding,
BatchNormalization
from tensorflow.keras.layers import Dense, Activation, Input, Dropout

seqnc_lngth = 128
embddng_dim = 64
vocab_size = 10000

(x_train, y_train), (x_test, y_test) = imdb.load_data(num_words=vocab_size,
                                        skip_top=20)

x_train = sequence.pad_sequences(x_train,
                    maxlen=seqnc_lngth).astype('float32')
```

```
x_test = sequence.pad_sequences(x_test,
                        maxlen=seqnc_lngth).astype('float32')
```

The layers of the model are defined as follows:

```
inpt_vec = Input(shape=(seqnc_lngth,))
l1 = Embedding(vocab_size, embddng_dim, input_length=seqnc_lngth)(inpt_vec)
l2 = Dropout(0.3)(l1)
l3 = SimpleRNN(32)(l2)
l4 = BatchNormalization()(l3)
l5 = Dropout(0.2)(l4)
output = Dense(1, activation='sigmoid')(l5)

rnn = Model(inpt_vec, output)

rnn.compile(loss='binary_crossentropy', optimizer='adam',
            metrics=['accuracy'])
rnn.summary()
```

This model uses the standard loss and optimizer that we have used before, and the summary produced is the following:

```
Model: "functional"
```

Layer (type)	Output Shape	Param #
input_1 (InputLayer)	[(None, 128)]	0
embedding (Embedding)	(None, 128, 64)	640000
dropout_1 (Dropout)	(None, 128, 64)	0
simple_rnn (SimpleRNN)	(None, 32)	3104
batch_normalization (BatchNo	(None, 32)	128
dropout_2 (Dropout)	(None, 32)	0
dense (Dense)	(None, 1)	33

```
Total params: 643,265
Trainable params: 643,201
Non-trainable params: 64
```

Then we can train the network using the callbacks that we have used before: a) early stopping, and b) automatic learning rate reduction. The learning can be executed as follows:

```
from tensorflow.keras.callbacks import ReduceLROnPlateau, EarlyStopping
import matplotlib.pyplot as plt

#callbacks
reduce_lr = ReduceLROnPlateau(monitor='val_loss', factor=0.5, patience=3,
                              min_delta=1e-4, mode='min', verbose=1)

stop_alg = EarlyStopping(monitor='val_loss', patience=7,
                         restore_best_weights=True, verbose=1)

#training
hist = rnn.fit(x_train, y_train, batch_size=100, epochs=1000,
               callbacks=[stop_alg, reduce_lr], shuffle=True,
               validation_data=(x_test, y_test))
```

Then we save the model and display the loss like so:

```
# save and plot training process
rnn.save_weights("rnn.hdf5")

fig = plt.figure(figsize=(10,6))
plt.plot(hist.history['loss'], color='#785ef0')
plt.plot(hist.history['val_loss'], color='#dc267f')
plt.title('Model Loss Progress')
plt.ylabel('Brinary Cross-Entropy Loss')
plt.xlabel('Epoch')
plt.legend(['Training Set', 'Test Set'], loc='upper right')
plt.show()
```

The preceding code produces the plot shown in the following diagram, which indicates that the network starts to overfit after epoch #3:

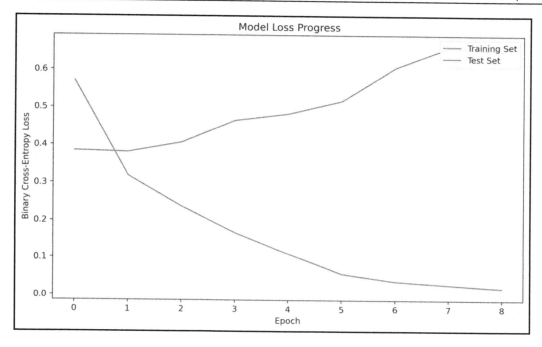

Figure 13.4. RNN loss during training

Overfitting is quite common in recurrent networks and you should not be surprised by this behavior. As of today, with the current algorithms, this happens a lot. However, one interesting fact about RNNs is that they also converge really fast compared to other traditional models. As you can see, convergence after three epochs is not too bad.

Next, we must examine the actual classification performance by looking at the balanced accuracy, the confusion matrix, and the **area under the ROC curve (AUC)**. We will do this only in the test set as follows:

```
from sklearn.metrics import confusion_matrix
from sklearn.metrics import balanced_accuracy_score
from sklearn.metrics import roc_curve, auc
import matplotlib.pyplot as plt
import numpy as np

y_hat = rnn.predict(x_test)

# gets the ROC
fpr, tpr, thresholds = roc_curve(y_test, y_hat)
roc_auc = auc(fpr, tpr)
```

```
# plots ROC
fig = plt.figure(figsize=(10,6))
plt.plot(fpr, tpr, color='#785ef0',
        label='ROC curve (AUC = %0.2f)' % roc_auc)
plt.plot([0, 1], [0, 1], color='#dc267f', linestyle='--')
plt.xlim([0.0, 1.0])
plt.ylim([0.0, 1.05])
plt.xlabel('False Positive Rate')
plt.ylabel('True Positive Rate')
plt.title('Receiver Operating Characteristic Curve')
plt.legend(loc="lower right")
plt.show()

# finds optimal threshold and gets ACC and CM
optimal_idx = np.argmax(tpr - fpr)
optimal_threshold = thresholds[optimal_idx]
print("Threshold value is:", optimal_threshold)
y_pred = np.where(y_hat>=optimal_threshold, 1, 0)
print(balanced_accuracy_score(y_test, y_pred))
print(confusion_matrix(y_test, y_pred))
```

First, let's analyze the plot produced here, which is shown in *Figure 13.5*:

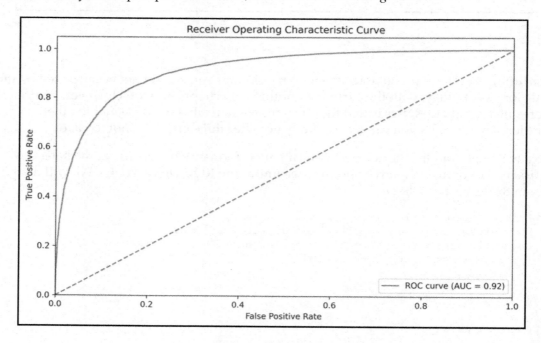

Figure 13.5. ROC and AUC of the RNN model calculated in the test set

The diagram shows a good combination of **True Positive Rates** (TPR) and **False Positive Rates (FPR)**, although it is not ideal: we would like to see a sharper step-like curve. The AUC is 0.92, which again is good, but the ideal would be an AUC of 1.0.

Similarly, the code produces the balanced accuracy and confusion matrix, which would look something like this:

```
Threshold value is: 0.81700134

0.8382000000000001

[[10273 2227]
 [ 1818 10682]]
```

First of all, we calculate here the optimal threshold value as a function of the TPR and FPR. We want to choose the threshold that will give us the maximum TPR and minimum FPR. The threshold and results shown here **will vary** depending on the initial state of the network; however, the accuracy should typically be around a very similar value.

Once the optimal threshold is calculated, we can use NumPy's `np.where()` method to threshold the entire predictions, mapping them to {0, 1}. After this, the balanced accuracy is calculated to be 83.82%, which again is not too bad, but also not ideal.

One of the possible ways to improve on the RNN model shown in *Figure 13.3* would be to somehow give the recurrent layer the ability to *remember* or *forget* specific words across layers and have them continue to stimulate neural units across the sequence. The next section will introduce a type of RNN with such capabilities.

Long short-term memory models

Initially proposed by Hochreiter, **Long Short-Term Memory Models (LSTMs)** gained traction as an improved version of recurrent models [Hochreiter, S., *et al.* (1997)]. LSTMs promised to alleviate the following problems associated with traditional RNNs:

- Vanishing gradients
- Exploding gradients
- The inability to remember or forget certain aspects of the input sequences

The following diagram shows a very simplified version of an LSTM. In *(b)*, we can see the additional self-loop that is attached to some memory, and in *(c)*, we can observe what the network looks like when unfolded or expanded:

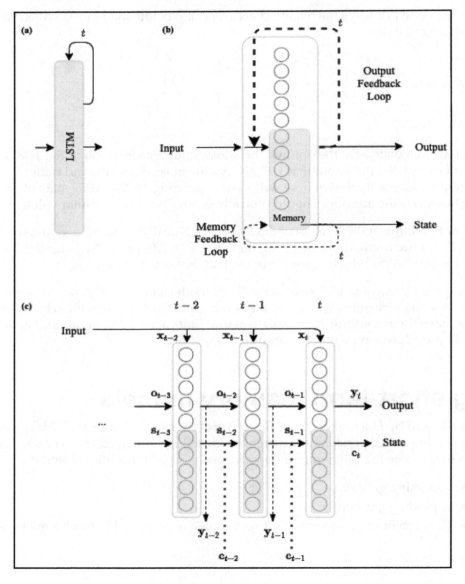

Figure 13.6. Simplified representation of an LSTM

There is much more to the model, but the most essential elements are shown in *Figure 13.6*. Observe how an LSTM layer receives from the previous time step not only the previous output, but also something called **state**, which acts as a type of memory. In the diagram, you can see that while the current output and state are available to the next layer, these are also available to use at any point if they are needed.

Some of the things that we are not showing in *Figure 13.6* include the mechanisms by which the LSTM remembers or forgets. These can be complex to explain in this book for beginners. However, all you need to know at this point is that there are three major mechanisms:

- **Output control**: How much an output neuron is stimulated by the previous output and the current state
- **Memory control**: How much of the previous state will be forgotten in the current state
- **Input control**: How much of the previous output and new state (memory) will be considered to determine the new current state

These mechanisms are trainable and optimized for each and every single dataset of sequences. But to show the advantages of using an LSTM as our recurrent layer, we will repeat the exact same code as before, only changing the RNN by an LSTM.

The code to load the dataset and build the model is the following:

```
from keras.datasets import imdb
from keras.preprocessing import sequence
from tensorflow.keras.models import Model
from tensorflow.keras.layers import LSTM, Embedding, BatchNormalization
from tensorflow.keras.layers import Dense, Activation, Input, Dropout

seqnc_lngth = 128
embddng_dim = 64
vocab_size = 10000

(x_train, y_train), (x_test, y_test) = imdb.load_data(num_words=vocab_size,
                                                      skip_top=20)
x_train = sequence.pad_sequences(x_train,
maxlen=seqnc_lngth).astype('float32')
x_test = sequence.pad_sequences(x_test,
maxlen=seqnc_lngth).astype('float32')
```

The model can be specified as follows:

```
inpt_vec = Input(shape=(seqnc_lngth,))
l1 = Embedding(vocab_size, embddng_dim, input_length=seqnc_lngth)(inpt_vec)
l2 = Dropout(0.3)(l1)
l3 = LSTM(32)(l2)
l4 = BatchNormalization()(l3)
l5 = Dropout(0.2)(l4)
output = Dense(1, activation='sigmoid')(l5)

lstm = Model(inpt_vec, output)

lstm.compile(loss='binary_crossentropy', optimizer='adam',
             metrics=['accuracy'])
lstm.summary()
```

This produces the following output:

```
Model: "functional"
```

Layer (type)	Output Shape	Param #
input (InputLayer)	[(None, 128)]	0
embedding (Embedding)	(None, 128, 64)	640000
dropout_1 (Dropout)	(None, 128, 64)	0
lstm (LSTM)	(None, 32)	12416
batch_normalization (Batch	(None, 32)	128
dropout_2 (Dropout)	(None, 32)	0
dense (Dense)	(None, 1)	33

```
Total params: 652,577
Trainable params: 652,513
Non-trainable params: 64
```

This essentially replicates the model shown in the following diagram:

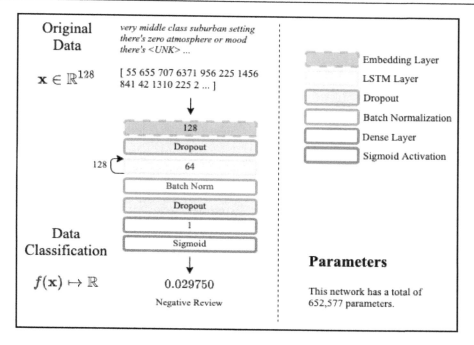

Figure 13.7. LSTM-based neural architecture for the IMDb dataset

Notice that this model has nearly 10,000 more parameters than the simple RNN approach. However, the premise is that this increase in parameters should also result in an increase in performance.

We then train our model the same as before, like so:

```
from tensorflow.keras.callbacks import ReduceLROnPlateau, EarlyStopping
import matplotlib.pyplot as plt

#callbacks
reduce_lr = ReduceLROnPlateau(monitor='val_loss', factor=0.5, patience=3,
                              min_delta=1e-4, mode='min', verbose=1)

stop_alg = EarlyStopping(monitor='val_loss', patience=7,
                         restore_best_weights=True, verbose=1)

#training
hist = lstm.fit(x_train, y_train, batch_size=100, epochs=1000,
                callbacks=[stop_alg, reduce_lr], shuffle=True,
                validation_data=(x_test, y_test))
```

Next we save the model and display its performance as follows:

```
# save and plot training process
lstm.save_weights("lstm.hdf5")

fig = plt.figure(figsize=(10,6))
plt.plot(hist.history['loss'], color='#785ef0')
plt.plot(hist.history['val_loss'], color='#dc267f')
plt.title('Model Loss Progress')
plt.ylabel('Brinary Cross-Entropy Loss')
plt.xlabel('Epoch')
plt.legend(['Training Set', 'Test Set'], loc='upper right')
plt.show()
```

This code will produce the plot shown in the following diagram:

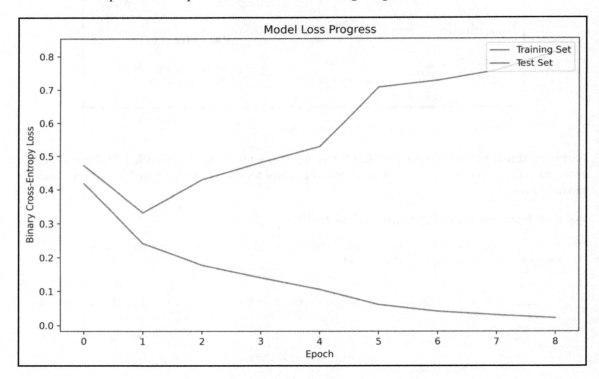

Figure 13.8. Loss across epochs of training an LSTM

Notice from the diagram that the model begins to overfit after **one epoch**. Using the trained model at the best point, we can calculate the actual performance as follows:

```
from sklearn.metrics import confusion_matrix
from sklearn.metrics import balanced_accuracy_score
from sklearn.metrics import roc_curve, auc
import matplotlib.pyplot as plt
import numpy as np

y_hat = lstm.predict(x_test)

# gets the ROC
fpr, tpr, thresholds = roc_curve(y_test, y_hat)
roc_auc = auc(fpr, tpr)

# plots ROC
fig = plt.figure(figsize=(10,6))
plt.plot(fpr, tpr, color='#785ef0',
         label='ROC curve (AUC = %0.2f)' % roc_auc)
plt.plot([0, 1], [0, 1], color='#dc267f', linestyle='--')
plt.xlim([0.0, 1.0])
plt.ylim([0.0, 1.05])
plt.xlabel('False Positive Rate')
plt.ylabel('True Positive Rate')
plt.title('Receiver Operating Characteristic Curve')
plt.legend(loc="lower right")
plt.show()

# finds optimal threshold and gets ACC and CM
optimal_idx = np.argmax(tpr - fpr)
optimal_threshold = thresholds[optimal_idx]
print("Threshold value is:", optimal_threshold)
y_pred = np.where(y_hat>=optimal_threshold, 1, 0)
print(balanced_accuracy_score(y_test, y_pred))
print(confusion_matrix(y_test, y_pred))
```

This produces the ROC shown in the following diagram:

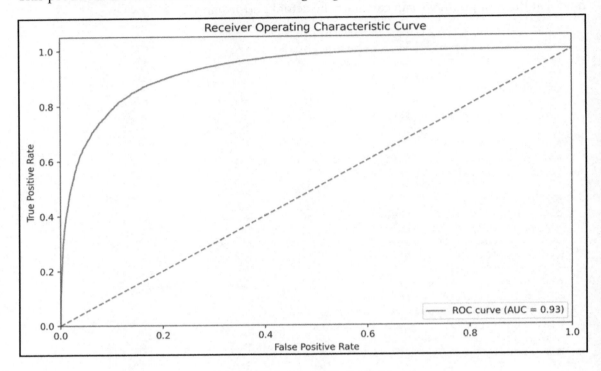

Figure 13.9. ROC curve of an LSTM-based architecture

From the plot, we can see that there is a slight gain in the model, producing an AUC of 0.93 when the simple RNN model had an AUC of 0.92.

When looking at the balanced accuracy and the confusion matrix, which was produced by the preceding code, this shows numbers like these:

```
Threshold value is: 0.44251397
0.8544400000000001
[[10459 2041]
 [ 1598 10902]]
```

Here, we can appreciate that the accuracy was of 85.44%, which is a gain of about 2% over the simple RNN. We undertook this experiment simply to show that by switching the RNN models, we can easily see improvements. Of course there are other ways to improve the models, such as the following:

- Increase/reduce the vocabulary size
- Increase/reduce the sequence length
- Increase/reduce the embedding dimension
- Increase/reduce the neural units in recurrent layers

And there may be others besides.

So far, you have seen how to take text representations (movie reviews), which is a common NLP task, and find a way to represent those in a space where you can classify them into negative or positive reviews. We did this through embedding and LSTM layers, but at the end of this, there is a dense layer with one neuron that gives the final output. We can think of this as mapping from the text space into a one-dimensional space where we can perform classification. We say this because there are three main ways in which to consider these mappings:

- **Sequence-to-vector**: Just like the example covered here, mapping sequences to an *n*-dimensional space.
- **Vector-to-sequence**: This goes the opposite way, from an *n*-dimensional space to a sequence.
- **Sequence-to-sequence**: This maps from a sequence to a sequence, usually going through an *n*-dimensional mapping in the middle.

To exemplify these things, we will use an autoencoder architecture and MNIST in the next sections.

Sequence-to-vector models

In the previous section, you *technically* saw a sequence-to-vector model, which took a sequence (of numbers representing words) and mapped to a vector (of one dimension corresponding to a movie review). However, to appreciate these models further, we will move back to MNIST as the source of input to build a model that will take one MNIST numeral and map it to a latent vector.

Unsupervised model

Let's work in the autoencoder architecture shown in the following diagram. We have studied autoencoders before and now we will use them again since we learned that they are powerful in finding vectorial representations (latent spaces) that are robust and driven by unsupervised learning:

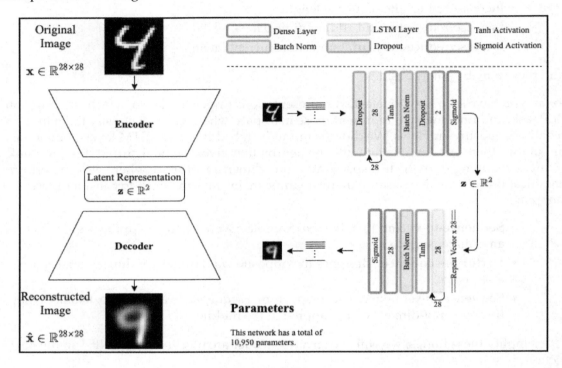

Figure 13.10. LSTM-based autoencoder architecture for MNIST

The goal here is to take an image and find its latent representation, which, in the example of *Figure 13.10*, would be two dimensions. However, you might be wondering: how can an image be a sequence?

We can interpret an image as a sequence of rows or as a sequence of columns. Let's say that we interpret a two-dimensional image, 28x28 pixels, as a sequence of rows; we can look at every row from top to bottom as a sequence of 28 vectors whose dimensions are each 1x28. In this way, we can use an LSTM to process those sequences, taking advantage of the LSTM's ability to understand temporal relationships in sequences. By this, we mean that, for example in the case of MNIST, the chances that a particular row in an image will look like the previous or next row are very high.

Notice further that the model proposed in *Figure 13.10* does not require an embedding layer as we did before when processing text. Recall that when processing text, we need to embed (vectorize) every single word into a sequence of vectors. However, with images, they already are sequences of vectors, which eliminates the need for an embedding layer.

The code that we will show here has nothing new to show except for two useful data manipulation tools:

- `RepeatVector()`: This will allow us to arbitrarily repeat a vector. It helps in the decoder (see *Figure 13.10*) to go from a vector to a sequence.
- `TimeDistributed()`: This will allow us to assign a specific type of layer to every element of a sequence.

These two are part of the `tensorflow.keras.layers` collection. These are implemented in the following code:

```
from tensorflow.keras.models import Model
from tensorflow.keras.layers import Dense, Activation, Input
from tensorflow.keras.layers import BatchNormalization, Dropout
from tensorflow.keras.layers import Embedding, LSTM
from tensorflow.keras.layers import RepeatVector, TimeDistributed
from tensorflow.keras.datasets import mnist
from tensorflow.keras.callbacks import ReduceLROnPlateau, EarlyStopping
import numpy as np

seqnc_lngth = 28      # length of the sequence; must be 28 for MNIST
ltnt_dim = 2          # latent space dimension; it can be anything reasonable

(x_train, y_train), (x_test, y_test) = mnist.load_data()

x_train = x_train.astype('float32') / 255.
x_test = x_test.astype('float32') / 255.

print('x_train shape:', x_train.shape)
print('x_test shape:', x_test.shape)
```

After loading the data we can define the encoder part of the model as follows:

```
inpt_vec = Input(shape=(seqnc_lngth, seqnc_lngth,))
l1 = Dropout(0.1)(inpt_vec)
l2 = LSTM(seqnc_lngth, activation='tanh',
          recurrent_activation='sigmoid')(l1)
l3 = BatchNormalization()(l2)
l4 = Dropout(0.1)(l3)
l5 = Dense(ltnt_dim, activation='sigmoid')(l4)
```

```
# model that takes input and encodes it into the latent space
encoder = Model(inpt_vec, 15)
```

Next we can define the decoder part of the model as follows:

```
16 = RepeatVector(seqnc_lngth)(15)
17 = LSTM(seqnc_lngth, activation='tanh', recurrent_activation='sigmoid',
          return_sequences=True)(16)
18 = BatchNormalization()(17)
19 = TimeDistributed(Dense(seqnc_lngth, activation='sigmoid'))(18)

autoencoder = Model(inpt_vec, 19)
```

Finally we compile and train the model like this:

```
autoencoder.compile(loss='binary_crossentropy', optimizer='adam')
autoencoder.summary()

reduce_lr = ReduceLROnPlateau(monitor='val_loss', factor=0.5, patience=5,
                              min_delta=1e-4, mode='min', verbose=1)

stop_alg = EarlyStopping(monitor='val_loss', patience=15,
                         restore_best_weights=True, verbose=1)

hist = autoencoder.fit(x_train, x_train, batch_size=100, epochs=1000,
                       callbacks=[stop_alg, reduce_lr], shuffle=True,
                       validation_data=(x_test, x_test))
```

The code should print the following output, corresponding to the dimensions of the dataset, a summary of the model parameters, followed by the training steps, which we omitted in order to save space:

```
x_train shape: (60000, 28, 28)
x_test shape: (10000, 28, 28)

Model: "functional"
```

Layer (type)	Output Shape	Param #
input (InputLayer)	[(None, 28, 28)]	0
dropout_1 (Dropout)	(None, 28, 28)	0
lstm_1 (LSTM)	(None, 28)	6384
batch_normalization_1 (Bat	(None, 28)	112

```
.
.
time_distributed (TimeDist (None, 28, 28)     812
========================================================
Total params: 10,950
Trainable params: 10,838
Non-trainable params: 112
```

```
Epoch 1/1000
600/600 [==============================] - 5s 8ms/step - loss: 0.3542 -
val_loss: 0.2461
.
.
.
```

The model will eventually converge to a valley where it is stopped automatically by the callback. After this, we can simply invoke the `encoder` model to literally convert any valid sequence (for example, MNIST images) into a vector, which we will do next.

Results

We can invoke the `encoder` model to convert any valid sequence into a vector like so:

```
encoder.predict(x_test[0:1])
```

This will produce a two-dimensional vector with values corresponding to a vectorial representation of the sequence `x_test[0]`, which is the first image of the test set of MNIST. It might look something like this:

```
array([[3.8787320e-01, 4.8048562e-01]], dtype=float32)
```

However, remember that this model was trained without supervision, hence, the numbers shown here will be different for sure! The encoder model is literally our sequence-to-vector model. The rest of the autoencoder model is meant to do the reconstruction.

If you are curious about how the autoencoder model is able to reconstruct a 28x28 image from a vector of just two values, or if you are curious about how the entire test set of MNIST would look when projected in the learned two-dimensional space, you can run the following code:

```
import matplotlib.pyplot as plt
import numpy as np

x_hat = autoencoder.predict(x_test)
```

```
smp_idx = [3,2,1,18,4,8,11,0,61,9]        # samples for 0,...,9 digits
plt.figure(figsize=(12,6))
for i, (img, y) in enumerate(zip(x_hat[smp_idx].reshape(10, 28, 28),
y_test[smp_idx])):
  plt.subplot(2,5,i+1)
  plt.imshow(img, cmap='gray')
  plt.xticks([])
  plt.yticks([])
  plt.title(y)
plt.show()
```

Which displays samples of the original digits, as shown in Figure 11.

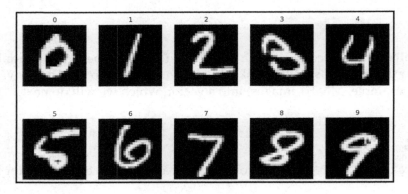

Figure 11. MNIST original digits 0-9

The following code produces samples of the reconstructed digits:

```
plt.figure(figsize=(12,6))
for i, (img, y) in enumerate(zip(x_test[smp_idx].reshape(10, 28, 28),
y_test[smp_idx])):
  plt.subplot(2,5,i+1)
  plt.imshow(img, cmap='gray')
  plt.xticks([])
  plt.yticks([])
  plt.title(y)
plt.show()
```

The reconstructed digits appear as shown in *Figure 12:*

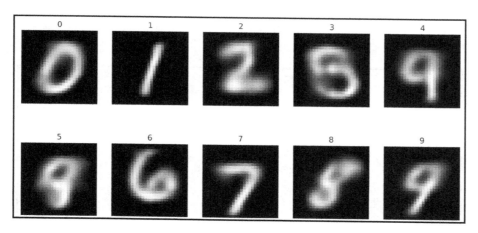

Figure 12. MNIST reconstructed digits 0-9 using an LSTM-based autoencoder

The next piece of code will display a scatter plot of the original data projected into the latent space, which is shown in *Figure 13*:

```
y_ = list(map(int, y_test))
X_ = encoder.predict(x_test)

plt.figure(figsize=(10,8))
plt.title('LSTM-based Encoder')
plt.scatter(X_[:,0], X_[:,1], s=5.0, c=y_, alpha=0.75, cmap='tab10')
plt.xlabel('First encoder dimension')
plt.ylabel('Second encoder dimension')
plt.colorbar()
```

Recall that these results may vary due to the unsupervised nature of the autoencoder. Similarly, the learned space can be visually conceived to look like the one shown in *Figure 13*, where every dot corresponds to a sequence (MNIST digit) that was made a vector of two dimensions:

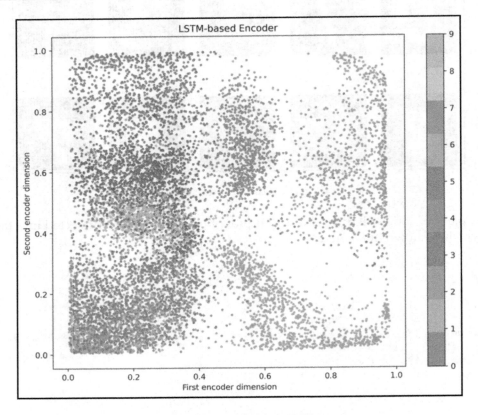

Figure 13. Learned vector space based on the MNIST dataset

From *Figure 13*, we can see that the sequence-to-vector model is working decently even when the reconstruction was based only in two-dimensional vectors. We will see larger representations in the next section. However, you need to know that sequence-to-vector models have been very useful in the last few years [Zhang, Z., *et al.* (2017)].

Another useful strategy is to create vector-to-sequence models, which is going from a vectorial representation to a sequential representation. In an autoencoder, this would correspond to the decoder part. Let's go ahead and discuss this next.

Vector-to-sequence models

If you look back at *Figure 10*, the vector-to-sequence model would correspond to the decoder funnel shape. The major philosophy is that most models usually can go from large inputs down to rich representations with no problems. However, it is only recently that the machine learning community regained traction in producing sequences from vectors very successfully (Goodfellow, I., et al. (2016)).

You can think of *Figure 10* again and the model represented there, which will produce a sequence back from an original sequence. In this section, we will focus on that second part, the decoder, and use it as a vector-to-sequence model. However, before we go there, we will introduce another version of an RNN, a bi-directional LSTM.

Bi-directional LSTM

A **Bi-directional LSTM (BiLSTM)**, simply put, is an LSTM that analyzes a sequence going forward and backward, as shown in *Figure 14*:

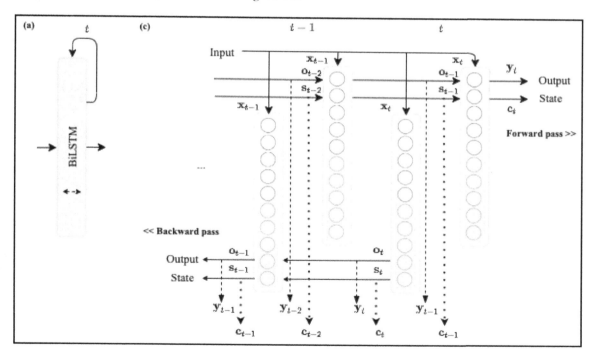

Figure 14. A bi-directional LSTM representation

Consider the following examples of sequences analyzed going forward and backward:

- An audio sequence that is analyzed in natural sound, and then going backward (some people do this to look for *subliminal* messages).
- A text sequence, like a sentence, that is analyzed for good style going forward, and also going backward since some patterns (at least in the English and Spanish languages) make reference backward; for example, a verb that makes reference to a subject that appears at the beginning of the sentence.
- An image that has peculiar shapes going from top to bottom, or bottom to top, or from side to side and backwards; if you think of the number 9, going from top to bottom, a traditional LSTM might forget the round part at the top and remember the slim part at the bottom, but a BiLSTM might be able to recall both important aspects of the number by going top to bottom and bottom to top.

From *Figure 14 (b)*, we can also observe that the state and output of both the forward and backward pass are available at any point in the sequence.

We can implement the bi-directional LSTM by simply invoking the `Bidirectional()` wrapper around a simple LSTM layer. We will then take the architecture in *Figure 10* and modify it to have the following:

- 100 dimensions in the latent space
- A BiLSTM replacing LSTM layers
- An additional dropout layer going from the latent space into the decoder

The new architecture will look like *Figure 15*:

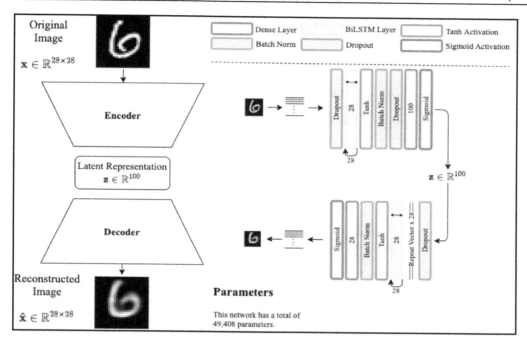

Figure 15. Implementing BiLSTMs with a view to building a vector-to-sequence model

Recall that the most important point here is to make the latent space (the input to the vector-to-sequence model) as rich as possible in order to generate better sequences. We are trying to achieve this by increasing the latent space dimensionality and adding BiLSTMS. Let's go ahead and implement this and look a the results.

Implementation and results

The code to implement the architecture in *Figure 15* is the following:

```
from tensorflow.keras.models import Model
from tensorflow.keras.layers import Dense, Activation, Input
from tensorflow.keras.layers import BatchNormalization, Dropout
from tensorflow.keras.layers import Bidirectional, LSTM
from tensorflow.keras.layers import RepeatVector, TimeDistributed
from tensorflow.keras.datasets import mnist
from tensorflow.keras.callbacks import ReduceLROnPlateau, EarlyStopping
import numpy as np

seqnc_lngth = 28
ltnt_dim = 100
```

```
(x_train, y_train), (x_test, y_test) = mnist.load_data()

x_train = x_train.astype('float32') / 255.
x_test = x_test.astype('float32') / 255.
```

We define the encoder portion of the model as follows:

```
inpt_vec = Input(shape=(seqnc_lngth, seqnc_lngth,))
l1 = Dropout(0.5)(inpt_vec)
l2 = Bidirectional(LSTM(seqnc_lngth, activation='tanh',
                       recurrent_activation='sigmoid'))(l1)
l3 = BatchNormalization()(l2)
l4 = Dropout(0.5)(l3)
l5 = Dense(ltnt_dim, activation='sigmoid')(l4)

# sequence to vector model
encoder = Model(inpt_vec, l5, name='encoder')
```

The decoder portion of the model can be defined as follows:

```
ltnt_vec = Input(shape=(ltnt_dim,))
l6 = Dropout(0.1)(ltnt_vec)
l7 = RepeatVector(seqnc_lngth)(l6)
l8 = Bidirectional(LSTM(seqnc_lngth, activation='tanh',
                  recurrent_activation='sigmoid',
                  return_sequences=True))(l7)
l9 = BatchNormalization()(l8)
l10 = TimeDistributed(Dense(seqnc_lngth, activation='sigmoid'))(l9)

# vector to sequence model
decoder = Model(ltnt_vec, l10, name='decoder')
```

Next we compile the autoencoder and train it:

```
recon = decoder(encoder(inpt_vec))
autoencoder = Model(inpt_vec, recon, name='ae')

autoencoder.compile(loss='binary_crossentropy', optimizer='adam')
autoencoder.summary()

reduce_lr = ReduceLROnPlateau(monitor='val_loss', factor=0.5, patience=5,
                              min_delta=1e-4, mode='min', verbose=1)

stop_alg = EarlyStopping(monitor='val_loss', patience=15,
                         restore_best_weights=True, verbose=1)

hist = autoencoder.fit(x_train, x_train, batch_size=100, epochs=1000,
                       callbacks=[stop_alg, reduce_lr], shuffle=True,
                       validation_data=(x_test, x_test))
```

There is nothing new here, except for the `Bidirectional()` wrapper used that has been explained previously. The output should produce a summary of the full autoencoder model and the full training operation and will look something like this:

```
Model: "ae"

Layer (type)            Output Shape        Param #
=================================================================
input (InputLayer)      [(None, 28, 28)]    0

encoder (Functional)    (None, 100)         18692

decoder (Functional)    (None, 28, 28)      30716
=================================================================
Total params: 49,408
Trainable params: 49,184
Non-trainable params: 224

Epoch 1/1000
600/600 [==============================] - 9s 14ms/step - loss: 0.3150 -
val_loss: 0.1927
.
.
.
```

Now, after a number of epochs of unsupervised learning, the training will stop automatically and we can use the `decoder` model as our vector-to-sequence model. But before we do that, we might want to quickly check the quality of the reconstructions by running the same code as before to produce the images shown in the following diagram:

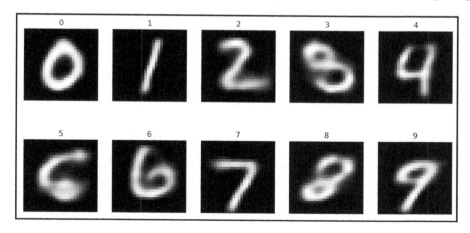

Figure 16. MNIST digits reconstructed with a BiLSTM autoencoder

If you compare *Figure 11* with *Figure 16*, you will notice that the reconstructions are much better and the level of detail is better when compared to the previous model reconstructions in *Figure 12*.

Now we can call our vector-to-sequence model directly with any compatible vector as follows:

```
z = np.random.rand(1,100)
x_ = decoder.predict(z)
print(x_.shape)
plt.imshow(x_[0], cmap='gray')
```

This produces the following output and the plot in *Figure 17*:

```
(1, 28, 28)
```

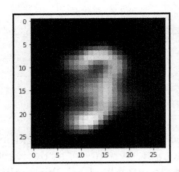

Figure 17. Sequence produced by a model from a random vector

You can generate as many random vectors as you wish and test your vector-to-sequence model. And another interesting thing to observe is a sequence-to-sequence model, which we will cover next.

Sequence-to-sequence models

A Google Brain scientist (Vinyals, O., et al. (2015)) wrote the following:

> *"Sequences have become first-class citizens in supervised learning thanks to the resurgence of recurrent neural networks. Many complex tasks that require mapping from or to a sequence of observations can now be formulated with the **sequence-to-sequence (seq2seq)** framework, which employs the chain rule to efficiently represent the joint probability of sequences."*

This is astoundingly correct because now the applications have grown. Just think about the following sequence-to-sequence project ideas:

- Document summarization. Input sequence: a document. Output sequence: an abstract.
- Image super resolution. Input sequence: a low-resolution image. Output sequence: a high-resolution image.
- Video subtitles. Input sequence: video. Output sequence: text captions.
- Machine translation. Input sequence: text in source language. Output sequence: text in a target language.

These are exciting and extremely challenging applications. If you have used online translators, chances are you have used some type of sequence-to-sequence model.

In this section, to keep it simple, we will continue using the autoencoder in *Figure 15* as our main focus, but just to make sure we are all on the same page with respect to the generality of sequence-to-sequence models, we will point out the following notes:

- Sequence-to-sequence models can map across domains; for example, video to text or text to audio.
- Sequence-to-sequence models can map in different dimensions; for example, a low-res image to high-res or vice versa for compression.
- Sequence-to-sequence models can use many different tools, such as dense layers, convolutional layers, and recurrent layers.

With this in mind, you can pretty much build a sequence-to-sequence model depending of your application. For now, we will come back to the model in *Figure 15* and show that the autoencoder is a sequence-to-sequence model in the sense that it takes a sequence of rows of an image and produces a sequence of rows of another image. Since this is an autoencoder, the input and output dimensions must match.

We will limit our showcase of the previously trained sequence-to-sequence model (autoencoder) to the following short code snippet, which builds up from the code in the previous section:

```
plt.figure(figsize=(12,6))
for i in range(10):
  plt.subplot(2,5,i+1)
  rnd_vec = np.round(np.mean(x_test[y_test==i],axis=0))    # (a)
  rnd_vec = np.reshape(rnd_vec, (1,28,28))                  # (b)
  z = encoder.predict(rnd_vec)                              # (c)
  decdd = decoder.predict(z)                                # (d)
  plt.imshow(decdd[0], cmap='gray')
```

```
        plt.xticks([])
        plt.yticks([])
        plt.title(i)
    plt.show()
```

Let's explain some of these steps. In *(a)*, we calculate the average sequence for every single number; this is in response to the question: what can we use as our input sequence since doing random is so easy? Well, using the average sequences to form the test set sounds interesting enough.

Next, *(b)* is simply to make the input compatible with the encoder input dimensions. Then, *(c)* takes the average sequence and makes a vector out of it. Finally, *(d)* uses that vector to recreate the sequence, producing the plot shown in the following diagram:

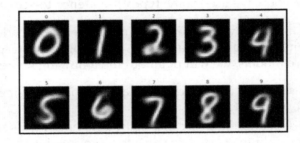

Figure 18. Sequence-to-sequence example outputs

From the diagram, you can easily observe well-defined patterns consistent with handwritten numbers, which are generated as sequences of rows by bi-directional LSTMs.

Before we finish this, let's have a word on the ethical implications of some of these models.

Ethical implications

With the resurgence of recurrent models and their applicability in capturing temporal information in sequences, there is a risk of finding latent spaces that are not properly being fairly distributed. This can be of higher risk in unsupervised models that operate in data that is not properly curated. If you think about it, the model does not care about the relationships that it finds; it only cares about minimizing a loss function, and therefore if it is trained with magazines or newspapers from the 1950s, it may find spaces where the word "women" may be close (in terms of Euclidean distance) to home labor words such as "broom", "dishes", and "cooking", while the word "man" may be close to all other labor such as "driving", "teaching", "doctor", and "scientist". This is an example of a bias that has been introduced into the latent space (Shin, S., et al. (2020)).

The risk here is that the vector-to-sequence or sequence-to-sequence models will find it much easier to associate a doctor with a man than with a woman, and cooking with a woman than with a man, just to name a couple of examples. You can take this to images of faces as well and find that certain people with certain features might be associated incorrectly. This is why it is so important to undertake the type of analysis we are doing here, trying to visualize the latent space whenever possible, trying to look at what the model outputs, and so on.

The key takeaway here is that, while the models discussed here are extremely interesting and powerful, they also carry the risk of learning things about our societies that are particularly perceived as unwanted. If the risk exists and goes undetected, it might cause bias (Amini, A., et al. (2019)). And if bias goes undetected, it might lead to several forms of discrimination. Please always be careful about these things as well as things beyond your own societal context.

Summary

This advanced chapter showed you how to create RNNs. You learned about LSTMs and its bi-directional implementation, which is one of the most powerful approaches for sequences that can have distant temporal correlations. You also learned to create an LSTM-based sentiment analysis model for the classification of movie reviews. You designed an autoencoder to learn a latent space for MNIST using simple and bi-directional LSTMs and used it both as a vector-to-sequence model and as a sequence-to-sequence model.

At this point, you should feel confident explaining the motivation behind memory in RNNs founded in the need for more robust models. You should feel comfortable coding your own recurrent network using Keras/TensorFlow. Furthermore, you should feel confident implementing both supervised and unsupervised recurrent networks.

LSTMs are great in encoding highly correlated spatial information, such as images, or audio, or text, just like CNNs. However, both CNNs and LSTMs learn very specific latent spaces that may lack diversity. This can cause a problem if there is a malicious hacker that is trying to break your system; if your model is very specific to your data, it may create certain sensitivity to variations, leading to disastrous consequences in your outputs. Autoencoders solve this by using a generative approach called the variational autoencoder, which learns the distribution of the data rather than the data itself. However, the question remains: How can we implement this idea of generative approaches in other types of networks that are not necessarily autoencoders? To find out the answer, you cannot miss the next chapter, `Chapter 14`, *Generative Neural Networks*. The next chapter will present a way of overcoming the fragility of neural networks by attacking them and teaching them to be more robust. But before you go, quiz yourself with the following questions.

Questions and answers

1. **If both CNNs and LSTMs can model spatially correlated data, what makes LSTMs particularly better?**

   Nothing in general, other than the fact that LSTMs have memory. But in certain applications, such as NLP, where a sentence is discovered sequentially as you go forward and backward, there are references to certain words at the beginning, middle, and end, and multiples at a time. It is easier for BiLSTMs to model that behavior faster than a CNN. A CNN may learn to do that, but it may take longer to do so in comparison.

2. **Does adding more recurrent layers make the network better?**

   No. It can make things worse. It is recommended to keep it simple to no more than three layers, unless you are a scientist and are experimenting with something new. Otherwise, there should be no more than three recurrent layers in a row in an encoder model.

3. **What other applications are there for LSTMs?**

   Audio processing and classification; image denoising; image super-resolution; text summarization and other text-processing and classification tasks; word completion; chatbots; text completion; text generation; audio generation; image generation.

4. **It seems like LSTMs and CNNs haver similar applications. What makes you choose one over the other?**

   LSTMs are faster to converge; thus, if time is a factor, LSTMs are better. CNNs are more stable than LSTMs; thus, if your input is very unpredictable, chances are an LSTM might carry the problem across recurrent layers, making it worse every time, in which case CNNs could alleviate that with pooling. On a personal level, I usually try CNNs first for image-related applications, and LSTMs first for NLP applications.

References

- Rumelhart, D. E., Hinton, G. E., and Williams, R. J. (1986). *Learning representations by backpropagating errors. Nature,* 323(6088), 533-536.
- Mikolov, T., Sutskever, I., Chen, K., Corrado, G. S., and Dean, J. (2013). *Distributed representations of words and phrases and their compositionality.* In *Advances in neural information processing systems* (pp. 3111-3119).
- Pennington, J., Socher, R., and Manning, C. D. (October 2014). *Glove: Global vectors for word representation.* In *Proceedings of the 2014 conference on empirical methods in natural language processing* (EMNLP) (pp. 1532-1543).
- Rivas, P., and Zimmermann, M. (December 2019). *Empirical Study of Sentence Embeddings for English Sentences Quality Assessment.* In *2019 International Conference on Computational Science and Computational Intelligence* (CSCI) (pp. 331-336). IEEE.
- Hochreiter, S., and Schmidhuber, J. (1997). *Long short-term memory. Neural computation,* 9(8), 1735-1780.
- Zhang, Z., Liu, D., Han, J., and Schuller, B. (2017). *Learning audio sequence representations for acoustic event classification. arXiv preprint* arXiv:1707.08729.
- Goodfellow, I., Bengio, Y., and Courville, A. (2016). *Sequence modeling: Recurrent and recursive nets. Deep learning,* 367-415.
- Vinyals, O., Bengio, S., and Kudlur, M. (2015). *Order matters: Sequence to sequence for sets. arXiv preprint* arXiv:1511.06391.
- Shin, S., Song, K., Jang, J., Kim, H., Joo, W., and Moon, I. C. (2020). *Neutralizing Gender Bias in Word Embedding with Latent Disentanglement and Counterfactual Generation. arXiv preprint* arXiv:2004.03133.
- Amini, A., Soleimany, A. P., Schwarting, W., Bhatia, S. N., and Rus, D. (January 2019). *Uncovering and mitigating algorithmic bias through learned latent structure.* In *Proceedings of the 2019 AAAI/ACM Conference on AI, Ethics, and Society* (pp. 289-295).

14
Generative Adversarial Networks

Reading about making sushi is easy; actually cooking a new kind of sushi is harder than we might think. In deep learning, the creative process is harder, but not impossible. We have seen how to build models that can classify numbers, using dense, convolutional, or recurrent networks, and today we will see how to build a model that can create numbers. This chapter introduces a learning approach known as generative adversarial networks, which belong to the family of adversarial learning and generative models. The chapter explains the concepts of generators and discriminators and why having good approximations of the distribution of the training data can lead to the success of the model in other areas such as *data augmentation*. By the end of the chapter, you will know why adversarial training is important; you will be able to code the necessary mechanisms for training a generator and a discriminator on questionable data; and you will code a **Generative Adversarial Network (GAN)** to generate images from a learned latent space.

This chapter is organized as follows:

- Introducing adversarial learning
- Training a GAN
- Comparing GANs and VAEs
- Thinking about the ethical implications of generative models

Introducing adversarial learning

Recently, there has been interest in adversarial training using adversarial neural networks (Abadi, M., et al. (2016)). This is due to adversarial neural networks that can be trained to protect the model itself from AI-based adversaries. We could categorize adversarial learning into two major branches:

- **Black box**: In this category, a machine learning model exists as a black box, and the adversary can only learn to attack the black box to make it fail. The adversary arbitrarily (within some bounds) creates fake input to make the black box model fail, but it has no access to the model it is attacking (Ilyas, A., et al. (2018)).
- **Insider**: This type of adversarial learning is meant to be part of the training process of the model it aims to attack. The adversary has an influence on the outcome of a model that is trained *not* to be fooled by such an adversary (Goodfellow, I., et al. (2014)).

There are pros and cons to each of these:

Black box pros	Black box cons	Insider pros	Insider cons
It gives the ability to explore more generative approaches.	Does not have a way to influence or change the black box model.	The model that is trained adversarially can be more robust to specific black box attacks.	The options for generating attacks are currently limited.
It is usually fast and likely to find a way to break a model.	The generator usually focuses only on perturbing existing data.	The generator can be used to *augment* datasets.	It is usually slower.
	The generator may not be usable in *augmenting* datasets.		

Since this book is for beginners, we will focus on one of the simplest models: an insider model known as a GAN. We will look at its parts and discuss the batch training of it.

GANs have historically been used to generate realistic images (Goodfellow, I., et al. (2014)), generally solving multi-agent problems (Sukhbaatar, S., *et al.* (2016)), and even cryptography (Rivas, P., et al. (2020)).

Let's briefly discuss adversarial learning and GANs.

Learning using an adversary

A machine learning model can learn traditionally to do classification or regression and other tasks, among which there may be a model trying to learn to distinguish whether the input is legitimate or fake. In this scenario, an machine learning model can be created to be an adversary that produces fake inputs, as shown in *Figure 14.1*:

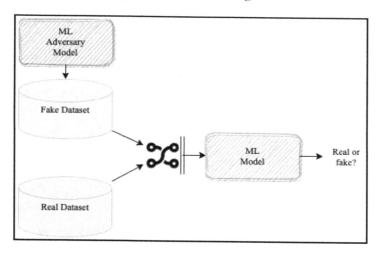

Figure 14.1 - Adversarial learning

In this paradigm, a machine learning model needs to learn to distinguish between true inputs and fake ones. When it makes a mistake, it needs to *learn* to adjust itself to make sure it properly recognizes true input. On the other hand, the adversary will need to keep producing fake inputs with the aim of making the model fail.

Here is what success looks like for each model:

- The **machine learning main model** is successful if it can successfully distinguish fake from real input.
- The **Adversary model** is successful if it can fool the machine learning main model into passing fake data as real.

As you can see, they are competing against each other. One's success is the failure of the other, and vice versa.

During the learning process, the machine learning main model will continuously call for batches of real and fake data to learn, adjust, and repeat until we are satisfied with the performance, or some other stopping criteria have been met.

In general in adversarial learning, there is no specific requirement on the adversary, other than to produce fake data.

 Adversarial robustness is a new term that is used to certify that certain models are robust against adversarial attacks. These certificates are usually designated for particular types of adversaries. See Cohen, J. M., *et al.* (2019) for further details.

A popular type of adversarial learning takes place within a GAN, which we will discuss next.

GANs

A GAN is one of the simplest neural-based models that implements adversarial learning, and was initially conceived in a bar in Montreal by Ian Goodfellow and collaborators (Goodfellow, I., et al. (2014)). It is based on a min-max optimization problem that can be posed as follows:

$$\min_{G} \max_{D} V(D, G) = \mathbb{E}_{\mathbf{x} \sim p_{\text{data}}(\mathbf{x})}\left[\log D(\mathbf{x})\right] + \mathbb{E}_{\mathbf{z} \sim p_{\mathbf{z}}(\mathbf{z})}\left[\log(1 - D(G(\mathbf{z})))\right]$$

There are several parts to this equation that require an explanation, so here we go:

- $D(\mathbf{x})$: In a GAN, this is the discriminator, which is a neural network that takes input data $\mathbf{x} \in \mathbb{R}^n$ and determines whether it is fake or real, as shown in *Figure 14.2*.
- $G(\mathbf{x})$: In a GAN, this is the generator, which is also a neural network, but its input is random noise, $\mathbf{z} \in \mathbb{R}^d$, with the probability $p(\mathbf{z})$:

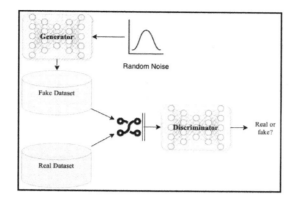

Figure 14.2 - GAN main paradigm

Ideally, we want to maximize the correct predictions of the discriminator D, while, at the same time, we want to minimize the error of the generator, G, producing a sample that does not fool the discriminator, which is expressed as $\log(1 - D(G(z)))$. The formulation of expectations and logarithms comes from the standard cross-entropy loss function.

To recap, in a GAN, the generator and the discriminator are neural networks. The generator draws random noise from a random distribution, and uses that noise to generate *fake* input to fool the discriminator.

With this in mind, let's proceed and code a simple GAN.

Training a GAN

We will begin our implementation with a simple MLP-based model, that is, our generator and discriminator will be dense, fully connected, networks. Then, we will move on to implementing a convolutional GAN.

An MLP model

We will now focus in creating the model shown in *Figure 14.3*. The model has a generator and discriminator that are distinct in terms of their numbers of layers and total parameters. It is usually the case that the generator takes more resources to build than the discriminator. This is intuitive if you think about it: the creative process is usually more complex than the process of recognition. In life, it might be easy to recognize a painting from Pablo Picasso if you see all of his paintings repeatedly.

However, it might be much harder, in comparison, to actually paint like Picasso:

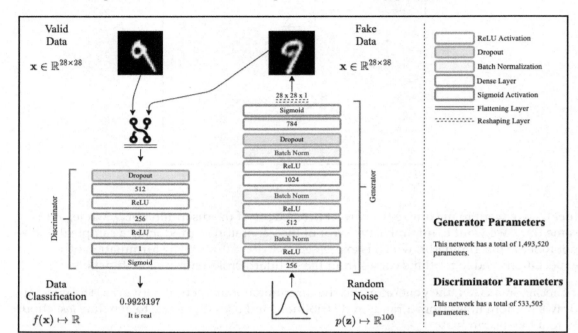

Figure 14.3 - MLP-based GAN architecture

This figure depicts an icon that simply represents the fact that the discriminator will be taking both fake and valid data and learning from both worlds. One thing that you must always remember about GANs is that they **generate** data from **random noise**. Just think about that for a minute and you will realize that this is very cool.

So, the architecture in *Figure 14.3* does not have any new items we have not discovered before. However, the design itself is what is original. Also, the way to create it in Keras is quite the task. So, we will show the whole code, with as many comments as possible to make things clear.

Here is the full code:

```python
from tensorflow.keras.models import Model
from tensorflow.keras.layers import Dense, Activation, Input, Flatten
from tensorflow.keras.layers import BatchNormalization, Dropout, Reshape
from tensorflow.keras.optimizers import Adam
from tensorflow.keras.datasets import mnist
import numpy as np
import matplotlib.pyplot as plt
```

```
img_dims = 28
img_chnl = 1
ltnt_dim = 100

(x_train, y_train), (x_test, y_test) = mnist.load_data()

x_train = x_train.astype('float32') / 255.
x_test = x_test.astype('float32') / 255.

# this makes sure that each image has a third dimension
x_train = np.expand_dims(x_train, axis=3)     # 28x28x1
x_test = np.expand_dims(x_test, axis=3)

print('x_train shape:', x_train.shape)
print('x_test shape:', x_test.shape)
```

Next, we define the generator as follows:

```
# building the generator network
inpt_noise = Input(shape=(ltnt_dim,))
gl1 = Dense(256, activation='relu')(inpt_noise)
gl2 = BatchNormalization()(gl1)
gl3 = Dense(512, activation='relu')(gl2)
gl4 = BatchNormalization()(gl3)
gl5 = Dense(1024, activation='relu')(gl4)
gl6 = BatchNormalization()(gl5)
gl7 = Dropout(0.5)(gl6)
gl8= Dense(img_dims*img_dims*img_chnl, activation='sigmoid')(gl7)
gl9= Reshape((img_dims,img_dims,img_chnl))(gl8)
generator = Model(inpt_noise, gl9)
gnrtr_img = generator(inpt_noise)
# uncomment this if you want to see the summary
# generator.summary()
```

Next, we can define the discriminator as follows:

```
# building the discriminator network
inpt_img = Input(shape=(img_dims,img_dims,img_chnl))
dl1 = Flatten()(inpt_img)
dl2 = Dropout(0.5)(dl1)
dl3 = Dense(512, activation='relu')(dl2)
dl4 = Dense(256, activation='relu')(dl3)
dl5 = Dense(1, activation='sigmoid')(dl4)
discriminator = Model(inpt_img, dl5)
validity = discriminator(gnrtr_img)
# uncomment this if you want to see the summary
# discriminator.summary()
```

The next step is to put things together as follows:

```
# you can use either optimizer:
# optimizer = RMSprop(0.0005)
optimizer = Adam(0.0002, 0.5)

# compiling the discriminator
discriminator.compile(loss='binary_crossentropy', optimizer=optimizer,
                      metrics=['accuracy'])

# this will freeze the discriminator in gen_dis below
discriminator.trainable = False

gen_dis = Model(inpt_noise, validity)     # full model
gen_dis.compile(loss='binary_crossentropy', optimizer=optimizer)
```

Next, we will make the training happen inside a loop that will run for as many epochs as we want:

```
epochs = 12001      # this is up to you!
batch_size=128      # small batches recommended
sample_interval=200     # for generating samples

# target vectors
valid = np.ones((batch_size, 1))
fake = np.zeros((batch_size, 1))

# we will need these for plots and generated images
samp_imgs = {}
dloss = []
gloss = []
dacc = []

# this loop will train in batches manually for every epoch
for epoch in range(epochs):
  # training the discriminator first >>
  # batch of valid images
  idx = np.random.randint(0, x_train.shape[0], batch_size)
  imgs = x_train[idx]
  # noise batch to generate fake images
  noise = np.random.uniform(0, 1, (batch_size, ltnt_dim))
  gen_imgs = generator.predict(noise)

  # gradient descent on the batch
  d_loss_real = discriminator.train_on_batch(imgs, valid)
  d_loss_fake = discriminator.train_on_batch(gen_imgs, fake)
  d_loss = 0.5 * np.add(d_loss_real, d_loss_fake)
```

```
# next we train the generator with the discriminator frozen >>
# noise batch to generate fake images
noise = np.random.uniform(0, 1, (batch_size, ltnt_dim))

# gradient descent on the batch
g_loss = gen_dis.train_on_batch(noise, valid)
# save performance
dloss.append(d_loss[0])
dacc.append(d_loss[1])
gloss.append(g_loss)

# print performance every sampling interval
if epoch % sample_interval == 0:
  print ("%d [D loss: %f, acc.: %.2f%%] [G loss: %f]" %
        (epoch, d_loss[0], 100*d_loss[1], g_loss))

  # use noise to generate some images
  noise = np.random.uniform(0, 1, (2, ltnt_dim))
  gen_imgs = generator.predict(noise)
  samp_imgs[epoch] = gen_imgs
```

This produces output similar to the following:

```
0 [D loss: 0.922930, acc.: 21.48%] [G loss: 0.715504]
400 [D loss: 0.143821, acc.: 96.88%] [G loss: 4.265501]
800 [D loss: 0.247173, acc.: 91.80%] [G loss: 4.752715]
.
.
.
11200 [D loss: 0.617693, acc.: 66.80%] [G loss: 1.071557]
11600 [D loss: 0.611364, acc.: 66.02%] [G loss: 0.984210]
12000 [D loss: 0.622592, acc.: 62.50%] [G loss: 1.056955]
```

This might look different in your system because this is all based on **random** noise. This randomness aspect will most likely take your model in a different direction. However, what you will see is that your generator's loss should decrease gradually, and if the generator is working properly, the accuracy should be getting closer to random change, that is, close to 50%. If your discriminator is always 100%, then your generator is not good enough, and if your discriminator is around 50% accuracy, then your generator might be too good or your discriminator too weak.

Now, let's plot a couple of things; the learning curves (losses and accuracy), and the samples generated across epochs.

The following code will plot the learning curves:

```
import matplotlib.pyplot as plt

fig, ax1 = plt.subplots(figsize=(10,6))
ax1.set_xlabel('Epoch')
ax1.set_ylabel('Loss')
ax1.plot(range(epochs), gloss, '-.', color='#dc267f', alpha=0.75,
         label='Generator')
ax1.plot(range(epochs), dloss, '-.', color='#fe6100', alpha=0.75,
         label='Discriminator')
ax1.legend(loc=1)
ax2 = ax1.twinx()
ax2.set_ylabel('Discriminator Accuracy')
ax2.plot(range(epochs), dacc, color='#785ef0', alpha=0.75,
         label='Accuracy')
ax2.legend(loc=4)
fig.tight_layout()
plt.show()
```

This generates the plot shown in the following diagram:

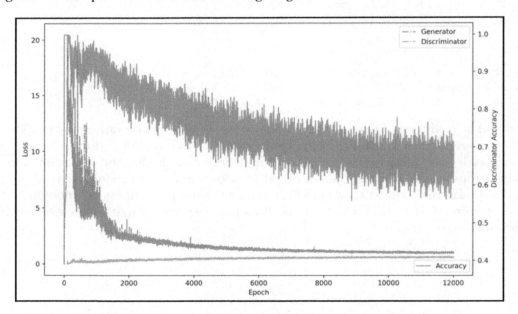

Figure 14.4 - Loss of generator and discriminator across epochs. Accuracy across epochs for an MLP-based GAN

As the plot indicates, the loss of the discriminator is initially low, as also indicated by the accuracy. However, as epochs advance, the generator gets better (loss decreases) and accuracy slowly decreases.

Figure 14.5 shows a couple of images at every sampled epoch that were produced from random noise:

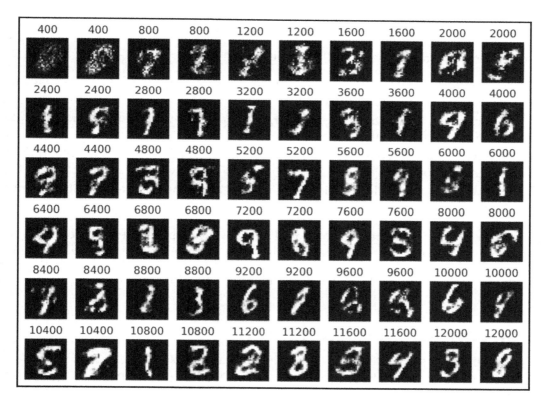

Figure 14.5 - GAN-generated images across epochs

As you can see, the initial images look noisy, while the later images have more detail and familiar shapes. This would confirm the decrease in the discriminator accuracy since these images can easily pass as real. *Figure 14.5* was produced using the following code:

```python
import matplotlib.pyplot as plt

fig, axs = plt.subplots(6, 10, figsize=(10,7.5))
cnt = sample_interval
for i in range(6):
  for j in [0, 2, 4, 6, 8]:
```

```
            img = samp_imgs[cnt]
            axs[i,j].imshow(img[0,:,:,0], cmap='gray')
            axs[i,j].axis('off')
            axs[i,j].set_title(cnt)
            axs[i,j+1].imshow(img[1,:,:,0], cmap='gray')
            axs[i,j+1].axis('off')
            axs[i,j+1].set_title(cnt)
            cnt += sample_interval
    plt.show()
```

Let's consider a few takeaways from this model:

- The model, as it has been presented, has room for improvements if we make the model larger where needed.
- If what we need is a good generator, we can extend the generator, or change it into a convolutional one (next section).
- If we want, we could save the discriminator and retrain it (fine-tune it) for the classification of digits.
- If we want, we could use the generator to augment the dataset with as many images as we want.

In spite of the *decent* quality of the MLP-based GAN, we can appreciate that the shapes might not be as well defined as original samples. However, convolutional GANs can help.

Let's proceed and change the MLP-based model into a convolutional one.

A convolutional model

The convolutional approach to a GAN was made popular by Radford, A., *et al.* (2015). The proposed model was called **Deep Convolutional GAN (DCGAN)**. The primary goal is to make a series of convolutional layers learn feature representations to produce *fake* images or to *distinguish* between valid or fake images.

Moving forward, we will be **intentionally** using a different name for the discriminator network, which we will call **critic**. Both terms are used in the literature. However, there is a new trend to use the term *critic* and the old term may go away at some point. Regardless, you should know that both terms refer to the same thing: a network that is tasked with determining whether input is valid (from the original dataset) or fake (from an adversarial generator).

We will be implementing the model depicted in the following diagram:

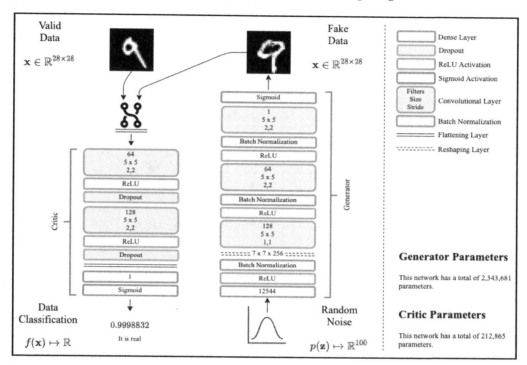

Figure 14.6 - CNN-based GAN architecture

This model has something new never before seen in this book: `Conv2DTranspose`. This type of layer is exactly like the traditional convolutional layer, `Conv2D`, except that it works in the exact opposite direction. While a `Conv2D` layer learns filters (feature maps) that split the input into filtered information, a `Conv2DTranspose` layer takes filtered information and joins it together.

Some people refer to `Conv2DTranspose` as *deconvolution*. However, I personally think it is incorrect to do so since *deconvolution* is a mathematical operation significantly different from what `Conv2DTranspose` does. Either way, you need to remember that if you read *deconvolution* in the context of CNNs, it means `Conv2DTranspose`.

The remainder of the elements in the model are things that we have already discussed previously. The full code, which omits comments, is the following:

```
from tensorflow.keras.models import Model
from tensorflow.keras.layers import Dense, Activation, Input,
Conv2DTranspose, Flatten
from tensorflow.keras.layers import BatchNormalization, Dropout, Reshape,
Conv2D
from tensorflow.keras.optimizers import Adam
from tensorflow.keras.datasets import mnist
import numpy as np
import matplotlib.pyplot as plt

img_dims = 28
img_chnl = 1
ltnt_dim = 100

(x_train, y_train), (x_test, y_test) = mnist.load_data()

x_train = x_train.astype('float32') / 255.
x_test = x_test.astype('float32') / 255.

x_train = np.expand_dims(x_train, axis=3)
x_test = np.expand_dims(x_test, axis=3)
```

Next we define the generator as follows:

```
# building the generator convolutional network
inpt_noise = Input(shape=(ltnt_dim,))
gl1 = Dense(7*7*256, activation='relu')(inpt_noise)
gl2 = BatchNormalization()(gl1)
gl3 = Reshape((7, 7, 256))(gl2)
gl4 = Conv2DTranspose(128, (5, 5), strides=(1, 1), padding='same',
                      activation='relu')(gl3)
gl5 = BatchNormalization()(gl4)
gl6 = Conv2DTranspose(64, (5, 5), strides=(2, 2), padding='same',
                      activation='relu')(gl5)
gl7 = BatchNormalization()(gl6)
gl8 = Conv2DTranspose(1, (5, 5), strides=(2, 2), padding='same',
                      activation='sigmoid')(gl7)
generator = Model(inpt_noise, gl8)
gnrtr_img = generator(inpt_noise)
generator.summary()  # print to verify dimensions
```

Then we define the critic networks as follows:

```
# building the critic convolutional network
inpt_img = Input(shape=(img_dims,img_dims,img_chnl))
```

```
dl1 = Conv2D(64, (5, 5), strides=(2, 2), padding='same',
             activation='relu')(inpt_img)
dl2 = Dropout(0.3)(dl1)
dl3 = Conv2D(128, (5, 5), strides=(2, 2), padding='same',
             activation='relu')(dl2)
dl4 = Dropout(0.3)(dl3)
dl5 = Flatten()(dl4)
dl6 = Dense(1, activation='sigmoid')(dl5)
critic = Model(inpt_img, dl6)
validity = critic(gnrtr_img)
critic.summary()   # again, print for verification
```

Next we put things together and set the parameters of the model as follows:

```
optimizer = Adam(0.0002, 0.5)

critic.compile(loss='binary_crossentropy', optimizer=optimizer,
               metrics=['accuracy'])

critic.trainable = False

gen_crt = Model(inpt_noise, validity)
gen_crt.compile(loss='binary_crossentropy', optimizer=optimizer)

epochs = 12001
batch_size=64
sample_interval=400
```

Then we train using the following cycle:

```
valid = np.ones((batch_size, 1))
fake = np.zeros((batch_size, 1))

samp_imgs = {}
closs = []
gloss = []
cacc = []
for epoch in range(epochs):
  idx = np.random.randint(0, x_train.shape[0], batch_size)
  imgs = x_train[idx]

  noise = np.random.uniform(0, 1, (batch_size, ltnt_dim))
  gen_imgs = generator.predict(noise)
  c_loss_real = critic.train_on_batch(imgs, valid)
  c_loss_fake = critic.train_on_batch(gen_imgs, fake)
  c_loss = 0.5 * np.add(c_loss_real, c_loss_fake)

  noise = np.random.uniform(0, 1, (batch_size, ltnt_dim))
```

```
g_loss = gen_crt.train_on_batch(noise, valid)
closs.append(c_loss[0])
cacc.append(c_loss[1])
gloss.append(g_loss)

if epoch % sample_interval == 0:
  print ("%d [C loss: %f, acc.: %.2f%%] [G loss: %f]" %
         (epoch, d_loss[0], 100*d_loss[1], g_loss))
  noise = np.random.uniform(0, 1, (2, ltnt_dim))
  gen_imgs = generator.predict(noise)
  samp_imgs[epoch] = gen_imgs
```

About 70% of the preceding code is the same as before. However, the convolutional network design was new. The code would print summaries for both the generator and critic. Here is the summary for the generator:

```
Model: "Generator"
```

Layer (type)	Output Shape	Param #
input_1 (InputLayer)	[(None, 100)]	0
dense_1 (Dense)	(None, 12544)	1266944
batch_normalization_1 (Batch	(None, 12544)	50176
reshape (Reshape)	(None, 7, 7, 256)	0
conv2d_transpose_1 (Conv2DTran	(None, 7, 7, 128)	819328
batch_normalization_2 (Batch	(None, 7, 7, 128)	512
conv2d_transpose_2 (Conv2DTr	(None, 14, 14, 64)	204864
batch_normalization_3 (Batch	(None, 14, 14, 64)	256
conv2d_transpose_3 (Conv2DTr	(None, 28, 28, 1)	1601

```
Total params: 2,343,681
Trainable params: 2,318,209
Non-trainable params: 25,472
```

Here is the summary for the critic:

```
Model: "Critic"
```

Layer (type)	Output Shape	Param #

```
==================================================================
input_2 (InputLayer)  [(None, 28, 28, 1)]    0

conv2d_1 (Conv2D)     (None, 14, 14, 64)     1664

dropout_1 (Dropout)   (None, 14, 14, 64)     0

conv2d_2 (Conv2D)     (None, 7, 7, 128)      204928

dropout_2 (Dropout)   (None, 7, 7, 128)      0

flatten (Flatten)     (None, 6272)           0

dense_2 (Dense)       (None, 1)              6273
==================================================================
Total params: 212,865
Trainable params: 212,865
Non-trainable params: 0
```

A sample output for the training steps would look like the following:

```
0 [C loss: 0.719159, acc.: 22.66%] [G loss: 0.680779]
400 [C loss: 0.000324, acc.: 100.00%] [G loss: 0.000151]
800 [C loss: 0.731860, acc.: 59.38%] [G loss: 0.572153]
.
.
.
11200 [C loss: 0.613043, acc.: 66.41%] [G loss: 0.946724]
11600 [C loss: 0.613043, acc.: 66.41%] [G loss: 0.869602]
12000 [C loss: 0.613043, acc.: 66.41%] [G loss: 0.854222]
```

From the training output, we can see that the convolutional network is able to reduce the loss of the generator faster than its MLP counterpart. It appears that for the remainder of the epochs, the critic learns slowly to be more robust against the generator of fake input. This can be more clearly observed by plotting the results using the following code:

```
import matplotlib.pyplot as plt

fig, ax1 = plt.subplots(figsize=(10,6))

ax1.set_xlabel('Epoch')
ax1.set_ylabel('Loss')
ax1.plot(range(epochs), gloss, '-.', color='#dc267f', alpha=0.75,
        label='Generator')
ax1.plot(range(epochs), closs, '-.', color='#fe6100', alpha=0.75,
        label='Critic')
ax1.legend(loc=1)
ax2 = ax1.twinx()
```

```
ax2.set_ylabel('Critic Accuracy')
ax2.plot(range(epochs), cacc, color='#785ef0', alpha=0.75,
         label='Accuracy')
ax2.legend(loc=4)

fig.tight_layout()
plt.show()
```

The code produces the plot shown in *Figure 14.7*. From the diagram, we can appreciate the claims made on faster convergence to small losses and slow recovery of the critic's accuracy:

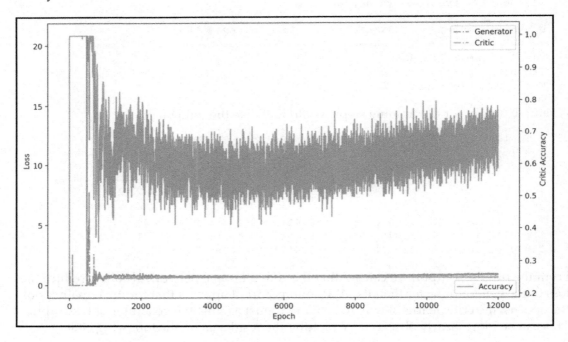

Figure 14.7 - Learning curves for CNN-based GANs

We can also display the samples generated as the convolutional GAN was being trained. The results are shown in *Figure 14.8*. These results are consistent with a poor-quality generator trained under 2,000 epochs. After 5,000 epochs, the generator is able to produce well-defined numerals that can easily pass as valid:

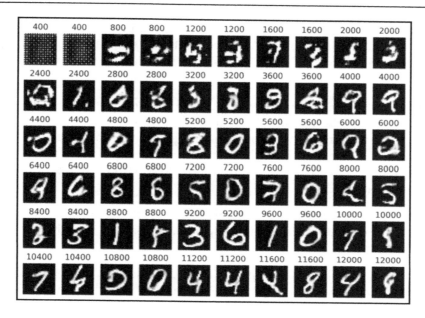

Figure 14.8 - Samples generated during training

For reference, we can compare *Figure 14.5* and *Figure 14.8* for the MLP-based and convolutional-based approach, respectively. Such a comparison can offer insights on the fundamental differences between a general-purpose GAN (MLP-based) or a GAN specialized in spatial relationships (CNN-based).

Now, we would like to discuss briefly the generative abilities that **Variational Autoencoders** (**VAEs**) and GANs bring to the table.

Comparing GANs and VAEs

In `Chapter 9`, *Variational Autoencoders*, we discussed VAEs as a mechanism for dimensionality reduction that aims to learn the parameters of the distribution of the input space, and effect reconstruction based on random draws from the latent space using the learned parameters. This offered a number of advantages we already discussed in `Chapter 9`, *Variational Autoencoders*, such as the following:

- The ability to reduce the effect of noisy inputs, since it learns the distribution of the input, not the input itself
- The ability to generate samples by simply querying the latent space

On the other hand, GANs can also be used to generate samples, like the VAE. However, the learning of both is quite different. In GANs, we can think of the model as having two major parts: a critic and a generator. In VAEs, we also have two networks: an encoder and a decoder.

If we were to make any connection between the two, it would be that the decoder and generator play a very similar role in VAEs and GANs, respectively. However, an encoder and a critic have very different goals. An encoder will learn to find a rich latent representation, usually with very few dimensions compared to the input space. Meanwhile, a critic does not aim to find any representations, but to solve a growing complex binary classification problem.

We could make a case that the critic is certainly learning features from the input space; however, the claim that features in the deepest layers are similar in both the critic and encoder requires more evidence.

One thing we can do to make a comparison is to take the deep VAE model shown in Chapter 9, *Variational Autoencoders, Figure 14.7*, train it, and draw some random samples from the generator in the VAE, and do the same for the convolutional GAN.

We can start by displaying the samples from the convolutional GAN and executing the following code immediately after the last piece of code in the previous section, which contains the trained GAN. Here is the code:

```
import matplotlib.pyplot as plt
import numpy as np

plt.figure(figsize=(10,10))
samples = np.random.uniform(0.0, 1.0, size=(400,ltnt_dim))
imgs = generator.predict(samples)
for cnt in range(20*20):
  plt.subplot(20,20,cnt+1)
  img = imgs[cnt]
  plt.imshow(img[:,:,0], cmap='gray')
  plt.xticks([])
  plt.yticks([])
plt.show()
```

This code will produce 400 numerals from random noise! The plot is shown in *Figure 14.9*:

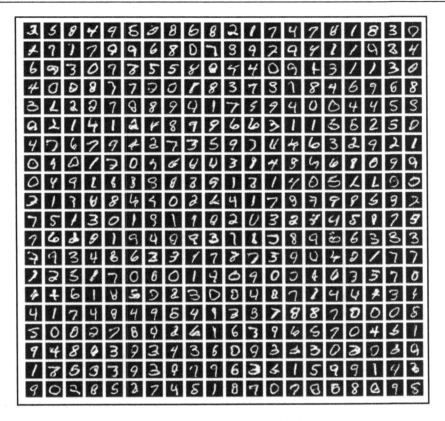

Figure 14.9 - 400 numerals produced by a convolutional GAN

Recall that these numerals were produced after 12,000 epochs. The quality seems relatively good. Most of these numerals could actually fool a human being into thinking they were really written by a human.

Now, we want to take a look at the quality of the numerals generated with a VAE. For this, you will need to go to Chapter 9, *Variational Autoencoders*, and use the code provided to implement the deep VAE and train it for, say, 5,000 epochs. After training it, you can use the decoder to generate samples from random noise by choosing random parameters.

Here is the code you should use *once* the training of the VAE is complete:

```
import matplotlib.pyplot as plt
import numpy as np

plt.figure(figsize=(10,10))
samples = np.random.normal(0.0, 1.0, size=(400,ltnt_dim))
```

```
imgs = decoder.predict(samples)
for cnt in range(20*20):
  plt.subplot(20,20,cnt+1)
  img = imgs[cnt].reshape((28,28))
  plt.imshow(img, cmap='gray')
  plt.xticks([])
  plt.yticks([])
plt.show()
```

A couple of visible differences is that the VAE assumes that the parameters of the latent space follow a normal distribution; also, the output needs to be reshaped to 28x28, as opposed to the GAN, which gives the output already in its correct shape thanks to the 2D convolutional output layer. The output of this code is shown in *Figure 14.10*:

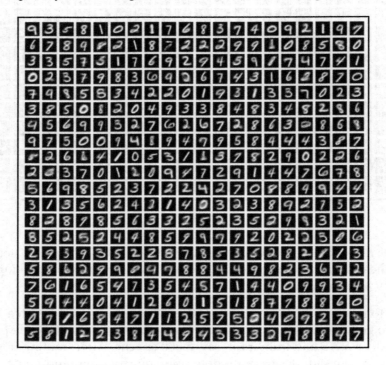

Figure 14.10 - 400 samples of numerals generated by the decoder of a VAE using random noise

As you can see from the diagram, some of these numerals look very good; some might say too good. They look smooth, well-rounded, and perhaps we can say noise-free. The numerals produced by the VAE lack the distinctive quality of looking noisy compared to the ones produced by the GAN. However, this can be a good thing or a bad thing depending on what you want to do.

Say that you want to have clean-looking samples that might be easily identified as *fake,* then a VAE is the best choice. Now, say that we want samples that can easily fool a human into thinking they are not produced by a machine; here, perhaps a GAN fits better.

Regardless of these differences, both can be used to augment your datasets if you need to have more data.

Thinking about the ethical implications of GANs

Some ethical thoughts about generative models have already been provided in Chapter 9, *Variational Autoencoders.* However, a second round of thoughts is in order given the adversarial nature of GANs. That is, there is an implicit demand from a GAN to *trick* a critic in a min-max game where the generator needs to come out victorious (or the critic as well). This concept generalized to adversarial learning provides the means to *attack* existing machine learning models.

Very successful computer vision models such as VGG16 (a CNN model) have been attacked by models that perform adversarial attacks. There are *patches* that you can print, put on a t-shirt, cap, or any object, and as soon as the patch is present in the input to the models being attacked, they are fooled into thinking that the existing object is a completely different one (Brown, T. B., et al. (2017)). Here is an example of an adversarial patch that tricks a model into thinking that a banana is a toaster: https://youtu.be/i1sp4X57TL4.

Now that these types of adversarial attacks are known to exist, researchers have found vulnerabilities in their current systems. Therefore, it has become almost an obligation for us, the deep learning practitioners, to make sure our models are robust against adversarial attacks. This is particularly important for systems that involve sensitive information, or systems that make decisions that affect human life.

For example, a deep learning model that is deployed in an airport to assist security efforts needs to be tested so as to avoid a person wearing a t-shirt with a printed adversarial patch aiming to avoid being recognized as a person in a restricted area. This is critical for the security of the population. However, a deep learning system to automatically tune the audio of a person singing might not be particularly critical.

What is required from you is to look into testing your models for adversarial attacks. There are several resources online being updated frequently that you can easily find if you search for them. If you come to find a vulnerability in a deep learning model, you should report it to the creators immediately, for the well-being of our society.

Summary

This advanced chapter showed you how to create GAN networks. You learned the major components of GANs, a generator and a critic, and their role in the learning process. You learned about adversarial learning in the context of breaking models and making them robust against attacks. You coded an MLP-based and a convolutional-based GAN on the same dataset and observed the differences. At this point, you should feel confident explaining why adversarial training is important. You should be able to code the necessary mechanisms to train a generator and a discriminator of a GAN. You should feel confident about coding a GAN and comparing it to a VAE to generate images from a learned latent space. You should be able to design generative models, considering the societal implications and the responsibilities that come with using generative models.

GANs are very interesting and have yielded amazing research and applications. They have also exposed the vulnerabilities of other systems. The present state of deep learning involves combinations of AEs, GANs, CNNs, and RNNs, using specific components of each, and gradually increasing the potential of applications of deep learning across different fields. The world of deep learning is exciting right now, and you are now ready to embrace it and dive deeper into whatever area you feel you like. Chapter 15, *Final Remarks on the Future of Deep Learning*, will present brief comments on how we see the future of deep learning. It attempts to use some kind of *prophetic* voice about the things to come. But before you go, quiz yourself with the following questions.

Questions and answers

1. **Who is the adversary in a GAN?**

   The generator. It acts as a model whose sole purpose is to make the critic fail; it is the critic's adversary.

2. **Why is the generator model bigger than the critic?**

   This is not always the case. The models discussed here were more interesting as generators of data. However, we could use the critic and retrain it for classification, in which case, the critic model might be bigger.

3. **What is adversarial robustness?**

It is a new field in deep learning tasked with researching ways to certify that deep learning models are robust against adversarial attacks.

4. **Which is better – a GAN or a VAE?**

This depends on the application. GANs tend to produce more "interesting" results than VAEs, but VAEs are more stable. Also, it is often faster to train a GAN than a VAE.

5. **Are there any risks associated with GANs?**

Yes. There is a known problem called *mode collapse*, which refers to the inability of a GAN to produce novel, different, results across epochs. It seems like the network gets stuck on a few samples that can cause sufficient confusion in the critic so as to produce a low loss, while having no diversity of generated data. This is still an open problem with no universal solution. A lack of diversity in a GAN's generator is an indication that it has collapsed. To find out more about mode collapse, read Srivastava, A., et al. (2017).

References

- Abadi, M., and Andersen, D. G. (2016). *Learning to protect communications with adversarial neural cryptography. arXiv preprint* arXiv:1610.06918.
- Ilyas, A., Engstrom, L., Athalye, A., and Lin, J. (2018). *Black box adversarial attacks with limited queries and information. arXiv preprint* arXiv:1804.08598.
- Goodfellow, I., Pouget-Abadie, J., Mirza, M., Xu, B., Warde-Farley, D., Ozair, S., and Bengio, Y. (2014). *Generative adversarial nets.* In *Advances in neural information processing systems* (pp. 2672-2680).
- Sukhbaatar, S., and Fergus, R. (2016). *Learning multi-agent communication with backpropagation.* In *Advances in neural information processing systems* (pp. 2244-2252).
- Rivas, P., and Banerjee, P. (2020). *Neural-Based Adversarial Encryption of Images in ECB Mode with 16-bit Blocks.* In *International Conference on Artificial Intelligence*.
- Cohen, J. M., Rosenfeld, E., and Kolter, J. Z. (2019). *Certified adversarial robustness via randomized smoothing. arXiv preprint* arXiv:1902.02918.

- Radford, A., Metz, L., and Chintala, S. (2015). *Unsupervised representation learning with deep convolutional generative adversarial networks. arXiv preprint* arXiv:1511.06434.
- Brown, T. B., Mané, D., Roy, A., Abadi, M., and Gilmer, J. (2017). *Adversarial patch. arXiv preprint* arXiv:1712.09665.
- Srivastava, A., Valkov, L., Russell, C., Gutmann, M. U., and Sutton, C. (2017). *Veegan: Reducing mode collapse in GANs using implicit variational learning.* In *Advances in Neural Information Processing Systems* (pp. 3308-3318).

Final Remarks on the Future of Deep Learning

15

We have been through a journey together, and if you have read this far you deserve to treat yourself with a nice meal. What you have accomplished deserves recognition. Tell your friends, share what you have learned, and remember to always keep on learning. Deep learning is a rapidly changing field; you cannot sit still. This concluding chapter will briefly present to you some of the new exciting topics and opportunities in deep learning. If you want to continue your learning, we will recommend other helpful resources from Packt that can help you move forward in this field. At the end of this chapter, you will know where to go from here after having learned the basics of deep learning; you will know what other resources Packt offers for you to continue your training in deep learning.

This chapter is organized into the following sections:

- Looking for advanced topics in deep learning
- Learning with more resources from Packt

Looking for advanced topics in deep learning

The future of deep learning is hard to predict at the moment; things are changing rapidly. However, I believe that if you invest your time in the present advanced topics in deep learning, you might see these areas developing prosperously in the near future.

The following sub-sections discuss some of these advanced topics that have the potential of flourishing and being disruptive in our area.

Deep reinforcement learning

Deep reinforcement learning (DRL) is an area that has gained a lot of attention recently given that deep convolutional networks, and other types of deep networks, have offered solutions to problems that were difficult to solve in the past. Many of the uses of DRL are in areas where we do not have the luxury of having data on all possible conceivable cases, such as space exploration, playing video games, or self-driving cars.

Let's expand on the latter example. If we were using traditional supervised learning to make a self-driving car that can take us from point A to point B without crashing, we would not only want to have examples of the positive class with events of successful journeys, but we would also need examples of the negative class with bad events such as crashes and terrible driving. Think about this: we would need to crash as many cars as we have successful events to keep the dataset balanced. This is not acceptable; however, reinforcement learning comes to the rescue.

DRL aims to **reward** good driving aspects; the models learn that there is a reward to be gained, so we don't need negative examples. In contrast, traditional learning would need to crash cars in order to **penalize** bad outcomes.

When you use DRL to learn using a simulator, you can get AI that can beat pilots on simulated flights (`https://fortune.com/2020/08/20/f-16-fighter-pilot-versus-artificial-intelligence-simulation-darpa/`), or you can get AI that can win on a video game simulator. The gaming world is a perfect test scenario for DRL. Let's say that you want to make a DRL model to play the famous game *Space Invaders*, shown in *Figure 15.1*; you can make a model that rewards destroying space invaders.

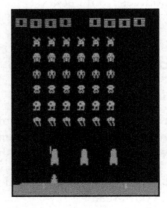

Figure 15.1 – Space invaders video game simulator

If you make a traditional model to teach the user to **not die**, for example, then you will still lose because you will eventually be invaded from space. So, the best strategy to prevent invasion is both not dying and destroying space invaders. In other words, you reward the actions that lead to survival, which are to destroy the space invaders quickly while avoiding being killed by their bombs.

In 2018, a new DRL research tool was released, called **Dopamine** (Castro, P. S., et al. 2018). Dopamine (`https://github.com/google/dopamine`) is meant for fast prototyping of reinforcement learning algorithms. Back in Chapter 2, *Setup and Introduction to Deep Learning Frameworks*, we asked you to install Dopamine for this moment. We simply want to give you an idea of how easy Dopamine is so that you can go ahead and experiment with it if you are interested. In the following lines of code, we will simply load a pre-trained model (agent) and let it play the game.

This will make sure the library is installed, then load the pre-trained agent:

```
!pip install -U dopamine-rl

!gsutil -q -m cp -R gs://download-dopamine-
rl/colab/samples/rainbow/SpaceInvaders_v4/checkpoints/tf_ckpt-199.data-0000
0-of-00001 ./
!gsutil -q -m cp -R gs://download-dopamine-
rl/colab/samples/rainbow/SpaceInvaders_v4/checkpoints/tf_ckpt-199.index ./
!gsutil -q -m cp -R gs://download-dopamine-
rl/colab/samples/rainbow/SpaceInvaders_v4/checkpoints/tf_ckpt-199.meta ./
```

The sample trained agent, which in this case is called `rainbow`, is provided by the authors of Dopamine, but you can also train your own if you want.

The next step is to make the agent run (that is, decide to take actions based on the rewards) for a number of steps, say `1024`:

```
from dopamine.utils import example_viz_lib
example_viz_lib.run(agent='rainbow', game='SpaceInvaders', num_steps=1024,
                    root_dir='./agent_viz', restore_ckpt='./tf_ckpt-199',
                    use_legacy_checkpoint=True)
```

This piece of code may take a while to run. Internally, it connects to PyGame, which is a resource of game simulators for the Python community. It makes several decisions and avoids space invasion (and dying). As shown in *Figure 15.2*, the model describes the cumulative rewards obtained across time steps and the estimated probability of return for every action taken, such as stop, move left, move right, and shoot:

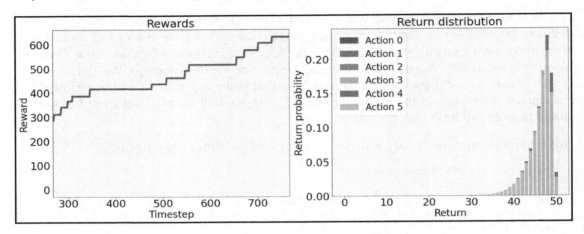

Figure 15.2 – Left: Calculated rewards of the model across time steps. Right: Estimated probability of returns for every action

One of the interesting things about this is that you can visualize the agent at any of the time steps (frames) and see what the agent was doing at that specific time step using the plot in *Figure 15.2* as a reference to decide which time step to visualize. Let's say that you want to visualize steps 540 or 550; you can do that as follows:

```
from IPython.display import Image
frame_number = 540    # or 550
image_file = '/<path to current
directory>/agent_viz/SpaceInvaders/rainbow/images/frame_{:06d}.png'.format(
frame_number)
Image(image_file)
```

You substitute `<path to current directory>` with the path to your current working directory. This is because we need an absolute path, otherwise we could have used a relative path with `./` instead.

From this, it is self-evident that all frames are saved as images in the `./agent_viz/SpaceInvaders/rainbow/images/` directory. You can display them individually or even make a video. The preceding code produces the images shown in *Figure 15.3*:

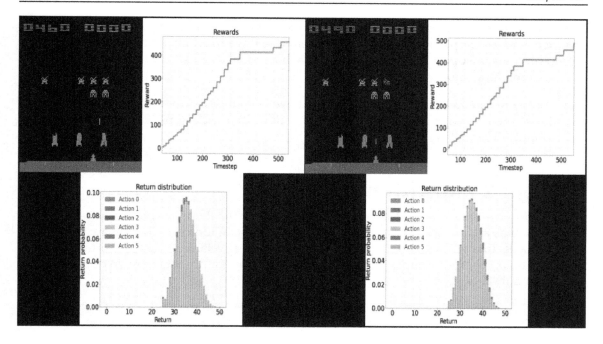

Figure 15.3 – Left: step 540. Right: step 550

Dopamine is as simple as that. We hope that you will be inspired by reinforcement learning and investigate further.

Self-supervised learning

Yann LeCun, one of the 2018 ACM Turing Award winners, said at the AAAI conference in 2020: *"the future is self-supervised."* He was implying that this area is exciting and has a lot of potential.

Self-supervision is a relatively new term used to move away from the term *unsupervision*. The term "unsupervised learning" might give the impression that there is no supervision when, in fact, unsupervised learning algorithms and models typically use more supervisory data than supervised models. Take, for example, the classification of MNIST data. It uses 10 labels as supervisory signals. However, in an autoencoder whose purpose is perfect reconstruction, every single pixel is a supervisory signal, so there are 784 supervisory signals from a 28 x 28 image, for example.

Self-supervision is also used to mean models that combine some of the stages of unsupervised and supervised learning. For example, if we pipeline a model that learns representations unsupervised, then we can attach a model downstream that will learn to classify something supervised.

Many of the recent advances in deep learning have been in self-supervision. It will be a good investment of your time if you try to learn more about self-supervised learning algorithms and models.

System 2 algorithms

The famous economist Daniel Kahneman made popular the theory of dual process with his book *Thinking Fast and Slow* (Kahneman, D. 2011). The main idea is that there are highly complex tasks that we, as humans, are good at developing relatively fast and often without thinking too much; for example, drinking water, eating food, or looking at an object and recognizing it. These processes are done by *System 1*.

However, there are tasks that are not quite simple for the human mind, tasks that require our fully devoted attention, such as driving on an unfamiliar road, looking at a strange object that does not belong within the assumed context, or understanding an abstract painting. These processes are done by *System 2*. Another winner of the 2018 ACM Turing Award, Yoshua Bengio, has made the remark that deep learning has been very good at System 1 tasks, meaning that existing models can recognize objects and perform highly complex tasks relatively easily. However, deep learning has not made much progress on System 2 tasks. That is, the future of deep learning will be in solving those tasks that are very complex for human beings, which will probably involve combining different models across different domains with different learning types. Capsule neural networks might be a good alternative solution to System 2 tasks (Sabour, S., et al. 2017).

For these reasons, System 2 algorithms will probably be the future of deep learning.

Now, let's look at resources available from Packt that can help in further studying these ideas.

Learning with more resources from Packt

The following lists of books is not meant to be exhaustive, but a starting point for your next endeavor. These titles have come out at a great time when there is a lot of interest in the field. Regardless of your choice, you will not be disappointed.

Reinforcement learning

- *Deep Reinforcement Learning Hands-On - Second Edition*, by Maxim Lapan, 2020.
- *The Reinforcement Learning Workshop*, by Alessandro Palmas *et al.*, 2020.
- *Hands-On Reinforcement Learning for Games*, by Micheal Lanham, 2020.
- *PyTorch 1.x Reinforcement Learning Cookbook*, by Yuxi Liu, 2019.
- *Python Reinforcement Learning*, by Sudharsan Ravichandiran, 2019.
- *Reinforcement Learning Algorithms with Python*, by Andrea Lonza, 2019.

Self-supervised learning

- *The Unsupervised Learning Workshop*, by Aaron Jones *et. al.*, 2020.
- *Applied Unsupervised Learning with Python*, by Benjamin Johnston *et. al.*, 2019.
- *Hands-On Unsupervised Learning with Python*, by Giuseppe Bonaccorso, 2019.

Summary

This final chapter briefly covered new exciting topics and opportunities in deep learning. We discussed reinforcement learning, self-supervised algorithms, and System 2 algorithms. We also recommended some further resources from Packt, hoping that you will want to continue your learning and move forward in this field. At this point, you should know where to go from here, and be inspired by the future of deep learning. You should be knowledgeable of other recommended books in the area to continue with your learning journey.

You are the future of deep learning, and the future is today. Go ahead and make things happen.

References

- Castro, P. S., Moitra, S., Gelada, C., Kumar, S., and Bellemare, M. G. (2018). Dopamine: A research framework for deep reinforcement learning. arXiv preprint arXiv:1812.06110.
- Kahneman, D. (2011). *Thinking, Fast and Slow. Macmillan.*
- Sabour, S., Frosst, N., and Hinton, G. E. (2017). Dynamic routing between capsules. In *Advances in neural information processing systems* (pp. 3856-3866).

Other Books You May Enjoy

If you enjoyed this book, you may be interested in these other books by Packt:

Advanced Deep Learning with TensorFlow 2 and Keras - Second Edition
Rowel Atienza

ISBN: 978-1-83882-165-4

- Use mutual information maximization techniques to perform unsupervised learning
- Use segmentation to identify the pixel-wise class of each object in an image
- Identify both the bounding box and class of objects in an image using object detection
- Learn the building blocks for advanced techniques - MLPs, CNN, and RNNs
- Understand deep neural networks - including ResNet and DenseNet
- Understand and build autoregressive models – autoencoders, VAEs, and GANs
- Discover and implement deep reinforcement learning methods

Applied Deep Learning and Computer Vision for Self-Driving Cars
Sumit Ranjan, Dr. S. Senthamilarasu

ISBN: 978-1-83864-630-1

- Implement deep neural network from scratch using the Keras library
- Understand the importance of deep learning in self-driving cars
- Get to grips with feature extraction techniques in image processing using the OpenCV library
- Design a software pipeline that detects lane lines in videos
- Implement a convolutional neural network (CNN) image classifier for traffic signal signs
- Train and test neural networks for behavioral-cloning by driving a car in a virtual simulator
- Discover various state-of-the-art semantic segmentation and object detection architectures

Leave a review - let other readers know what you think

Please share your thoughts on this book with others by leaving a review on the site that you bought it from. If you purchased the book from Amazon, please leave us an honest review on this book's Amazon page. This is vital so that other potential readers can see and use your unbiased opinion to make purchasing decisions, we can understand what our customers think about our products, and our authors can see your feedback on the title that they have worked with Packt to create. It will only take a few minutes of your time, but is valuable to other potential customers, our authors, and Packt. Thank you!

Index

M

Markov Chain Monte Carlo (MCMC) 253
MaxPooling2D 314
mean absolute error (MAE) 106
mean squared error (MSE) 24, 96, 177, 231
ML algorithms
  training, from data 14, 15
ML ecosystem 12, 13, 14
ML main model 373
MLP model
  about 144, 146, 147
  implementing 375, 378, 380, 381
MNIST data
  preparing 179
MNIST dataset
  about 216, 217
  autoencoders 180, 182
  binarizing 51
  deep VAE, versus shallow VAE 238, 239
  images, binarizing 52, 53, 54
  targets, binarizing 54, 55
model parameters 114
multi-class classification 91, 92, 93
Multilayer Perceptron (MLP) 222, 270
multiple classes
  dealing with 101, 102, 103, 104, 105
MXNET
  URL 42

N

n-dimensional convolutions 310
neuron model 15, 17
non-linearly separable data
  perceptron model, implementing 134
non-numeric categorical data 56
normal distribution 68
normal equations 97
numbers
  string labels, converting to 56, 57, 58
numeric categorical data 56

O

one-dimensional convolution 305, 306, 307
one-hot encoding

about 56
  categories, converting to 59, 60, 61
one-layer encoder
  with MNIST test data 188
Ordinal Encoding 58
over-parametrization 272
overfitting curve 116
overfitting
  about 116
  identifying 109

P

pandas 48
perceptron learning algorithm (PLA)
  about 17, 18, 19, 89, 127, 131, 270
  implementing, in Python 131, 133, 134
perceptron model
  about 127
  implementing, on non-linearly separable data
  134
  tensor operations 129, 130
  visual concept 128
Persistent Contrastive Divergence (PCD) 255
pocket algorithm 139
pooling strategies 313, 314
principal component analysis (PCA) 75
probability density function (PDF) 68
processed data 13
pseudo-inverse 97
Python
  PLA, implementing 131, 133, 134
PyTorch 38, 39

Q

Quantile Transformation 68

R

R2 score 106
random noise 379
random search 119
raw data 12
re-parameterization 224, 227
real-valued data
  about 61
  scaling, to specific range of values 62, 63, 64

V

VAE model
  decoder, modeling 230
  examining 223, 224
  loss, minimizing 230, 231
  posterior's parameters, in encoder 228, 229, 230
  re-parameterization 227
  sampling 228
  training 232, 233, 234
validation dataset 108
vanishing gradient 195
Variational Autoencoders (VAEs)
  data, generating from 235, 236
  versus GANs 389, 391
vector-to-sequence model
  about 359
  Bi-directional LSTM (BiLSTM) 359, 360, 361
  implementation 361, 362, 363, 364
  results 361, 362, 363, 364

visualization
  applications 179

W

wide layers
  about 271
  names 273
  summaries 272, 273
wide neural networks
  about 270
  learning process, stopping 278, 279
  learning rate, reducing 277
  models, loading 276
  models, saving 275
  results 281, 282, 283
  training tools 275
word embedding
  about 333
  on IMDb 335, 336, 337, 338, 340, 341, 342, 343

Made in United States
North Haven, CT
23 June 2022

20552826R00239